OCT 2 7 2004

W9-APO-164

3 1170 00654 0433

DATE DUE

OMAHA

D-DAY

BEACH

JUNE 6, 1944

JOSEPH BALKOSKI

940.542142
BAL

STACKPOLE
BOOKS

Glenview Public Library
1930 Glenview Road
Glenview, Illinois

Copyright © 2004 by Stackpole Books

Published by
STACKPOLE BOOKS
5067 Ritter Road
Mechanicsburg, PA 17055
www.stackpolebooks.com

All rights reserved, including the right to reproduce this book or portions thereof in any form or by any means, electronic or mechanical, including photocopying, recording, or by any information storage and retrieval system, without permission in writing from the publisher. All inquiries should be addressed to Stackpole Books, 5067 Ritter Road, Mechanicsburg, Pennsylvania 17055.

Endsheet photo: U.S. Army Signal Corps, National Archives

Printed in the United States of America

10 9 8 7 6 5 4 3 2 1

FIRST EDITION

Library of Congress Cataloging-in-Publication Data

Balkoski, Joseph.
  Omaha Beach : D-Day, June 6, 1944 / by Joseph Balkoski.— 1st ed.
    p. cm.
  Includes bibliographical references and index.
  ISBN 0-8117-0079-8
  1. Operation Neptune. I. Title.
D756.5.N6 B343 2004
940.54'21422—dc22

2003021928

*This book is dedicated to
the American and British servicemen,
living and dead,
who participated in the
Omaha Beach invasion,
June 6, 1944*

Unita Fortior
"In Unity There is Strength"

Contents

Maps

Preface

They couldn't stop thinking about the ships. There were just so many of them. To those who witnessed it, anything that had transpired in their lives beforehand seemed trivial in comparison. Here was something worthy of telling your grandchildren—but if events shaped up as the top brass expected, a lot of good men aboard those ships would not be alive by sunset, and virtually every soldier and sailor involved in the operation surely wondered whether or not he would be one of those.

The ships had secret appointments in the predawn darkness of June 6, 1944, off the coast of Normandy. Their anchor chains would soon slip thunderously into the sea a few miles off beaches code-named Omaha, Utah, Sword, Juno, and Gold, and one of the most momentous struggles in world history would begin. The conferences, the plans, the exercises were meaningless now: soon, real bullets would fly and men would be killed; and the destiny of millions would hinge on the success or failure of the invasion the world would come to know simply as "D-Day."

It is axiomatic that no military operation ever unfolds according to plan, and D-Day was no exception. Compared to other amphibious operations that had come before it in World War II, however, the Normandy invasion was, for the most part, remarkably successful, thanks in large measure to the Allies' colossal concentration of force and meticulous preparation for an assault they deemed to be the war's most significant military undertaking.

Shortly after dawn, British and Canadian troops stormed ashore on Sword, Juno, and Gold Beaches, breaking through the enemy's coastal defenses quickly, despite the four years of preparation the Germans had had to prepare for the inevitable Allied invasion. Meanwhile, on and beyond Utah Beach in the eastern Cotentin Peninsula, American infantrymen, paratroopers, and glider troops methodically reduced German defenses in a coordinated airborne-amphibious assault that early invasion planners had once considered much too risky to include as part of Operation Overlord.

When the first sketchy intelligence reports of the fighting in Normandy reached Gen. Dwight Eisenhower's SHAEF headquarters on the morning of June 6, Ike and his staff officers breathed a sigh of relief: after all the doubts and uncertainty, the invasion was clearly succeeding. But not all news from the front was positive. On a beach code-named Omaha, the critical connector between the American forces in the Cotentin, and British-Canadian forces to the east, the invasion had started calamitously. Rumors of terrible casualties among the first waves, paralysis on the beach, and unyielding enemy defenses were filtering into SHAEF headquarters all morning. The only course of action was to wait out the crisis and hope that the fighting men on the beach would have the know-how to sort out the chaos on their own initiative, and bring the invasion timetable back on track.

That the GIs on Omaha Beach did indeed possess the essential fighting skills to save the day has become an elemental moral of American history. No one realized it at the time, particularly the unfortunate men who were subjected to the enemy's relentless barrage of bullets and shells, but Omaha Beach would become one of those exceptional moments in history when Americans defined themselves by their actions as a people worthy of the principles upon which the nation was founded. Yet it is particularly ironic that sixty years after D-Day, Americans still do not know all the details about that momentous day in June 1944 when their soldiers stormed ashore in France to begin the liberation of Europe.

In truth, only one person has attempted to write a comprehensive history of the assault—and that effort was made while World War II still raged. Lt. Col. Charles Taylor, a former Harvard history professor, was an accomplished U.S. Army historian—and his work *Omaha Beachhead*, written for a military audience and published by the War Department in 1945, proves it. But Taylor's work was crafted when the proverbial dust kicked up by the

Omaha invasion had not yet settled. Perspective has a vital impact on any historian's work, and surely Taylor's perspective of the Omaha Beach invasion was nearly as close as it was possible to be.

Six trips to Normandy thus far in my life have convinced me that, nearly sixty years after the publication of *Omaha Beachhead*, the time has come to write a new history of the Omaha invasion. During those Normandy trips, I guided several Omaha Beach tours, some for World War II veterans, others for current American soldiers as part of what the U.S. Army designates "Battlefield Staff Rides." But pinpointing where many key events of the invasion took place in response to questions from the groups was neither easy nor precise. Unlike American Civil War battlefields, notably Gettysburg, where Civil War veterans saw to it that hundreds of memorials and explanatory plaques would thoroughly document the fighting to the uninitiated, the four-mile stretch of beach that Americans and French alike have come to call Omaha is only sparsely memorialized and features virtually no indicators of the vital military actions that swirled on and beyond that shore line on D-Day.

If the history of a battle is a tapestry of hundreds of distinct and decisive actions by individuals, the Omaha tapestry is surprisingly indistinct. Where, for example, did Gen. Norman Cota of the 29th Division lead the GIs off the deadly beach on the morning of D-Day? Where did Lt. Jimmie Monteith of the 1st Division perform the heroics for which Eisenhower personally insisted he be awarded the Medal of Honor—posthumously? Where did Capt. Ralph Goranson and his Rangers climb Omaha's bleak western cliffs to knock out a key German strongpoint holding up the invasion? The answers to these and many other unresolved questions are conspicuously absent from D-Day histories, but they are answers that future generations of Americans deserve to know, just as earlier generations grasped the magnitude of the Civil War as a consequence of the U.S. government's resolution to preserve and interpret the notable battlefields of that conflict.

Omaha Beach lies beyond the boundaries of the United States, and as a consequence, its physical preservation is uncertain. Spiritually, however, the Omaha story is entirely preservable; and based on more than a quarter century of effort exploring archival material related to the invasion, I am unreservedly confident that a thorough historical record of the Omaha landing is feasible. But amassing voluminous quantities of original records is only a first step—in truth, the easy part. Much more problematic is a critical analysis of those records: separating useful information from the useless, organizing that information into a framework of a coherent and meaningful story, and relating that story in a readable and engaging way.

The ideas that led to this book came together for me in the summer of 2001, when my family and I resided in Normandy. For part of that time, we rented a farmhouse in Colleville-sur-Mer, the embodiment of a rural Norman village that also happened to be a crucial American D-Day objective. From the Colleville farm, it was possible to walk to all points of historical significance on Omaha Beach, and on countless hikes of exhausting duration, I did exactly that. I undertook some of these treks in the incredibly early dawn light of a Norman summer, and the stark loneliness of the beach and its adjacent bluffs under those conditions was remarkable. Some hikes took me into areas so remote they can hardly be classified as part of Omaha Beach. On other walks, initiated at a more reasonable hour, I strolled for miles down a beach filled with locals whose only interest in Omaha was to swim and sunbathe. At high tide, when the beach is surprisingly narrow, they moved their blankets and umbrellas beyond the high-water mark to the shingle, a sloping wall of stones that had provided meager protection for thousands of dazed American soldiers on a June morning only fifty-seven years previously.

Every walk triggered mixed and entirely surprising emotions, a combination of satisfaction at having tracked down through archival records the exact spots where the mostly forgotten events of the Omaha invasion occurred; sadness at having come across the precise places where fellow countrymen died; respect at the contemplation of what those men accomplished in the grand scheme of World War II; astonishment that for the Normans, life goes on as if nothing unusual had ever happened there; and determination that a thorough story of the landing must be written while there were still those alive who had actually lived it.

Nowadays it is exceptionally difficult to imagine that this peaceful shoreline once boiled with fury. But to figure out exactly what happened there, one must have no hesitation to envisage that fury. Armed with eyewitness accounts and official D-Day action reports, I retraced the footsteps of dozens of outfits on and beyond Omaha Beach into places that in 1944 were decidedly deadly. For many of those whose D-Day movements I followed, these were the last walks of their lives. Some hikes took me on a path that coursed directly through the U.S. Cemetery outside Colleville, where the remains of 9,386 Americans killed in Normandy are buried. It was especially difficult to imagine that the immaculate, somber cemetery grounds once were a battlefield, and in fact, many of the soldiers buried there are resting only a few dozen yards from where they fell in battle.

The meditative moods generated by Omaha exploration helped immensely to clarify the invasion's sometimes murky history. Formerly inscrutable official reports abruptly became clear; the locations of key events previously deemed unfindable unexpectedly turned out to be obvious; the state of mind of the GIs in the luckless first waves, who at first perceived virtually no means of escape from the deadly inferno generated by an unseen enemy, seemed entirely understandable and dreadfully real.

The net result for me was an epiphany: Enough information pertaining to Omaha Beach could indeed be assembled to chronicle the invasion thoroughly and coherently. The most sensible and compelling means of fulfilling such a project, in my view, would be to weave the words of those actually involved in the invasion's planning and execution—from generals to privates—directly into a chronological narrative, for the eloquence of even the most diligent historian can never hope to equal the poignancy of a participant's eyewitness account.

But I also resolved to be exceptionally selective in using such accounts, for I feared that a book depending heavily on an "I was there" approach would have obvious drawbacks. If there is one firm lesson that serious World War II researchers have learned, it is that the reliability of human memory varies drastically from one veteran to another. There is a fair chance that any eyewitness account provided decades after D-Day will be incomplete, if not inaccurate. The passage of a half century or more can play subtle tricks on the mind, and the historian's thorniest problem is to separate those rare fully substantiated accounts from the more typical yarns that time has embellished.

Furthermore, when eyewitness accounts of World War II fighting are presented to the reader in an unceasing and protracted sequence, unaccompanied by thorough explanatory narratives of the larger context in which those incidents occurred, much of the emotional power of these accounts is typically squandered. In a military operation as grandiose as the Omaha invasion, individuals are mere specks in the immense panorama of war. Personal experiences usually make for riveting reading, but they can be infinitely more riveting when the reader knows the exact time and place of that experience, the unit to which the observer belonged, the mission that unit was supposed to accomplish, whether it in fact was accomplished, and how it fit into the grand scheme of an incredibly ambitious military operation. In short, warfare is too colossal an enterprise to be understood by individual experiences alone.

Rather than use eyewitness accounts as the primary means of telling the Omaha Beach story, I therefore resolved to employ them selectively in support of a conventional narrative. In effect, those first-person accounts would serve as powerful evidence to the reader that events did indeed transpire as described. Moreover, they could help clarify the potentially bewildering choreography of military maneuvers on and beyond the beach that characterized the Omaha battle. Finally, appropriate eyewitness accounts would surely heighten the human drama of the story, for in the end, the enduring impact on those who survived the D-Day invasion was that it was an overwhelming and dreadful experience. Any book that does not impart those sentiments to readers is incomplete.

I held to three simple rules when considering whether to insert a first-person account into the narrative: First, the events related in the account had to be positively recognized as having taken place at a specific time and place on D-Day so that it could fit properly into the larger story. Second, whenever possible, I strove to confirm the most vital details of all eyewitness accounts, and if any significant parts of them egregiously contradicted established historical truths, I avoided using them. Third, and probably most important, I endeavored to use first-person accounts written as close in time as possible to June 6, 1944.

Anyone familiar with D-Day research understands that the most powerful and reliable first-person observations were those generated in 1944, only weeks or months after D-Day, when those men who had survived the Omaha ordeal—sometimes still in hospitals recovering from wounds suffered on June 6—were first approached by army historians. These primary accounts are surely the Rosetta Stone of Omaha Beach. The twenty-first-century reader may be surprised at how thoroughly the units participating in the Omaha invasion documented their D-Day activities, a process that continued until 1945. Within this vast array of eyewitness accounts and unit reports, written when D-Day memories were still fresh, lies the truth of the Omaha invasion. For the historian, however, locating and analyzing these archival materials is a vast undertaking, a methodical investigative process in which patience is an essential virtue.

As a rule, I judged these contemporaneous accounts more relevant and accurate than those written decades after D-Day. But the Omaha story is highly complex, and there are several mystifying gaps in the June 6 timeline not covered by 1944–45 reports. In these cases, by necessity I relied on veterans' memories of the Omaha assault given years after D-Day, although I still strove whenever possible to use accounts written by participants when they were still young men. The most noteworthy source for eyewitness accounts of this kind is the Cornelius Ryan Memorial Collection of World War II Papers at the Ohio University Library in Athens, Ohio. For his seminal book, *The Longest Day*, Ryan began collecting D-Day reminiscences in the 1950s, and the preserved collection is a proverbial goldmine for any serious D-Day researcher.

In short, the closer in time to D-Day an eyewitness recorded his observations of Omaha, the more I trusted it. In narrating a history of the Omaha invasion, this book provides a total of more than 500 eyewitness accounts, official reports, quotes, citations for valor, and other primary source material generated by the people and units that planned and participated in the assault. More than half of these accounts originated in 1944 (or earlier, in the chapters dealing with the origins of the invasion); about two-thirds were generated before 1950, when memories of D-Day were still fresh.

Twelve of the men who provided eyewitness observations of their Omaha experiences in this book, or whose actual words on the beach are quoted, did not survive the war: Carter, Fair, Fellers, Fettinger, Golas, Hawks, Howie, McGrath, Mullins, Nash, Schenk, and Schilling. Five are buried in the U.S. Military Cemetery on the bluff behind Omaha Beach.

Eyewitness accounts and unit reports recorded under harsh wartime conditions pose several curious problems for twenty-first-century historians. Some of those archival documents were written in nearly illegible penmanship; others employed perplexing phraseology and a style of English that would have made the soldiers' high school writing teachers wince. But grammatically acceptable English was hardly the prime concern of a soldier in a frontline dugout who had just witnessed the unspeakable proceedings of war. Nevertheless, I considered it mandatory in this book to facilitate readers' comprehension of the participants' Omaha observations, and as a consequence, when I transcribed those accounts and reports, I corrected spelling mistakes and egregious syntax errors. Furthermore, I sometimes added explanatory notes in brackets to help readers grasp the essence of what the D-Day observer was trying to express. Aside from such corrections and comments, I left the observers' prose alone.

Each eyewitness statement is identified by its originator and his military role at the time he wrote or spoke it. In the case of official reports written by unnamed persons, only the units to which those individuals belonged are provided. If an account or report was drafted shortly after D-Day (or before D-Day in the chapters dealing with the invasion's origins), the date of that statement is provided as specifically as possible. However, many accounts' precise dates of origin are unknown, and for others drafted or spoken a decade or more after D-Day, I considered the date irrelevant to the historical narrative. These kinds of accounts are therefore not specified by date, although the reader is invited to consult the Notes section for more detailed information.

U.S. ARMY WORLD WAR II ORGANIZATION

Archival documents pertaining to Omaha Beach are filled with expressions that may baffle the modern reader. The following explanatory background is intended to assist those unfamiliar with World War II military terminology and organization.

The soul of the U.S. Army in World War II was its divisions, of which there were a total of eighty-nine primed and ready for combat, or already involved in combat, in the spring of 1944. The Omaha invasion involved two such units: the 1st and 29th Infantry Divisions, each of which consisted of close to 14,300 men under normal circumstances. In this book, the word "Infantry" is generally omitted from their designations, thus 1st Division or 29th Division. On D-Day, thousands more specialized troops were temporarily attached to each division for the invasion.

The primary components of a division were its three 3,100-man regiments. In the 1st Division, these were the 16th, 18th, and 26th Infantry Regiments; in the 29th Division, they were the 115th, 116th, and 175th. (The 16th and 116th were the first infantry units to land on Omaha Beach on D-Day and will be heard from frequently in this narrative.) According to a venerable army custom, the word "Regiment" is considered superfluous when referring to units of regimental size, and hence references such as the 16th Infantry or 116th Infantry imply regiments.

A regiment was configured into three 870-man battalions, designated simply 1st, 2nd, and 3rd. Battalions in turn were broken down into companies: A, B, C, and D Companies in the 1st; E, F, G, and H in the 2nd; I, K, L, and M in the 3rd. On D-Day, 16th and 116th Infantry companies typically discarded their normal organization, and each split up into six or seven thirty-one-man "boat teams," a designation representing the optimal number of men that could fit into a single assault landing craft.

U.S. Army divisions also included thousands of specialized soldiers, among them artillerymen, engineers, reconnaissance troops, signalmen, military policemen, and medical personnel. Although their responsibilities were somewhat overshadowed by their infantry brethren, they all played vital roles in the invasion.

HIGHER U.S. AND ALLIED COMMAND ECHELONS

The Omaha Beach invasion was planned and executed by the U.S. Army's V Corps, the command to which the 1st and 29th Divisions, as well as dozens of other diverse outfits, belonged. The V Corps was a component of the U.S. First Army, which in turn was subordinated to the multinational 21st Army Group led by Gen. Sir Bernard Montgomery, Britain's most celebrated military commander of World War II and Eisenhower's chief ground planner for the D-Day assault.

CAST OF PRINCIPAL COMMANDERS

Gen. George Marshall, Chief of Staff, U.S. Army

Gen. Dwight Eisenhower, Supreme Commander, Allied Expeditionary Force

Gen. Sir Bernard Montgomery, Commander, 21st Army Group

Adm. Harold Stark, Commander, U.S. Naval Forces, Europe

Lt. Gen. Omar Bradley, Commander U.S. First Army

Rear Adm. Alan Kirk, Commander, Western Naval Task Force (Task Force 122)

Lt. Gen. Carl Spaatz, Commander, U.S. Strategic Air Forces, Europe

Lt. Gen. Frederick Morgan, Chief of Staff to Supreme Allied Commander (COSSAC)

Maj. Gen. Leonard Gerow, Commander, U.S. V Corps

Maj. Gen. Clarence Huebner, Commander, U.S. 1st Infantry Division

Maj. Gen. Charles Gerhardt, Commander, U.S. 29th Infantry Division

Rear Adm. John Hall, Commander, Assault Force "O" (Task Force 124)

Brig. Gen. Willard Wyman, Assistant Division Commander, U.S. 1st Infantry Division

Brig. Gen. Norman Cota, Assistant Division Commander, U.S. 29th Infantry Division

Brig. Gen. William Hoge, Commander, Provisional Engineer Special Brigade Group

Rear Adm. Carleton Bryant, Commander, Naval Bombardment Group, Force "O"

Col. George Taylor, Commander, 16th Infantry Regiment, 1st Division

Col. Charles Canham, Commander, 116th Infantry Regiment, 29th Division

Col. Benjamin Talley, Deputy Chief of Staff and Senior Observer,
V Corps
Col. Doswell Gullatt, Commander, 5th Engineer Special Brigade
Col. Paul Thompson, Commander, 6th Engineer Special Brigade
Capt. Lorenzo Sabin, Commander, Naval Close Gunfire Support
Group, Force "O"

MILITARY TIMEKEEPING

During World War II, the American military denoted time by means of the
twenty-four-hour clock, and numerous reports and eyewitness accounts
included in this book adhere to that system. When observers employed this
style, I refrained from translating times into the more familiar A.M. and P.M.
method. Within my own narrative, however, I specify time in the conventional manner.

The twenty-four-hour clock denotes a specific time by a four-digit
number. The first two digits represent the hour; the last two, the minute.
Hours "00" to "11" are A.M. hours and are self-explanatory. Hours "12" to
"23" are P.M. hours. To translate hours 13 and higher into conventional
time, simply subtract 12 from the hour number. For example, 2345 = 11:45
P.M.; 0015 = 12:15 A.M.

In June 1944, Great Britain adhered to "Double British Summer
Time," which was a special wartime measure similar to daylight saving
time, except that the clock was advanced two hours, not one. All Allied
military formations followed this arrangement, and times expressed in this
book adhere to it as well.

LANDING CRAFT

Any story of a World War II seaborne invasion demands frequent references to the diverse family of landing craft employed by the Allies to disembark troops and equipment ashore. The following notes are provided to
give the reader a basic impression of those landing craft mentioned in the
narrative, listed in order from smallest to largest.

LCVP (Landing Craft, Vehicle, Personnel): Basic U.S. Navy and
Coast Guard assault vessel, carrying 31 troops.
LCA (Landing Craft, Assault): Basic Royal Navy assault vessel,
carrying 31 troops. Preferred by GIs over LCVP because of its
armor and its benches, which allowed embarked troops to sit.

The U.S. Navy favored the LCVP because of its slightly higher speed.

LCM (Landing Craft, Mechanized): Capable of transporting one tank, although on D-Day LCMs typically carried up to 50 engineers and their demolition equipment.

LCT (Landing Craft, Tank): Produced in many varieties, carrying 3 or 4 tanks directly to the beach or for launching at sea.

LCT(A) (Landing Craft, Tank [Armored]): LCT variant with added armor for protection against enemy fire. LCT(A)s were the first landing craft to land on Omaha Beach.

LCT(R) (Landing Craft, Tank [Rocket]): LCT variant with more than 1,000 fixed rocket launchers added for close-in bombardment of the beach prior to the assault.

LCG (Landing Craft, Gun): LCT variant armed with guns for shore bombardment.

LCI (Landing Craft, Infantry): Large vessel, carrying 200 troops, considered too vulnerable to land under direct enemy fire.

LST (Landing Ship, Tank): Largest of the landing vessels, carrying up to 20 tanks and 200 troops, but considered too vulnerable to land under direct enemy fire.

CODE WORDS

"D-Day" was merely a code word indicating the day on which Allied forces would launch the invasion of Europe. As late as mid-May 1944, Eisenhower had not yet specified D-Day's actual date. Eventually he selected June 5, then postponed it one day to June 6 due to bad weather. In official reports, "H-Hour" refers to the exact time when assault forces would first storm ashore in Normandy, a time that in late May Eisenhower specified as 6:30 A.M. for Omaha Beach. References in eyewitness accounts and official reports of "D" or "H" plus a number signify the indicated number of days after D-Day or hours after H-Hour. For example, "D+1" means June 7; "H+4" denotes 10:30 A.M.

"Operation Overlord" was the code word for the Anglo-American plan to invade German-occupied France and build up a large Allied army and logistical infrastructure ashore for the ultimate purpose of liberating western Europe from Nazi domination. "Operation Neptune" was that part of the Overlord plan dealing specifically with the amphibious invasion of Normandy, including the Omaha Beach assault.

ABBREVIATIONS

AAA	antiaircraft artillery
AAF	U.S. Army Air Force
AEAF	Allied Expeditionary Air Force
Adm.	admiral[a]
BAR	Browning automatic rifle
Brig. Gen.	brigadier general
Capt.	captain[a]
CG	commanding general
Cmdr.	commander[a]
CO	commanding officer
Col.	colonel
CP	command post
Cpl.	corporal
CW	combat wing
DD	duplex drive (amphibious) tank
Ens.	ensign[a]
F.O.	field order (or forward observer)
HQ	headquarters
Lt. Col.	lieutenant colonel
Lt. Cmdr.	lieutenant commander[a]
Lt. Gen.	lieutenant general
Lt. (jg)	lieutenant, junior grade[a]
Maj.	major
Maj. Gen.	major general
M/Sgt.	master sergeant[b]
NCO	non-commissioned officer
PFC	private first class
Pvt.	private
RCN	Royal Canadian Navy
RCT	regimental combat team
RN	Royal Navy
Sgt.	sergeant[b]
Sgt. Maj.	sergeant major[b]
S/Sgt.	staff sergeant[b]
Sub-Lt.	sub-lieutenant[a]
T/Sgt.	technical sergeant[b]
T/3	technician grade 3[c]
T/4	technician grade 4[c]

T/5	technician grade 5[c]
USCG	U.S. Coast Guard
USN	U.S. Navy
WN	*Widerstandsnest* (German resistance nest)
W.O.	warrant officer[a]
XO	executive officer (2nd-in-command)
1st Lt.	first lieutenant
2nd Lt.	second lieutenant
1st Sgt.	first sergeant[b]

[a] U.S. Navy, U.S. Coast Guard, or Royal Navy rank. A navy captain was equal to an army colonel.

[b] The order of rank for WWII U.S. Army sergeants, from highest to lowest, was master sergeant, technical sergeant, staff sergeant, and sergeant (sometimes called "buck" sergeant). First sergeant and sergeant major were not ranks, but positions within a company, battalion, or regiment as its ranking NCO.

[c] Technician grades 3, 4, and 5 were equivalent in rank to staff sergeant, sergeant, and corporal, respectively, but technicians had no command authority.

CHAPTER 1

The End of the Beginning

WE WILL LAND IN FRANCE

One had to admit in May 1944 that perhaps the Americans did not really know war as well as they thought they did.

It was almost two and a half years after Pearl Harbor, and only eleven U.S. Army divisions had so far fought the German Army in battle. The two American generals who bore full responsibility for destroying that enemy army, Dwight Eisenhower and Omar Bradley, had not even served overseas in World War I, and prior to Pearl Harbor, neither had commanded anything larger than a battalion of 800 men.

True, the United States could outproduce any nation in the world when it came to war matériel, and by May 1944 the U.S. Army had almost 8 million men under arms. But less than four years previously, when the German Army had occupied Paris in June 1940, the American Army, including Air Corps personnel, consisted of only 190,000 men, a smaller military force than that of Sweden, Switzerland, Hungary, or Yugoslavia. Only a few U.S. Army divisions had existed then, none of which could be deployed overseas without extensive augmentation and training. In truth, an assault against the German-occupied coast of France was inconceivable—the army and the navy barely had the resources to practice a landing on an island in the Chesapeake Bay.

Could the millions of civilians who had been hastily converted to soldiers stand against the elite SS, the *Panzertruppen*, the *Fallschirmjäger*—the German soldiers who had overrun France in one month, the men whose actions had defined for the world the meaning of the new word "blitzkrieg"? The American high command was confident that they could, but some outside observers disagreed: little more than a year before D-Day, one of Prime Minister Winston Churchill's most esteemed generals, Sir Harold Alexander, had labeled the Americans as "mentally and physically rather soft and very green." Even more to the point: Could the United States tolerate a campaign that might produce casualties on the scale of Verdun or the Somme in the First World War?

No one knew, but they were about to find out.

The GIs were certainly ready for their big test. The army's top soldier, Gen. George C. Marshall, had made sure of that. Ever since Grant and Sherman, Americans had aimed to win their wars swiftly, ruthlessly, completely—and this war would be no exception. Nearly every GI, from the greenest private to Marshall himself, passionately held to the clear-cut military principle that the fastest way home was to pummel the enemy into extinction. If a cause was worth fighting for, and this one certainly was, could there be a more sensible method of fighting a war?

The problem, as Marshall saw it, was that Allied troops would need to inflict a lot of pummeling on the renowned German Army to make it extinct, and to do so without respite required American war production of almost unimaginable magnitude. However, given the imprudence of America's lax rearmament after war had broken out in Europe in the fall of 1939, such production levels had taken considerable time to achieve. General Marshall, who was not a man to overstate a case, declared ruefully in the postwar years that had the United States initiated a vigorous rearmament program in 1939 rather than the following year, it could have hastened the end of the war by one year, saved billions of dollars, and avoided 100,000 American casualties.

But by the spring of 1944, the economy was finally in full swing, and the army was ready. Marshall once said that it took U.S. Army divisions almost two years to gain the necessary training, spirit, and tactical finesse they would require to defeat their formidable German or Japanese counterparts on the battlefield, and by mid-1944 most of the army's eighty-nine divisions had already proved their worth or were ready to do so. With prudence and good luck, there would be no more disasters as at Kasserine Pass in North Africa in February 1943. And if, as President Roosevelt and Prime Minister Churchill had so forcefully declared, Germany—not

Japan—was the Allies' first enemy, the most pressing issue from Marshall's perspective was to initiate a land campaign that would set as many of those divisions as possible against the *Wehrmacht*. In the past, the strategy of annihilation had worked for Grant and Pershing, and now Marshall hoped it would work again for him. As long as the Soviets would continue to tie down the bulk of the German Army, the enemy could not hope to stand against the weight of Anglo-American military might and industrial production.

For years, General Marshall had known where that decisive campaign must take place. It was no secret: In May 1942, he had announced it openly when he spoke to the graduating class of West Point cadets gathered in the cavernous field house down near the old polo flats on the banks of the Hudson River.

Gen. George C. Marshall
Chief of Staff, U.S. Army, speech to graduating cadets, U.S. Military Academy, May 29, 1942
This struggle will be carried to a conclusion that will be decisive and final. . . . There is no possible compromise. We must utterly defeat the Jap and German war machines. . . . Current events remind me of questions which were put to me by members of Congress prior to December 7 as to where American soldiers might be called upon to fight, and just what was the urgent necessity for the Army that we were endeavoring to organize and train. . . . No one could tell what the future might hold for us, but one thing was clear to me: we must be prepared to fight anywhere, and with a minimum of delay. The possibilities were not overdrawn, for today we find American soldiers throughout the Pacific, in Burma, China, and India. Recently they struck at Tokyo. They have wintered in Greenland and Iceland. They are landing in Northern Ireland and England and they will land in France. [At this point, Marshall was interrupted by sustained applause.] It is on the young and vigorous that we must depend for the energy and daring and leadership in staging a Great Offensive. I express my complete confidence that you will carry, with a proud and great resolution, into this new army of citizen-soldiers at their American best, all the traditions, all the history and background of your predecessors at West Point—and may the good Lord be with you.

But it had taken Marshall years to persuade others of his strategy's worth, and herein lay the most challenging impediment to his management of America's war effort: In coalition warfare, one does not always get one's way—and to pursue one's favored military strategy, it becomes necessary to negotiate with allies from a position of strength. Unhappily for Marshall,

America's military unpreparedness and inexperience in 1941 and 1942 in comparison with Great Britain and the Soviet Union forced him to carry out the war against Germany and Italy in ways that were decidedly contrary to the crushing war of annihilation he was resolved to execute. Later, as American military production swelled and GIs flowed into Britain like a torrent, Marshall would find it easier to get his way. But in the meantime, a humbled Marshall learned a lesson of incalculable value: The German military machine was so mighty that the Americans could not hope to win the war by themselves, at least in Europe. Air superiority for his cherished "Great Offensive" could not be achieved without Royal Air Force fighters; the German economy could not be effectively smashed without RAF's Bomber Command; the seas could not be controlled without Royal Navy battleships, nor could invasion routes be swept clear of mines without Royal Navy minesweepers; and perhaps most important of all, an amphibious assault against the coast of France could not be carried out on the massive scale necessitated by the German defenses without British transports, landing craft, and skilled boat crews.

And then there was the monumental Soviet contribution, indirect and remote, but without which Marshall's Great Offensive would have been much more problematic. For every bloodbath through which the German Army struggled on the eastern front—and there had been many since June 1941—the Western Allies faced more favorable prospects when they would, as Marshall hoped, open up a western front in France.

It was, as Grant and Sherman had said, the quickest way home.

Among the great military clashes of history, D-Day is one of the few that is not formally designated by a geographic name, nor is it generally referred to as a "battle." In fact, the term "D-Day," much in vogue in the English-speaking world during the war years, was used by Anglo-American war planners in dozens of different military operations in both Europe and the Pacific. Suitably cryptic and concise, D-Day was very much an expression of modern warfare, and as such, the term attracted people's attention and stimulated their imagination. Few, however, had any idea what it actually meant.

Although many "D-Days" occurred in World War II, history recognizes only one. Such an ambiguous title for one of the world's most decisive battles is perhaps the consequence of the fact that World War II combats had become so grandiose and multidimensional compared with past wars that simple geographic names no longer applied. The Normandy invasion took place on five separate beachfronts along a coastline more than fifty miles in length. Simultaneously, large bodies of American and

"We will land in France." U.S. Army Chief of Staff Gen. George Marshall shakes hands with Gen. Omar Bradley on Omaha Beach, June 12, 1944. Gen. "Hap" Arnold, commander of the U.S. Army Air Force, is on the right.
U.S. Army Signal Corps, National Archives.

Anglo-Canadian paratroopers landed miles behind the coast, and Allied naval and air forces fought their own distinct battles in the seas adjacent to and the skies above Normandy. Meanwhile, the French Resistance erupted into action deep inside France. The very scope of the Normandy invasion was one of the Allies' greatest advantages, for the bewildered Germans simply could not discern the invasion's limits for several days. Nothing in history could compare to it.

Even given the accepted subdivision of the Normandy invasion into a dozen or so semi-independent battles, few of the myriad D-Day histories written in the past half century have focused a narrow historical beam on their subject matter. Rather, D-Day historians have tended to group the separate battles into a larger whole. And yet each of D-Day's sub-battles was, by its own measurement, of such considerable size and supreme significance to the war as a whole that all deserve thorough historical analyses of their own. Contrary to the proverb that censures a viewer for failing to see the forest for the trees, standard D-Day research fails to see the trees for the forest.

The American landing on the coastal strip between the Norman villages of Vierville-sur-Mer and Colleville-sur-Mer, a beach forever since known as Omaha, is a case in point. Although the Omaha Beach invasion was just one of many D-Day battles, it was in itself larger in scale than most World War II engagements that had preceded it involving American troops. Of the 1,348 days in which the United States was a participant in the Second World War, few had a daily count of American casualties exceeding those the Americans suffered on Omaha Beach on June 6, 1944.

The Omaha Beach landing typified the American World War II experience: a disastrous beginning during which hundreds of soldiers were slaughtered with shocking ease by an unseen enemy; the swift abandonment of prearranged plans that were not working; a hardening of American resolve that a solution to the crisis must be initiated; a hard fight against resolute enemy soldiers who simply would not quit; and eventual victory—followed by exhaustion, grief, and ultimately satisfaction that the task had been achieved despite seemingly insurmountable difficulties.

This is the story of that invasion.

IT WON'T WORK

D-Day was the product of several years of dialogue between high-powered diplomats and military professionals in Britain and the United States who directed the Allied war effort. Conceptually, the origins of the invasion plan may be traced back to the establishment of the Anglo-American alliance in 1941, when Britons and Americans agreed that should the United States enter the war, the defeat of Germany must be their primary goal. The more immediate genesis of the Normandy invasion, however, occurred on March 12, 1943, when the Allied combined chiefs of staff appointed Lt. Gen. Frederick Morgan of the British Army as the chief planner for a future invasion of northwest Europe, entitling him the "Chief of Staff to the Supreme Allied Commander" (COSSAC).

From the earliest days of American involvement in World War II, General Marshall, speaking as President Franklin Roosevelt's senior military counselor, had made the American position on European grand strategy plain: An invasion of German-occupied France and a subsequent ground campaign aimed at the heart of Germany would be the surest and swiftest course to Allied victory in Europe, and the sooner this invasion was launched, the faster the war would be won. When Morgan took up his position in March 1943, the American military chiefs had only recently conceded—grudgingly—that the invasion of Europe could not take place in 1943, as Marshall had fervently hoped. Instead, thanks to Churchill's persistence, the Allies would pursue a Mediterranean strategy in 1943, hoping to knock Italy out of the war and exploit what the prime minister had labeled in a November 1942 war report "the soft underbelly of the Axis." With an American concession to adhere to that strategy, however, came an insistence from Marshall that the invasion of northwest Europe must take place in 1944.

For their part, the British service chiefs, led by the austere and brilliant Chief of the Imperial General Staff, Gen. Sir Alan Brooke, asserted that an invasion of Europe must not be rushed, and should, in fact, be undertaken only when military conditions favored it—namely, when the occupying German Army in France and the Low Countries was thinned in response to Allied pressure in other war theaters. That the British and Americans did not agree on grand strategy was unmistakably demonstrated in the written dialogue that ensued when the Allies attempted to specify the date in 1944 on which the invasion of France would occur. A resolute Marshall would not accept ambiguity on this issue, and his staff boldly declared that the COSSAC guiding principle would be "a full-scale invasion in the spring of 1944." Upon reading the directive, the British chiefs bounced it back to the Americans with the defining word "spring" eliminated. The Americans immediately sent it back again with "spring" replaced. This game of ping-pong semantics could have gone on forever had someone not prompted a compromise. Ultimately, the agreed-upon phraseology stated: "A full-scale assault against the Continent in 1944 as early as possible."

Sir Winston Churchill
Prime Minister, United Kingdom
While I was always willing to join with the United States in a direct assault across the Channel on the German sea front in France, I was not convinced that this was the only way of winning the war, and I knew that it would be a very heavy and hazardous adventure. The fearful price that we had had to pay in human life and blood from the great offensives of the First World War was graven in my mind. Men of the Somme and Passchendaele and many larger frontal attacks upon the Germans were not to be blotted out by time or reflection.

Any enthusiasm General Morgan may have possessed about his COS-SAC role surely dissipated when, in March 1943, he walked into General Brooke's office to be briefed on the dubious resolution that France would be invaded in 1944. Brooke blurted as he handed Morgan the "Most Secret" strategic guidelines for COSSAC agreed upon by the combined chiefs: "Well there it is. It won't work but you must bloody well make it."

In short, Morgan was obliged to address two fundamental questions: Would an Allied invasion of France in the spring of 1944 have a reasonable chance of success? If so, could sufficient troops and supplies be built up in the bridgehead to launch a subsequent grand offensive aimed at defeating the German Army in the West? The COSSAC staff dedicated itself to the challenging task of answering these questions, prodded by Morgan's blunt statement at an April 1943 meeting: "I am to plan nothing less than the reconquest of Europe."

But the uncertain nature of COSSAC's job was obvious to all, for the supreme allied commander, for whom Morgan was supposed to be a chief of staff, did not even exist—and nobody had the slightest idea who he would be or when he would be named. Even worse, COSSAC had little notion of the manpower and logistical resources that the Allies would ultimately commit to the invasion, and could not possibly predict with certainty the state of German defenses on the Continent when the invasion would be launched. Given the huge significance of the invasion to the Allied war effort, it was a peculiar way to run a war.

Lt. Gen. Frederick Morgan
COSSAC, Letter to Brig. Leslie Hollis, secretary to British chiefs of staff, August 1943

Essentially what we are here trying to do is to make an impossible situation reasonably possible for practical purposes. . . . Never were so few asked to do so much in so short a time.

Despite the Americans' impatience for an invasion of France, they had given little thought to exactly where that landing should be made. Planners at the highest levels of the British military infrastructure, however, had been considering this issue for years, and Morgan and his COSSAC team inherited this invaluable groundwork. The British had seriously contemplated only two regions of France as potential invasion sites: Pas de Calais and Normandy. The most logical invasion site was the Pas de Calais ("Pass of Calais," the French name for the Strait of Dover, but also the name of the local French administrative district bordering the coast in that region). The strait is so narrow here that on a clear day, the French shoreline can easily be seen with the naked eye from England. If the invasion would be made at Pas de Calais, the Allied invasion fleet would have only a short journey, thereby reducing its exposure to enemy attack. Moreover, Allied air cover would be at its strongest.

The Strategic Options, 1944

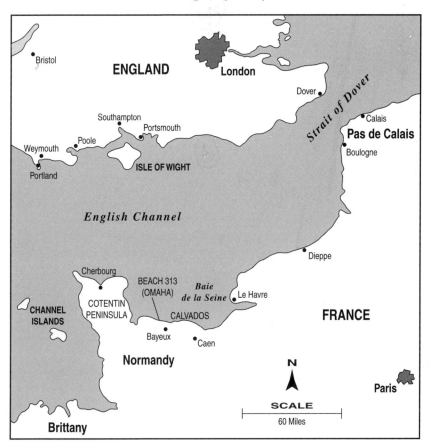

In contrast, one needed only to glance at a map of western Europe to see that Normandy hardly made sense as an Allied invasion site compared to Pas de Calais. Normandy was not only much more distant from England, but also farther away from the Allies' ultimate objective, Germany. Its only decent port, Cherbourg, was hardly adequate to support the Allies' considerable logistical needs.

But the British had reasoned that geography alone must not dictate military strategy. Based on its inherited paperwork and its own thorough studies of the invasion issue, the COSSAC staff concluded that Normandy, although by no means a perfect invasion site, offered greater chances of success than Pas de Calais. In his report outlining the operation the Allies had christened "Overlord," Morgan noted, "The Pas de Calais is the most strongly defended area on the whole French coast." In suggesting Normandy as an alternative, he wrote, "An attempt has been made to obtain tactical surprise by landing in a lightly defended area. . . . [The] Germans consider a landing there unlikely to be successful."

With so little information available to him concerning Allied resources and enemy capabilities, Morgan's report was, by necessity, vague. The main body of the COSSAC outline was, in fact, only thirty-seven short paragraphs, and aside from specifying the operation's intended target date, May 1, 1944, and recommending its landing site—Normandy—most of these paragraphs dealt only in generalities.

Lt. Gen. Frederick Morgan
Cover letter to COSSAC Overlord plan, July 15, 1943
I have come to the conclusion that, in view of the limitations in resources imposed by my directives, we may be assured of a reasonable chance of success on the 1st of May, 1944, only if we concentrate our efforts on an assault across the Norman beaches about Bayeux. As regards circumstances that we can control only indirectly, it is, in my opinion, necessary to stipulate that the state of affairs existing at the time, both on land in France and in the air above it, shall be such as to render the assault as little hazardous as may be so far as it is humanly possible to calculate. The essential discrepancy in value between the enemy's troops, highly organised, armed and battle-trained, who await us in their much vaunted impregnable defences, and our troops, who must of necessity launch their assault at the end of a cross-Channel voyage with all its attendant risks, must be reduced to the narrowest possible margin. Though much can be done to this end by the means available and likely to become available to us in the United Kingdom to influence these factors, we are largely dependent upon events that will take place on other war fronts, principally on the Russian front, between now and the date of the assault.

But in addressing the selection of the precise locations on the Normandy coast at which the invasion would be made, Morgan strove to be comprehensive. The COSSAC report included twenty-four annexes, some of which provided remarkably accurate details on the Normandy shoreline based largely on air photography, reports from the French Resistance, old French postcards, British tourists' fuzzy photographs taken on summer holidays—even offshore depth soundings taken in the Napoleonic era.

That area of Normandy suggested by Morgan as the actual invasion site is known as Calvados, a name originating according to local legend from the ship *El Salvador*, which wrecked on the Normandy coast as the Spanish Armada passed by in 1588. In selecting Calvados beaches on which the invasion would have a reasonable chance of success, Morgan's planners were severely limited by natural factors. Sheer cliffs and offshore rocks, features that would make large-scale amphibious assaults in those sectors nearly impossible, mark much of the Calvados coast. Furthermore, English Channel weather is notoriously capricious. The invasion could be compromised if a severe storm whipped in a few days after the initial assault. Finally, Normandy's tidal changes are among the most dramatic in the world. At high tide, the waves lap right up against coastal seawalls; five hours later, a soldier exiting a landing craft might have to cross 600 yards of open beach to reach that seawall. It was an invasion planner's nightmare.

The three beaches designated by COSSAC as promising invasion sites were situated, noncontiguously, along a twenty-five-mile coastal strip and were referred to in the plan by number, not name. Morgan assigned the westernmost beach the lifeless label "Beach 313," later changed by the Americans to the equally dreary "Beach 46." No one who closely examined the four-mile strip of Beach 313 could ever say honestly that it would be an easy site at which to make an invasion. When viewed from close offshore, the beach appeared to be backed up by a seemingly impenetrable green wall of bluffs that would be easy for a determined enemy to defend. If, as Morgan recommended, the Allies began the liberation of western Europe at Calvados, Beach 313 would have to do. There simply were no other locations in this part of Normandy that were any better.

In April 1944, the Americans would rechristen that beach "Omaha."

Roosevelt, Churchill, and their combined military chiefs accepted the judgments of Morgan's Overlord report. But if, as all parties seemed to agree, Overlord would be the Allies' most decisive military operation of World War II, a supreme commander must clarify the number of men and amount of matériel that would be committed to the endeavor. As of late fall of 1943, however, this commander had not yet been named. Morgan, in effect, was chief of staff to a phantom—and phantoms cannot make decisions.

The crucial impetus that transformed Overlord from an imprecise framework into an explicit and focused war plan was triggered by the "Big Three"—Roosevelt, Churchill, and Stalin—at the summit in Tehran from November 28 to December 1, 1943, codenamed "Eureka." Aside from his persistent calls for a "Second Front" to relieve German pressure on his Soviet armies, Marshal Stalin had so far played no direct role in shaping Overlord. He had met Churchill only once, Roosevelt and Marshall never. But at Tehran, Stalin joined the debate in earnest.

The Tehran summit filled in many of the missing pieces of the Overlord scheme. In a trinity, two votes are a majority; and at Tehran, Stalin sided unequivocally with the American view that the invasion of western Europe must be the Western Allies' primary military focus for 1944—and it must be launched that spring. All operations other than the invasion of France, according to Stalin, would be superfluous, a disheartening sentiment to Churchill. The prime minister, famous for his novel military schemes, actively supported Mediterranean operations, called for future Allied action in the Balkans, and hoped to energize Turkey to enter the war on the Allied side.

The Eureka summit concluded that Overlord must be taken seriously. To do so, a supreme commander must be chosen as soon as possible, and extraordinary efforts must be made to provide the matériel required for its success. In concurring with the U.S. Army's vision of the war, Stalin—the antithesis of an American democratic leader—had verified that war, too, makes strange bedfellows.

Marshal Josef Stalin
Premier of the Soviet Union, Eureka Conference, Tehran, Iran,
November 28, 1943
We Russians believe that the best result would be yielded by a blow at the enemy in northern or northwestern France. The best course would be to make Overlord the basic operation for 1944.

President Franklin D. Roosevelt
Letter to Marshal Stalin, December 6, 1943
The immediate appointment of General Eisenhower to command of the Overlord operation has been decided upon. [To this handwritten note was appended the following:]

Cairo, Dec. 7, 1943
Dear Eisenhower: I thought you might like to have this as a memento. It was written very hurriedly by me as the final meeting [in Cairo, Egypt] broke up yesterday, the President signing it immediately. George C. Marshall

A guiding principle of any successful military operation is concentration of force. Morgan's Overlord outline could not achieve this object, for it had neither the authority nor the support of higher command echelons to do so. However, Eisenhower's January 1944 transfer from the Mediterranean to Britain as head of Supreme Headquarters Allied Expeditionary Force (SHAEF) supplied the critical stimulus that would be required if D-Day was to be carried out by a force sufficient in men and matériel. Furthermore, Gen. Sir Bernard Montgomery, the Allies' most famous combat commander in the war so far, also shifted to Britain, assuming the role of Eisenhower's senior ground force commander and chief invasion planner. Monty's insufferable ego promised to generate command friction, but he was a proven winner, and his involvement in Overlord bolstered the will of skeptics who still believed the invasion would most likely fail.

If the invasion of German-occupied France would be the Western Allies' decisive military operation of World War II, Eisenhower and Montgomery lobbied vigorously for more weight in the initial assault, and they got what they wished for. What was to have been an initial seaborne invasion of three divisions was transformed overnight into one of more than five. Furthermore, by adding two new invasion beaches to Morgan's original three, the length of Normandy coast against which the invasion would fling itself was doubled. The additional landing craft required by the new plan, however, would force the invasion's postponement by one month, from early May to early June 1944. Not a single man went on record opposing this delay.

General Morgan had ably addressed the questions asked of him in the spring of 1943, but only the intervention of big-name politicians and generals could provide the resources to make the forthcoming invasion succeed. Later, Morgan would aptly describe his work as an "overture to Overlord."

Competent generals fully understand that no war can ever be won on paper. Sooner or later, bullets must fly, hand grenades must be flung, and people must be killed. For the United States, the invasion of France would be a decisive gauge of the effectiveness of America's abrupt militarization. No one doubted that American soldiers were good. But would they prove capable of dedicating themselves to the thoroughly deadly and prolonged task of bringing down the Nazis? In America, that question affected nearly everyone, from the lowliest GI peeling potatoes at Camp Kilmer to the chief of staff in the Pentagon; from the housewife in Des Moines to the munitions worker in Detroit; from the sailor in the South Pacific to the senator on Capitol Hill.

Gen. George C. Marshall
Chief of Staff, U.S. Army, letter to General Eisenhower, May 1, 1944
Consider only Overlord and your own heavy burden of responsibility for its success. Everything else is of minor importance.

Gen. Dwight D. Eisenhower
Supreme Commander, Allied Expeditionary Force, letter to chiefs of staff, January 23, 1944
I have now had an opportunity of discussing the Overlord plan with my Commanders-in-Chief. We are convinced that in all discussions full weight must be given to the fact that this operation marks the crisis of the European war. Every obstacle must be overcome, every inconvenience suffered, every priority granted, and every risk taken to ensure that our blow is decisive. We cannot afford to fail.

Unhappily for the Americans, the beach Morgan had designatcd "313" had the appearance of a place where a seaborne invasion could indeed fail. Averting that failure was clearly going to be both difficult and costly. Now the time had come to convey to the men who would face death in that invasion the momentous events in which they were about to participate.

CHAPTER 2

Realism, Not Pessimism

A MAN NAMED GEE

It is unprecedented in American military history that such an obscure general successfully directed a battle of such profound historical significance as Omaha Beach. The name of Maj. Gen. Leonard T. Gerow, commanding general of the American ground force that assaulted Omaha Beach on D-Day, is assuredly not among those in the pantheon of brilliant American military leaders. But Gerow's résumé will forever carry on it the fact that he carefully planned and ultimately victoriously led a military operation that only a short time previously had been deemed almost impossible. Further, although he wore only two stars on his helmet as commanding general of the U.S. Army's V Corps, in June 1944 he commanded a number of men that had all the trappings of a small army.

Gerow's enduring obscurity is perhaps traceable to the fact that D-Day was a military operation of such momentous proportions that its better-known leaders, such as Eisenhower, Montgomery, and Bradley, represented the limits of the public's captivation. At fifty-six years of age, "Gee" Gerow had reached the army's unspoken upper age limit, causing Chief of Staff Marshall to wonder whether an active combat assignment was a good idea.

A graduate of the Virginia Military Institute in 1911, Gerow had put in more army years than his friends Omar Bradley or Dwight Eisenhower. As

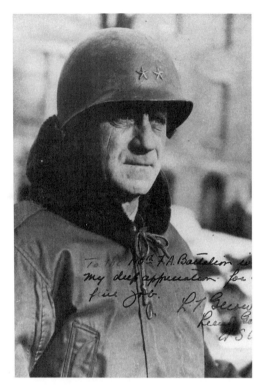

"Unselfishness is the most important quality of any officer." Maj. Gen. Leonard Gerow, leader of the U.S. Army V Corps on Omaha Beach.
<small>COURTESY MARYLAND NATIONAL GUARD.</small>

an assistant chief of staff in the War Plans Division, working closely with Marshall in Washington from December 1940 to February 1942, Gerow seemingly possessed an almost assured ticket to high command. However, there was nothing in Gerow that triggered in Marshall the same high regard he held for Eisenhower and Bradley. Despite obvious military proficiency, Gerow lacked flamboyance and did not impress people. Chronic ulcers contributed to his impassive, somber personality. Worse, for two and a half years after Pearl Harbor, Gerow had not heard a shot fired in anger. In an army that highly valued officers who had led men in battle, this was a shortcoming that would be difficult to overcome.

With all his limitations, Gerow was an affable man. He and Bradley, the commander of the U.S. First Army and Gerow's immediate boss, had forged a strong camaraderie during their residency at Fort Benning's Infantry School in 1924. Gerow finished first in the class, Bradley second. An enduring comradeship with "Ike" Eisenhower—Gerow's subordinate until 1942—kindled Gerow's wartime career despite his lack of combat experience and advanced age, no doubt cementing his role as V Corps commander and chief planner for the crucial Omaha Beach assault. Influential friends can never hurt a general's career, and Gerow's friends were among the most influential in the U.S. Army.

Maj. Gen. Leonard T. Gerow
Commander, V Corps
In my opinion unselfishness is the most important quality of any officer, be he a staff officer or a commander.

Lt. Gen. Dwight D. Eisenhower
Commander, European theater of operations, Letter to General Marshall, September 19, 1942
I am quite well aware that you do not fully share my very high opinion of General Gerow's abilities. But I submit that his loyalty, sense of duty, and readiness to devote himself unreservedly to a task, are all outstanding. Moreover, he is a very close personal friend of mine and for that reason alone would strain every nerve to meet any requirements I might place upon him.

Capt. J. Milnor Roberts
Aide-de-camp to Major General Gerow, V Corps
Gerow expected a lot. . . . He was not dramatic at all, and he didn't cater to the press. . . . [He] never called anybody by their first name. That was too familiar. And the only people who called him anything other than "General," who I came across, were either Bradley or Eisenhower, who called him "Gee." He was a pretty strict, out-of-the-old-school type of soldier.

Lt. Gen. Dwight D. Eisenhower
Letter to Major General Gerow, February 24, 1943
I can never get over the feeling, one that I have held ever since I made second lieutenant, that in every respect you have deserved recognition far above myself. . . . But you must know, as well as I do, that certain fortuitous circumstances, more than any indication of peculiar merit, were responsible for my advancement. . . .

The only thing on which I would venture to give the slightest advice is that you must be tough. You may not be able to discover among your men those that will be the best battle leaders, but you can find those who are this minute endangering the battle success of your whole command. They are the lazy, the slothful, the indifferent or the complacent. Get rid of them if you have to write letters the rest of your life.

After a disappointing spring 1944 amphibious training exercise in Britain, Eisenhower chided Gerow for his pessimism. According to Ike's aide Harry Butcher, "Gee said he wasn't pessimistic, he was merely realistic." Given the challenging task assigned to Gerow, perhaps realism and pessimism were synonymous. In truth, if Gerow had any misgivings in the spring of 1944 concerning his duty, they were justified: For a military operation of such major importance to American grand strategy in World War II, many complications that could lead to catastrophe on the beach had not yet been worked out. By D-Day, Gerow had been commanding troops at division and corps level in Britain for nearly twenty months. Few, if any, senior American generals—including Eisenhower and Bradley—knew more than he did about the enemy's infamous Atlantic Wall and the capacity for the U.S. Army to crack it.

Of all Gerow's concerns, the most critical was the obvious necessity that the invasion must come by sea. He needed no grounding in history to know that an amphibious assault against prepared enemy defenses was a dreadfully dubious operation of war. Gallipoli hung over his blueprints like the proverbial Sword of Damocles. That Anglo-French invasion against the Turkish beaches of the Dardanelles in April 1915 was defined by its almost inconceivable futility. More than a quarter of a million Allied soldiers suffered death or wounds in little more than eight months of fighting, ultimately accomplishing nothing except the killing and wounding of almost equal numbers of Turks. Even the greenest recruit understood that soldiers entrenched on coastal bluffs held an immeasurable advantage over troops invading by sea. And yet on Omaha Beach, Gerow would somehow have to figure out a method of overcoming an enemy more formidable than the Turks, dug into a shoreline even more challenging than Gallipoli.

By early 1944, Allied experience in World War II had plainly demonstrated that successful amphibious warfare doctrine was a dicey proposition. Despite the Allies' successful invasions of North Africa, Sicily, and Italy, each of those landings had come dangerously close to disaster. Problems in the November 1942 North African invasions could be blamed simply on inexperience. But at Sicily, Salerno, and Anzio, real crises had erupted when slim Allied beachheads felt the wrath of German counterattacks, usually with dreaded panzers, threatening to drive the invaders back into the sea. Gerow was certain that the Germans would try to repeat that performance in Normandy.

And then there was Dieppe. On August 19, 1942, the Allies had tested the German coastal defenses in France by launching more than 6,000 troops, mostly Canadian, on a large-scale raid against this small port city situated almost exactly halfway between London and Paris. It was the type of operation the Allies needed to perfect if a seaborne invasion of a heavily defended coast was to take place in the future. But the result was an unmitigated disaster, in which nearly two-thirds of the participants were lost. Nothing of substance was accomplished other than the dearly bought lesson that next time much more thought and practice would have to be applied to such an operation.

In the Pacific, a theater in which seaborne invasions were the norm, amphibious doctrine was equally fraught with peril. In November 1943, Japanese defenders slaughtered U.S. Marines on the beach of Tarawa. Although the Americans emerged victorious after a bitter four-day struggle, had Gerow ever viewed the stark newsreel footage of dead, bloated marines floating in the shallow waters of Tarawa lagoon, he could be forgiven for harboring pessimistic thoughts about his Omaha Beach assignment. No matter how carefully staffs planned for this type of warfare, it seemed as if the odds hadn't changed since Gallipoli.

Even the top brass at high-powered summits agreed that amphibious warfare was fundamentally risky, leading Gerow to wonder whether this form of attack could ever be done right. Failure could set the Allied war effort back months, even years. Realism, not pessimism . . .

Tehran (Eureka) Conference
Transcript, November 29, 1943

General Marshall said that the difference between a river crossing, however wide, and a landing from the ocean is that the failure of a river crossing is a reverse while the failure of a landing from the sea is a catastrophe, because a failure in the latter case means the almost utter destruction of the landing craft and personnel involved. General Marshall went on to say that his military education had been based on roads, rivers, and railroads. . . . During the last two years, however, he had been acquiring an education based on oceans, and he had to learn all over again. General Marshall said that prior to the present war he had never heard of any landing craft except a rubber boat. Now he thinks about little else.

Marshal [Kliment] Voroshilov [of the Soviet Army] replied, "If you think about it, you will do it." Marshal Voroshilov said that he wished to emphasize that if in Operation Overlord our forces were launched against the hostile coast without previously destroying the enemy positions, there could, of course, be no success. . . . First the enemy positions must be destroyed with artillery fire and bombing from the air. . . . He felt that if the operation were conducted in this way, it would prove to be a brilliant success and not result in a catastrophe.

General Marshall emphasized that no catastrophe was expected, but that everyone was planning for success.

Lt. Gen. Henry Crerar
Commander, First Canadian Army, address to Canadian Officers, June 7, 1944

Although at the time the heavy cost to Canada, and the non-success of the Dieppe operation, seemed hard to bear, I believe that when this war is examined in proper perspective, it will be seen that the sobering influence of that operation on existing Allied strategical conceptions, with the enforced realization by the Allied governments of the lengthy and tremendous preparations necessary before invasion could be attempted, was a Canadian contribution of the greatest significance to final victory.

Despite Hitler's boasts about the impregnability of his coastal defenses in western Europe, that section of Gerow's staff responsible for monitoring the enemy provided surprisingly reassuring details about the German troops deployed on Omaha Beach. In early May 1944, the Americans reported that only a single battalion of enemy infantry, amounting to fewer than 1,000 men, guarded the four-mile beach. Gerow presumed that there would be many holes in the coastal defenses, given such a low density of enemy troops. The hammer blow the enemy would receive at the hands of bombarding Allied warships and heavy bombers, followed by a direct assault delivered by two well-trained American divisions and two elite Ranger battalions—a total of 35,000 men—would surely be fatal.

Even more encouraging to Gerow was the report that the quality of the enemy beach defenders, drawn from the 716th *Bodenständige* (static defense) Division, was inferior. Intelligence declared that at least 40 percent of the division consisted of non-German soldiers, mostly Poles, who supposedly were not enthusiastic about risking their lives for the Third Reich. Further, much to Gerow's surprise, the classic German tactic of prompt and violent counterattack against Allied incursions, usually with panzers, did not appear a very realistic threat against an American beachhead. Gerow's intelligence staff asserted that only a single enemy battalion was positioned close enough to counterattack on D-Day, and it possessed no armored vehicles.

Clearly Gerow's men held a significant preponderance of force over the enemy and, perhaps more important, were unquestionably more highly motivated. If success in war depended on these two factors alone, the Americans could not lose. Warfare, however, is never so simple. Even with the encouraging intelligence about the enemy's meager numbers, Gerow fretted about the enemy's fixed defenses: concrete pillboxes, minefields, barbed wire, trenches, antitank ditches, beach obstacles. All knowledgeable military men appreciated that even reluctant soldiers would fight hard behind fortifications—the better the fortifications, the firmer their resolve. Moreover, Allied invasion planners were well aware that the enemy's coastal defenses were being supervised by Field Marshal Erwin Rommel, the wily "Desert Fox" who had confounded British and American commanders in North Africa. Allied intelligence suggested that Rommel was decidedly keen on toughening the Atlantic Wall.

Gerow also knew that terrain would certainly augment the enemy's courage, for any soldier armed with a machine gun, entrenched atop the harsh bluffs and cliffs backing up Omaha Beach, would possess a strong sense of invulnerability, coupled with a profound impression of power that his weapon could easily kill dozens of enemy troops who had no place to hide on the featureless beach.

Amphibious assaults present few opportunities for shrewd generalship—and Omaha Beach would be no exception. No matter how thoroughly V Corps planned for the invasion, there was no getting around the fact that it was a direct assault on a fixed enemy position. Past conflicts, from Pickett's Charge to Gallipoli, promised that such an assault would be challenging and costly, and despite the Americans' vast advantages in numbers and morale, the risk was great and failure was a distinct possibility.

Maj. Gen. Leonard T. Gerow
Commander, V Corps, letter to Major General Gerhardt, Commander,
29th Division, May 13, 1944
The whole success of the operation may depend on the speed with which commanders can get out their orders and the familiarity of subordinate commanders with the tasks that may be assigned to them. . . . Your people must not look at these problems from an academic standpoint. They are very real situations involving the lives of men, and every effort must be made to solve them along realistic lines.

Since his elevation to command of V Corps in July 1943, before anyone had heard of Beach 46, General Gerow had pondered the complexities of a cross-Channel attack against Hitler's Atlantic Wall. Upon the transfer of Eisenhower, Montgomery, and Bradley from the Mediterranean to

Britain in late 1943, however, Gerow found himself in the delicate role of subordinate to three new bosses, each of whom had forged a strong reputation as a combat leader in North Africa and Sicily. Empowered by Eisenhower with near-absolute power in the Overlord planning process, Bradley and Montgomery professed passionate ideas about how the invasion should be carried out, and Gerow was obligated to adhere to these decrees, even if they occasionally did not correspond with his own views.

But there was also much common ground. No one could deny that the addition of more men and matériel to the initial invasion force than General Morgan had first recommended would offer a greater chance of success. Similarly, all generals agreed that the invasion must be accompanied by supporting firepower on a scale unprecedented in military history, an essential that, at Eisenhower's insistence, would be provided mostly by the U.S. Eighth Air Force and RAF Bomber Command.

But perhaps due to Gerow's closer affiliation to the men who would actually execute the assault, he focused on some of the finer tactical elements of the Omaha landing plan. Prior to his current job as V Corps commander, Gerow had led the 29th Infantry Division, one of the two divisions scheduled to land on Omaha Beach on D-Day, and thus he identified closely with the tasks demanded of the common infantryman to accomplish the job. To Gerow, the preinvasion air and naval bombardments were comforting, but they by no means assured success. More so than its superior command organizations, V Corps perceived the upcoming struggle as a straightforward infantry fight, to be won by men who would root Germans out of pillboxes with rifles, grenades, and bangalore torpedoes.

In past Mediterranean and Pacific amphibious assaults, Allied troops had not coped with fixed fortifications, barbed wire, and beach obstacles at anywhere near the level of the Germans' Normandy defenses. Unprecedented problems demand extraordinary solutions, and at Gerow's insistence, V Corps spent a considerable amount of planning time contemplating effective means by which the Americans could rupture these defenses in the first hours of the invasion. In combat of this nature, the infantryman's best friend is the engineer, and consequently, V Corps allocated combat engineer outfits to the initial assault at a level unmatched in any previous amphibious invasion in history. For D-Day alone, Gerow scheduled twelve engineer battalions to land with the infantry on Omaha Beach—a force of nearly 10,000 sappers that virtually amounted to a division in its own right. Two of these battalions would land in the first minutes of the assault, and the rest within the next several hours.

They say that adaptable armies win wars. Probably the clearest evidence that the U.S. Army in Britain did indeed adapt to meet the challenge at Omaha Beach was the transformation of its soldiers from standard infantrymen to assault specialists. Virtually every American infantryman who would land on Omaha Beach on D-Day attended a rigorous three-week course at the U.S. Army Assault Training Center in Devon, on England's southwestern coast. There they learned landing craft drill, demolition techniques, mine clearing, and assault tactics with special weapons.

In addition to enhancing the troops' physical condition and preparing them mentally for the difficulties they would soon endure, the Assault Training Center managed to narrow the differences between an infantryman and an engineer. Soldiers who had formerly been proficient only with rifles and machine guns were taught how to use the complex array of weapons formerly associated only with sappers, such as bangalore torpedoes, flamethrowers, wire cutters, and satchel charges. But most important of all, the center imparted confidence to the soldiers who would soon storm Omaha Beach that the German defenses could indeed be overcome. Soon, when those enemy pillboxes were churning out real bullets by the thousands on D-Day, that confidence would help the Americans avert disaster.

Maj. Gen. Leonard T. Gerow
Commander, V Corps, Overlord Planning Conference, December 21, 1943
The thing that concerns me most is the man being held up on that beach by physical obstacles which he can't get by without getting out there with an implement and doing it by hand in daylight.

Lt. Col. Lucius Chase
Chief of training, U.S. Army Assault Training Center, Woolacombe, U.K.
This was approximately all [the U.S. manual on amphibious operations] had to say about fortifications: "Fortified areas are avoided in the initial assault and taken from the rear." Our feeling was—nice work if you can get it!

Col. Paul Thompson
Commander, U.S. Army Assault Training Center, Woolacombe, U.K.
Engineers had a great deal to do with the landing assault on the Normandy beaches on June 6, 1944. When I say "engineers," I have in mind not only conventional engineers like all of us know, but also the fact that the infantry of the assault divisions had been trained in engineer skills, had become so to speak

"engineer-like infantry." These infantry combat teams had received their engineer-like training at the U.S. Assault Training Center. . . . Our mission, we said, is to insure that our side wins the fight for the first 1,000 yards, which generally speaking would take us across the beach, up the exits, and onto the immediate uplands.

Eisenhower's adage that no American troops under his command would ever stop training was strictly adhered to by Gerow. Ultimately, this policy reaped dividends on Omaha Beach, not only due to the U.S. troops' enhanced combat skills, but also because every American soldier who had emerged from the Assault Training Center considered himself a superior fighter than anyone the tired German Army could produce. The Americans were ready.

Maj. Gen. Leonard T. Gerow
Commander, V Corps, Outline of Omaha Beach invasion plan,
May 17, 1944
The plan of the V Corps is comparatively simple. . . . Well organized strongpoints and tank obstacles [are] located on the beach and the high ground in rear thereof. All exits from the beach inland are mined and strongly guarded by wired-in strongpoints. Additional positions are located on the heights at either extremity of the beach. It is estimated that the beach defenses are garrisoned at the present time with about one infantry battalion, reinforced. Preliminary air and naval bombardment will effect some destruction of these defenses, but we are relying on infantry assault teams to finally take them out.

NO MISSION TOO DIFFICULT

Of the seven Allied divisions relocated from the Mediterranean to Britain in late 1943 to bulk up Overlord, one—the U.S. Army's 1st Infantry Division—will forever be linked to Omaha Beach. The "Fighting First" had existed continuously since 1917 and had forged a lengthy and impressive combat record in North Africa and Sicily in 1942–43. However, their outfit's transfer to Britain could hardly have pleased 1st Division fighting men. The 1st already had two major amphibious assaults to its credit, and in truth, any of its infantrymen who had survived North Africa and Sicily unscathed could not fail to realize that they were lucky men indeed. A soldier did not have to be an expert in probability to grasp that in combat, luck could only hold so long, and Beach 46 did not appear to be a place where good luck would be common.

General Bradley had observed that many soldiers of the 1st Division had an attitude that could only be generously described as immodest. The old saying went that the U.S. Army consisted entirely of the 1st Infantry Division—and eight million replacements. One credible rumor that had circulated after the close of the North African campaign asserted that Brig. Gen. Teddy Roosevelt, Jr., the son of the former president and the assistant division commander of the 1st, had informed the division's enlisted men that they shouldn't salute officers from commands other than the 1st. Yet another avowed that the 1st Division's commander, Maj. Gen. Terry Allen, had barged into an Algiers bar to lend a hand to some of his men who were battering an unfortunate group of MPs.

These were not the kinds of acts the U.S. Army expected of its generals, and at Bradley's instigation, both Allen and Roosevelt had found themselves unemployed by the close of the Sicilian campaign in August 1943. The new commander, a man 1st Division GIs would soon come to know simply as "The Coach," was Maj. Gen. Clarence Huebner, a grizzled veteran of thirty-four years of army service, including his first six as an enlisted man. His affiliation with the 1st Division dated to World War I, and his deeds in the AEF's first offensive on the Western Front at Cantigny in May 1918 were celebrated not only within the ranks of the 1st Division, but in the army as a whole.

Col. Stanhope Mason
Chief of Staff, 1st Division
Sincerity just oozed from [Huebner]. He had a fatherly interest in everybody in the Division, and he had a sense of humor. . . . [In Sicily,] he assembled all the officers and NCOs and made a short talk to them. This talk was simple, straight from the heart, utterly sincere, and was on the subject of the heritage of the 1st Infantry Division: Its World War One accomplishments, modestly covering his own involvement, what it had accomplished so far in World War Two, and what still had to be done. . . . Huebner had the God-given gift of making a person fear him, love him, and respect him—all at the same time.

Maj. Gen. Clarence Huebner
Commander, 1st Division, conversation with Col. Stanhope Mason, fall 1943
Somebody in this Division has got to be a son-of-a-bitch. . . . I'll chew 'em out—and if they're worth keeping, you pick 'em up and be sure we don't lose 'em.

To men who took special pride in their outfit, SHAEF's initial order to the 1st Division upon its arrival in England must have been infuriating: Every member of the Fighting First was to remove the distinctive divisional patch from his left shoulder, the one featuring the memorable "Big Red One," so that any German spies roaming Britain would not detect the 1st's transfer. Furthermore, the SHAEF top brass insisted that several 1st Division units rotate through the Assault Training Center, dismaying the combat veterans of North Africa and Sicily, who wondered why facing real enemy bullets for nearly eight months had not provided an education in combat at least equal to an ordinary camp of instruction.

Although the 1st Division had suffered immense turnover in its previous campaigns, the division still retained much of the regional affiliation it had gained based on nearly two decades of recruiting in the New York City vicinity. Indeed, the 16th Infantry, which would lead the assault on Omaha Beach, had been stationed on Governor's Island in the heart of New York harbor as recently as 1941, and even on D-Day the regiment still carried on its rolls many soldiers with the distinctive ethnic names of New York's legendary melting pot: Bracciale, Danchak, Friedman, Gallagher, Sohatski, Streczyk, Zukowski.

Brig. Gen. Clift Andrus
Commander, 1st Division Artillery
Training and planning were constant and there was no rest period. Terry Allen never had such a long period for polishing his division, and battlefield experience had to take its place. . . . All of Gen. Huebner's actions were directed at the infantry and every detail in every unit was carefully supervised. He personally handled the various infantry weapons and he even went into a foxhole and let a tank run over him. As one infantry G.I. told me, "The Old Man surely knows his business."

Capt. Charles Hangsterfer
1st Battalion, 16th Infantry, 1st Division
Some of our catchwords that I remember were: "No mission too difficult," "No sacrifice too great," "Duty first"—these were inherently instilled in all the soldiers of the 1st Infantry Division. There was no morale problem as far as we were concerned. We were all scared, but we felt that all we had to do was to turn our shoulder around, show them our Big Red One—and they would all run away.

Gen. Dwight D. Eisenhower
Supreme Commander, SHAEF, Address to 16th Infantry, July 2, 1944
You are one of the finest regiments in our army. I know your record from the day you landed in North Africa and through Sicily. I am beginning to think that your

regiment is a sort of Praetorian Guard which goes along with me and gives me luck. I know you want to go home, but I demanded if I came up here, that you would have to come with me. You've got what it takes to finish the job.

U.S. Army infantry divisions, the principal American ground combat organizations of World War II, were supposed to be homogeneous and interchangeable. However, the two V Corps divisions selected by Bradley to participate in the D-Day assault on Omaha Beach, the 1st and 29th, were practically opposites. In March 1944, during a V Corps landing exercise on Slapton Sands designated "Fox," the scruffy Willies and Joes of the Fighting First noted with amazement and pity that the 29ers, who had never heard an enemy bullet, carried on with innocent enthusiasm, clad strictly according to regulations: helmet chin straps always hooked; web gear just right; leggings fastened perfectly. And their jeeps! How did the rookies keep them so clean? And more to the point—why?

Raised in 1917 from historic state militia units that had fought on opposing sides in the Civil War, thereby gaining its "Blue and Gray" nickname, the 29th Division had fought in the trenches of the Great War, returning home in 1919 to heroes' welcomes at their local National Guard armories. In the interwar period, the 29th Division, now drawn from Maryland, Virginia, and District of Columbia National Guard units, had existed only in the War Department's imagination. About the most anyone could expect of the part-time soldiers, having had only one night of drill per week and two weeks of summer training per year, was a solid grasp of fundamental military skills. Given America's indifference to all things military in the 1920s and 1930s, however, soldierly proficiency was a rare commodity, and those who had mastered it would be highly valued when the United States was suddenly swept into World War II.

For Maryland and Virginia guardsmen, the long road to Omaha Beach began on February 3, 1941, when the War Department mobilized the 29th Division for one year of full-time military service. This commitment was less than two months from expiration when Pearl Harbor abruptly redefined each soldier's military obligation with the ominous phrase "for the duration."

The Blue and Gray's long association with General Gerow began in March 1942 at Fort Meade, Maryland, when he assumed command of the enthusiastic—but unready—division. Infused with thousands of new draftees, and minus hundreds of former guardsmen deemed unfit or too old for combat operations, the 29th Division shipped out to England in September 1942 aboard the Cunard liners *Queen Mary* and *Queen Elizabeth*—only the fourth U.S. Army division in the Second World War to make the trans-Atlantic journey. For the invasion of North Africa in November 1942, the top brass committed three of the four American divisions in England, including the 1st Division. Only the 29th Division stayed behind. It would remain in England for twenty months, right up until D-Day, and was known during that interminable training period by the cynical nickname "England's Own."

Upon Gerow's promotion to the command of V Corps, the higher organization to which the 29th Division belonged, the army assigned the Blue and Gray a new commander, Maj. Gen. Charles Gerhardt. A former cavalryman, Gerhardt armed the skeptical 29ers with a new battle cry, "Twenty-Nine, Let's Go!" and hardened the division to its upcoming role in the invasion of Europe. Gerhardt sensed that Eisenhower and Bradley had doubts about the combat abilities of his green division, especially in comparison with the skilled 1st Division. He therefore insisted that his men look like first-class soldiers and continued Gerow's policy of incessant training. But even he must have wondered whether the 29ers could fight up to the standards of the 1st Division veterans.

On the eve of D-Day, the 29th Division still carried with it the reputation of a National Guard division, which in many army circles was categorically negative. By that stage of the war, however, the truth was that less than 20 percent of division personnel had National Guard origins. The rest were draftees and products of officer candidate schools, with a handful of officers who had been educated at West Point. A majority of the conscripts were natives of Maryland, Pennsylvania, and Virginia, so the division retained much of the regional flavor of the interwar period.

The 29th Division's June 1944 rolls show that most of the key leadership positions among both officers and enlisted men, such as battalion and company commanders, first sergeants, platoon sergeants, and squad leaders, were filled by Maryland and Virginia guardsmen who had endured Gerow's and Gerhardt's rigorous weeding-out process and were highly proficient in military skills. Furthermore, more than 600 of the 29ers had completed an almost unimaginably harsh training course at the British Commando School in Scotland, and for about six months in 1943, they held the proud title of 29th Ranger Battalion. Although the army disbanded the unit in October of that year and returned the men to their regular units, every Ranger was a first-class soldier whose commando-style training would prove invaluable on D-Day.

Maj. Sidney Bingham
Commander, 2nd Battalion, 116th Infantry, 29th Division
The men of the 116th Infantry [one of the three infantry regiments making up the 29th Division] were predominantly from rural Virginia and were in large measure steeped in the traditions of the Confederacy. They were proud that the 116th was a direct descendant of the "Stonewall Brigade," which had been Stonewall Jackson's first command during the Civil War. They were magnificently trained, superbly equipped, had confidence in one another and their leaders, and were equally confident of their ability to do the job assigned to them.

M/Sgt. Paul Ritter
HQ Battery, 110th Field Artillery Battalion, 29th Division
I don't think there was ever a better-trained outfit than ours. In training, they practically killed us on the moors, ran us up and down cargo nets . . . forced marches, bitter cold, invasion landings, maneuver after maneuver. But it paid off. . . . The morning we pulled out of our camps to load on the landing craft, we passed a group from the 1st Infantry Division as we were chanting "Twenty-Nine, Let's Go!" They kept chanting back: "Go ahead, Twenty-Nine, we'll be right behind you!"

Maj. Gen. Charles Gerhardt
Commander, 29th Division, letter to U.S. Army Chief of Military History,
April 26, 1956
For a new outfit to succeed, subordinate commanders must be pushed. I had seen and studied with one of the commanders present at the disaster of Alta Villa, connected with the Salerno landings, [involving] a National Guard division that you can no doubt identify [the 36th, from Texas]. We in the 29th Division had all decided that we would not have anything like that on our record. During the training phases [for D-Day], another National Guard division [the 28th, from Pennsylvania], which had been picked for the assault, didn't measure up and was replaced by the 1st Division. Again, we had decided that we would not be placed in such a predicament.

Capt. Norval Carter
Surgeon, 1st Battalion, 115th Infantry, 29th Division, journal entry,
May 31, 1944
We realize that we are to hit soon and on D-Day (early). We have been chosen very carefully and found to be the best troops in the army today. This is no idle boast, it is fact. Another division goes in with us who are equally well trained, and their advantage is they have seen combat. To bed with minds too heavy for thinking. Everyone sleeps, but restlessly.

Among Gerow's other notable outfits scheduled to land on Omaha Beach, the most distinctive were the 2nd and 5th Ranger Battalions. Trained for special combat missions according to the extraordinarily rigorous model of the legendary British commandos, the Rangers rightfully considered themselves the U.S. Army's best. In its entirety, the Omaha Beach invasion would be a risky venture, but the riskiest of the assault tasks would in large measure be assumed by the Rangers, and their performance would determine whether they were indeed worthy of their lofty reputation.

1st Lt. Charles Parker
Commander, Company A, 5th Ranger Battalion

I was driven by the need to test myself. I volunteered for the paratroopers and the Rangers. The Rangers got there first and accepted me, thank God. . . . There was no wasted time: the thoroughness of the training and physical conditioning—we were supposed to be elite, and we were getting there. . . . Officers did everything the enlisted men did. Non-coms were expected to conduct themselves with high standards. Trouble-makers of any rank were dismissed. . . . As far as ésprit was concerned, I saw tough, rough Rangers literally cry at the threat of being sent away. We knew we were the best.

In truth, every outfit on Gerow's troop list considered itself unique. An old Ohio National Guard unit, "Cleveland's Own" 112th Engineer Battalion, held vital orders to clear one of Omaha's beach exits early on D-Day. Two other engineer battalions, the 146th and 299th, were assigned the almost impossible task of clearing enemy obstacles from the beach as the first waves of infantry landed. The men of the 146th had been acting as school troops at the Assault Training Center since late 1943 and probably knew more about amphibious assault techniques than any unit in the army. The 299th, which consisted mostly of men drawn from the Finger Lakes district of New York, had only departed the United States in early April 1944.

Armies are always developing secret weapons, but on the eve of D-Day, the most secret of all was the Duplex Drive (DD) amphibious tank. Of the army's three tank battalions trained to operate this British invention, two—the 741st and 743rd—were attached to Gerow's V Corps. The thoroughly trained tankers of these two outfits had the unenviable but downright critical job of bringing their tanks ashore on Omaha Beach before anyone else, even the infantry. That would certainly be something to tell their grandchildren about—if they survived.

The burden of command. Gen. Charles Gerhardt (at right), commander of the 29th Division, converses with Gen. Omar Bradley, leader of the First U.S. Army. Gen. Clarence Huebner (behind Bradley), commander of the "Fighting 1st" Division, listens attentively. U.S. NAVY, NATIONAL ARCHIVES.

Even thirty months after Pearl Harbor, U.S. Army units that had seen combat were still scarce. Bradley and Gerow cherished the battle-hardened 1st Division, not only because its troops had experienced combat in two different campaigns, but also because its staff was scrupulously professional and had proved that it could operate effectively amid the chaos of battle. Despite the fact that the 1st Division had joined the Overlord planning process several months after the 29th Division, the top brass bestowed upon General Huebner tactical control over most 29th Division units on D-Day. According to the invasion plan, General Gerhardt would not assume command of his 29th Division until June 7.

Aside from the 1st Division, Gerow's V Corps was by no means entirely green. Several units had seen combat in North Africa and Sicily, among them the 58th and 62nd Artillery Battalions, each of which fielded eighteen 105-millimeter howitzers mounted on self-propelled armored vehicles. The cannoneers of the 58th and 62nd were supposed to be the first artillerymen to bring their guns ashore on D-Day. Gerow also had the 20th Engineer Battalion, a unit that had opened the Moroccan port of Casablanca to American shipping shortly after the North African invasion. In January 1943, the engineers had provided security for the Casablanca summit attended by Roosevelt, Churchill, and their military staffs. But the 20th's D-Day task, which required it to open the largest of Omaha's five beach exits, promised to make their earlier work seem easy in comparison.

Maj. Gen. Leonard T. Gerow
Commander, V Corps, message to the officers and men of V Corps,
May 18, 1944

You have been selected by the Supreme Allied Commander to perform the most important military operation in the history of the world. Your task will be to destroy the Nazi defenders of the gate to Western Europe and to lead our victorious forces on to Berlin. The way has been prepared for you—the Hun has been driven from the sea, annihilated by the Russians, kicked out of Africa, bombed from the air and is now nervously and hopelessly waiting for you to deliver the knockout blow. You are well prepared to do the job. No troops have ever entered battle better trained or more magnificently equipped. Supporting us will be the tremendous resources of the Allied Naval and Air Forces. Success is assured. With victory will come the eternal gratitude of freedom-loving nations the world over. I have implicit confidence in your professional ability, your courage, and your determination. Hit hard and keep going forward. We fight on God's side and cannot fail. Good luck to all of you.

The American melting pot that was V Corps was ready for war.

CHAPTER 3

Festung Europa

DEFEND EVERYTHING, DEFEND NOTHING

Initiative—that prime determinant of military success—can shift in war like the swing of a pendulum. Stalingrad, Tunisia, and the surrender of Italy had confirmed that the Allies had at last halted the prolonged and remarkably successful German swing. Starting in late 1943, Germany possessed neither the resources nor the spirit to carry out any military strategy except the retention of the territories it currently occupied. Still, from Hitler's perspective, even a static pendulum favored Germany, for German success in 1944 could be measured by denying the Allies their strategic goals while Nazi scientists finalized Hitler's "wonder" weapons, such as rockets and jet fighters, that could ultimately win the war.

The supreme effort carried out by the Western Allies to preserve the Overlord secret could not prevent the Germans from detecting the presence of plentiful numbers of unused American, British, and Canadian divisions in Britain. In a period of little more than one month in the early fall of 1943, four new American divisions arrived in England, a fact that could hardly have escaped the attention of German intelligence. Even a man so devoid of strategic insight as Adolf Hitler could perceive that such a large and growing force of combat troops would unquestionably launch a major seaborne invasion of northwest Europe sometime in 1944.

A transformation of Germany's war strategy was about to occur. Hitler reasoned that the enemy force poised to strike in the west would most likely land on the coast of France, Belgium, or Holland. German garrisons had occupied these countries for over three years and had grown complacent. In comparison with the mortal dangers of an active front, the relatively quiet western theater had become known as a "soldier's rest camp" to the contented occupiers. At Hitler's specific order, however, this state of affairs would quickly change. The garrison troops would be toughened, coastal defenses enhanced. Moreover, the führer would no longer allow the best German garrison units in France and the Low Countries to be drawn off by the ravenous needs of the Russian front, which had been devouring German manpower and matériel at a prodigious rate since June 1941, with no end in sight.

In short, Hitler would strive to transform his *Festung Europa* ("Fortress Europe") from an empty boast to a formidable truth.

Adolf Hitler
Führer Conference, May 1943
Most dangerous for us is the creation of a second front in the West. You know that I have never yet capitulated, but I must frankly admit here that a major landing of the enemy in the West would bring us to a generally critical position. . . . Most probable is a landing in France because this would require the least shipping. Therefore we must prepare the coastline for defense. . . . Alone through the creation of an Atlantic Wall on the model of the West Wall can the security of Europe be insured.

Field Marshal Erwin Rommel
Conversation with Lt. Gen. Fritz Bayerlein, July 1943
You know, Bayerlein, we have lost the initiative, of that there is no doubt. . . . We must have a completely new approach. There can be no question of taking the offensive for the next few years, either in the West or the East, and so we must try to make the most of the advantages which normally accrue to the defense. . . . Our main effort must be directed towards beating off any attempt of the western Allies to create a second front, and that is where we must concentrate our defense. If we can once make their efforts fail, then things will be brighter for us.

Gen. Alfred Jodl
Chief of the operations staff, German high command, November 1943
My most profound conviction is based on the fact that at the head of Germany there stands a man who . . . can only have been destined by Fate to lead our peo-

ple into a brighter future. . . . I must testify that he is the soul not only of the political but also of the military conduct of the war, and the force of his will-power and the creative riches of his thought animate and hold together the whole of the *Wehrmacht*.

Adolf Hitler
Führer Directive 51, November 3, 1943
For the last two and one-half years the bitter and costly struggle against Bolshevism has made the utmost demands upon the bulk of our military resources and energies. This commitment was in keeping with the seriousness of the danger, and the overall situation. The situation has since changed. The threat from the East remains, but an even greater danger looms in the West: the Anglo-American landing! In the East, the vastness of the space will, as a last resort, permit a loss of territory even on a major scale, without suffering a mortal blow to Germany's chance for survival. Not so in the West! If the enemy here succeeds in penetrating our defenses on a wide front, consequences of staggering proportions will follow within a short time. All signs point to an offensive against the Western Front of Europe no later than spring, and perhaps earlier. For that reason, I can no longer justify the further weakening of the West in favor of other theaters of war. I have therefore decided to strengthen the defenses in the West, particularly at places from which we shall launch our long-range war [with V-rockets] against England. . . .

During the opening phase of the battle, the entire striking power of the enemy will of necessity be directed against our forces manning the coast. Only an all-out effort in the construction of fortifications, an unsurpassed effort that will enlist all available manpower and physical resources of Germany and the occupied areas, will be able to strengthen our defenses along the coasts within the short time that still appears to be left to us. . . . Should the enemy nevertheless force a landing by concentrating his armed might, he must be hit by the full fury of our counterattack. . . . I expect that all agencies will make a supreme effort toward utilizing every moment of the remaining time in preparing for the decisive battle in the West.

Supreme Headquarters Allied Expeditionary Force
Combined Intelligence Committee Report, March 15, 1944
Germany's only hope for the future lies in inflicting a decisive defeat upon the Allies in the West, the repercussions of which, both political and military, might lead at best to the gaining of a compromise peace, and at worst to the gaining of time and the opportunity once more to seize the initiative. Germany's primary task for 1944, to which all considerations on the fronts must be subordinated, is to defeat the Allied invasion of the West.

If the führer's *Festung Europa* would become a reality, its outer crust known as the Atlantic Wall would have to be hardened by a considerable degree. Organization Todt, the Nazi labor force composed heavily of foreign workers, would provide the muscle. The inspiration would derive from Field Marshal Rommel, who at Hitler's behest in December 1943 had inaugurated an inspection of the Atlantic Wall from the North Sea coast to the English Channel. In early 1944, Hitler solidified Rommel's role in the imminent battle by assigning him to the command of a group of two armies responsible for the defense of the French and Belgian seaboard where military logic dictated that the Allies would invade. Currently one of the führer's favorites, Rommel symbolically represented to both friend and foe that the defense of northwest Europe would now be taken seriously.

The clearest possible evidence that Germany's military machine had peaked by early 1944 was offered by Hitler's appointment of Rommel as the principal defender of the west. For this master of the blitzkrieg to be relegated to a command that was essentially defensive was certainly incongruous. Nevertheless, Rommel had earned his reputation due to his unconventional solutions to military challenges. In his analysis of the difficulties posed by a future Allied invasion of Europe, Rommel remained in character.

Conventional military wisdom declares that he who defends everything defends nothing. Given that the German Army was obligated to defend 3,000 miles of coast from Norway to the Pyrenees, most German officers, including Field Marshal Gerd von Rundstedt, Hitler's senior commander in the west, adhered firmly to this principle—even when their führer did not. However, Rommel offered the intriguing possibility that under certain rigidly defined conditions, the Atlantic Wall just might work. First, the German high command must greatly enhance the existing coastal fortifications in the locales the enemy would most likely invade. Second, the defenders of these areas must be increased in number and trained to carry out an unyielding defense with all possible firepower directed on the landing beaches. Third, Rommel himself must be given the freedom to control the deployment and combat operations of mobile reserves placed in close proximity to the coast in order to execute immediate counterattacks against all enemy beachheads.

Had Rommel worked under a sensible supreme commander, these conditions might have been met. Whether they would have worked, however, will never be known. Rommel owed his position to Hitler—a petty tyrant with little military sense, a man who in his years of complete control over German political and military matters had terrorized the once proud German

General Staff. Rommel's wants could not be fulfilled, and the German Army would ultimately fight the enemy on the beaches of Normandy under a highly compromised defensive scheme.

As future events would suggest, a compromised strategy was perhaps the worst strategy of all.

Field Marshal Erwin Rommel
Commander, Army Group B, Atlantic Wall Inspection Report, April 22, 1944

The enemy most likely will try to land at night and by fog after a tremendous shelling by [naval] artillery and bombers. They will employ hundreds of boats and ships unloading waterproofed amphibious vehicles and submersible tanks. We must stop him in the water, not only delaying him but destroying all enemy equipment while still afloat. . . . We must succeed in the short time left until the invasion starts to bring all defenses to such a standard that they will hold up against the strongest attack. Never in history was there a defense of such an extent, with such an obstacle, as the sea. The enemy must be annihilated before he reaches our main battlefield. . . .

From day-to-day, week-to-week, the Atlantic Wall will be stronger, and the equipment of our troops will be better. Considering the strength of our defenses, and the courage, ability, and the willingness of our soldiers to fight, we can look forward with utmost confidence to the day when the enemy will attack the Atlantic Wall. It will and must lead to the destruction of the attackers, and that will be our contribution to the revenge we owe the English and Americans for the inhuman warfare they are raging against our homeland.

Field Marshal Gerd von Rundstedt
Commander-in-Chief, western theater, 1948

[Rommel] was a brave man, and a very capable commander in small operations, but not really qualified for high command. . . . I had over 3,000 miles of coastline to cover from the Italian frontier in the south to the German frontier in the north, and only 60 divisions with which to defend it. Most of them were low-grade divisions, and some of them were skeletons.

Albert Speer
Reich minister for armaments and munitions

Given the great length of the French, Belgian, and Dutch coasts, a complete line of pillboxes spaced close enough to offer mutual protection would have far exceeded the capacity of the German construction industry. Moreover, there were not enough soldiers available to man such a large number of pillboxes. . . . For [the Atlantic Wall] we consumed, in barely two years of intensive building, 17,300,000 cubic yards of concrete worth 3.7 billion DM [*Deutsch marks*]. In addition the armaments factories were deprived of 1.2 million metric tons of iron. All this expenditure and effort was sheer waste.

Gen. Geyr von Schweppenburg
Commander, Panzer Group West

The Atlantic Wall was an outpost position. Therefore, the whole defense theory of Hitler, Jodl, and Rommel was unjustified. Since Hannibal, decisive battles had not been fought in outpost positions. With their theory, Hitler, ignorant of military matters; Rommel, the pure tactician; and Jodl, who was untouched by the holy spark as far as strategy was concerned, stamped themselves as indistinguishable from the trench-war soldiers of 1918.

Field Marshal Erwin Rommel
Commander, Army Group B, Letter to Gen. Alfred Jodl, April 23, 1944

If in spite of the enemy's air superiority, we succeed in getting a large part of our mobile force into action in the threatened coast defense sectors in the first few hours, I am convinced that the enemy attack on the coast will collapse completely on its first day.

Within the 3,000-mile front covered by von Rundstedt's command, Rommel's two armies guarded 800 miles of French and Belgian shoreline, and without precise intelligence of where the Allies would land, the Desert Fox resolved to defend it all. The zone for which he was responsible was remarkably diverse, from the cliffs and coves of Brittany to Belgium's low sand dunes. Local topography would dictate how Rommel would defend each area: Jagged and precipitous coastlines with narrow beaches, particularly those distant from Germany, would be defended sparsely; those with wide sands and gentle shorelines would be fortified in strength, especially those close to the Fatherland.

From Rommel's perspective, the Calvados shoreline in Normandy, on which four of the Allies' five D-Day invasion beaches would later be sited, lay somewhere between an illogical and a practical choice for an enemy invasion site. The Calvados beaches were much more distant from Germany than the coastal sectors farther east, and no strategic objectives of any great importance, such as a major port, were situated within immediate striking distance of the coast. Furthermore, almost two-thirds of Calvados's forty-five miles of shoreline was marked by cliffs and offshore rocks that would make a large-scale enemy landing in those vicinities virtually unworkable. Conversely, several areas of Calvados would clearly be attractive enemy invasion targets because they featured wide beaches, firm sands, and offshore waters suitable for the approach of large numbers of landing craft. Altogether, Rommel resolved to defend Calvados, but not with the fervor reserved for the more obvious potential invasion sites in Flanders and Pas de Calais.

Furthermore, the Allies contributed to Rommel's uncertainty concerning the location of the invasion by embarking on an ingenious deception plan labeled Operation Fortitude, which imparted false intelligence information to the German high command that the cross-Channel assault would come at the Pas de Calais. Even when the actual D-Day assault was initiated on June 6 against Normandy, Fortitude induced Hitler and many senior German leaders to believe that the invasion could be a feint, and that the major Allied effort would be made later against the Pas de Calais. That the Calvados beaches were not in actuality defended by the Germans as forcefully as they might have been was due in large measure to the success of Operation Fortitude. But to Gerow and Huebner, who were about to experience how vigorously the Germans would fight even with decidedly imperfect defenses, it must have been a sobering thought that the invasion might have been much worse had the enemy not been fooled at the strategic level.

Viewed from a military standpoint, the most unusual Calvados beach was to be found between the tiny villages of Vierville-sur-Mer and Colleville-sur-Mer—the one Allied planners were secretly referring to as "Omaha." To either an attacker or a defender, the most obvious characteristic of this beach was its isolation: Flanking the beach on both its eastern and western extremities for a distance of several miles were vertical cliffs and strips of sand and rock no more than a few feet wide, areas where it would be practically impossible for invading troops to move inland. The nearest town of any military significance, Bayeux, was ten miles distant, and the closest sector that could sustain a large-scale amphibious invasion was "Gold" Beach, thirteen miles to the east. "Utah" Beach, where the American VII Corps would land on June 6, was almost thirty miles distant. If the Americans failed to break out of the Omaha beachhead on D-Day, therefore, little or no help could be expected from British troops storming ashore on Gold and Americans on Utah. Although Rommel's resolution that the Allies be denied even the most narrow toehold in Europe dictated that the beach between Vierville and Colleville be forcefully prepared for defense, its remoteness surely caused him to view this spot as an unlikely invasion site.

And yet, from the Allies' perspective, the four-mile beach was a decent place for landing craft of all sizes to convey assault troops to shore. Marked by a modest beach gradient and generally placid waters in warm-weather months, a large amphibious invasion on a broad front was decidedly practical on this shoreline. True, it was not by any means a perfect beach on which to make a landing, but the invasion planners worried more about the terrain beyond the beach than they did about the beach itself.

Between the cliffs at its eastern and western extremities, the beach features a gentle curve, like a clothesline dangling loosely between two poles. That crescent shape gives the coast the feel of a giant amphitheater, with the high ground beyond the sand reserved for the audience and the offshore bay serving as the stage. It is an arena with a highly favorable perspective for the spectators, for the coastal heights rise spectacularly to 130 or more feet over the sea only a short distance inland. Truly, had this stretch of coast not been positioned to figure prominently in the history of World War II, it would have always been a popular tourist spot as a consequence of its expansive beach and arresting sea vista.

The line of bluffs between Vierville and Colleville lay unbroken and apparently unassailable save for five breaks, referred to as "draws" by Allied invasion planners. Centuries of erosion produced by water running down to the sea had formed the draws, each of which had a distinctive appearance, from a narrow, steep-walled gap to a broad valley with gently sloping sides. Within each draw, a single road varying in quality from a narrow dirt track to a paved thoroughfare climbed from the beach to the inland plateau. To both attacker and defender, the roads embodied the critical significance of the draws, for no vehicle could ever get off the beach except by climbing inland through one of these gaps—and no invasion on a scale contemplated by the Allies could succeed unless vehicles could move inland as quickly as possible after the initial landing.

LOOK UPON MY WORKS YE MIGHTY AND DESPAIR

Altogether, the beach that the world would soon know as Omaha was a highly defensible piece of terrain, and a soldier might unhesitatingly draw the conclusion that an assault against this sector, when defended by a resolute enemy who had had years to prepare its fortifications, would be as foolhardy and costly as a World War I–style frontal attack across no-man's-land. A German machine gunner positioned on the high ground at either end of the coastal crescent could fire his weapon lengthwise down the beach, perpendicular to the axis of an Allied attack, and would not fail to hit someone. Furthermore, it would be a relatively simple task for soldiers as skilled in the science of war as the Germans to drop, with deadly accuracy, a continuous barrage of bursting artillery and mortar shells on top of any enemy troops huddled on the beach. In effect, a confident German might reason that on a beach with no place for concealment, the combined effect of unremitting flat trajectory and high-angle fire would surely kill a considerable number of the invaders.

Japanese Naval Attaché to Germany
ULTRA intercept, radio message to Tokyo, May 1944
Since his inspection in autumn 1943, Rommel's policy has been to destroy Allies near coast, most of all on beaches, without allowing penetration inland. . . . Since Rommel took command strengthening coastal defenses and movement of troops to coastal sector particularly noticeable. . . . Allies must expect heavy losses in any landing operations which follow familiar pattern, and chances of success considered very slight indeed.

V Corps
Intelligence summary, March 1944
The concave shape of Beach 46 permits grazing fire by flat trajectory weapons sited anywhere along the beach or on the flat strip directly to the rear. Weapons located at Pointe et Raz de la Percée and in the strongpoints north of Colleville can enfilade the entire beach and coastal strip.

Warfare is distinguished by natural and human variables, and as a result, it is a noticeably unpredictable pursuit. The most pronounced natural variable by far on Omaha Beach was the tide, which rose and fell with spectacular energy. On average, low tide yielded 500 yards of open beach, and under certain lunar conditions that figure would grow by another 100 yards. Little more than five hours later, high tide left a strip of sand so narrow that in some places a man could not lie prone on it without getting his feet wet. Expressed in blunter terms, a soldier standing on the edge of the surf at low tide would be floating in water twenty-three feet deep at high tide.

This dramatic tidal change offered the Germans an opportunity to transform an already favorable defensive position into a nearly perfect one. Even the youngest German grenadier could foretell a slaughter should the enemy be so foolish as to land at low tide and cross 500 yards of open beach in the face of dozens of machine guns, firing from within the protective cover of concrete pillboxes. And should the enemy land at high tide,

Field Marshal Rommel's impenetrable belts of mined beach obstacles would prevent any landing craft from ever reaching shore.

Rommel was obsessed with the idea that the key to defensive success within his sector rested in obstructing and mining the entire coast of northern France and Belgium on an unprecedented scale. In theory, the scheme was nearly foolproof, but a general rarely enjoys sufficient time and resources to fulfill a military plan absolutely—and in 1944 Germany, the project was founded on matériel and labor demands that bordered on fantasy. Nevertheless, had even three-quarters of Rommel's concept been completed in Normandy, the Allies would have found it much more difficult, if not impossible, to invade successfully on D-Day.

The Desert Fox ambitiously envisioned an impenetrable mine belt lining the coast at a depth of nearly five miles, amounting to the astonishing number of 200 million mines. Coastal waters would be edged with four bands of steel obstacles, many of which would be submerged and invisible to landing craft crews—even during Normandy's famously low tides. These beach obstacles would be interlocked with thick, crisscrossed bands of barbed wire.

Rommel occasionally sketched an optimal beach defense scheme, and some of these drawings survive. Had Gerow gotten hold of one of these, his supposed pessimism might have heightened markedly, for Rommel's illustrations gave the distinct impression that an amphibious assault against such perfect defenses would be suicidal, no matter what tide. Rommel's sketches emphasized that his coastal defense scheme depended primarily on inanimate objects rather than on soldiers. If all went according to plan, most of the enemy's landing craft would be wrecked offshore, and the German defenders would do nothing more than mop up the dazed survivors who managed to reach the beach.

Field Marshal Erwin Rommel
Commander, Army Group B, Atlantic Wall Inspection Report,
April 22, 1944
Minefields will contain mines of all kinds and are likely to be highly effective. If the enemy should ever set foot on land, an attack through the minefields against the defense works sited within them will present him with a task of immense difficulty. He will have to fight his way through the zone of death in the defensive fire of the whole of our artillery. . . . [Beach obstructions] consist of a wide variety of obstacles armed by mines or shells. Every effort will be made to have them installed in depth and make them effective at all states of the tide. . . . The more time the enemy

gives us, the stronger will be the obstacles, and we may sooner or later expect all battalions to be in a position to report that their barriers are dense, deep, and armed.

Col. Benjamin Talley
Deputy chief of staff for plans, V Corps, letter to U.S. Army historian, February 18, 1948

In addition to the minefields, wire, and antitank ditches, the Germans had hung several hundred 10-inch and 12-inch high explosive shells immediately below the top of the cliffs at intervals of about 100 to 200 feet throughout their length. It was reported by some of the demolition teams that these shells were wired to detonate either by increased tension, a release of tension on a trip wire, or by disturbing additional wires hung down the cliff side.

In the end, Rommel did not get the time he needed. When the Americans stormed ashore on Omaha Beach on June 6, 1944, the German defenses did not in the least resemble Rommel's vision. Less than half of his beach obstacles had been installed, and many of the earliest invasion impediments erected by the Germans had deteriorated and were no longer effective due to incessant pounding by the tides and the Norman weather. Finally, the division assigned to defend this sector, the 716th, had deployed only a tiny fraction of the land mines and barbed wire that Rommel had envisioned if his plan was to have any chance of working. Thus the initial American waves that came ashore shortly after low tide on D-Day were in no way physically obstructed.

Field Marshal Erwin Rommel
Commander, Army Group B, Atlantic Wall Inspection Report, April 22, 1944

Here and there I noticed units that do not seem to have recognized the graveness of the hour and who do not even follow instructions. There are also reports of cases in which my orders have not been followed—for instance, that all minefields on the beach should be live at all times. . . . I do not intend to issue unnecessary orders every day. I give orders only when and if necessary. I expect, however, that my orders will be executed at once and to the letter. . . .

A lot has to be done until the defenses are complete. Right now, most battalion sectors show only a few mines, do not have any depth, and beach obstructions are much too weak and cannot even stop small boats. Officers down to company commanders must supervise the installations and see to it that all defenses in their respective sectors are dense and effective. . . .

Army Talks **magazine**
U.S. Army, European theater of operations, May 31, 1944
They [the Germans] would like for you to think that they have the entire coast of Europe organized into one mighty fortress—pillboxes for miles inland, heavy defense guns covering the entire coast, a sort of Siegfried Line around Europe. Actually this discouraging picture is straight from the propaganda mill. They have built powerful defenses, but the coast of Europe is a long one and they have to spread themselves pretty thin. We can go in where we choose. The pillboxes which they have built we can knock down. . . . In the Pacific, we captured Kwajalein, one of the Marshall Islands which was defended by pillboxes as thick as raisins in a Christmas cake. We killed more than 4,000 Japs but lost less than 200 men ourselves.

Special Tactical Study Number 30
British intelligence, German views on the Normandy Landing,
November 28, 1944
Troops employed in coastal defenses were suffering from overstrain as a result of incessant laboring on the fieldworks—as they were ordered to do from first light to dusk for weeks before the invasion. Sentries, especially the 17-year-old recruits, often went to sleep from weariness.

Given Germany's fixation with ethnic purity, the outfit selected to defend the beaches of Calvados against Allied invasion cannot have been considered very battle-worthy. Despite the 716th Infantry Division's status as a part of the German Army, it contained considerable numbers of non-Germans, mostly Poles and various ethnic groups drawn from ex-prisoners of war captured on the eastern front. For one reason or another, these unenthusiastic warriors succumbed to the severities of German military life rather than face an uncertain future at home under Nazi occupation. Their division's identifying number exposed their low standing within the *Heer* (army), for divisions numbered in the 700 series were generally immobile, manned by very young or overage soldiers, and equipped with mediocre weapons. The German high command recognized the 716th's shortcomings, rating it at *Gefechtswert* (combat value) level III—suitable only for static defense missions.

Although the men of the 716th may have been second-rate soldiers, Rommel reasoned that first-rate coastal fortifications might compensate for their human deficiencies. The German scheme for the defense of the Vierville-Colleville coastal sector did not endeavor to establish a continuous defensive belt in the manner of a World War I trench line, nor did it attempt to give the position any depth. Instead, the men of the 716th, aided by the laborers of the Todt Organization, constructed fifteen semi-independent strongpoints (*Widerstandsnest*, or WN), numbered consecutively WN60 to WN74 from east to west. Most of these positions were concentrated on ground dominating the five draws leading inland from the beach, for the Germans presumed that an invading enemy would have to attempt to move off the beach through those gaps. Along the lengthy bluff crests between the draws, however, the 716th made little effort to build solid fortifications because the movement of large bodies of enemy troops up those forbidding slopes was not deemed feasible—a decision that would have profound consequences on D-Day.

With an expertise acquired from six years as Hitler's prime military contractor, the Todt Organization knew how to build sophisticated fortifications. Nearly all Omaha Beach *Widerstandsnest* included one or more Todt pillboxes, some of which were mammoth structures with sloping concrete faces several feet thick, big enough to contain large-caliber guns. Generally only a direct hit from a heavy naval shell could hope to penetrate the concrete, although a bazooka round or flamethrower blast fired directly through a pillbox's narrow aperture might kill or wound the occupants. The Germans, however, structured their defenses so that enemy infantry would find it extraordinarily difficult to get that close to a pillbox.

Rommel fully understood that any Allied seaborne invasion would be preceded by a large volume of naval gunfire, and as a consequence many German coastal pillboxes were cleverly positioned in folds of the ground so that they would be virtually invisible when viewed from the sea and nearly impossible to destroy with naval gunfire. Their apertures permitted fire only in a lateral direction, down the length of the beach rather than directly out to sea. This type of enfilade fire not only would be difficult for enemy sailors to spot, but also would be much more lethal against Allied troops moving across the beach. The Germans generally built the sturdiest pillboxes directly in or immediately adjacent to the mouths of the five beach exits, and their remarkable durability is confirmed by their survival to the present day, for the most part intact. Furthermore, the German defensive positions were sited with interlocking fields of fire so that Allied troops who attempted to exit the beach by moving up the draws would be met by withering crossfires that the Germans hoped would be impenetrable.

Rommel did not consider the Calvados coast of Normandy the most likely place the Allies would invade, yet he had to consider the possibility that they would do so. Before March 15, 1944, the 716th Infantry Division alone covered this forty-five-mile front, a remarkably long distance for an

June 6, 1944: Omaha Beach

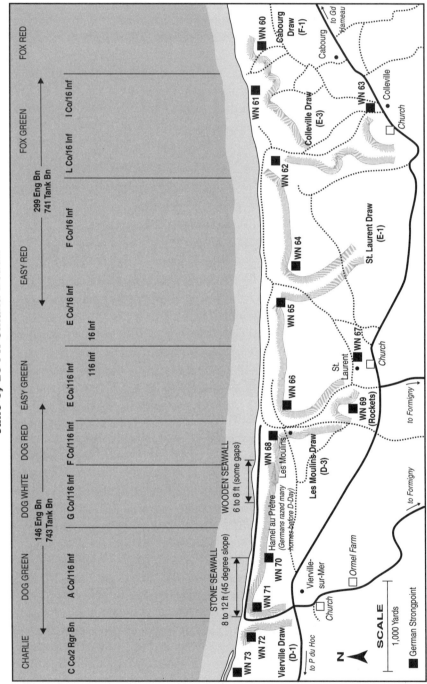

immobile division of less than 10,000 men. On the four-mile front from Vierville to Colleville, 600 troops were available for coastal defense, with little hope of reinforcement within the first twenty-four hours. Even Rommel's commitment of the more agile 352nd Infantry Division to the defense of the Calvados coast on March 15, a decision that nearly doubled the number of coastal defenders on Omaha, conspicuously failed to provide sufficient manpower to counter the rapidity with which the British and Americans could bring troops ashore. On D-Day, within the first hour of the Omaha invasion alone, the Americans planned to land a force almost seven times as large as the German garrison. True, the Germans had near-perfect defensive terrain and formidable fortifications, but against such an overwhelming ratio, they would sooner or later be crushed unless their beach obstructions and minefields could be significantly enhanced to fulfill Rommel's defensive scheme.

SOMEONE HAD BLUNDERED

Sometime in the chaos of the first two hours of the invasion, an American intelligence officer made an astonishing deduction after interrogating the first batch of German prisoners captured on Omaha Beach: The German beach defenders, who an Allied intelligence report had confidently promised would be inferior and few in numbers, had been reinforced by a fresh infantry division, the 352nd, which that same report had asserted could not possibly reach the coast from its bivouac area around St. Lô until June 7 at the earliest. The GIs surely wondered how an invasion plan that had been meticulously prepared with the full support of the seemingly omnipotent Allied intelligence teams could have missed the presence of an entire German division. Some of the boys in Omar Bradley's G-2 section had missed this one—and if they missed something so fundamental, what else did they get wrong?

The 352nd was rumored to be a top-quality mobile outfit containing numerous battle-hardened veterans of the Russian front and equipped with superior weapons relative to the static 716th Division. For those perplexed Americans seeking an immediate explanation for the enemy's unexpectedly ferocious resistance in the first few hours of the invasion, the 352nd's presence provided a hasty, if imperfect, answer. After conducting interviews with the first prisoners from the 352nd on the beach, American interrogators concluded sullenly that the GIs had been the recipients of a massive dose of bad luck on D-Day. According to the captives, the 352nd was not deployed on the coast, but by coincidence had been conducting anti-invasion exercises when the American landing commenced and had promptly been swept into the battle.

16th Infantry, 1st Division
S-3 D-Day Action Report, June 1944

From one of the first German prisoners, it was learned on D-Day that on D-1 [June 5] the 352nd Infantry Division moved out of the St. Lô vicinity to the coastal area of beach Omaha for maneuver purposes. At 0630 hours on D-Day, when CT [Combat Team] 16 assaulted beach Omaha, the 352nd Infantry Division was behind the coastal strongpoints, which were manned by personnel of the 726th Infantry Regiment [of the 716th Division].

Despite the perpetuation and broad acceptance of this report for decades after D-Day, it was entirely untrue—and several Allied officers at the time knew it. In truth, Rommel had transferred the 352nd from St. Lô to the Calvados coast on March 15, 1944, almost three months prior to the Allied invasion, a move that neither the Allies' top secret ULTRA intercepts of German radio messages nor their conventional intelligence sources had managed to detect. The fact that the 352nd Division had moved up to the coast in support of, rather than displacing, 716th units had perhaps helped screen its relocation from the Allies, but for a military operation as momentous as the invasion of Omaha Beach, the Allies' failure to detect the transfer of an entire German division directly into the combat zone was one of their most notable intelligence slips of the war.

Oberleutnant Hans Heintze
Number 5 Company, 916th Infantry Regiment, 352nd Division

These Frenchmen and others later knew exactly where we—and the entire [352nd] division were relocated. . . . It's hard for me to believe that the French underground and, through them, Allied intelligence didn't find out that information. Supposedly, the Allies only knew that the 716th was there and were totally surprised that we'd been deployed [to the coast] as well. I can't imagine that. No one was discreet. On the contrary—we had such a good relationship with the French in the area that we communicated with each other, and there were no secrets. . . . I can't believe no one knew unless they were really sleeping on the job.

Oberstleutnant Fritz Ziegelmann
Assistant chief of staff, 352nd Division

It became gradually clearer that an invasion might occur which in particular would concern the sectors of the 352nd Infantry Division that summer. . . . From a conversation my division commander [Gen. Dietrich Kraiss] had in May with Field Marshal Rommel—whom he knew very well—he seemed to expect the beginning of the invasion in early August. . . . The grouping of the reserves was a hobby of Field Marshal Rommel. It was his opinion that he could destroy the enemy with an attack in front of the Main Line of Resistance—consequently, in the water. All heavy weapons of the infantry were incorporated in the defensive installations, or had joined new combat installations. On the occasion of his visit in May, I was reproached because I did not bring the reserves close enough to the coast. He wished every soldier to be able to concentrate his fire on the water. My query, that the width of the division sector (53 kilometers) and the weakness of our rearward defenses made possible an infiltration through the less heavily occupied sections, and that to counter this, assault reserves were necessary behind the lines, remained unanswered. . . . My division commander agreed with me.

V Corps
G-2 intelligence estimate, May 15, 1944
Probable Enemy Action: 1) Strong defense of Beach 46 by one battalion of the 726th Infantry Regiment, 716th Division; 2) Company-size counterattacks to re-establish beach defenses.

Since the end of the Second World War, history has largely failed to record that late on June 4, the highest levels of Allied intelligence correctly deduced that the enemy's 352nd Division was positioned on the Calvados coast and would surely become involved early in the D-Day fighting, both on Omaha and Gold Beaches. However, at that late date—about thirty hours before the invasion would commence—even an intelligence break-through of this magnitude could not affect the impending battle. Though enemy resistance on the beaches in the early hours of the invasion would now be fiercer than anticipated, it was much too late to alter invasion plans and reset D-Day objectives. According to Col. Benjamin "Monk" Dickson, Bradley's chief intelligence officer, this key information "was transmitted to V Corps [Gerow] and the HQ 1st Division [Huebner]," which were already onboard the transport USS *Ancon* heading to Normandy.

If Gerow or Huebner took any action in response to this piece of alarming news, history does not record it. They may have judged it imprac-tical—if not impossible, due to obligatory radio silence on the Channel crossing—to inform subordinate units at that late hour. Or they may have sensed that passing on such a piece of disturbing intelligence would have demoralizing effects on the assault troops with no balancing positive impact. For whatever reason, by the time the invasion began, no troops below 1st Division headquarters were aware of the 352nd Division's deployment on the Normandy coast in the sectors that encompassed parts of Gold Beach and all of Omaha. Indeed, after the end of the war, few learned that in truth, the 352nd had been positioned there since March.

Before Gerow learned about the presence of the 352nd Division on the coast, his invasion plan assumed 600 Germans would initially resist the assault on Omaha Beach. Given that the V Corps invasion front would cover more than four miles, Gerow considered 600 enemy defenders, belonging to a second-rate coastal defense division, to be no match for the 35,000 Americans who would soon swarm across the beach on D-Day. He fretted more about GIs being blocked by obstacles and minefields than he did about the troop ratio.

Until June 5, Gerow remained blissfully ignorant of the fact that Rommel's transfer of the 352nd Division to the coast in March had altered that troop ratio by a considerable degree. Instead of 600 defenders, the real number would be more like 1,100—and made up of troops the German high command rated in its highest combat category, meaning they were fully mobile and capable of launching large-scale attacks. Also, the Allies' original intelligence estimate had declared that only a single enemy battalion posted in reserve behind Omaha could counterattack on D-Day. But when the 352nd was moved to the coast, that number was increased to at least five.

21st Army Group
Intelligence Estimate, June 4, 1944
For some time now in other areas coastal divisions have been narrowing their sectors, while divisions the role of which has hitherto been read as lay-back have nosed forward into the gaps provided by the reduced responsibility of the coastal divisions. . . .The evidence that the same has happened on the left in the case of 716th Division is slender indeed; yet it should not be surprising if we discovered that it has two regiments in the line and one in reserve, while on its left the 352nd has one regiment up and two to play.

According to Rommel, even the deployment of the 352nd Division to the coast would not be sufficient to stop the Allied onslaught—and he was right. Though 1,100 beach defenders were better than 600, they would still at best be capable only of slowing down an Allied landing. And if the Allies landed on a broad front in several different places at once, as they did indeed do, the 352nd's five reserve battalions would be dissipated responding to different threats, and hardly capable of throwing the enemy back into the sea. What Rommel really needed was a few panzer divisions deployed near the coast. But happily for Gerow, there were none near Omaha Beach—the closest was located at Caen, nearly thirty miles away.

Like most of Adolf Hitler's flawed military schemes, theory and reality did not coincide in the Atlantic Wall. On Hitler's orders, Germany had committed vast resources over several years to the coastal defense venture, but no one dared tell the führer of the plan's fundamental flaw: By spring 1944, the German Army simply could not commit sufficient manpower to defend the entire coast adequately, except at the most obvious invasion sites such as Belgium and Pas de Calais. When General Morgan of COSSAC recommended Normandy as an invasion site and the Allied top brass accepted his proposal, Hitler's faith that the Atlantic Wall would prevent the Allies from establishing a secure foothold in northwest Europe was crushed in a single stroke. The wall's limited capacity to impede the Allied invasion, particularly in Normandy, utterly failed to justify its immense cost.

CHAPTER 4

Fortune Favors the Bold

MOTHER NATURE'S WARRIORS

In a military operation as complex as Overlord, the wishes of mere mortals were generally subservient to the unbending laws of nature. In truth, the Allies could not hope to achieve their invasion goals without a profound knowledge of the natural conditions characteristic of Normandy, and to generals such as Eisenhower, Montgomery, Bradley, and Gerow, a keen fluency in Norman tides, weather, and currents was as weighty as a grasp of strategy. In war, nature is a neutral; but if only for an instant, Allied planners strove to make nature an ally by setting an invasion day and time so precisely that natural conditions would collectively benefit the invaders.

Churchill and Roosevelt had promised Stalin at the Tehran conference that the invasion of Europe would occur by May 1, 1944. This was a guarantee that the Allies made every effort to keep, as Stalin had in turn pledged to initiate a supporting Soviet offensive on the eastern front simultaneously. As the invasion plan expanded in scope in early 1944, however, SHAEF concluded that the assault must be delayed by one month so that the Allies could gather more landing craft, and therefore Eisenhower set a tentative invasion target date of June 1, declaring that date "Y-Day" with a code name of "Halcyon."

In April 1944, as SHAEF learned more about the German defenses of Calvados—particularly the profusion of obstacles erected on the beaches—its choice of a target invasion date became more problematic, as any assault during a high or mid-tide could be thwarted by the enemy's obstructions. Therefore, to enlist nature as an ally, Eisenhower and his senior commanders resolved in early May to launch the invasion on Y+4 (June 5), Y+5 (June 6), or—at last resort—Y+6 (June 7). All three days featured low tides at or near sunrise, which would enable first-wave landing craft to beach soon after dawn well short of the enemy beach obstacles. Before the rising tide submerged those obstacles, they could then be demolished by engineers, allowing later craft to land unimpeded as the tide climbed. Furthermore, June 6 featured a full moon, an important aid for nocturnal flying that would positively improve predawn parachute drops and heavy bomber assemblies in the night skies over England. Two or three days before and after June 6 would also offer bright lunar light.

Omaha Beach Natural Conditions
Bigot-Neptune top secret monograph, April 21, 1944
First Twilight June 6: 5:16 A.M.
Sunrise June 6: 5:58 A.M.
Sunset June 6: 10:10 P.M.
End of Twilight June 6: 10:48 P.M.
Moonrise June 5: 8:33 P.M. (sets 5:31 A.M. June 6)
Moonrise June 6 (Full Moon): 9:44 P.M. (sets 6:04 A.M. June 7)
1st Low Water June 6: 5:18 A.M. (4 ft. above datum)
1st High Water Stand June 6: 9:42 A.M. to 12:40 P.M. (22 ft. above datum)*
2nd Low Water June 6: 5:41 P.M. (3.5 ft. above datum)
2nd High Water Stand June 6: 10:00 P.M. to 1:00 A.M. June 7 (22.7 ft. above datum)*
Mean Daily Maximum Air Temperature: 66° F
Mean Daily Minimum Air Temperature: 55° F
Average Sea Temperature: 56° F
Mean Daily Maximum Air Temperature: 66° F
Chance of Breaking Waves 1 ft. or less: 57%
Chance of Breaking Waves 1 to 4 ft.: 28%
Chance of Breaking Waves 4 to 8 ft.: 1.5%
Chance of Breaking Waves 8 to 12 ft: 1.3%
Chance of Breaking Waves Greater than 12 ft.: 0%
Chance of Moderate Chop due to Offshore Winds: 12%

*Owing to the character of the high water stand near Port-en-Bessin [Omaha Beach], it is not feasible to indicate the precise time of high water, and so the times of beginning and end of high water stand are given instead.

NOTE: "High Water Stand" is defined as the period, near the time of high water, during which the tide does not vary by more than one foot. Heights of tides are referred to a "datum" plane, which is the approximate level of lowest low water.

If Eisenhower feared one thing about the Germans, it was their proclivity to counterattack as swiftly as possible in response to Allied attacks. Inevitably, or so SHAEF thought, the enemy would strike back at the Allied beachheads as early as the night of D-Day—or certainly within the next day or two. Accordingly, probably the most inflexible of the SHAEF invasion designs was to commence all five beach assaults as soon as possible after sunrise, thereby allowing almost seventeen hours—the length of daylight in Normandy at that time of year—to land such a multitude of fighting troops that even the fiercest enemy counterattack could not smash the beachheads, however narrow they might be.

And so SHAEF passed the word down to all ground, naval, and air commanders involved in invasion planning: D-Day would be June 5, 6, or 7. However, should harsh weather or some other unforeseen circumstance compel a postponement, the next invasion dates with suitable tidal conditions would not occur until June 19, 20, or 21. Those later dates would feature no moonlight at all. Furthermore, the delay would offer the enemy two additional weeks to improve its beach defenses, a potential development that could yield ruinous consequences.

On May 8, with the invasion dates narrowed down to three, Eisenhower polled the commanders of his five beach assault forces about their preferences for the precise date and time of the assault in their sectors. A reply would have to be in SHAEF hands within one week so that the invasion plan could be finalized. One of the factors SHAEF learned as a result of this inquiry was that each of the five invasion beaches exhibited highly distinctive tidal conditions, thereby forcing a reluctant Eisenhower to allow each assault a different starting time—designated "H-Hour." However, Eisenhower limited the maximum variance between earliest and latest H-Hour to sixty-five minutes, thereby lessening any ill effects that might occur due to an unsynchronized invasion.

Gerow's terse May 13 reply to Eisenhower concerning the timing of the Omaha Beach invasion summarized his preferences:

Maj. Gen. Leonard T. Gerow
Commander, V Corps, memorandum to SHAEF, May 13, 1944
OBJECTIVES:

A. Permit a minimum of 20 minutes in which obstacles will be dry-shod [i.e., not submerged by rising tide].

B. Permit a minimum of 87 minutes after first light for aerial bombardment and naval gunfire. NOTE: The Air Force plan for employment of heavy bombers calls for a minimum of 57 minutes after first light to reach the target area and 30 minutes for bombing.

C. Permit DD [duplex drive] tanks to debark during darkness.

D. Permit LCT(A)'s to touch down and unload.

D-DAY AND H-HOUR

1. Y+4 [June 5], 0610 hours, will just meet objective "A" with no factor of safety for minor delays which may occur. It fails by 34 minutes to meet objective "B". It will meet objectives "C" and "D".

2. Y+5 [June 6], 0645 hours, will just meet objective "A". It will just meet objective "B" if the time for the fulfillment of the mission assigned to heavy bombers is reduced from an estimated 87 minutes to 83 minutes. It will meet objective "C". DD tanks will debark 12 minutes prior to sunrise.

3. In considering Y+6 [June 7] or Y+7 [June 8], objectives "A", "B" and "D" can be met, the controlling factor for these days being objective "A"; namely, breaching of underwater obstacles. Objective "C" cannot be met. A study of the beach gradients indicates that objective "D" can be met on any date under consideration.

RECOMMENDATION

It is recommended that D-Day be set as Y+5 [June 6] and H-Hour at 0635 hours, provided the Air Force will give assurance that the heavy bombers can accomplish this mission; otherwise 0645 hours on the same date.

Eisenhower did not grant Gerow's wish; on May 17, the supreme commander selected D-Day as Y+4, or June 5. Ironically, when Eisenhower was later forced to postpone D-Day by twenty-four hours to June 6 due to inclement weather, Gerow by default got the exact invasion date he had requested of SHAEF on May 13.

YOUNG MEN LOOKING OLD

Allied planners christened that stage of the Overlord operation concerned with the initial landing of Allied forces in Normandy as "Operation Neptune." As an amphibious invasion, Neptune was a cooperative venture among naval, ground, and air forces. From the naval perspective, Neptune's most perilous phase was the passage of large numbers of ground troops, crammed into slow and vulnerable transports, over the open sea to the Normandy coast. The overall success of a World War II seaborne invasion depended entirely on fulfillment of this stage of the operation, and yet when it was carried out flawlessly, and troops were deposited on their target beaches in a timely fashion, history has typically overlooked this phase as nothing more than a precursor to the more noteworthy land battle.

In 1944, the English Channel was generally not a safe place for Allied ships, given the close proximity of German air and naval forces in France. Wisecracking GIs appreciated the dangers, professing a preference for the land because no one had yet figured out how to dig a foxhole in the water. A single torpedo from a dreaded German U-boat or patrol vessel could send one of those large transports to the bottom in a matter of minutes—and with it more than 1,000 embarked troops. That the enemy was indeed capable of such carnage was proved on April 28, 1944, when German torpedo boats attacked an American convoy rehearsing off the south coast of England for the upcoming Utah Beach landing and sank two large landing craft with the loss of 749 lives. If a small enemy force could deal such a devastating blow in a training exercise, what would the Germans achieve on D-Day?

The English Channel had no road map, but that is precisely what Rear Adm. John Hall needed to navigate his command, designated "Force O," successfully across the Channel to Omaha Beach. Hall's Force O consisted of nearly 700 ships of fifty varieties, figures that did not include the hundreds of small landing craft slung aboard those ships' davits during the Channel crossing. In addition, Force O embarked 35,000 soldiers from the 1st and 29th Infantry Divisions, plus dozens of smaller army commands, all set to land on Omaha Beach on D-Day. Hall was a grizzled, white-haired U.S. Navy veteran with plenty of amphibious warfare expertise gained in the Mediterranean, but the enormity of his Neptune task must have been daunting even to him.

The journey from England to Normandy was only about 120 miles, but 5 of those miles traversed a reportedly formidable German mine belt that would wreak havoc on the transports if they were not preceded by minesweepers. Even minesweepers did not guarantee success: given the enemy's penchant for using new "wonder weapons," there existed the distinct possibility that no matter how carefully the Allies swept for mines, many ships would still be sunk by mines that could not be detected. Furthermore, at this time of year in northern Europe, darkness was of especially

"No troops have ever entered battle better trained or more magnificently equipped." Somewhere near Plymouth, England, troops from the 115th Infantry, 29th Division, head to their landing craft for the journey to Normandy, June 1944. U.S. Army Signal Corps, National Archives.

short duration, and therefore Force O would have to make the Channel crossing mostly in daylight—with all its attendant dangers of enemy air and naval attack.

The enemy, however, was not the only element that menaced Hall's ships. Force O would have to share limited sea room with 2,000 Allied warships and transports bound for the other four invasion beaches, and despite the short period of darkness the fleets would endure, nighttime traffic snarl-ups and collisions would be a real hazard. Even worse, to minimize the enemy mine threat, the Neptune plan dictated that near the midpoint of their journey, assault convoys such as Force O funnel into specially designated swept channels 40 miles in length—but only 400 yards wide. Accordingly, convoy sailing schedules would have to be carefully preplanned and rigidly enforced, and even then the vast quantity of ships at Hall's disposal would necessitate a tightly bunched column of slow-mov-

June 5, 1944: Force O Movement to Normandy

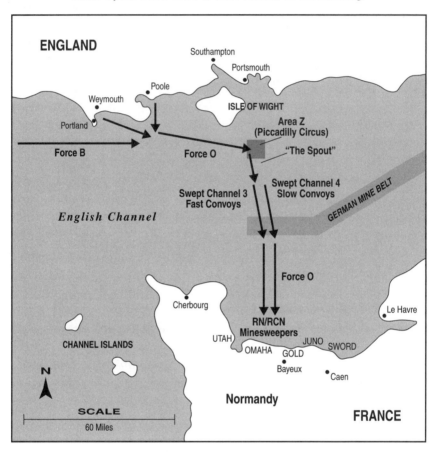

ing vessels 20 miles long. Such a snakelike procession would be especially difficult to protect.

Neptune would not be an operation for rookie sailors.

Rear Adm. John Hall
Commander, Force O, Operation Neptune Action Report, July 1944
Several subordinate commanders within the Force have commented adversely upon the extreme length of the assault convoys and their consequent unwieldiness and vulnerability. The Force Commander recognized these facts while the operation was being planned, but saw no way to change them. They were imposed by conditions beyond his control. . . . In the opinion of the Force Commander the enemy missed a golden opportunity by not attacking the assault convoys while they were in the vulnerable formation and restricted waters of the swept channels leading to the Transport Area. A determined torpedo plane attack positively could not have been stopped, and had it been driven home, resulting in the loss of several of the large transports, it would have been extremely serious.

Ninth Air Force
IX Fighter Command, Report of D-Day Operations, July 1944
P-38s had been chosen to afford cover over the main shipping route and its flanks because the relative ease of their identification would afford a guarantee against friendly fire. [P-38s, known as "Lightnings," had highly distinctive twin tails, and for Operation Neptune, their wings were specially painted with alternating black and white stripes.] Two Ninth Air Force Groups, together with four groups from VIII Fighter Command [of the Eighth Air Force] were assigned to this task. Patrols of four squadron strength [each squadron of sixteen P-38s, totaling sixty-four aircraft] were to maintain continuous cover from 1600 hours D-1 [June 5] on, and to operate at heights of from 3,000 to 5,000 feet or below clouds. Each patrol was scheduled to be over the shipping area for 90 minutes.

On May 25, 1944, shortly before midnight, Admiral Hall and all Force O naval officers holding requisite security clearances were commanded to open their top secret operation orders for the invasion—700 pages long and three inches thick—with the simple but momentous directive, "Execute Operation Neptune." Although more than a week remained until Eisenhower's designated invasion date, June 5, the sailors had many intricate tasks to fulfill. Warships, transports, and landing craft located at distant harbors throughout Britain and Northern Ireland had to gather at the southern English ports of Portland and Poole, from where Force O would depart for

Normandy; troops must be embarked, plentiful ammunition and supplies loaded; and most important, all sailors from admirals down to the youngest swabbies would have to prepare for their D-Day roles.

Ens. J. J. Terranella
Executive, LCI(L)-554 Action Report, June 20, 1944

We all felt we had a job to do and hoped we wouldn't have to remain inactive too long. It was a relief to see the Army come aboard; we now knew we didn't have to wait as long as these other ships that had been here for several months. Although we had not been briefed, the Army had, and since we were all restricted to the ship we learned a great deal about the plans on D-Day in our conversations with the troops. Their information did very much to bolster our morale. When we shoved off for the invasion we were pleasantly amazed at the terrific mass of ships that were continually collecting as we proceeded along the English coast, and then across the Channel. The tremendous air power overhead added to our ever-growing confidence that this invasion would be a great success. All of us tried to sleep that night, but most of us only rested.

1st Lt. George Bryan
HQ Company, 2nd Battalion, 116th Infantry, 29th Division, July 1944

The ship was crowded, but the extra food made the men happy to be aboard. Most of the time was spent readjusting equipment and having debarkation drills. Every man seemed to be very much interested in making certain that he and his equipment were in top-notch condition.

By the evening of June 3, Force O had completed all its preparatory jobs, and a few hours later, the first of its convoys set sail for Normandy. However, all vessels were hastily recalled to Portland and Poole when Eisenhower canceled the June 5 invasion due to bad weather. Indeed, Channel conditions on June 4 were so rough that many vessels could hardly beat their way back to port against the gale-force westerly winds. Early on June 5, word passed down from SHAEF that the invasion would now take place the following day, and so after a rest of only a few hours at anchor at Portland and Poole, Force O convoys recommenced their journey to Normandy.

Army Talks Magazine
U.S. Army, European Theater of Operations, May 31, 1944

As you move onward and look at the destruction and misery around you, thank God that your own land has been spared the agony of German occupation. The peoples of Europe have suffered. Do everything you can to make them know that with your coming, their suffering is eased and may soon be over. . . . Bear in mind continuously that the operation for which we have been assembled in Great Britain—the invasion of Europe—must be successful, or we have lost World War II. Think that over.

Capt. Norval Carter
Surgeon, 1st Battalion, 115th Infantry, 29th Division, journal entry,
May 31, 1944
Well, the further briefing has been given. It is so fascinating not only to sit and listen to the plan, but also to watch the facial expressions of the officers. No smiles except one officer. Everyone dead serious. Faces immobile and deeply lined. Young men look old. No fear shown, no nervous finger-tapping, just quiet, deeply thoughtful immobility.

Capt. Lawrence Bour
HQ Company, 2nd Battalion, 16th Infantry, 1st Division
Personally the one thing that upset me was finding out how short the voyage was scheduled to be. I had put off worrying until the last minute. Then upon boarding I found out the next day was the initially scheduled D-Day [June 5]. I spent an hour that evening alone on deck, mentally adjusting myself to the possibilities.

Motor Machinist's Mate 1st Class Clifford Lewis
U.S. Coast Guard, LCI(L)-94, Diary, June 5, 1944
At about 1700 we got underway. Skipper called us all into the crew quarters and had a long diagram or photograph of the beach on the mess table. All pillboxes, machine guns, mines, entanglements & other obstacles. Our beach is to be Red Dog, close to Easy Green. He said we could expect plenty of mines & that subs & E-Boats would be active. New weapons were expected and 1,950 enemy planes were available for use against us. He wished us the best of luck and then Mr. Mead checked over all our names for correct serial numbers & beneficiaries.

The first leg of the journey was the easy part: Divided into five convoys, each of which was in turn separated into a fast (twelve-knot) and slow (five-knot) group, Force O sailed eastward, hugging the southern English coast, heading straight for an assembly point that Neptune orders designated "Area Z." Christened "Piccadilly Circus" by the British, Area Z was a theoretical circle, ten miles in diameter, off the southeast coast of the Isle of Wight. Here, Force O's mission turned complex, for 2,700 Allied ships involved in the invasion would be making ninety-degree turns to the south within this circle, all in a period of only about twelve hours. Unless all sailors knew exactly what they were doing, chaos loomed.

And danger, too, for the southward turn out of Area Z led Force O down a narrow channel, appropriately nicknamed "The Spout," which headed directly into the dreaded German mine belt.

Rear Adm. John Hall
Commander, Force O
Having participated in amphibious assault landings in French Morocco as Chief of Staff to Admiral Hewitt, and in Sicily and Italy as Attack Force Commander, the crossing to me was perhaps not so momentous as to those who were participating for the first time. Our chief concern was enemy minefields. Could my ships conform to swept channels? Could the gunfire support vessels gain effective support positions in waters where thorough sweeping was impossible?

Unlike the Royal Navy, which held the reputation as the world's best World War II minesweeping force, the U.S. Navy considered mine warfare an inglorious job and in 1944 was unqualified to deal with the ever-increasing threat of enemy mines in the European theater. As a consequence, only about 10 percent of the minesweepers involved in Operation Neptune were American, and of those, only four vessels had had the experience of sweeping live mines. If any American ever needed proof that the United States could not win World War II on its own, the fact that the fleet carrying American assault troops to Omaha Beach did not contain a single U.S. Navy minesweeper should have been sufficient evidence. Instead, British and Canadian minesweepers did the job—and they did it flawlessly.

Minesweeping is a task that is generally noted only when it fails. The fact that Force O was able to fulfill its complex and hazardous minesweeping mission without revealing to the enemy where the invasion would take place was attributable not only to the skill of the British and Canadian sailors who carried it out, but also to the almost total failure of the enemy to conduct mine warfare aggressively. In retrospect, by far the best chance the Germans had to defeat the invasion was with sea mines. Yet the five-mile mine belt that the Allies had worried so much about turned out to be almost empty. Allied minesweepers detected and neutralized only twenty-nine mines throughout the mine barrier—none of which were located in Force O's two swept channels.

Adm. Harold Stark
Commander, U.S. Naval Forces Europe , Report on Neptune Mine-sweeping Operations, 1945
In order to assure that the channels cut would be located in the proper positions, ten sonic underwater buoys were laid in positions to mark the edge of the enemy

mine barrier in the Assault approach channels. These buoys were laid so as to come alive on D-1 [June 4] when they would be utilized by [launches], acting as marker boats, to enable the minesweepers to commence sweeping the approach channels in the correct positions.

Special Tactical Study Number 30
British intelligence, German views on the Normandy Landing,
November 28, 1944
Mines were laid along the coast without the assistance of the Navy, and therefore this task was not properly done.

Earlier in the war, Hitler had committed many of his scientists to the task of developing an unsweepable mine, and by 1943, they had come up with an ingenious device called a pressure mine. Such a weapon worked by lurking unseen below the surface, moored to the sea bottom with a chain and armed with a fuse that would detonate the mine when nearby water pressure was altered by a passing enemy vessel overhead. The Allies were aware of this weapon, but try as they might, they could develop no certain means of neutralizing it short of primitive remedies such as a "suicide" barge. Had the Germans laid these mines in appreciable numbers in their mine belt off Normandy, they surely would have hindered—if not crippled—the Allied invasion fleet. However, such a tactic of course would have worked only if the Germans had deduced ahead of time that the Allies would invade Normandy—a deduction that they did not make. Instead, Hitler had decreed that pressure mines be withheld from deployment until after the Allied invasion commenced, at which point he would direct the Luftwaffe to drop hundreds of pressure mines directly on the shipping route between England and the Allied beachheads. In actuality, Allied minesweepers experienced great difficulty dealing with pressure mines when the Germans first employed them in the weeks following D-Day. But by then it was too late for them to have any significant impact on the campaign.

Adolf Hitler
Führer Conference Summary, May 17, 1944
The Commander-in-Chief Navy announces his renewed intention to increase minefields off the invasion ports along the southern coast of England with the most varied types of mines. He expresses his doubts concerning the use of pressure mines since . . . there is the danger that the secret may be discovered. . . . The Führer agrees and directs the Reichsmarschall [Hermann Göring] to take care that under no condition mines of this type fall into the hands of the enemy in case of an invasion through careless disposition of them along the coast.

Dragging their long mine-clearing cables behind them, the little British and Canadian sweepers chugged through the German mine barrier and beyond, all the way to within a mile of Omaha Beach. Not a single enemy mine was located, a heartening revelation to the crews of the hundreds of vessels following in the sweepers' wakes. As they neared the French coast, the minesweepers toiled under the cover of darkness, but the failure of German beach sentries to notice such intense enemy activity so close to shore and the inability of German coastal radar to detect the approach of such a vast enemy armada provided the first firm evidence that the Allies had indeed achieved surprise. Much of Force O would soon be anchoring off the beach. The cross-Channel journey was over; the invasion was about to begin.

Rear Adm. Alan Kirk
Commander, Western Naval Task Force, Operation Neptune Action Report,
July 25, 1944
It can be said without fear of contradiction that minesweeping was the keystone of the arch in this operation. All of the waters were suitable for mining. . . . The performance of minesweepers can only be described as magnificent.

FOR A SHORT MOMENT IN THE ANNALS OF TIME
The soul of Force O was its fifteen troopships, aboard which were the first 10,000 infantrymen who would storm Omaha Beach. Eight of these vessels sailed under British colors, more proof that the Omaha Beach invasion, although limited to American ground troops, was in truth a multinational operation. The British transports carried seventy-six Royal Navy LCAs, slung on davits on their port and starboard sides. These were crewed by veteran sailors who had already experienced the hazards of amphibious operations against a skilled and ruthless enemy in the Mediterranean. In fact, the Royal Navy was responsible for landing the Americans on the three most perilous spots in the Omaha sector: the beach's extreme eastern and western flanks, both of which were covered by nearly unapproachable and indestructible enemy pillboxes; and the vertical cliffs of Pointe du Hoc, which would be assaulted by U.S. Rangers in a semi-independent operation. The remaining seven Force O troopships were American, six manned by the U.S. Navy and one by the U.S. Coast Guard.

Admiral Hall prized no vessels in Force O more than his fifteen troopships, and he did everything in his power to protect them. The entire invasion hinged on the preservation of these critical vessels, and under no

"The soul of Force O." The British troopship SS Empire Javelin *conveyed a battalion of the 116th Infantry to Normandy. The LCAs of the Royal Navy assault flotillas that carried the GIs to the beach are slung on the ship's davits.*
COURTESY ROYAL NAVY.

circumstances would Hall put them at risk, if avoidable. Neptune's thorough intelligence summary had pinpointed several German heavy coastal guns along the Calvados shoreline, and when officers armed with compasses and maps plotted the precise ranges of these enemy guns, they concluded that no Allied vessel under eleven miles from Omaha Beach, especially anchored transports packed with troops, would be safe from bombardment. The catastrophe that might be triggered by a direct hit from a heavy, plunging shell on an unarmored transport was apparently too fearsome for Hall to contemplate, and the Neptune plan therefore dictated that all fifteen transports must anchor eleven miles off Omaha Beach prior to disembarking their assault troops into landing craft. The primary and obvious drawback of this scheme, however, was that those diminutive landing craft, each tightly packed with about thirty troops, would have to travel eleven miles to reach the beach. Including loading and time spent circling, that journey would last three hours, in some cases four, on a violently pitching sea, for the most part in near total darkness. Such a voyage would surely not leave the landing craft's occupants in a mood to fight.

Adm. Sir Bertram Ramsay
SHAEF, Senior SHAEF naval commander, Operation Neptune Report, November 1944

It was always the intention to make the "lowering positions" [of landing craft] as near the beaches as it was thought the enemy long-range coastal batteries would permit. In the Eastern Task Force [British-Canadian] area they were therefore established seven miles from the shore. The U.S. forces, however, preferred to select positions 11 miles from the coast. Actually it was found that the [troop-

ships] of the Eastern Task Force were not menaced by enemy fire, and the reduction of the length of the trip to the beach must have been most welcome to the
British troops in the unpleasant conditions that occurred.

Orders demanded that the sailors deposit ninety-two landing craft on
seven predesignated beach sectors in the first three minutes of the Omaha
assault. In large measure, the invasion's overall success would depend on
the navy's ability to beach each landing craft group precisely on the sector
prescribed by Neptune orders as close to 6:30 A.M. as possible. Since darkness would prevent observation of the coastline during most of the journey,
fulfillment of this task would require exceptional skill on the part of the
landing craft crews. Even the hazy light yielded by a 5:58 A.M. sunrise
would barely illuminate the shoreline's few distinctive landmarks. Furthermore, the seamen's instructions had been supplemented with a stark warning: Watch out for the currents! At the moment of the first landings,
intelligence reports asserted that an offshore current would be streaming
eastward at almost three knots. Amazingly, six hours later, it would be flowing in the opposite direction at the same speed. Under such remarkable conditions, it is not surprising that some pessimistically believed that confusion
would promptly set in once the invasion began.

Omaha Beach offshore currents
Bigot-Neptune top secret monograph, April 21, 1944
5:30 A.M.: Current 0.2 knots to east
7:30 A.M.: Current 2.7 knots to east
9:30 A.M.: Current 1.6 knots to east
Noon: Current 0.1 knots to west
1:30 P.M.: Current 2.7 knots to west
3:30 P.M.: Current 2.5 knots to west
5:30 P.M.: Current 0.2 knots to west

NOTE: Current speeds are estimated for positions five miles offshore.

Admiral Hall did everything within his power to prevent that confusion. Neptune orders designated several diminutive U.S. Navy warships as
control vessels, and as these ships had drafts of seven feet or less, each was
instructed to sail close inshore before dawn to a preselected position and
mark the proper path to its corresponding beach sector with buoys. Each
would also fly a distinctive flag to identify itself. Similar vessels and even

smaller launches, most of which were equipped with sophisticated radar sets that could identify coastal landmarks even at night and in haze, would guide the groups of landing craft directly to their proper beaches.

Ens. Richard Crook
Executive Officer, PC-553, Force O

The PCs' [patrol craft's] job called for us to be in precise positions to serve as reference points for the landing craft. We had British QH [radio navigation] gear installed; it was the antecedent of American LORAN. The gear was able to pick up radio signals that gave us lines of position. When we plotted the intersection of those lines, we had a navigational fix. . . . The landing craft had a long run in before reaching the control vessels. By going past the PCs, the waves of LCVPs would be able to orient themselves and get into the right position for the final run-in to the beach.

No military scheme had ever generated more paper. To the participants, the thick sheaves of Force O's Neptune plans yielded confidence—surely such a meticulously conceived operation had dealt with every imaginable contingency. The plans featured complex charts and diagrams, detailing the positions and movements of the assault vessels like the choreography of a grand ballet. Ship captains and army officers were provided with top secret Omaha Beach maps, portraying hydrographic and coastal terrain features with astonishing thoroughness. Updated just a few days before the invasion from information acquired from air photographs, these maps reputedly displayed the correct locations of all the different types of German beach obstacles, as well as enemy pillboxes, barbed wire belts, and minefields. Superimposed along the bottom of the map was a detailed panoramic sketch of the coastline as it would appear from about one mile offshore. The scales of both sketch and map matched precisely: To determine what any point on the map actually looked like from the perspective of a landing craft approaching the shore, a coxswain simply had to glance at the corresponding point on the sketch.

Omaha Beach map
Bigot-Neptune, scale 1:7,920, April 21, 1944

Note to coxswain or navigator: Building landmarks, especially near the beach, may be destroyed before any craft land. Terrain features, therefore, are much more reliable for visual navigation from panoramic shoreline sketch.

*A rare 1943 air photo of "Beach 313" (Omaha Beach). The area shown is the
St. Laurent (E-1) draw. After this photo was taken, the Germans would build a
formidable strongpoint (WN65) on the bluff to the right (west) of the road
heading straight inland.* COURTESY MARYLAND NATIONAL GUARD.

67th Tactical Reconnaissance Group, Ninth Air Force
Monthly Report, March 1944
What is believed to have been the most secret photographic mission of the war has
been accomplished by the 67th Tactical Reconnaissance Group without the loss or
damage of a single aircraft. The mission was to make Merton Oblique photographs
of approximately 160 miles of French coastline. . . . Many runs had to fly directly
over or within effective range of heavily defended flak areas. During the photographic run, the photo ship had to maintain a constant altitude of 3,500 feet and fly
an absolutely straight flight line on a predetermined heading for an average of four
minutes. It became apparent that such flying was an anti-aircraft gunner's dream.

10th Photographic Group, Ninth Air Force
Monthly Report, May 1944
Heading the list of accomplishments for the month . . . is the number of "Dicing"
missions flown by this organization over the beaches of Western Europe. These
missions were flown with F-5 type aircraft, mounting a 12-inch focal length nose
camera shooting straight forward and tilted approximately ten degrees down from
the horizon. . . . These missions are flown at minimum altitude, some having been
completed at 25 feet. These were the first missions of this type to have been flown
in this part of the European Theater. As a result of these missions, two pilots were

awarded the DFC (Distinguished Flying Cross), and one pilot is listed as missing in action.

10th Photographic Group, Ninth Air Force
Low-altitude photo mission 31/419, May 19, 1944
Port-en-Bessin to Mouth of the Vire River. [Includes area of Omaha Beach.] Flown to 1st Lt. Rufus (NMI) [no middle initial] Woody, O-672919, 31st Photo Reconnaissance Squadron, at 1650 Hours.

Oberstleutnant Fritz Ziegelmann
Assistant chief of staff, 352nd Infantry Division
I must say that never in my entire military life have I been so impressed as in that hour when I held in my hands the [captured] operational order of the American V Army Corps.

With such detailed information at their disposal, the sailors of Force O and the soldiers of V Corps had come to know well a piece of terrain that none of them had ever seen. When sunrise on June 6, 1944, illuminated this coast, these men would recognize all of its natural and man-made landmarks. However, an unseen enemy lay somewhere beyond the beach, an adversary who had had four years to study his own intelligence reports and prepare his defenses accordingly. No matter how comprehensive the Allied maps and sketches of Omaha Beach were, nothing could alter the fact that the beachhead could not be won without a fierce battle.

The soldiers who would make the initial landings on Omaha Beach had been confined to their troopships for up to a week. They had little to do but think, and by the time Force O anchored eleven miles off Omaha Beach in the predawn darkness of June 6, many surely wondered whether they would live to see another day. Such sentiments are generally not beneficial to soldiers' morale, and yet somehow, as the GIs assembled on deck in the dark to board their landing craft for the long journey to the beach, most retained supreme confidence in their units' ability to accomplish their missions. One sensed that the darkness cloaked not only the soldiers' physical surroundings, but also the dangers that lay ahead.

Capt. Walter Schilling
Commander, Company D, 116th Infantry, 29th Division, 0200 hours, June 6, 1944
This is "The Real McCoy." The dry runs are over, the amphibious assault training is concluded. I am proud to lead this company into battle. . . . Cross the beach fast,

gain the high ground and get into a perimeter defense. . . . When I call the roll tonight in Isigny, I want everyone to say "Here!" Good luck!

Lt. Col. Robert Pratt
Assistant G-3, V Corps, September 1944

The picture of an army afloat is a mighty one, and I certainly was proud to have a small part in the conception and execution. Barnum and Bailey have lost their title to the Greatest Show on Earth. This for a short moment in the annals of time was IT.

Capt. John Moglia
Antitank Company, 16th Infantry, 1st Division

Some were convinced that they could not possibly make it—the law of averages would catch up with them. One friend offered me two cigars to be smoked after the beachhead was established. I told him to keep one and we would smoke them together. He stated that he would not be around at that time, and asked me to smoke his for him. I did.

T/Sgt. William McClintock
HQ Company, 741st Tank Battalion

I slept for about four hours. My gear was in good order, and I thought I knew what I was going to do. Turned out I didn't know as much as I thought I did.

2nd Lt. John Spalding
Company E, 16th Infantry, 1st Division

We cheered each other up and "whistled in the dark" by pointing out that the battle orders called for the Air Force to flatten out the beaches, clear them of all anti-personnel, anti-tank mines, etc., in addition to supplying ready-made foxholes in the form of bomb holes to assist in advancing across the exposed beach. We had been led to believe German troops would be in a state of shock from aerial and naval bombardment. How little we knew, how great our faith! The Navy promised us that we would be dumped ashore without even getting our shoes wet.

Sgt. Roy Stevens
Company A, 116th Infantry, 29th Division

Ray [Stevens's twin brother] said he wasn't afraid, but I was. . . . We made a point that we would meet each other at the Vierville crossroads when we landed. I got ready to go off [the *Empire Javelin*] and he was standing there. He put out his hand to shake mine, and I said, "I'll shake your hand at the crossroads." It actually didn't happen, and I've regretted not shaking his hand because that was the last time I saw him.

CHAPTER 5

The Greatest Show on Earth

A BEACH DRENCHED WITH FIRE

The Willies and Joes who had been lucky enough to survive combat in the Mediterranean theater had learned a hard lesson: The Krauts were damn good fighters, make no mistake about that. Every moment of the Tunisian and Sicilian campaigns had been grueling, and each foot of ground gained had cost good men, too many good men. By the spring of 1944, that warning had reached as far as the training camps in Britain, and for the soldiers who had heeded it, it was not encouraging. If the Germans had fought so ferociously around the peripheries of Europe, how hard would they resist to retain France and protect their own homeland? More to the point, given nearly four years to construct the Atlantic Wall, what would be the chances of survival for Allied soldiers who had drawn the mission of battering down that wall?

One could hardly suppress a sense of amazement at the enemy's fighting tenacity. By the date scheduled for D-Day, a mere eleven U.S. Army divisions had engaged in combat in the African, Sicilian, and Italian campaigns—and after a few months of combat, most of those were depleted and exhausted. In contrast, the Germans seemed to conduct military operations on a higher plane. For the invasion of Russia in June 1941, Hitler had deployed 153 Axis divisions of more than 3.5 million men.

In the army, negativity could spread like a plague, with potentially disastrous consequences. If the prospects of survival were slim, would Allied soldiers carry out their duties? Allied generals involved in Operation Neptune recognized the profound implications of this question and took steps to answer it: First, know your jobs as well as the enemy knows his, the generals said, and you will boost your chance of survival; second, you will be supported by firepower at unprecedented levels by air, sea, and land, which will shatter the Germans, no matter how good they are.

Lt. Gen. Omar Bradley
Commander, First U.S. Army, Overlord Conference, December 21, 1943
The attack will be preceded by a bombing which may last up to six hours. In other words, the present plan is that every bomber in Great Britain will be used in this operation. . . . This area will be drenched by heavy bombers and everything they can throw on it. . . . They are going to use big stuff, including blockbusters. [This] may have some effect on the morale of the [Germans] around there.

Combined Operations Headquarters
Report of Lessons Learned on Dieppe Raid, October 1942
The lesson of greatest importance is the need for overwhelming fire support, including close support, during the initial stages of the attack . . . [by] heavy and medium naval bombardment, by air action, by special vessels or craft working close inshore, and by using the firepower of the assaulting troops while still seaborne.

V Corps
Summary, Overlord Conference, February 3, 1944
Every house and other building with observation over the beach will be knocked out. Also, all possible pillboxes.

Capt. Harry Butcher
U.S. Navy aide to General Eisenhower, diary, April 28, 1944
Gerow seemed a bit pessimistic, and finally Ike said to him that he should be optimistic and cheerful because he has behind him the greatest firepower ever assembled on the face of the earth.

Maj. Sidney Bingham
Commander, 2nd Battalion, 116th Infantry, 29th Division
General Omar Bradley visited the 29th Division in late May 1944, during which he said: "You men should consider yourselves lucky and are to be congratulated. You have ring-side seats at the Greatest Show on Earth."

To imply to soldiers who would soon experience combat that they would be mere spectators at a deadly theater of battle at first seems peculiar. But Bradley's point was convincing: His "show" would be a sensational aerial and naval firepower display, dwarfing anything ever seen before in war. Everywhere the Americans turned, there would be warships and airplanes plastering the beach, and if the plan worked, the German beach defenders wouldn't even know what had hit them. Willie and Joe might even allow themselves a few seconds of pity for those poor bastards—if it weren't for the fact that they were Nazis.

General Bradley was Ike's chief practitioner of the confidence school, but his expectations relating to the application of firepower on Omaha Beach fell conspicuously into the realm of overconfidence. Even under perfect conditions, there were but few examples in recent military history of firepower alone overcoming fixed defenses. Furthermore, after months of sanguine talk of "drenching" the beach with massive firepower, Bradley's "Greatest Show on Earth" was severely compromised by several unchallengeable facets of the invasion plan. The most significant of these was Bradley's determination to commence the landing of troops on Omaha Beach as soon as possible after dawn to assure surprise and maximize the number of GIs who could be put ashore by nightfall. A commitment to such a strict landing schedule severely curtailed the navy's and the army air force's ability to provide the grandiose levels of fire support that Eisenhower and Bradley had promised the troops for so long.

With the first troops scheduled to storm ashore on Omaha Beach at 6:30 A.M., the navy and air force were budgeted little more than a half hour to bombard the beach prior to the invasion—hardly the drenching Bradley had in mind. At the invasion of Tarawa atoll in November 1943, a heavy naval bombardment of nearly three hours had utterly failed to dent the Japanese defenses. Even worse, the Omaha Beach bombardment would take place immediately after dawn in such dim light that even the most experienced naval gunners and air bombardiers would not be able to perform their duties effectively. Under such restrictive time limitations and natural conditions, the navy and air force could do little more than to force the Germans to take cover, and their chances of destroying the enemy's expertly camouflaged concrete pillboxes would be virtually nil.

Robert Sherrod
Reporter, with U.S. Marine Corps at Tarawa, November 1943
The facts were cruel, but inescapable: probably no amount of shelling and bombing could obviate the necessity of sending in foot soldiers to finish the job. . . . There is no panacea which will prevent men from getting killed.

Rear Adm. John Hall
Commander, Force O, Operation Neptune Action Report, July 1944
In general, it is believed that the time available for pre-landing bombardment was not sufficient. German defensive positions were well camouflaged and strong. It is considered that these positions should be destroyed by slow aimed fire from close range, prior to the landing. Something more than temporary neutralization is required when troops face beach mines, wire, antitank ditches, and similar obstacles after landing.

If the bombardment of Omaha Beach would be the Greatest Show on Earth, the U.S. Eighth Air Force would be the main act in the center ring. The Eighth's B-17 Flying Fortresses and B-24 Liberators, which had been pummeling enemy targets with regularity from the air since the fall of 1942, represented a new form of warfare. But if Lt. Gen. Carl Spaatz, the senior American airman in Europe, had taken stock of the Eighth Air Force's short history on the eve of D-Day, his mood would have been decidedly uneven. On the positive side, the Eighth had grown steadily to the point at which it could regularly launch more than 1,000 bombers against German industrial targets on days with reasonably clear weather. Even better, America's ongoing production of bombers provided Spaatz with nearly unlimited resources at a level the enemy could never hope to match. Henry Ford's Willow Run plant outside Detroit proved this point by churning out 500 B-24 Liberators per month. Supported by production levels of such immensity, the American proponents of strategic airpower believed that the Eighth Air Force, along with RAF Bomber Command, could eventually bring Germany to its knees with bombing alone.

What troubled Spaatz, however, was how much reality differed from theory. Army Air Force bombardiers had bragged for years about putting their bombs in a "pickle barrel" from lofty altitudes, but precision bombing of this kind, so cherished a few years previously, had nearly vanished. In truth, every element of the strategic bombing campaign against Germany had been compromised in one form or another since it had begun. Enemy resistance had been unexpectedly ferocious; American casualties had been tragically high. The Nazis always appeared to have an effective response to every American stratagem; and as the air war endured seemingly without end, the Eighth Air Force sporadically experienced bouts of wretched morale. But there was no going back: The AAF top brass resolved that precision bombing would continue until war's end, no matter what, and as a result, the Eighth Air Force would have to adapt—or die.

What Bradley had asked the Eighth to do on Omaha Beach on D-Day had never been done before. Omaha Beach was a lot bigger than a pickle barrel, and surely an entire bomb division of 450 Liberators would be able to smash the German defenders into oblivion. However, Bradley's conception of strategic airpower on D-Day was scarcely compatible with the methods by which the Eighth Air Force made war. Under Bradley's strict and unforgiving invasion timetable, the chance the Eighth Air Force could achieve what Bradley wanted was almost zero—and several airmen knew it.

Eighth Air Force
Action Report, Tactical Operations in Support of Landings in Normandy, July 1944
Heavy bomber operations in close support of ground forces involved a tactical concept differing greatly in many particulars from the customary strategic bombing activities of the Eighth Air Force. Problems were posed in relation to assemblies, formations, routings, bomb loadings, fuzings, and overcast bombing techniques; details of briefing and mission reporting had to be worked out; coordination with other Air Forces and with naval planners was necessary to a far greater degree than heretofore required . . . and most important, the requirements of the ground forces had to be translated into a feasible air support program, and the ground force commanders had to be thoroughly informed as to the capabilities and limitations of the heavy bombers.

From the airmen's perspective, Operation Neptune promised to be a hair-raising adventure, even if the Luftwaffe did not make an appearance. To reach the Normandy coast at the appointed hour, the B-24s would have to take off and assemble large, tight groups in darkness. This was a tactic the Eighth Air Force was not trained to do, and had rarely done on the enormous scale demanded by the Neptune plan. Furthermore, there was a strong possibility of "10/10 cloud"—the aviators' phrase for total overcast. The light conditions a few minutes after dawn would be abysmal, and the enemy could put up severe antiaircraft fire during the bomb run.

But above all, the Liberators would have to hit their targets with pinpoint accuracy from a high altitude when all lessons learned so far in the strategic bombing offensive against Germany had clearly indicated that precision bombing in the prevailing weather conditions of northern Europe was close to unattainable. Moreover, first-wave assault troops would be a scant 3,000 yards from the bomb line when the first of thousands of bombs would cascade toward Omaha Beach, leading to the awful conclusion that errant bombs could kill far more Americans than Germans on D-Day should the bombardiers make a mistake. It was one thing to have precision bombing fail when the object of an attack was a Nazi city; it was quite another when thousands of friendly troops could be the victims of an error.

Lt. Gen. Carl Spaatz
Commander, U.S. Strategic Air Forces Europe, letter, January 23, 1944
The weather here is the most discouraging of all factors and I am sure that it will result in the loss of remaining hairs on my head, or at least will turn what is left of the red into white. Nothing is more exasperating than trying to run an Air Force continuously hampered or grounded by weather.

But the clock continued to tick, and harried Allied staff officers all over Britain took advantage of every waking moment to review their top secret Neptune orders again and again. By early May 1944, only a few weeks before the Normandy invasion would be launched, Gerow's V Corps had carefully designated the Omaha Beach targets that the Eighth Air Force must neutralize, and although the airmen knew that such a task would be difficult, they had agreed in principle that the entire 2nd Bombardment Division of the Eighth Air Force, consisting of over 400 B-24 Liberators, could carry it out. How exactly they would carry it out, the airmen did not say. Transcripts of vital May 1944 conferences between senior ground and air leaders make no reference whatsoever to the steps the airmen would take to avoid hitting friendly troops, nor do they mention the potential disruptive effect of 10/10 overcast on D-Day. Apparently General Bradley was content to leave the details to the airmen.

Brig. Gen. Frederic Smith
Chief of operations, Allied Expeditionary Air Force
I explained to [army commanders] that the effect which each commander wanted on his particular beach was his prerogative. He could tell us what effect he wanted; if it were anti-personnel, and cutting above-ground communications—tell us that. . . . We would prescribe the bomb load to achieve that. [It] took a whole day to get the detailed effects which they desired. And based upon [that] and our knowledge of munitions, we prepared in late May the bomb loadings for D-Day and furnished them to all of the commands.

V Corps
Conference, Operation Neptune Air Support, May 17, 1944
Details of bombing of V Corps beach defense targets for D-Day were agreed upon as follows: For the V Corps, 8th Bomber Command will provide 75

squadrons of 6 heavy bombers each, a total of 450 planes. The following are details for each target:

Target	No. Squadrons	Bomb Tonnage	Fuse Type	Time
Pt. et Raz de la Perceé	6	129.0	delay	H-25 to H-5 minutes
Fortified house/barn	6	88.2	instant	H-25 to H-5 minutes
Vierville (D-1) draw	6	88.2	instant	H-25 to H-5 minutes
Hamel au Prêtre	6	129.0	delay	H-25 to H-5 minutes
Les Moulins (D-3) draw, west	6	88.2	instant	H-25 to H-5 minutes
Les Moulins (D-3) draw, east	6	88.2	instant	H-25 to H-5 minutes
St. Laurent (E-1) draw, west	6	88.2	instant	H-25 to H-5 minutes
St. Laurent draw (E-1), east	6	88.2	instant	H-25 to H-5 minutes
Colleville (E-3) draw, west	6	88.2	instant	H-25 to H-5 minutes
Colleville (E-3) draw, east	6	88.2	instant	H-25 to H-5 minutes
Cabourg (F-1) draw	6	129.0	delay	H-25 to H-5 minutes
Port-en-Bessin west	4	86.0	delay	H-20 to H-5 minutes
Port-en-Bessin east	5	107.5	delay	H-20 to H-5 minutes

Eighth Air Force
Interview with Col. John De Russey, Eighth Air Force liaison officer, 1945
Col. De Russey was present at the practice mission on which beaches in southern England were bombed prior to D-Day. He recalled that Generals Eisenhower, Montgomery, Bradley, airmen Spaatz, [Sir Arthur] Tedder, [Sir Trafford] Leigh-Mallory, and others were present. The Field Order stipulated that no elements would bomb subsequent to a certain time. After the time deadline had passed, Gen. [Orville] Anderson [operations officer, Eighth Air Force] asked Col. De Russey whether he was sure no other elements would bomb. De Russey replied that the Field Order definitely stated bombs were to be held up after the deadline. Gen. Eisenhower was anxious to go to the beach and see the results. [De Russey] recalls that as they prepared to leave the observation post, one group came over and dropped its bombs, causing consternation and embarrassment. Another bad time occurred when one group dropped several hundred yards short and ricocheting fragments splattered around the observation post, causing all the observers to hit the ground.

One detail, however, Bradley insisted upon: If, after Omaha Beach was secured, hundreds of deep craters caused by Eighth Air Force bombs were scattered over the sand, the innumerable jeeps, trucks, and tanks Bradley would need to support Gerow's inland push toward St. Lô could be prevented from leaving the beach. As the only traversable exits off Omaha Beach were its five narrow draws, bomb craters could trigger traffic jams far worse than those at 42nd Street and Broadway at rush hour, much to the detriment of the battle beyond the beachhead. Bradley therefore considered an avoidance of beach cratering a mandatory element of the bombardment plan. The airmen informed him, however, that the types of bombs and fuses that would achieve that end would have virtually no effect against a hardened position such as a concrete gun emplacement.

As a consequence, the Liberators would drop mostly 100-pound high explosive and fragmentation bombs—some of the lightest pieces of ordnance in the Eighth Air Force's inventory. When armed with instantaneous rather than delayed fuses, these bombs would have about as much effect on a concrete pillbox as a pistol bullet. But the instantaneous fuses, which directed blasts outward rather than down, would ensure lethal results against troops in the open and reasonably destructive effects on minefields, barbed wire, and obstacles. Above all, small bombs with instant fuses would not cause the cratering Bradley was so anxious to avoid.

To the uninitiated, a 100-pound bomb may seem to have been a fearsome weapon. It was not. Only a fraction of the bomb's total weight consisted of explosive material, generally TNT and ammonium nitrate. The detonation of such a bomb yielded a relatively small blast. Troops standing in the open fifteen yards away from the explosion would have a good chance of emerging unscathed, and if they were prone or in a foxhole, their chance of survival would be greatly improved. A concrete pillbox or underground shelter would be safest of all, as these were virtually impregnable.

Generals must make difficult decisions, and for Bradley, some tough choices lay ahead. He had to balance the tactical needs of the assault troops on D-Day with the strategic necessities of the overall campaign, and in this instance, the strategic needs prevailed. The strict Overlord timetable dictated that the beachhead must grow at a rapid pace, and severe cratering of the beach by bombs would surely paralyze that effort. Had Bradley sought proof after D-Day that this paralysis indeed would have occurred, he needed only to examine the German strongpoint at Pointe du Hoc, several miles to the west of Omaha, which was hit repeatedly with heavy bombs armed with delayed fuses prior to the invasion. The result was countless craters of such immensity that they continue to impress even today. Had Omaha Beach been transformed into this moonscape by heavy bombs, it is hard to believe that a single vehicle could have exited the beach within twenty-four hours of the invasion.

Eighth Air Force
Action Report, Tactical Operations in Support of Landings in Normandy, July 1944
The probability that direct hits on gun emplacements would not be in excess of 2% of the tonnage dropped, and that little damage would result in most instances was emphasized. . . . It was agreed that the air support should aim primarily at the demoralization of front-line troops with a possible bonus in the destruction of barbed wire and other obstacles.

A GREAT THUNDER FROM THE SEA

Bradley's show would begin shortly before dawn, as soon as Admiral Hall's Force O bombardment ships could make out their coastal targets. Gerow's Omaha Beach target list was remarkably comprehensive, specifying beach sites down to individual houses and pillboxes. Each target was assigned a number, description, and an X-Y map coordinate so that naval gunners could pinpoint the objects of their fire on their detailed Omaha Beach maps. Gerow had selected about sixty targets, each of which would be engaged by at least one warship. However, if sunrise would be at 5:58 A.M. and the first waves of ground troops would land at 6:31 A.M., the naval bombardment would have to lift after only about thirty-five minutes.

Admiral Hall's main Force O bombardment group consisted of eighteen warships, eleven of which belonged to the U.S. Navy, including the aged battleships USS *Texas* and USS *Arkansas*. Hall had once been skipper of the *Arkansas*, which was the oldest battleship in the U.S. Navy but had never fired a shot against an enemy in its thirty-two-year career. The battleships and cruisers would engage the enemy from about four miles offshore, seven miles closer to the coast than the transports. The smaller destroyers would close to a range of less than two miles from the beach. To enhance the accuracy of the ships' fire, the U.S. Navy had formed a special squadron of spotter planes, equipped with British-made Spitfires and flying from a southern English airfield. A pair of these Spitfires would fly over Omaha Beach continuously, reporting by radio directly to the warships on the accuracy of their shelling. When the Spitfires ran low on fuel, they would be replaced by a fresh pair and would return to England.

Force O, Bombardment Group
Rear Adm. C. F. Bryant, commander, June 6, 1944
Battleships
  USS *Texas*   USS *Arkansas*

Light Cruisers

HMS *Glasgow*	*Montcalm* (French)
HMS *Bellona*	*Georges Leygues* (French)

Destroyers

USS *Frankford*	USS *Harding*
USS *McCook*	USS *Satterlee*
USS *Carmick*	USS *Thompson*
USS *Doyle*	HMS *Tanatside*
USS *Emmons*	HMS *Talybont*
USS *Baldwin*	HMS *Melbreak*

Hall had also formed a second "fire support group," consisting of landing craft to which bombardment rockets and small-caliber guns had been affixed. These vessels had shallow drafts and could therefore approach their targets more closely than larger warships, even the nimble destroyers. In fact, this group held the daunting mission of landing U.S. Army tanks on Omaha Beach at H-Hour by means of sixteen LCT(A)s (landing craft, tank armored) recently handed over by the Royal Navy to the Americans and specially modified with extra armor and raised platforms allowing embarked Sherman tanks to fire as their craft headed for shore. All LCTs were notoriously clumsy sailers in rough seas, and most had experienced harsh cross-Channel journeys en route to Normandy. One had sunk, and several others were late because they could not keep station in their convoys.

Also a part of Force O's fire support group were nine ungainly vessels with the unimposing label of LCT(R)s. These were modified LCTs, each armed with 1,080 five-inch rockets, and if Admiral Hall was to drench Omaha Beach with fire, these were the vessels to fulfill that job. According to the fire support plan, each LCT(R) would approach to within about one and a half miles from shore, and when the first-wave assault troops were only three minutes short of the beach—6:27 A.M. if the invasion was on schedule—the LCT(R)s would let loose with continuous barrages of rockets until their supply was depleted. The object was to lay a curtain of fire in front of the assault troops, demolishing any obstacles or barbed wire that stood in the way and killing any enemy defenders who dared to stick their heads above ground. In theory, the rocket salvos could devastate an area more than forty acres in size in a matter of seconds. However, the fundamental issue was whether or not the skippers could hit what they were aiming at. The odds were not good. Because the rocket racks were fixed rigidly on deck, a skipper could alter the rockets' aiming and range only by the highly unscientific method of maneuvering the vessel itself. Given the strict

Force O: Transports and Naval Bombardment

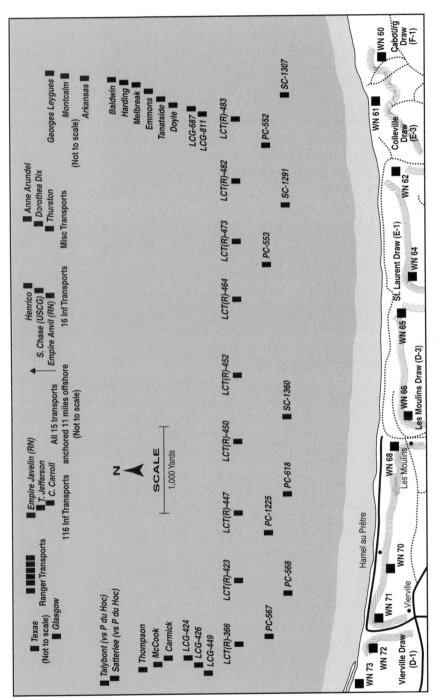

invasion schedule and the poor lighting conditions when the rocket ships would open fire, this would be a nearly impossible task.

In actual fact, the Germans triggered the battle of Omaha Beach. At 5:30 A.M., as the pink light on the eastern horizon steadily brightened prior to dawn, revealing the murky silhouettes of the Allied fleet, a few German guns opened fire from their coastal emplacements near Port-en-Bessin, about four miles east of the landing beaches. This fire accomplished nothing other than to help Force O pinpoint the location of enemy batteries, and in fact, it allowed some Allied warships to commence firing twenty minutes earlier than they otherwise would have.

Having silenced the pesky enemy guns, the fleet opened fire in earnest at its preselected beach targets at about 5:50 A.M., eight minutes before dawn. But the light was too muted and the German pillboxes too well disguised for the sailors to determine whether their shells were having the desired effect. Sunrise did not improve matters, for illumination revealed only patches of coast, the rest being obscured by drifting clouds of smoke. From the limited perspective of the assault troops in their little landing craft en route to shore, the smoke was beneficial, for if the Allies could see little, the enemy probably could see even less. Even better, within or beyond those smoke clouds, perhaps the naval shells were pummeling the Germans into oblivion.

In truth, the naval bombardment's chief contribution to the invasion was the morale boost it provided to the assault troops. If the fleet had neither adequate firepower nor time to obliterate the German beach defenders, it at least provided solid encouragement to the soldiers who were forced to endure journeys to the beach of three hours or more, crammed like cattle into rolling and plunging landing craft with a whipping southwest wind slamming spray into their faces. As terrifying and stomach-churning as was the voyage to the beach, it was surely healthier than being the target of a persistent torrent of shells. Or so it seemed . . .

The assault troops could at first see nothing of the fleet, for they boarded their landing craft and headed for the beach in complete darkness. Only six or seven miles into their shoreward journey did the gloomy predawn light reveal the presence of warships, and even then, all the troops could make out was the bulky battleship *Texas* and a British cruiser a few miles to their right, and another battleship, the *Arkansas*, plus two French cruisers off to their left. So far, the fleet did not appear particularly impressive—but it had not yet commenced shooting. In just a few minutes, the battlewagons would indeed open fire, and no soldier in a nearby landing craft would ever forget their great flaming muzzle flashes and booming aftershocks.

Lt. Col. Robert Pratt
Assistant G-3, V Corps, September 1944
Around us the vaporous clouds of billowing yellow smoke hovered over the battlewagons and cruisers, and I could follow the curving course of the brilliant tracers as they sped to shore to end up in a greyish black waterspout of smoke and dust. . . . The continuous dull rumble and ominous thunder of the bursting charges filled the air with a nightmare of sound. Added to this devil's symphony was the melodious drone of many planes shuttling back and forth over us on their mission of help and protection. The raucous beat of unmuffled [boat] engines cropped off from time to time as the exhausts were squeezed underwater by the unsubduable swell, and the clamor of a squawking loud-hailer added a macabre rhythm to this unholy cadenza.

Ens. Victor Hicken
Officer-in-command, LCT(A)-2227, Gunfire Support Group, Force O
We went right in front of the bow of the battleship *Texas* just when it fired a full salvo. It was just like a giant door slamming, and it really shook me up. You could actually see the shells flying through the air toward the shoreline.

Don Whitehead
Reporter, Associated Press
We headed for the beach, and I noticed that everyone in our boat appeared to be trembling violently. I knew that everyone was scared—but not that scared. And then I realized that the appearance of trembling was caused by the concussion from the big guns of the navy. The air vibrated from the sound.

As the landing craft passed the battleships and headed closer inshore, sunrise clarified the tableau. On either side of the wide boat lane cleared for the assault troops' approach to the beach, eight U.S. and Royal Navy destroyers stood about 3,000 yards offshore, hammering the coastal defenses with rapid, flat trajectory gunfire. Through the intermittent gaps in the floating smoke, the steep, green bluffs beyond the beach loomed dead ahead. The nine rocket-armed LCT(R)s were parked close inshore, and when the first-wave landing craft sailed past them and swung into line, no one needed to be told that H-Hour was not far off. Then the rocket ships let fly with their crashing and whooshing salvos directly over the infantrymen's heads, startling the already anxious and seasick men packed into the nearby landing craft. This impressive display was what General Bradley had meant when he gave his "Greatest Show on Earth" peptalk. In a few minutes, the troops would land directly in the center ring.

But for all their noisy fireworks, the rockets accomplished little. According to some witnesses, most rockets fell into the sea short of the beach, harming no one and failing to break up any obstacles or wire. Other observers failed to see a single rocket impact anywhere in sight, a suggestion that some vessels may have overshot their targets.

So much for the Greatest Show on Earth.

1st Lt. Edward McNabb
Company H, 116th Infantry, 29th Division, July 1944

There were a number of warships out at different distances letting go some big guns and mortars, and rocket craft inshore were blasting away at the cliffs and bluffs inland from the beach. There was some comment from a more optimistic PFC about what a shambles those bombs and the ships' guns were going to make of that beach. It did sound too good at the time. . . . It looked like another big tactical scheme off Slapton Sands, and I couldn't get the feeling out of my head that it was going to be another miserable two-day job with a hot shower at the end.

USS *Texas*
Action Report, Bombardment Summary, June 6, 1944

Time	Target	Gun	Rounds
0550–0624 hours	Pointe du Hoc	14-inch	115 AP, 100 HC
0626–0630 hours	Pointe du Hoc	14-inch	11 AP
0550–0624 hours	Vierville draw	5-inch	91 HC, 99 COM

AP: Armor piercing; COM: Common shell; HC: High capacity (high explosive)

USS *Doyle*
Action Report, 0630 hours, June 6, 1944

Commenced indirect fire on target [Cabourg Draw] . . . to aid in clearing beach exit now completely obscured by smoke and dust.

Sgt. Gilbert Murdoch
Company A, 116th Infantry, 29th Division, 1947

As we went toward the beach we could see the colored flares that the [navy] had placed to mark the route. As we passed the last flare, after being in the water for

"There go our holes on the beach!" A U.S. Navy LCT(R) fires a rocket salvo.
U.S. ARMY SIGNAL CORPS, NATIONAL ARCHIVES.

almost two hours, the battleship *Texas* fired. We could see the flash, then hear the roar of the shell overhead, then hear the report of it as it left the muzzle, then see the flash on the shore, and then hear the bursting shell explode. . . . Rocket barges gave us our first real fright. They started to fire their huge banks. They seemed to fire on the upward roll and dropped their huge load of rockets a few hundred yards in front of us, still a good two miles offshore. [The actual distance was probably 300 to 400 yards offshore.] One guy yelled, "Well there goes our holes on the beach!"

THE BEST LAID SCHEMES GO OFT ASTRAY

One of the most persistent recollections among American survivors of the Omaha landing was their disappointment at seeing no bomb craters on the beach. Although long before the invasion, General Bradley had dictated that no craters were desired in the assault area, somehow along the GI grapevine, the story spread within the marshaling areas that Omaha Beach would be littered with craters courtesy of the Eighth Air Force. And if the

Germans managed to survive the deadly deluge of bombs, so the rumor
went, the craters would turn out to be handy foxholes in which the GIs
could take cover. So, when the first-wave assault troops approached the
beach and saw that the sands were as flat as a billiard table, they shook
their heads and cursed yet another army snafu. They were right: A snafu of
enormous magnitude had indeed occurred—but the GIs could not have
imagined how it had come about.

A few minutes shy of midnight on June 5, 1944, the crews of the
Eighth Air Force's 2nd Bombardment Division were awakened to learn the
particulars of Field Order 328. If the Eighth could genuinely carry out precision bombing, they would now have to prove it, for F.O. 328 dictated that
hundreds of B-24s must pave the way for the D-Day assault troops by
blasting Omaha Beach with a carpet of bombs just a few minutes before
the first wave of landing craft touched down on the sand. Such a mission
had never been part of the Eighth's repertoire, and as tasks of this sort dis-
tracted the airmen from their main job of demolishing German industry,
Spaatz was not as zealous as Bradley about the bombers' D-Day role. The
Eighth would nevertheless fulfill its D-Day duty loyally, but to Spaatz the
Omaha Beach mission was akin to asking a first baseman to pitch: it could
be done, but don't expect much.

To examine F.O. 328 is to open a window to an esoteric form of warfare
that surely would have baffled traditional infantrymen like Eisenhower and
Bradley. This order, dated 3:25 P.M. on June 5, dictated down to the minute
what every Liberator unit in the 2nd Bomb Division must do to carry out the
aerial assault against Omaha Beach successfully. The document is notable
for its profusion of inscrutable jargon and acronyms, such as "Buncher,"
"PFF bombing," "Splasher," "H2X radar," "GEE," "Step Down Trails," and
much more.

The great paradox of F.O. 328 was that the Liberator crews carried out
this complex and exceedingly dangerous mission flawlessly, if not brilliantly—but not a single bomb fell anywhere near Omaha Beach. At the
close of D-Day, the ground troops on Omaha Beach wondered, Where
were the bombers? To which the airmen replied, We did what we told you
we could do, and we did it damn well.

A bitter General Bradley later professed shock at the 2nd Bomb Division's failure to soften up the beach, blaming the useless result on the airmen's timidity. Bradley, however, ought to have been more forgiving, for
he himself had designed an inflexible landing plan that had positioned
thousands of army troops and dozens of landing craft two miles or less
from shore when the Liberators would fly directly overhead and release

their bombs. Under those conditions—made even more hazardous by the cloud blanket over Normandy on D-Day—one could hardly blame the airmen for being apprehensive, for accidental bomb releases just a few seconds too soon could have caused hundreds of American and British deaths. By leaving the details of F.O. 328 to the air force, Bradley allowed the airmen to determine the means by which they would avoid accidentally bombing friendly troops. The air force's perspective of the problem was vastly different from Bradley's, and lacking specific orders to the contrary, the 2nd Bomb Division would take an extraordinary precaution to avert friendly casualties.

Had the weather been clear on D-Day, the differences between Bradley and the airmen would have narrowed appreciably. But the skies over Normandy were overcast on June 6, and as a consequence, the B-24s were forced to bomb blindly through the clouds. When a bombardier could not even see the proverbial pickle barrel, precision bombing lost much of its meaning, although by 1944, a basic airborne radar known as H2X—affectionately referred to as "Mickey" by the crews—at least enabled the bombers to try. Throughout the Eighth Air Force, the pre-D-Day briefings had stressed that if crews were forced to bomb through overcast using Mickey, the bombardiers must delay their "Bombs away!" calls by five to thirty seconds, depending on how close to H-Hour the bombers would pass over their targets; the closer to H-Hour a Liberator flew over the beach, the longer its delay. To the airmen, this precaution was perfectly logical; to Bradley, it was anything but.

96th Combat Wing, 2nd Bomb Division, Eighth Air Force
Special Instructions, June 5, 1944
Greatest possible care will be taken to prevent accidental releases and to insure that all bomb drops are overages due to dangers of shorts causing loss of Allied lives and damage to landing points. Troops will be 400 yards to one mile offshore during attack.

Eighth Air Force
Action Report, D-Day Heavy Bomber Activities, June 1944
It was deemed advisable to adopt further precautionary measures to prevent bombs from falling on friendly troops. . . . Accordingly, in conjunction with HQ A.E.A.F., it was decided that if cloud cover should prevent visual synchronization, bombs would be dropped on Pathfinder indications in the normal manner except that the release would be delayed so that the Mean Point of Impact would be no less than 1,000 yards from the forward wave of the water-borne assault forces.

Eighth Air Force
Action Report: Tactical Operations in Support of Landings in Normandy,
July 1944
[The Eighth Air Force's] safety features represented the final compromise between the desire of the ground forces to exploit immediately the demoralization resulting from the bombing at the risk of casualties and the inclination of the air forces to impose considerably greater intervals to minimize the dangers from possible bombing errors.

When the men of the 2nd Bomb Division retreated to their spartan quarters on June 5, they had no notion of the momentous event that would occur in a few hours. But when war room teleprinters whirred into action with the initial transmission of F.O. 328, officers were suddenly called to a surprise midnight briefing, and the first thing the briefer told them was that they must say nothing to their air crews about the upcoming mission until the Liberators were in the air. Whispers of "this is it" filled the air. Briefers armed with sheets of teleprinter paper and pointers meticulously began explaining the dozens of details that made up their mission.

Lt. Col. Philip Ardery
Operations officer, 2nd Combat Wing, 2nd Bomb Division,
Eighth Air Force
We were briefed about eleven that night for takeoff at 1:30 A.M. At that briefing I saw the first reaction of the crews—a show of genuine enthusiasm. When it was announced that at last the invasion was beginning, a cheer stopped the briefing officer for almost a minute. The crews were cheering as they might have cheered the end of the war.

The time had come for the highly efficient 2nd Bomb Division ground crews to fuel and arm their beloved Liberators. Driving their wheeled trailers, coupled into trains of immense length and stacked high with 100- and 500-pounders, the crews hauled the ordnance from bomb dumps to the airfields. Here they were dropped off next to the airplanes into which they would be loaded. In the chilly dark of an English spring night, the men carefully inserted the long fuses into the bombs' noses and gingerly cranked them to their proper settings.

With a supreme efficiency only experienced crews could achieve, the men speedily carried out the strenuous and precise task of shifting bombs to trolleys, shoving the trolleys under the low B-24 bomb bays, jacking up the trolleys, and transferring the bombs to the racks. Each bomb was fitted into its designated position with all the care that would be given a newborn baby. As each bomb was inserted into the rack, the ground crew attached a safety wire to its nose, a safeguard that supposedly prevented an accidental activation of the fuse—a catastrophic event that would instantly vaporize the ship and its crew. When the ordnance was fully loaded, pilots and copilots carried out the eminently sensible practice of a safety check. According to F.O. 328, each of the thirteen Omaha Beach targets would be bombed by thirty-six Liberators, divided into six successive waves of six aircraft each. Typically, the groundcrew loaded each B-24 with fifty-two 100-pounders with instantaneous fuses, set to detonate the moment the bomb touched the earth.

Planes cannot fly without fuel, and a Liberator guzzled a lot of fuel in a hurry. Early on D-Day, each 2nd Division bomb group's fuel bowsers hurried along the airfields, halting to fill each airplane with 2,400 gallons of high-octane gasoline. With the thousands of Allied aircraft that flew on D-Day, many for two or more missions, the immensity of the Eighth Air Force's logistical endeavor was impressive.

F.O. 328 dictated a schedule of countless deadlines, and for each one missed the already challenging mission became even tougher. Takeoff times for the twelve participating bomb groups would be between 1:55 and 3:00 A.M. Each group would have only seventeen minutes to get its thirty-six aircraft airborne. At the appointed time, an officer stationed atop each airfield's control tower gave an appropriate signal, indicating the commencement of the mission. The bomb group's lead B-24 pilot promptly taxied his Liberator to its takeoff point, opened the throttle wide, raced down the runway, and roared into the darkness. Each group's remaining aircraft followed at intervals of forty-five seconds. The simple wristwatch was one of the 2nd Bomb Division's most valuable tools that night. B-24 copilots held responsibility for proper timing, both on the ground and in the air, and they peered intently at their watches, counting down to zero out loud to indicate to the pilots when a takeoff should commence. When airborne, orders strictly prescribed a speed of 155 miles per hour and a climb rate of 300 feet per minute.

On June 6, Liberator air crews feared the night far more than they feared the Germans. The Eighth Air Force was celebrated for flying tight formations, but flying "close up," as orders routinely demanded, was a hazardous thing to do even in daytime. At night, it was infinitely worse—like driving a car with no headlights in a tunnel. There was a full moon, but a heavy cloud cover at 2,500 feet diffused the glow considerably. Wing lights and Aldis lamps flashed by tail gunners also helped, but not much.

96th Combat Wing, 2nd Bomb Division, Eighth Air Force
Special Instructions, June 5, 1944
Single aircraft not making rendezvous with flight formations will proceed to the
target, joining formations and bombing if practical. If not, individual aircraft will
bomb the secondary target.

After takeoff, the Liberators circled their airfields on what was known
as a "racetrack course." This element of the mission, which had sounded
simple in the briefing room, was anything but. It involved sharp turns in
close proximity to friendly aircraft, all of which were climbing rapidly,
cloaked by the nearly impenetrable darkness. Furthermore, no radio talk
was permitted to announce when turns would be executed. Copilots again
played a critical role, as they vigilantly counted down upcoming turns with
their watches. At zero, a pilot would bank his B-24 sharply, as everyone on
the aircraft prayed that the other nearby Liberators would follow suit.

According to assembly plans, groups would circle their airfields on
racetrack courses, climbing until they reached predesignated altitudes, generally around 10,000 feet. Climbing with fully loaded bomb bays was
never easy, particularly when frigid air caused ice to accumulate on wings
and engines. Unknown to the pilot, ice could easily push an airplane over
its weight limit. Although the Omaha Beach mission took place only two
weeks prior to summer, ice did in fact cause trouble for Liberators during
their climbs. At around 8,000 feet, alert pilots who shone flashlights out of
their cockpits noticed the first signs of ice accumulation and compensated
by slightly lessening their rate of climb. Nevertheless, ice buildup caused
the one and only B-24 loss on this mission, the veteran 389th Bomb
Group's deputy lead ship, which crashed about twenty miles north of its
Hethel airfield, with the loss of all ten crew members. The first fatalities in
the Omaha Beach assault were neither soldiers nor sailors, but airmen—
whose deaths occurred nowhere near Normandy.

With all its dangers so far, the mission had only begun. The task ahead,
just as hazardous as the first, would be to assemble ever larger clusters of
bombers, from groups of 36, to wings of 108, to divisions of about 450,
and finally to the entire Eighth Air Force of more than 1,350 Fortresses and
Liberators, flying down a corridor less than ten miles wide. Here was the
most treacherous airspace in aviation history; a busy twenty-first-century,
big-city airport is empty in comparison.

The Eighth Air Force, famous for its progressive technology, set up
screeching radio beacons called "Bunchers" or "Splashers" at ground sta-

tions specified in field orders. These transmitted on secret frequencies that aircraft could home in on. Each Eighth Air Force combat wing had an assigned Buncher station, which changed its transmission frequency from mission to mission. The top brass considered Buncher frequencies highly sensitive information, insisting that this data be released only just prior to takeoff. The information was typed on razor-thin rice paper that, according to Eighth Air Force lore, was supposed to be eaten if capture was imminent. But as one airman pointed out, "Who could think of food at a time like that?" To assemble in a tidy formation around a Buncher beacon, Liberator navigators kept their eyes fixed on a radio compass dial, which accurately indicated the position of the aircraft in relation to the transmission. When a bomber flew directly over a Buncher, the dial abruptly flipped 180 degrees. Aircraft survival depended on continuous concentration and perfect crew teamwork.

On D-Day, a messy patchwork of clouds snarled the assembly procedure—and to any World War II bomber pilot, clouds were a purveyor of hard luck. Fortunately, hard luck was on holiday, and no midair collisions occurred among any Eighth Air Force aircraft. The price of good fortune, however, was high. Tight formations had dissipated within the clouds, and most groups would not recover prior to the bomb run.

Lt. Col. Warren Polking
392nd Bomb Group, 2nd Bomb Division, Eighth Air Force, D-Day Mission Critique, June 13, 1944
We were together pretty well until we hit a big cloud over Buncher 5. We did not see the cloud coming up, and when we did there was just one choice. We went in and when we came out, and there were only three ships with us.

Lt. Col. Lawrence Gilbert
392nd Bomb Group, 2nd Bomb Division, Eighth Air Force
The B-17, by the nature of the beast, was able to fly tighter, more compact formations than we were. We often joined the bomber stream in loose and scattered formations, whereas the Forts were very tight and compact. Most B-24 pilots will tell you that it was a difficult aircraft to hold in formation. It was physically demanding and after 20 or 30 minutes at altitude, you were worn out.

The higher the bombers climbed and the farther they flew from their home airfields, the greater the irresistible buildup of time pressure. This was no normal bomb mission, as all crews clearly understood. If they were even a few minutes late over Omaha Beach, they had better not drop their bombs over the primary target. There were GIs down there—and a court-martial could be awaiting them if they made a mistake.

20th Combat Wing, 2nd Bomb Division, Eighth Air Force
Special Instructions, June 5, 1944
Flights will depart Buncher 7 at their assembly altitudes at six minute intervals. First flight of each group will depart Buncher 7 at Zero minus 194 [3:16 A.M.].

As the B-24s clustered and circled, slumbering East Anglian farmers were woken by a throbbing roar growing in intensity by the minute. More than a few thought to themselves that the Americans were up to something special that night, hoping that old man Hitler was going to get it good. But the throbbing eventually passed off to the northwest—seemingly the wrong direction. The great paradox of the 2nd Bomb Division's D-Day mission was that more than half the time the Liberators spent in the air prior to bombing Omaha Beach, they actually flew northward, directly *away* from Normandy. Such a contradiction was the price the Eighth Air Force had to pay for SHAEF's simultaneous employment of every Allied warplane and transport in Britain on June 6, when crowded night skies forced staffs to formulate extraordinary flight plans. Had the B-24s flown directly to Normandy from their English bases, they would have arrived in little over one hour. In the actual mission, however, Liberators were in the air for nearly four hours prior to reaching their targets.

Finally, at about 4:30 A.M., the 2nd Bomb Division formed four immense columns, each composed of more than 100 Liberators deployed in V-formations of three ships each, and headed straight south for Omaha Beach. Twenty pathfinder B-24s equipped with the new H2X Mickey radar led the way, firing brightly colored flares at one-minute intervals to guide the many lost pilots to their proper stations.

Col. John Gibson
44th Bomb Group, 14th Combat Wing, 2nd Bomb Division,
Eighth Air Force
You can envision it sort of like this: picture a funnel, like you use to pour fuel in a gas tank. The large end would be the end up toward Scotland. As we kept going [south], the area kept getting smaller and smaller, so that finally we were just going through the neck of the funnel. This would be where we left the shores of England and progressed across the Channel.

Eighth Air Force: 2nd Bomb Division on D-Day

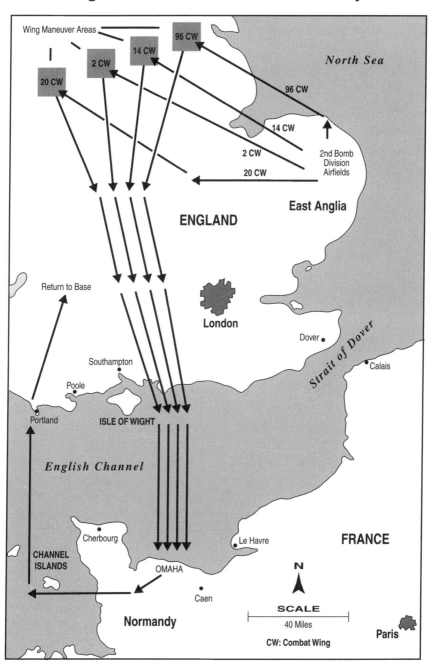

Wing Maneuver Areas

96 CW

14 CW

2 CW

20 CW

North Sea

96 CW

14 CW

2 CW

20 CW

2nd Bomb
Division
Airfields

East Anglia

ENGLAND

Return to Base

London

Dover

Strait of Dover

Calais

Southampton

Poole

Portland

ISLE OF WIGHT

English Channel

Cherbourg

Le Havre

FRANCE

CHANNEL
ISLANDS

OMAHA

Caen

N

SCALE

40 Miles

Normandy

CW: Combat Wing

Paris

A pink glow in the east hinted at the first appearance of the sun as the bombers raced down the 2nd Bomb Division's corridor like a torrent, passing over the south coast of England, just east of the Isle of Wight, headed straight for Omaha Beach—now only thirty minutes away. The pathfinders' H2X radar soon picked up the Allied invasion fleets off the Normandy coast, and the apparently infinite white blips on the radar scopes, each one representing a single ship, triggered astonishment in anyone who saw it. Liberator veterans who had survived Ploesti and raids on "The Big B"— Berlin—had witnessed many fantastic sights in the skies over Europe, but here was something entirely new, a spectacle they certainly would never see again.

Cloud cover so far in the mission had been heavy. As dawn broke and the 2nd Bomb Division approached the Normandy coast, grim pilots discerned total overcast. Bombing would have to take place through a complete blanket of clouds. Consequently, the twenty pathfinder aircraft leading the Liberators to Normandy would assume an importance far out of proportion to their numbers, for their H2X radar would be the only means by which crews could determine the proper bomb release points over Omaha Beach. Upon signals given by the pathfinders, the B-24s would soon drop more than 2.3 million pounds of bombs, so the entire mission depended on bombardiers, navigators, and Mickey operators who knew H2X thoroughly. If only a single mistake was made, disaster awaited.

H2X was a simple antenna that continuously revolved while emitting high-frequency radio pulses. On late-model Liberators, the H2X dome replaced the belly turret and could be lowered and retracted as needed. The bounce-back of the H2X set's electrical pulses revealed a radio picture of the earth below on the Mickey operator's scope. The intensity of bounce-back between the earth and the H2X set was the key: The greater the number of returning pulses, the brighter the image on the scope. A trained operator could easily recognize urban areas because the buildings' sharp corners produced a high rate of pulse return, in turn yielding very bright blips on the scope. In contrast, flat areas such as the ocean or pastures gave little return and appeared dark on the scope.

As the pathfinders approached Omaha Beach, Mickey operators noticed gloriously sharp returns on their H2X scopes. The coastal bluffs beyond the beach were easily discernible, and bombardiers would therefore be able to make reasonably accurate fixes on their targets despite complete overcast. The Liberators approached those targets rapidly, and pilots prepared by opening their bomb bay doors. Of the 450 B-24s on the mission, however, only the 20 pathfinders were equipped with H2X, meaning 20 men shouldered the weighty responsibility of determining the proper times for bomb release. When a pathfinder dropped, the B-24s of its group would follow suit. If bombers lagged behind their leader and could not see its drop, a pathfinder would also release colored smoke markers, clearly indicating to the stragglers the position where it had released its bombs.

The pathfinder Liberators were now over Omaha Beach, leading their flocks. But because of stern warnings at premission briefings to avoid accidental short bombing of friendly troops, pathfinder bombardiers shifted their gaze to their watches rather than releasing their bombs. The seconds ticked away unhurriedly: five, ten, fifteen, twenty. Sometime around twenty seconds, and apparently in some cases more than thirty, they finally pushed their bomb release buttons and made the momentous announcement the crews had been waiting for: "Bombs away!" Pathfinder pilots stared out their cockpits at the trailing B-24s and observed with satisfaction that all had dropped their bombs in unison with their leaders.

Thousands of bombs cascaded out of bomb bays, disappearing through the clouds. Crews could see no impacts and did not have the slightest idea where their bombs had actually landed. But the mission was almost over, and it was apparently a job well done. The nighttime assembly had been masterful; enemy opposition, almost nonexistent. Best of all, every bomber except for the one lost after takeoff would return to base safely. "Milk runs" didn't come any better than this.

Brig. Gen. Leon Johnson
Commander, 14th Combat Wing, Eighth Air Force, D-Day Mission Critique, June 13, 1944
I thought our plan worked out pretty well, personally.

Lt. Col. Philip Ardery
Operations officer, 2nd Combat Wing, 2nd Bomb Division,
Eighth Air Force
I called the bombardier to ask him whether he thought he had a good run. Of course we could see nothing below us but the deck of clouds into which our bombs disappeared. "Sir," he replied, "if that wasn't a good run I'd never count on one being good. I think we dropped them right in the bucket."

But numbers told a different story: A B-24 at cruising speed covered a lot of ground in a hurry—close to 100 yards per second. Bomb delays of twenty or more seconds caused virtually all bombs to impact at least a mile beyond their intended targets.

It was not an auspicious start to the invasion.

Lt. Gen. Omar Bradley
Commander, First U.S. Army, Autobiography, **A Soldier's Story**
In bombing through the overcast, air had deliberately delayed its drop to lessen the danger of a spill-over on craft approaching the shore. This margin for safety had undermined the effectiveness of the heavy air mission. To the seasick infantry . . . this failure in air bombing was to mean many more casualties upon Omaha Beach.

Capt. Lorenzo Sabin
Commander, U.S. Navy Gunfire Support Group, Force O
In the midst of the [naval] bombardment, Lt. Robert Lee Smith, . . . the operations officer for the close gunfire support group, shouted, "Where are the airplanes?" It was a question no one could answer at the time. Not one bomb was dropped on Omaha Beach by our airplanes during the assault.

CHAPTER 6

Forlorn Hope

A DEVICE CALLED DUPLEX DRIVE

Ever since the Germans had unleashed blitzkrieg in 1939, British and American generals had come to believe in the tank as a necessary ingredient of any offensive military operation. But the Allies would initially have to attack from the sea to gain a toehold in Europe, and in such an endeavor, tanks would seemingly have little or no immediate role. An operation as hazardous as Neptune, however, demanded innovative solutions to the immense challenge of landing a large military force on a hostile shore, and if the Allies could come up with a way to employ tanks in the early stage of an amphibious assault, Neptune's chance of success would increase dramatically. It required a monumental effort to devise and produce special equipment that would enable tanks to land in the invasion's first wave, but that effort would be well worth it if those tanks could help crack open the Atlantic Wall.

For years the British had advocated the use of special armored vehicles in amphibious warfare, and with their help, Generals Gerow and Bradley resolved to land 112 specially modified U.S. Army Sherman tanks on Omaha Beach before a single infantryman set foot in France. According to Gerow's plan, sixteen U.S. Navy LCT landing craft would launch a total of sixty-four duplex drive (DD) Shermans about three miles offshore. These tanks would proceed shoreward under their own power, landing on Omaha Beach at 6:25 A.M., five minutes before H-Hour. In the meantime, another sixteen armored LCT(A)s were to proceed straight to the beach, grounding themselves in the shallow surf to deposit forty-eight more Shermans onto the sand over the landing craft's bow ramps.

If this ambitious and unprecedented scheme actually worked, exultant GIs emerging from their landing craft minutes later would observe Shermans churning across the beach, spaced at intervals of roughly sixty yards, their big 75-millimeter cannons and machine guns blasting away at enemy pillboxes. Even if the occupants of those pillboxes survived the tanks' onslaught, the Shermans would make excellent shields against enemy fire as the foot troops hastily crossed the beach. And if enemy barbed wire or obstructions blocked the infantry's path, the tanks could handily remedy that situation too. Many were convinced that the tanks could be the much-needed modifiers that altered the amphibious warfare equation in favor of the invaders. But a few harbored misgivings that the tank plan sounded too good to be true.

Maj. Gen. Leonard T. Gerow
Commander, V Corps, Overlord Conference, December 21, 1943
I don't know whether it has been demonstrated or not: What will happen to those DD tanks with a three- or four-knot current? . . . I question our capability of getting them in with that current and navigation.

In a war noted for its technological innovations, the DD tank stands as one of the most curious developments of World War II. One would not expect a thirty-three-ton Sherman tank to be capable of driving off an LCT into the sea and then cruising to shore under its own power, but that is exactly what a DD tank was intended to do. A shroud made of rubber and canvas supported by metal struts enabled the tank to float; the duplex drive transmission powered two propellers, which also acted as rudders, for sea movement, although speed was a meager five miles per hour. Once on land, the driver switched the transmission to power the treads rather than the propellers, and the tank proceeded to travel on solid earth.

The Americans had learned to operate DDs from British Army personnel in early 1944 and were satisfied with the tanks' performance—in practice. A DD tank in the water with its shroud raised was almost entirely submerged; less than one foot of canvas remained above the water to prevent the sea from swamping the vehicle. The uninitiated would not have the slightest idea that a tank lay hidden behind that canvas, for a DD at sea

A device called duplex drive. A U.S. Army DD tank enters the water with its canvas shroud raised. The two propellers provide propulsion when the tank immerses fully. U.S. ARMY SIGNAL CORPS, NATIONAL ARCHIVES.

had the slightly ludicrous appearance of a floating bathtub, lacking any imaginable military application whatsoever.

Maj. William Duncan
S-3, 743rd Tank Battalion, top secret DD Tank Report, April 30, 1944
The following are limitations of the DD tank: A) It is given flotation by a very tender skin of canvas. This canvas is easily torn. . . . A tear greater than one foot may cause the tank to sink. B) The DD tank is limited to a maximum of Force 3 wind and sea. C) It is believed that a DD tank can be sunk by wash of LCT, LCS, and larger craft passing within a few yards of the tank. D) Six cases of carbon monoxide poisoning have been noted in launches of 4,000 yards or greater. No fatalities.

Lt. Dean Rockwell
Commander, U.S. Navy LCT Group 35, Evaluation of DD tank, April 30, 1944
I should like to make the following recommendations. . . . A) That the Army be notified immediately of the LCTs by number that will be assigned to each tank

battalion. This is imperative for future training to prepare for D-Day. B) Inasmuch as the Army is desirous of launching, if at all possible and feasible, the DD tanks on D-Day, an Army officer who is thoroughly cognizant of the limitations and peculiarities of said tanks should make the decision, in case of rough sea, whether or not the tanks shall be launched or taken directly to the beach. C) That the DD tanks be used on D-Day.

Duncan and Rockwell trained three tank battalions with these new secret weapons for the invasion. On Omaha, two would be employed: The 741st would swim thirty-two DDs ashore on the eastern half of the beach, and the 743rd would swim in thirty-two on the western half.

1st Lt. Edward Sledge
Company A, 741st Tank Battalion

[I recall] the complete confidence of the men in our tanks. . . . In all our training in England, we had not lost one DD tank.

The two tank outfits were almost indistinguishable: They handled the same equipment; followed identical training procedures; and shared the same mission. Their D-Day experiences, however, were anything but identical. The proficient tankers in both the 741st and 743rd were anxious to demonstrate their DD tanks' worth, but they also realized that these were delicate machines. Major Duncan had warned that Force 4 or worse wind and sea conditions could be disastrous for the DDs, and tankers and sailors who heeded this warning surely noted that at dawn's early light on D-Day, Force 4 conditions—eleven- to sixteen-knot winds and waves of three to five feet—seemed to be in effect.

The LCTs carrying the DD tanks had endured a tough Channel crossing. As H-Hour loomed, the task at hand promised to be even tougher. The 741st and 743rd had vital missions to fulfill, but given the current sea conditions, someone would have to make some difficult decisions. At 5:30 A.M., as the LCT columns wallowed at a speed of four knots through the dark, choppy sea toward Omaha Beach, now about three miles distant, the moment for that judgment had come.

Launch the DD tanks at sea or take them straight to the beach? Despite the parallel upbringings of the two tank outfits, their fates would diverge dramatically as a result of the choices soldiers and sailors were about to make.

H-Hour: 741st and 743rd Tank Battalions

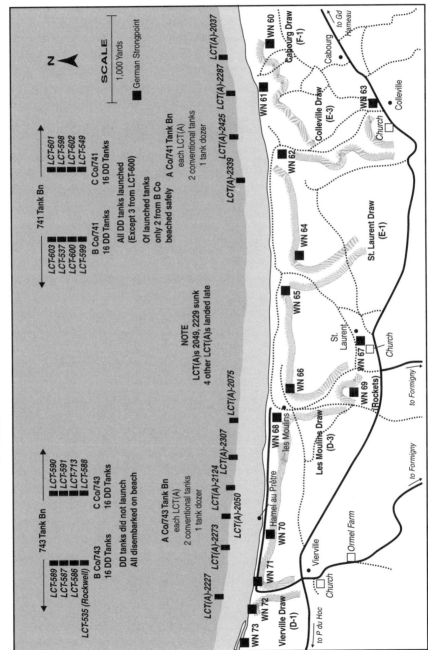

Force O, U.S. Navy
Top secret Neptune orders, LCTs carrying DD tanks, May 1944

Weather permitting, launch DD tanks about 6,000 yards offshore and land them at about H-10 minutes [6:20 A.M.]. If state of sea is such as to prevent their being launched and proceeding to the beach under their own power, land them with the first wave.

741st Tank Battalion
Loud-hailer message to LCT-602, carrying four 741st DD tanks, 0520 hours, June 6, 1944

You are 5,500 yards from the beach. It's up to your DDs now!

Ens. J. H. Metcalfe
Action Report, LCT-601, carrying 4 DD tanks of 741st Tank Battalion, June 1944

The tank corps men appeared confident of being able to reach the beach.

741st Tank Battalion
After-Action Report, July 19, 1944

At approximately H-60 [5:30 A.M.] the LCTs bearing the DD tanks of Companies B and C were in position off beach Omaha at a distance of approximately 6,000 yards from the beach. Company B was commanded by Capt. James Thornton, Company C was commanded by Capt. Charles Young. Capt. Thornton succeeded in contacting Capt. Young by radio and the two commanders discussed the advisability of launching the DD tanks, the sea being extremely rough—much rougher than the tanks had ever operated in. . . . Both commanders agreed that the advantage to be gained by the launching of the tanks justified the risk of launching the tanks in the heavy sea. Accordingly, orders were issued for the launching of the tanks at approximately H-50 [5:40 A.M.].

Lt. (jg) J. G. Barry
Action Report, LCT-549, carrying four DD tanks of 741st Tank Battalion, June 1944

No signal was received by me from the army concerning their intentions or anything else. When I endeavored to contact the next senior army officer by visual signal, he had already started to launch. . . . It was obvious even before launching that the sea at that distance was too choppy for the tanks.

Maj. William Duncan
S-3, 743rd Tank Battalion

Any Force 4 sea with choppy waters and waves of two feet or over were very dangerous, and Lt. Rockwell, USN, and the crews on his LCTs were well trained and very well aware of the danger. However, the Army directed that the senior captains of each battalion involved in the actual DD landing would make the decision on the spot as to whether to launch or not. Capt. Ned Elder (a wonderful officer), CO, Company C, 743rd Tank Battalion, determined that because of the heavy seas, the Navy LCTs should take the 743rd tanks to the beach.

Lt. Dean Rockwell
Commander, U.S. Navy LCT Group 35, Action Report, July 14, 1944

It was apparent that the sea would not be ideal for launching of the tanks. Before leaving Portland the question had been raised by this command as to the course to pursue in the event of a sea too rough for launching. Despite the insistence of this command that a decision be made by one senior army officer for both battalions, the question of launching was finally left to the senior army officer of each battalion, in this case Capt. Thornton of the 741st and Capt. Elder of the 743rd. This decision was agreed upon by Lt. Cols. Skaggs and Upham, commanding the 741st and 743rd, respectively. At 0505 this command contacted Capt. Elder via tank radio, and we were in perfect accord that the LCTs carrying tanks of the 743rd Battalion would not launch, but put the tanks directly on the designated beaches.

S/Sgt. Paul Ragan
Company B, 741st Tank Battalion, aboard LCT-600, July 1945

I saw the yellow flags go up, which meant to start launching. The ramp went down, and the first tank went off. I watched it clear the ramp and turned my head to start giving instructions to the other ones and at that time there was a big explosion near our craft, and all the tanks were pushed against each other and tore the screens. . . . [I saw] that the only tank that went off the LCT had sunk. The water was very rough. I went to the skipper and said that we must pick the men up. . . . We picked them up, and I also noticed a lot of others who were in life rafts, but we had to go on to the beach to drive our tanks off; this we did.

Ens. R. L. Harkey
Action Report, LCT-602, carrying four DD tanks of 741st Tank Battalion, June 1944

I am not proud of the fact, nor will I ever cease regretting that I did not take the tanks all the way to the beach.

On LCT-549, a concerned Lieutenant Barry had expressed doubt that his embarked DDs could successfully launch, but the tankers decided to try anyway. The first three tanks that drove off LCT-549's ramp sank after swimming only about 100 yards. Even after observing this disaster, Sgt. John Sertell, in charge of the fourth and last tank remaining on LCT-549, decided to launch despite an obvious tear in the canvas shroud of his DD. Said the astonished Barry, "It was a vain hope." Later that day, another LCT picked up Sertell's body.

The decision to launch the DD tanks of the 741st Tank Battalion at sea proved calamitous. All sixteen of Company C's tanks sank on the way to the beach, with the loss of considerable numbers of men. Only two of Company B's tanks made it to shore under their own power, although by sensible agreement of Ens. Henry Sullivan and 2nd Lt. P. J. O'Shaughnessy, LCT-600 later carried three more tanks directly to the beach after the unsuccessful launch of its first DD. The infantrymen of the 1st Division would therefore be lacking twenty-seven of the thirty-two DD tanks that the top brass had promised would be waiting for them on the beach at H-Hour. The men of the Fighting First would miss them greatly.

But thanks to Elder and Rockwell, the eight LCTs carrying Companies B and C of the 743rd made it to the beach without launching a single DD tank at sea. All eight landing craft successfully touched down at about 6:40 A.M., only a short time after the DD tanks had been scheduled to land. A few of Rockwell's LCTs experienced problems off-loading their tanks, for the beach was now under heavy fire, but in large measure most of the 743rd's DDs churned through the shallow surf toward the ominous belts of enemy beach obstacles dead ahead. The tanks were roughly where they were supposed to be, and the GIs of the 29th Division would sorely need them.

OVER THERE, AGAIN

Gerow's skepticism of the DD tanks—now proved valid—had led him to devise an invasion plan that did not depend entirely on duplex drive technology to deposit tanks in front of the infantry on Omaha Beach. A complementary scheme dictated that at H-Hour, sixteen ex-British LCT(A)s, enhanced with extra armor plating and still painted in the mostly white camouflage pattern favored by many Royal Navy landing craft, would each land three tanks directly on the beach over special ramp extensions meant to ease the task of disembarking vehicles in the deep surf. Two of the three tanks would be conventional Shermans; the third would be a Sherman specially fitted with a bulldozer blade to clear barbed wire and beach obstacles. To enable these tanks to land and operate in surf up to about seven feet deep, they had been specially waterproofed and had large metallic intake and exhaust ducts shaped like inverted fishhooks mounted over the rear engine.

Sailors assigned to a vessel that the navy had upgraded with supplementary armor harbored suspicions that they would be the invasion's proverbial guinea pigs—and they were right. Gerow's invasion diagrams could not be more blunt: The LCT(A)s would be the first landing craft to touch down on Omaha Beach. Intelligence summaries were equally blunt: The Germans had many large-caliber guns deployed in pillboxes, some rumored to be dreaded "88s," whose shells had sliced through Allied tanks in North Africa with astonishing precision even at ranges of a mile or more. If the preassault aerial and naval bombardment failed to produce results, the life expectancy of LCT(A) crews on Omaha could be very short.

Army tankers embarked on the LCT(A)s were less fatalistic. Tanks were designed to pave the way for the infantry, so their D-Day mission was not received with much surprise. If any Germans survived the bombardment, the tanks could disperse, take cover in the deep surf, and blast away at the enemy from there. For men who had drawn one of the invasion's toughest assignments, the tankers were surprisingly confident of success.

But the plan fell apart almost immediately. The arduous Channel crossing had caused many LCT(A)s to scatter, and in the predawn darkness off Omaha Beach, it proved impossible for them to gather in their proper assembly areas prior to the run to the beach.

Capt. Lorenzo Sabin
Commander, U.S. Navy Gunfire Support Group, Force O, Action Report, July 3, 1944
As we were behind schedule, all craft proceeded directly towards the beach at utmost speed and made no attempt to proceed to a position in front of the transport area and thence to the beach.

In addition to their treacherous fundamental mission, overwhelmed LCT(A) skippers were ordered to extend minesweeping gear on the approach to the beach—a task some simply ignored. They were also responsible for towing large LCM landing craft across the Channel, an obligation that no doubt contributed to the breakdown of their assembly schedule. About three miles off the beach, embarked army demolition engineers were supposed to shift from the LCT(A)s to the LCMs, an awkward procedure in the dark, rough seas off Calvados, and both landing craft would then head for the beach independently.

Burdened by so many hazardous tasks, Commander Sabin could hardly have been surprised that only ten of his sixteen LCT(A)s scheduled to land at 6:30 A.M. actually made it to the beach on time and successfully put their tanks ashore. The Germans promptly greeted them by opening fire with every weapon within range. For the LCT(A)s, an already risky mission suddenly became considerably riskier.

Capt. Lorenzo Sabin
Commander, U.S. Navy Gunfire Support Group, Force O, Action Report, July 3, 1944
During the approach to the beach, LCT(A)-2229 was sunk, presumably due to flooding, at a position about two miles off Dog Red beach. Two officers, four [enlisted] men, and three Army personnel were lost. . . . There was not much opposition from enemy defenses until the craft were right at the beach. At that time, a heavy barrage of shell, mortar, and machine gun fire was laid down.

Ens. Victor Hicken
Officer-in-command, LCT(A)-2227, Gunfire Support Group, Force O
On Dog Green, we landed "smack on," as the British would say, and right on time [6:30 A.M.]. On Dog Green there is a little spit which hooks out beyond the beach. We landed there and immediately drew mortar and machine gun fire. The tanks were discharged, but we couldn't get the anchor winch to retract. We were all huddled down in the wheelhouse, which was armored, listening to machine gun bullets hitting. A mortar shell blew off the ramp, and at that moment the heavy fire eased. I think Company A, 116th Regiment [29th Division] was landing and took the fire from us. In a sense we were saved by their sacrifice. . . . I will always remember a seaman coming up from below, shouting: "The mattresses are on fire!" With my foot I pushed him on the helmet and told him to go back and put out the fires. He did.

Ens. Edwin Kaufmann
Officer-in-command, LCT(A)-2124, Gunfire Support Group, Force O
While on the beach a shore battery placed at least ten shells of about 57mm caliber into LCT(A)-2124. The most serious problem was punctured fuel wing tanks and loss of the anchor, as a shell severed the anchor cable. We did retract but lost power about a mile from the beach because of saltwater in the fuel.

On a wide-open beach, the Shermans stood little chance against enemy antitank guns sited in fortified positions on commanding ground, all of which had easily survived the aerial and naval bombardment of the coast.

Vanguards of the invasion. The crippled U.S. Navy LCT(A)-2273, commanded by Ens. Lloyd McVey, sails off Omaha Beach on the morning of D-Day. Two Sherman tanks and a tank dozer are visible on her deck. The vessel broke in two and sank later that day. U.S. NAVY, NATIONAL ARCHIVES.

To prove that point, one DD tank of the 743rd Tank Battalion brought directly to the beach as per Elder's and Rockwell's orders was knocked out by a screeching enemy antitank shell only seconds after driving down LCT-591's bow ramp. To destroy the enemy pillboxes, the tanks would have to work in concert with the infantry, but lacking that support, they would be trapped on a beach with no exit, to be picked off one by one like the proverbial fish in a barrel. To postpone this fate, most tanks sought concealment in the shallow surf and returned fire from that skimpy cover as the tide rose. Across more than 400 yards of open beach, however, the well-concealed enemy pillboxes were nearly impossible to detect, and for the moment, the tankers could do little except wait for more favorable conditions to recommence their attack—assuming they could survive that interval. Unhappily for Bradley and Gerow, only a few minutes after H-Hour, the Germans proved themselves fully capable of thwarting the large numbers of tanks the Americans had deployed in the invasion's first wave. At least in this instance, tanks would not alter the balance of amphibious warfare in favor of the invader after all.

Ens. W. C. Cook
Officer-in-command, LCT-586, Action Report, June 1944

[After beaching,] machine gun fire was all around. . . . When I left the beach the tanks were in a group and half-underwater and were firing.

Ens. H. White
Officer-in-command, LCT-713, Action Report, June 1944

[We beached] a little to the left of Exit D-1 [Vierville draw]. Dead ahead appeared a pillbox made of cement and red brick, with two gun ports.

S/Sgt. Thomas Fair
Company A, 741st Tank Battalion, June 1944

The ramp was dropped in pretty deep water and we left the craft. I was in Number 1 tank, and Sgt. Larsen had Number 2 tank, and the dozer was Number 3. The water was up over our turret ring. We finally pulled up on the beach, but still stayed in the water enough for our protection. Our bow gunner and gunner started spraying the trees and hillside with .30 caliber [machine gun fire] while we looked for antitank guns and pillboxes.

Cpl. S. Schiller
Company A, 741st Tank Battalion, June 1944

Lt. [Gaetera] Barcelona's tank, named "Always in My Heart," upon approaching the beach was firing continuously upon targets. The main target was a house to the right of Exit E-1, into which several rounds were fired. After leaving the landing craft, our first target was a pillbox of a 75mm [antitank gun], which was stopped after [we fired] several rounds of high explosive.

743rd Tank Battalion
D-Day After-Action Report, June 23, 1944

The LCT on the extreme right landed its [four Company B] tanks OK. Captain [Charles] Ehmka in the next LCT hit the beach directly in front of the 88 at the Vierville exit. It sank his LCT before it landed, including Captain Ehmka's tank. Captain Ehmka and two lieutenants were KIA [killed in action], and another officer was WIA [wounded in action]. Lieutenant [Harold] Beavers was the only officer in B Company left.

T/5 Robert Jarvis
Company B, 743rd Tank Battalion

When we first came down the ramp of the LCT, we started firing immediately at whatever pillboxes or targets we could see. Being the assistant gunner, I didn't have much time to look out of my periscope [as I was] loading the 75mm cannon and the .30 caliber machine gun. I would get a call for AP [armor piercing] for pillboxes or HE [high explosive] for what looked like trenches or a machine gun nest. . . . I finally had a few slack moments in firing to look around. I figured by our firing that the beach should be pretty well secured. . . . As I was watching, the surf rolled a body of a sailor alongside of our tank. I recognized the sailor as being one of the crew of our LCT. . . . It was then that I realized everything was not going according to schedule.

Enclosed within their vehicles' steel hulls, with a severely limited field of vision, the tankers had a profound sense of isolation. What was going on? No one had the slightest idea—but if the tanks did not clear the beach soon, they stood a good chance of being turned into flaming wrecks. Help, in the form of American GIs, was on the way.

CHAPTER 7

The Momentous Now

TOP MEN AT THEIR CRAFT

For the foot soldiers who were about to storm *Festung Europa*, the first close-up view of the French coast was alarming. Where were the bombers? The top brass had promised that the shoreline would be smoldering from the Eighth Air Force's cascade of bombs, but the beach was obviously intact, and as smooth as slate. True, the naval shelling had been impressive, but it had hardly lasted long enough to accomplish much.

As the beach drew closer, troops and sailors peering over the sides of their landing craft could distinguish the terrain features they had been briefed so thoroughly about—but aside from some friendly tanks floundering in the shallow surf, the beach and coastal bluffs displayed no signs of life. Staff officers had assured the GIs that the Germans defending the beach were second-rate troops. Perhaps the brief naval barrage had caused most of the enemy to flee. Evidence of the Germans' presence here, however, was obvious: Hundreds of menacing beach obstacles loomed beyond the surf, among them wooden poles, steel tetrahedrons, and bulky metal gates—most of which were allegedly mined. If the enemy had indeed survived the naval barrage, the GIs of the first wave could not fail to notice that crossing that expanse of open beach under fire would be anything but easy.

It did not take long for the Germans to announce their presence. Foamy white geysers, apparently produced by mortar or howitzer shells, suddenly erupted from the sea amid the ragged lines of landing craft racing toward the beach, now just a few hundred yards distant. No machine gun fire yet—but the landing was clearly not going to be a walkaway after all.

Coxswains raced their engines, steering their landing craft through the rolling breakers toward touchdown points on the beach. Their wretched three-hour journey from transport to shore about to end, many desperately seasick men could barely wait to place their feet on solid ground again regardless of what the enemy had to offer. At a time like this, typical soldier chatter hardly seemed appropriate—just a reassuring glance at a buddy and a faint smile or nod in return would do. The landing craft's engines were too loud to permit normal conversation anyway. Nervous infantrymen adjusted equipment that had already been readjusted a dozen times, and as their craft noisily jolted to a halt, the men gripped their weapons tightly and prepared to carry out the job they had been trained to do.

Sub-Lt. Jimmy Green
Wave commander, Royal Navy 551 Assault Flotilla, Embarking
Company A, 116th Infantry

It was approaching the time to form line abreast and make our dash for the shore. I gave the signal and told Signalman Webb to stop pumping and take cover. [Coxswain] Martin pulled down the cover over his head and was guided by me through slits in his armor-plated cockpit. . . . Now we were alone, at the right beach at the right time. Taylor Fellers [CO, Company A, 116th Infantry] wanted to be landed to the right of the pass [Vierville draw]. We went flat out and crunched to a halt some 20 or 30 yards from the shoreline and 100 yards below the nearest beach obstacles.

PFC Paul McCormick
Company E, 16th Infantry, 1st Division

Going into shore on an LCVP, one of the boys looked up at me and said: "Mac, when a bullet hits you, does it go all the way through?"

2nd Lt. John Spalding
Company E, 16th Infantry, 1st Division, February 1945

The Navy had been firing, and the dust from debris plus the early morning mist made it difficult to see the coast. . . . As we came in there was considerable noise from the shore and sea. En route to the shore we passed several yellow rubber boats. They had personnel in them, but we didn't know who they were. They turned out to be tank personnel from the DD tanks which had foundered. . . . About 0630 we hit the line of departure; someone gave a signal and we swung

"The Momentous Now." Troops from the 1st Battalion, 16th Infantry, 1st Division, in a U.S. Coast Guard LCVP en route to Omaha Beach. The boat team leader, an officer, looks over the bow ramp toward the shore.
U.S. COAST GUARD, NATIONAL ARCHIVES.

into line. When we got about 200 yards offshore, the boat halted and a member of the Navy crew yelled for us to drop the ramp. S/Sgt. Fred A. Bisco and I kicked the ramp down.

Those foot soldiers who were lucky enough to have survived the initial landing at Omaha Beach would forever define D-Day by their experiences in the invasion's first few minutes. The first wave was transported to its destination—and its destiny—in fifty small landing craft, more than a quarter of them British. Each craft embarked at least 31 soldiers, yielding a force of more than 1,550 GIs to shoulder the burden of introducing the U.S. Army to the German occupiers of France at precisely H+1 minute, 6:31 A.M.

Omaha Beach was a big place. The first wave would land on a front of more than four and a half miles. Dispersed over such great length, the initial invaders might feel lonely at first, but thousands more comrades-in-arms would shortly follow in their wake. Of the fifty landing craft, twenty-four carried members of the 16th Infantry, 1st Division, to the eastern half of the beach; another twenty-four brought troops from the 116th Infantry, 29th Division, to the western half. The remaining two craft would convey Company C of the 2nd Ranger Battalion to Omaha's westernmost extremity, a sector Neptune planners had designated "Charlie."

When the army had created its elite Ranger units in World War II, Charlie was precisely the type of place where it planned to employ them. This was a foreboding and lonely sector, seemingly a cul-de-sac with the ocean on one side and cliffs higher than 100 feet on the other. At high tide, there was no beach save for a belt of boulders only a few feet wide. But the Rangers had been trained to consider cliffs and boulders as nothing more than temporary impediments. In fact, at the same time Company C stormed ashore on Omaha Beach, three more Ranger companies from the 2nd Battalion were scheduled to ascend similar cliffs at Pointe du Hoc, a critical objective four miles westward down the Calvados coast.

That Company C was a decidedly confident outfit was demonstrated when, in one of the two Royal Navy LCAs transporting them to the beach, the Rangers acknowledged Sgt. Walter Geldon, who was celebrating his third wedding anniversary, by singing in his honor. Geldon would be dead in less than an hour.

Capt. Ralph Goranson
Commander, Company C, 2nd Ranger Battalion
I was fortunate to have, in my humble pride, the best damn group of Rangers in the 2nd Battalion. I also felt that the Royal Navy and its landing craft were the very best. They beached us on time in the best place—exactly per our instructions. And they paid dearly for it.

In the Charlie sector, the beach abruptly terminated in a rocky promontory the locals called Pointe de la Percée. There the Germans had erected an apparently impregnable strongpoint atop the cliff, consisting of at least four pillboxes surrounded by two belts of barbed wire. Only a highly confident soldier could have imagined that sixty-five men landing by sea could capture such a position in daylight, but that was precisely what Company C was obliged to do. Such a treacherous mission could be accomplished only by soldiers who knew exactly what they were doing, but Goranson was certain that these were the type of men who populated his company. The task was critical. No American on Omaha Beach could move without being observed by the enemy from the Percée headland. Goranson's Rangers would be responsible for seeing to it that the enemy did not enjoy that advantage.

Lt. Col. James Rudder
Commander, 2nd Ranger Battalion, conversation with Goranson,
May 1944
You have the toughest goddamn job on the whole beach.

Captain Goranson devised two different attack plans. According to Plan One, Company C would shift eastward down the beach after landing and move inland through the Vierville draw, assuming 29th Division troops had already cleared that exit. The Rangers would then move west along the coast road and attack the enemy strongpoint from the landward side. However, if the 29ers had not yet seized the draw, Goranson would trigger Plan Two, a much more challenging scheme requiring the Rangers to ascend the sheer cliffs overlooking Charlie prior to moving inland around the strongpoint. Even if only a few Germans survived the preinvasion bombardment to resist the GIs from the clifftop, Plan Two would be extraordinarily difficult to execute, especially as Goranson's men lacked most of the specialized climbing gear that their fellow Rangers would deploy at Pointe du Hoc.

The LCA carrying Goranson was the westernmost of the fifty first-wave landing craft. Consequently, it drew attention from the German beach defenders, who indeed had survived the Allied bombardment. As the Rangers neared Omaha Beach, they stopped singing.

1st Sgt. Henry Golas
Company C, 2nd Ranger Battalion, 0630 hours, June 6, 1944
Gee, fellas, they're shooting back at us!

Capt. Ralph Goranson
Commander, Company C, 2nd Ranger Battalion
I told the men to get from the water's edge under the overhang of the cliffs as fast as they could because that's where safety will be. . . . Right after we landed we took at least three or four rounds of 88s. The first was wide, but number two took the landing ramp off. Number three hit in the rear, and number four amidships.

The Rangers' worst fears had been immediately realized: the enemy was decidedly active and seemingly had every foot of the beach zeroed in.

H-Hour: Vierville Draw

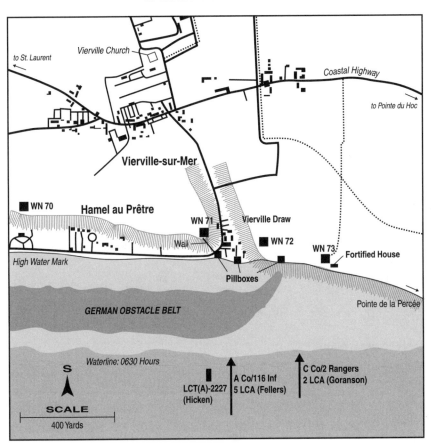

Goranson had a wrecked LCA and a dozen casualties to prove it, and not a single Ranger had thus far set foot on Omaha Beach. Was another Dieppe imminent?

On Company C's second landing craft, as the Royal Navy coxswain raced his engine for the final run to the beach, Lt. Sidney Salomon noticed sharp, metallic pings on the side of the LCA: machine gun fire. When the LCA grounded, Salomon was the first through its narrow armored door and down the bow ramp. Sgt. Oliver Reed followed but was immediately felled by a bullet. As the rest of the boat team trudged off the LCA, Salomon grabbed Reed's collar and dragged him through the waist-deep surf to dry sand. But the worst was yet to come . . .

1st Lt. Sidney Salomon
Company C, 2nd Ranger Battalion
After going a short distance, a mortar shell landed behind me, killing or wounding my mortar section, the concussion knocking me forward and on the ground. I thought that I was dead. . . . Just then sand was kicked in my face; I assumed that an enemy machine gunner was getting me in range, and decided that I had better move. I got up and ran to the base of the cliff.

PFC Nelson Noyes
Company C, 2nd Ranger Battalion
We went out onto the beach, and the Germans had us zeroed in. We waded in about a foot of water. . . . All of us ran across the beach as fast as we could. I ran about 100 feet before hitting the ground, when we ran into enemy crossfire from the right and in front.

Burdened by equipment and waterlogged uniforms, the Rangers found it hard to move swiftly across the soft sand, and the Germans cut many more of them down—including First Sergeant Golas and Sergeant Geldon. The stunned survivors who reached the base of the cliffs noted that more than half of the original sixty-five Rangers had failed to make it that far. In front of the Vierville draw off to his left, Goranson could observe tanks and 29th Division troops on the receiving end of even heavier enemy fire.

If the Rangers still had a job to do, the proper course of action was obvious. Lt. William Moody needed only to glance at Goranson and ask, "Plan Two?" Goranson replied, "Right." Reduced to about thirty men, the Rangers would climb the cliffs.

Accompanied by Sgt. Julius Belcher and PFC Otto Stephens, Moody followed the cliff base westward for about 300 yards. There they found a section of cliff that just might do. Stephens climbed first, thrusting his bayonet into the cliff face to gain successive holds. Belcher and Moody followed and brought up four sections of toggle rope to anchor on the cliff top, thereby easing the climb for any followers. The Rangers' war would begin from there.

PFC Otto Stephens
Company C, 2nd Ranger Battalion, Distinguished Service Cross Citation, June 1944
Proceeding across the fire-swept beach PFC Stephens scaled a 100-foot cliff and secured ropes to the top for other men to use in ascending. Without waiting for his comrades to reach the top, PFC Stephens proceeded to attack the enemy positions located there.

Capt. Ralph Goranson
Commander, Company C, 2nd Ranger Battalion
After we had crossed the beach and lay flat under the cliff overhangs, I heard this voice hollering, "Captain, mashed potatoes, mashed potatoes!" It was [PFC] Mike Gargas warning me that there was a potato masher grenade between my legs. I managed to creep ahead enough so when it went off, it did not hurt me. The name "Mashed Potatoes" stuck with Mike the rest of the war.

CAPTAIN FELLERS'S BOYS

The invasion plan hinged on the quick seizure of the Vierville draw, but the 29th Division unit with the mission to capture it faced a tactical dilemma just as challenging as the Rangers' task on Charlie. Gerow prized the draw because it was Omaha's best beach exit, featuring a good, hard-surfaced road that connected to the vital coastal highway at Vierville, only 500 yards inland.

The enemy, too, grasped the significance of the draw and fortified it with a fervor unmatched anywhere else on Omaha Beach. Packed into a front of only 600 yards, the Germans had constructed three autonomous strongpoints on ground so commanding that troops who attempted to move up the draw would be enveloped in a crossfire that would in all probability kill them all. At the draw's mouth, a concrete wall 9 feet high, 6 feet thick, and 125 feet long protruded from a massive pillbox situated on an embankment just beyond the beach, blocking all movement inland. Another pillbox sited slightly lower on the same embankment, about 100 yards to the west, had two apertures that allowed it to fire along the beach in either direction.

The entire resistance nest in front of the draw was surrounded by barbed wire and minefields, and its fighting positions were interconnected with trenches. With an efficiency for which the Germans were celebrated, they had ensured that no American soldier in the invasion's first wave would get anywhere near the Vierville draw.

Sub-Lt. Jimmy Green
Wave commander, Royal Navy 551 Assault Flotilla, Embarking
Company A, 116th Infantry

As we neared the shore I picked out a nasty looking pillbox and hoped it was not manned. . . . I was watching [the pillbox] and thinking that if it was manned we were going to be in trouble. There was a loud bang in my right ear, and I turned to see an LCG [landing craft, gun—probably USS LCG-424, with Royal Marine gun crews] blazing away with its 4.7-inch guns and scoring direct hits on the pillbox. I wished it could have stayed longer, but it disappeared as quickly as it had arrived.

"Heart of Oak." The Royal Navy's 551 Assault Flotilla, which carried the 1st Battalion, 116th Infantry, to Dog Green Beach at H-Hour. Sub-Lt. Jimmy Green is seated in the front row (see arrow). Sub-Lt. T. E. Arlidge, who saved many American lives by swinging his three LCAs to the east at about 7:00 A.M., is the second officer to the right of Green. COURTESY JIMMY GREEN.

The outfit drawing the assignment for this impossible mission was Company A, 116th Infantry, an old Virginia National Guard unit with highly treasured traditions harking back to Jackson and his legendary Stonewall Brigade, both fundamental icons of the Confederacy's "Lost Cause." Raised in the picturesque village of Bedford in the foothills of the Blue Ridge, the old Company A men styled their outfit "The Peaks of Otter Rifles" after the nearby summits known by all Virginians for their natural beauty. On February 3, 1941, Company A had been abruptly converted from a group of 98 part-time militiamen into an active component of the

U.S. Army. By D-Day, more than three years later, the army had made over Company A, and the Bedford guardsmen who had survived this transformation amounted to only a small minority—35 men out of the outfit's full complement of 210. However, most of the company's key leaders, including its commander, Capt. Taylor Fellers, its executive, Lt. Ray Nance, and 1st Sgt. John Wilkes, were Bedford men, as were many senior noncommissioned officers.

Capt. Taylor Fellers
Commander, Company A, 116th Infantry, 29th Division, letter to his mother, 1943
I am beginning to think it is hard to beat a Bedford boy for a soldier. . . . I am truly proud to be commanding my old hometown outfit, and just hope I can carry them right on through and bring all of them home.

Six Royal Navy LCAs under Green's command, all drawn from the British transport *Empire Javelin*, carried Fellers's Company A to its H-Hour appointment on Dog Green Beach. Fellers was suffering from the lingering effects of a nasty sinus infection that had nearly forced him to miss the invasion. He asked Green to land his men astride the mouth of the Vierville draw, three LCAs on either side. Green correctly surmised that the taciturn Fellers was troubled by the gravity and danger of his mission. Indeed, Fellers had recently blurted to Nance that, armed with a single machine gun, one enemy infantryman could hold off the entire company from the heights straddling the draw—and if the bombardment failed to work, Company A would be wiped out. Like Gerow, Fellers was a realist.

S/Sgt. John Schenk
Company A, 116th Infantry, 29th Division, letter to his wife, April 1944
All that will save us now is God, luck, and a deep foxhole. And the latter must be plenty deep too.

Green pledged his support. His landing craft crews were brave and highly competent, and they would take the Americans exactly where they wanted to go, on schedule. Unlike U.S. Navy LCVPs, Green's British LCAs were armored and could stop rifle and machine gun bullets. They also provided some measure of overhead protection and featured benches on which the GIs could sit during the long run to shore. Once Fellers's men disembarked, however, Green's craft would have to depart—and Company A would be on its own.

Misfortune struck Company A just before it landed, as the LCA in column immediately behind Green's swamped about 1,000 yards offshore due to an apparent leak. As the LCA disappeared beneath their feet, the men activated carbon dioxide capsules to inflate their life belts and waged frantic life-or-death struggles to shed heavy equipment before the sea swallowed them forever. Only one man, radio operator PFC Jim Padley, drowned. He was last seen on the crest of a swell, and then he was gone. The rest would later be rescued by Green and returned to *Empire Javelin*. Down to five boat teams, Fellers's already difficult task had suddenly become even more daunting.

Pvt. John Barnes
Company A, 116th Infantry, 29th Division
I had heard no noise nor felt any impact. Quickly the boat fell away below me, and I squeezed the CO_2 [carbon dioxide] tubes in my life belt. Just as I did [the life belt] popped away. The buckle was broken. I was going under. I turned and grabbed the back of the man behind me. I climbed on his back and pulled myself up in a panic. . . . The battle had started, and I wasn't there.

The Royal Navy, as promised, landed Company A on time on either side of the draw. On each of the five surviving LCAs, a crewman kicked open the steel door and dropped the bow ramp into the surf with a cracking splash. The men yearned to get off, but on an LCA, they would have to be patient; the steel door in the bow was narrow enough to permit only a single file of soldiers to exit at once, as opposed to three files in an American LCVP. Led by Fellers, and accompanied by simple exhortations of "Good luck!" from the British, the heavily laden GIs shuffled down the ramps into frigid waist-high water, holding their weapons aloft. Despite the lack of evidence that the Eighth Air Force had visited this beach, the men retained hopes that most of the enemy had fled with their first glimpse of the vast Allied armada. Could it be true? So far the Germans had offered mostly inaccurate mortar fire. Green observed every soldier exit his LCA safely and advance through the surf to the water's edge—still no enemy machine guns. Having done his duty, Green ordered his signalman to radio *Empire Javelin*: "Landed against light opposition. On target."

The men of Company A emerged from the water and pressed forward onto the beach. Off to the left, some Shermans were visible in the surf. A profuse jumble of German obstacles lay dead ahead, seemingly strewn randomly on the sand. Nearly 300 yards beyond them, the Vierville draw loomed. Company A needed only to seize that draw to accomplish its mission. But on an embankment directly between the GIs and their objective lay two sinister enemy pillboxes, apparently intact. Those 300 yards would seem a lot longer to Fellers and his men if the pillboxes suddenly turned active.

As Green prepared to return to *Empire Javelin*, he noted that Dog Green Beach was for the moment tranquil. Only the thud of waves smacking ashore and occasional shouts of command could be heard. On the beach, the men of Company A flopped into prone positions in a scraggly line just short of the obstacles, while Fellers, at the far right of the line, conferred with some of his noncommissioned officers. Meanwhile, the tide surged forward, so rapidly that it seemed to exhort the Americans to push ahead.

And then all hell broke loose.

No one could tell where the enemy machine gun fire came from; only its distinctive *rrrrrrp*, like a rag being torn, was audible. But no one could fail to notice its obvious effects, as thousands of bullets kicked up spouts of sand around the startled GIs, many of whom were promptly hit. A German machine gun spewed out 1,200 bullets per minute, and at that rate, it could kill a lot of Americans in a hurry—especially on a beach with no cover and no craters.

Fellers was probably one of the first to die, but it is impossible to determine how, because every member of his thirty-one-man boat team died with him. It was a slaughter. Of the 155 Company A soldiers who had just exited the LCAs, close to 100 died on Omaha Beach, and most of the rest were wounded. Nineteen of the dead were Bedford men, including a pair of brothers. Those few who survived did so only because they hastily retreated neck-high into the surf or hid behind some of the tanks located at the water's edge.

Company A, 116th Infantry, 29th Division
U.S. Army Historical Division, interview with PFC Leo Nash, September 1944

[Lt. Edward Tidrick] went on to the sands and flopped down fifteen feet from PFC Leo J. Nash. He raised up to give Nash an order. Nash saw him bleeding from the throat and heard his words: "Advance with the wire cutters!" It was futile. Nash had no wire cutters, and in giving the order, Tidrick had made himself a target for just an instant, and Nash saw machine gun bullets cleave him from head to pelvis. German machine gunners along the cliff directly ahead were now firing straight down into the party.

Company A, 116th Infantry, 29th Division
U.S. Army Historical Division, interview with PFCs Nash, Murdoch, and Grosser, September 1944

A medical boat team came in on the right of Tidrick's boat. [This was probably Company A's seventh LCA, led by Lt. Ray Nance, the company's executive officer. It was scheduled to land thirty minutes after the first six LCAs, but it beached about twelve minutes early. It had three medics, two of whom were killed.] The Germans machine-gunned every man in the section. [A few survived, including Nance and the third medic, Cpl. Cecil Breeden.] Their bodies floated with the tide. By this time the leaderless infantrymen had foregone any attempt to get forward against the enemy, and where men moved at all, their efforts were directed toward trying to save any of their comrades they could reach. [Witnesses noted Breeden treating several Company A wounded under heavy fire.] The men in the water pushed wounded men ahead of them so as to get them ashore.

One of the Bedford natives who perished by Fellers's side was S/Sgt. Elmere Wright, one of the most accomplished athletes in the 116th Infantry. Wright was a superb pitcher who had led the 116th Infantry's baseball team to the 1943 European Theater championship with a perfect 27–0 record. He had played minor league baseball in the St. Louis Browns' organization before the war, and after his dominating 1943 performance, he was delighted to hear from a Browns executive that a major league career was a distinct possibility upon his return to the States. In a 1943 team photograph, Wright's cheerful visage reveals a man who eagerly looked forward to that chance. The enemy saw to it that he would never get it.

So few Company A soldiers survived that it was almost impossible for wartime U.S. Army historians to determine precisely how the debacle had unfolded. In recent years, however, the reality of Company A's fate has become more clear. Captain Fellers had been correct: Only a few Germans—perhaps two or three machine gun teams—were responsible for the company's destruction. The primary source of the killing was probably an enemy pillbox camouflaged nearly perfectly in the folds of the bluff about 200 yards west of the Vierville draw. This pillbox was sited to fire only eastward, and through its firing slit, occupants had an ideal view of the beach where Company A disembarked. At about 400 yards range, a German manning a fixed machine gun with a perfect flank shot could hardly miss.

The Bedford Bulletin Weekly
"The War Comes Closer," July 20, 1944

The war was brought very close to all Bedford people Monday when a number of our homes received official notices of the loss of sons, brothers, and husbands on the beaches of Normandy. No home represented in the armed forces can escape the dread inherent in war, and this feeling of uneasiness and fear was intensified here when it became known in early June that the men who left Bedford with old Company A, 116th Infantry, were in the vanguard of the invasion forces which landed in France on the morning of the 6th. It was too much to hope that all of them could have escaped death or serious injury.

The men of Bedford had trained for almost three and a half years for this moment, only to be cut down in seconds like stalks of wheat felled by a scythe. Despite promises of unprecedented levels of support, Company A died alone. Eighth Air Force bombs had not hit the beach; the navy's guns had not knocked out the enemy's pillboxes; and aside from a few dozen Rangers racing to the cliffs on their right, not a single friendly infantryman was in sight.

OBEDIENT TO THEIR COMMANDS WE LIE

The invasion plan had seemed so neat on paper: At H-Hour, three companies from the 29th Division's 116th Infantry—G, F, and E—would simultaneously land adjacent to Company A on the east, extending its left flank along the beach by about one mile. Many of these men were old guardsmen from southside Virginia, close to the North Carolina border. The three companies, consisting of about 560 men, would land from eighteen U.S. Navy LCVPs drawn from the transport *Thomas Jefferson*, and if everything went according to plan, all four companies would advance across the beach in unison, each drawing confidence from the support of the others on its flanks. Accompanied by the 743rd's tanks, such a bold and concerted attack would surely overawe the supposedly second-rate German defenders who had survived the aerial and naval barrages.

But two factors conspired to throw this scheme awry before a single GI set foot on the beach, and neither of them had anything to do with the Germans. First, the naval bombardment had set grass on fire on the bluffs between the two westernmost draws. The thick smoke generated by this blaze drifted eastward, obscuring the coastal landmarks the navy coxswains had so carefully memorized. And then there was the notorious offshore current, which at H-Hour pushed landing craft relentlessly and with surprising force to their left, or east.

By daybreak's muffled light, the *Jefferson*'s coxswains were perplexed to discover as they neared the coast that they did not know with any certainty where they were. As a consequence, they landed Company E more than a mile off target to the east—so much so that its subsequent D-Day experience would fall within the realm of the 1st Division rather than its own 29th Division. As for F and G, the naval crews piloting their twelve LCVPs shoreward managed to discern some landmarks near the Les Moulins draw, but even so, they dropped their troops east of their assigned beach sectors.

Aside from Captain Fellers's Company A, the 116th's first wave had scattered badly. When Fellers came ashore in front of the Vierville draw at H-Hour, Company G was supposed to have been immediately on his left, but the navy put G ashore so far to the east that he could not even see them.

Companies F and G came ashore with little semblance of the neatness dictated by the plan. As the men exited in three files from their landing craft into the surf, officers and NCOs realized that they had been put down in the wrong place. A dozen or so little beach villas tucked into a break between the bluffs indicated that this must be the Les Moulins draw. Near the draw's mouth on the beachfront lay a landmark with which the troops were unfamiliar: a large three-story house with a distinctive mansard roof—more proof that the two outfits were on the wrong beach.

PFC John Robertson
Company F, 116th Infantry, 29th Division
Most of my boat team was seasick. I remember heaving over the side, and someone said, "Get your head down! You'll get killed!" I said: "I'm dying anyway!" So here we are, all seasick, ahead of everyone else, no bomb craters to get in, and heading straight into machine gun fire. That was my definition of Hell.

PFC August Bruno
Company G, 116th Infantry, 29th Division, September 1944
We didn't expect any trouble on the beach and had been told not to run.

Pvt. Rocco Russo
Company F, 116th Infantry, 29th Division
We landed in three or four feet of water, and the ramp failed to go down. Our lieutenant yelled to the tech sergeant, "What do we do, sergeant?" The sergeant yelled back: "Go over the side, lieutenant!" Each of us close to the lieutenant cupped our hands together to give him a boost up the side of the vessel. About the time [he] got on top, the ramp went down and we started leaving the boat. . . . Many of us fell down, but we had life preservers [actually life belts] on and did not drown.

Despite the absence of enemy fire when the first files of GIs started to exit their landing craft, the beach in front of Les Moulins would soon be a very hazardous place. The Germans had not been driven from their pill-

H-Hour: Les Moulins Draw

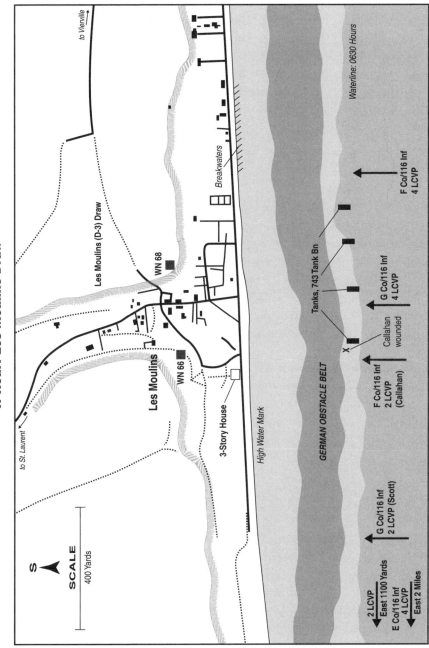

boxes, and the Americans had to cross 400 yards of open beach directly in front of those pillboxes to get at the enemy. Just as they had done at the Vierville draw, the Germans held their fire until most of the LCVPs had been emptied and the men had advanced through the surf up to the first belt of German beach obstacles.

With no place to hide, several F and G Company men, like their Company A brethren, were cut down the moment the enemy opened fire. Some of the remainder pressed on; others dropped to the sand and crawled forward to seek shelter behind the obstacles. They would not be able to remain there long, as the rapidly rising tide impelled them to move ahead or drown.

Although the two companies endured grave casualties, several factors saved them from the near total annihilation suffered by Company A. Drifting smoke from the grass fires partially masked German machine gunners who otherwise would have had perfect fields of fire. Moreover, the bluffs on this beach sector were strictly perpendicular to their line of advance, and the enemy was therefore incapable of achieving the flanking fire that had proved so lethal on Dog Green. Finally, several 743rd Tank Battalion Shermans had successfully beached in this sector, and more would arrive soon. As the tanks wove slowly through the belt of enemy beach obstacles, nearby GIs could follow closely behind and gain at least a fair degree of cover.

PFC John Robertson
Company F, 116th Infantry, 29th Division
I went in carrying 60 pounds of 60mm mortar ammo. My mortar crew was wiped out. It was a tank coming up behind me, as I was lying in the water, that got me up and across the beach. It looked like suicide, but better than getting run over.

Those lucky enough to have successfully traversed the beach fell to the ground in confused heaps at the base of a sharply sloping embankment, six feet high at its peak, consisting of thousands of weather-beaten off-white stones roughly the size of apples. This was the "shingle," an Omaha terrain feature with which the troops had become familiar by studying the invasion plan. Prone soldiers directly on its seaward side would be nearly invulnerable to enemy rifle and machine gun fire, but the shingle would pose no barrier to high-angle mortar shells. Happily for them, no such rounds were currently impacting in that area, but old soldiers knew that the Germans were too skilled at warfare to pass up such a golden opportunity. Surely the enemy's mortar tubes would soon cough their shells skyward to whistle down among them with deadly effect.

Pvt. Rocco Russo
Company F, 116th Infantry, 29th Division
I looked to my right and saw my friend, Sgt. John Cooney, with his head cocked over, his helmet lying on the beach. He was dead. He was the first soldier whom I saw dead on Omaha Beach. He and I used to go to Mass together in England. [I] headed for the seawall, running until fired at, then hitting the beach for a short period, then running again. It did not take me long to get to the wall, and I plopped down on the sand and rested.

On the opposite side of the shingle, the Germans had strung two coils of seemingly impenetrable barbed wire, and the GIs noted with disgust that the preassault bombardment had not affected it in the least. Just beyond the wire was a dirt track paralleling the beach and extending all the way to the 1st Division sector. Only about thirty-five yards past the track on the east side of the beach exit stood the conspicuous three-story house with its curious roof. The enemy had converted the house into a strongpoint, and it would be an obvious initial objective once the Americans could initiate an attack. From where Companies F and G lay on the shingle, a strong-armed soldier could have hit the house with a single well-aimed grenade toss, but no one could take it unless the troops could get off the beach—and this they could not do unless they penetrated the barbed wire.

Capt. William Callahan
Commander, Company F, 116th Infantry, 29th Division
I went in with my Number 3 assault team commanded by Lt. Theodore Lamb. . . . We suffered heavily crossing the beach, the weakened condition of the men contributing as well as heavy enemy fire. Unable to contact [743rd Tank Battalion] tanks by radio, I went back to the beach to direct their fire. This was a mistake. While directing fire [from atop a tank], I was wounded in both legs and right hip. In trying to get back to the shingle I was hit in the face and both hands.

The first prerequisite was to get organized. Key leaders had been killed or wounded, water and sand had fouled weapons, and boat team cohesion had evaporated. Stunned survivors could not fathom what to do next. Company G's few remaining leaders in front of the Les Moulins exit could gather only four depleted boat teams out of the company's original six, and they decided to try to move those teams 1,000 yards to the right along the shingle to reach the beach sector, about halfway between the Vierville and Les Moulins draws, on which G was supposed to have landed. But movement of any kind on the beach drew the enemy's undivided attention, and an already depleted Company G was reduced even further when it initiated this hazardous journey. About 400 yards down the beach, a series of stone and wood breakwaters protruded seaward perpendicular to the shingle, effectively blocking the company's axis of advance. Here its scant remnants took refuge between the breakwaters to await developments. Company G's six thirty-one-man boat teams, each theoretically an autonomous combat element, had thoroughly lost the cohesion they had trained so hard to retain.

Sgt. Theodore Fettinger
Company G, 116th Infantry, 29th Division, September 1944
The men were standing as [boat] sections; they were told to displace as a company, and as soon as they started to move to the right, along the crowded and embattled beach, sections became hopelessly mixed and little groups began to fall away from the company.

Company F had lost many more men than G, including its company commander, and for the moment was powerless to accomplish anything at all. Its worn-out survivors saw no alternative but to stay put behind the cover of the shingle. An invisible enemy atop the bluffs on either side of the Les Moulins draw unquestionably held the initiative, and any attempt by the GIs to move through the wire into the wide mouth of the beach exit would result in a massacre. According to the invasion plan, follow-on waves of 116th Infantry troops would soon arrive, and they could help rekindle the flagging assault. But grim Company F men lying prone behind the shingle realized that if something was not done soon, the company would be wiped out where it lay.

Pvt. Rocco Russo
Company F, 116th Infantry, 29th Division
In a little while Sgt. [Francis] Ryan got to the wall and ended up close to my spot. Ryan was an older man, probably 30 years old, and I had a lot of respect for him. Ryan suggested that we clean our rifles, and we did just that. . . . After the next shell came close to my position, I looked down and saw a big chunk of bloody meat in my lap. It had hit the top part of my assault jacket and fallen into my lap. I was shaken up and pointed it out to Ryan. He asked if it was part of me. I told him that I didn't think so, but I was so scared I wasn't really sure. . . . Sgt. Ryan and I went snooping around and saw an area that we thought we might be able to climb to get off the beach. We did not have enough people to help us, so we waited until more G.I.s got up to the wall.

THE THIRD TIME AROUND

On the eastern half of Omaha Beach, the 1st Infantry Division was about to initiate its third invasion in the past nineteen months. Compared with what the division was about to endure, the two previous invasions would seem easy in retrospect. It was true that the North African and Sicilian campaigns had turned the tide of war in the Allies' favor, an accomplishment the 1st Division had helped achieve, but Omaha Beach would have infinitely greater historical resonance, and would later define the division's World War II legacy. As difficult as it was for the battle-scarred veterans of Arzew and Gela to conceive, what had preceded Omaha Beach was only a foretaste of what was to come.

The 16th Infantry had led the 1st Division ashore twice before, and on June 6 it would do so yet again. The regiment had achieved a splendid combat record in the Mediterranean, and now, after an even more splendid ten-month interval away from combat, the rejuvenated 16th was ready for its new mission. The 16th's commanding officer, Col. George A. Taylor, was a forty-five-year-old, blue-eyed Oklahoman who had served in the infantry for virtually his entire professional career, starting in 1922 with his graduation from West Point. By D-Day, Taylor had led the 16th for more than a year and had enhanced his reputation as a master infantry tactician by successfully guiding his troops though the perilous fights at Hill 523 in Tunisia, and Troina in Sicily in 1943. In warfare, experience counts—and on Omaha Beach no one could accuse Taylor of being untested.

Col. George Taylor
Commander, 16th Infantry, 1st Division, May 1944
There will be lots of Germans left after [the navy] gets through shooting. We'll have to dig 'em out with bayonets and grenades.

The 16th's plan of attack mirrored that of the 116th Infantry on its right: Four companies totaling close to 750 men would be transported to the beach in twenty-four landing craft on a front of nearly two miles. According to the invasion timetable, twelve U.S. Navy LCVPs drawn from the transport *Henrico* would land Companies E and F astride the mouth of the St. Laurent draw at precisely 6:31 A.M. Concurrently, twelve British LCAs from the troopship *Empire Anvil* would carry Companies I and L to the easternmost of Omaha's beach sectors opposite the wide mouth of the Colleville draw. In theory, the troops forming the 16th's spearhead had a straightforward mission: push into the St. Laurent and Colleville draws, brushing aside any pockets of enemy resistance that had survived the prein-

vasion bombardment, and pave the way off the beach for follow-on waves
of infantry and engineers. However, the Germans reportedly had fortified
beach sectors on the 16th's front with their customary zeal, and if Colonel
Taylor was right, it would be not be easy for the 16th to accomplish its mission in a timely fashion.

The beach where Taylor's men would land on D-Day differed
markedly from the 116th's sector. Omaha's eastern half was a nearly pris-
tine shoreline with only a few signs of human habitation, and for most of
its length, grassy dunes and the ubiquitous rock shingle defined the border
between sand and soil. There would be no man-made seawalls or breakwaters to provide cover.

The two draws for which the 16th Infantry was responsible would be
difficult to capture. The St. Laurent draw was virtually a cul-de-sac, featuring acres of woods and thick undergrowth at its head that in places seemed
almost impenetrable. The exit's only road leading inland was a narrow dirt
track climbing the draw's precipitous western face toward the village of St.
Laurent, but two formidable enemy strongpoints sited on high ground on
either side of the draw's mouth effectively guarded this outlet. Minefields,
barbed wire, and a long water-filled moat would make any direct attack
against these strongpoints exceptionally difficult.

Similarly, the 500-yard mouth of the adjacent Colleville beach exit was
an exposed killing zone in which no American could live if the enemy's
sizable strongpoints on the dominating and seemingly unassailable ground
on either side of the draw were not eliminated. Even worse, at a length of
nearly a mile, the Colleville draw was by far Omaha's longest beach exit,
and should its enemy defenders resist resolutely, a direct attack straight up
the draw to the coastal highway at Colleville could be as fruitless and
deadly as Pickett's Charge.

Whereas both draws in the 116th Infantry's zone featured good paved
exit roads, not a single hard-surfaced road existed anywhere in Taylor's
beach sector. Consequently, the engineers' task of opening up the St. Laurent and Colleville draws for vehicular traffic would be an arduous job. But
before the engineers set out to accomplish this task, the 16th would have to
clear out the Germans, and Taylor's men had seen enough of them in
Africa and Sicily to know that they should never be underestimated. Somehow or other, according to the veterans, German soldiers would always surprise you.

The 16th's H-Hour landing was beset by the same difficulties as that of
the 116th Infantry on its right. The powerful coastal crosscurrent pushed

H-Hour: Cabourg Draw

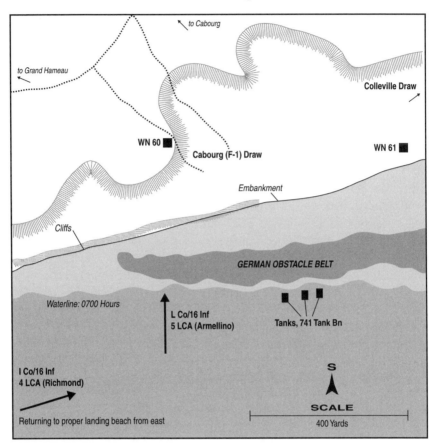

to Cabourg

to Grand Hameau

Colleville Draw

WN 60 ■

Cabourg (F-1) Draw

WN 61 ■

Embankment

Cliffs

GERMAN OBSTACLE BELT

Waterline: 0700 Hours

L Co/16 Inf
5 LCA (Armellino)

Tanks, 741 Tank Bn

I Co/16 Inf
4 LCA (Richmond)

Returning to proper landing beach from east

S

SCALE
400 Yards

landing craft inexorably eastward, and despite the warnings of the Neptune plan book, some coxswains apparently failed to compensate sufficiently for this flow's effect. Additionally, drifting smoke generated by grass fires made it difficult for naval crews to recognize coastal landmarks. The end results were that the 16th Infantry's entire first wave came ashore considerably to the east of its designated landing points, and instead of landing in unison at regular intervals across its front, the men landed in clumps staggered over a period of more than one hour. This allowed the Germans to concentrate their fire on the relatively narrow beachfronts where the GIs came ashore, and with superlative observation and fields of fire offered by the high ground beyond the beach, they could shift their fire at will as each group beached in turn.

The involuntary eastward shift of landing zones spared Companies I and L the hazardous mission of assaulting the Colleville draw head-on. However, the current's forceful push to the left also caused I and L to arrive on the beach separately, both considerably late, under circumstances even more treacherous than those they would have faced according to the original plan. Somehow the six *Empire Anvil* LCAs transporting Company I shoreward headed for the coast more than a mile east of its intended sector. Such a mistake was understandable, for the long line of vertical cliffs starting just east of the Colleville draw had a sameness that, in the dim light of dawn, could easily blur offshore navigation. But as the LCAs neared the shore, the men could see plainly that they were off course, for there was no beach ahead—only an unbroken line of gray-green cliffs.

3rd Battalion, 16th Infantry, 1st Division
D-Day After-Action Report, June 23, 1944

The alert company commander of I Company [Capt. Kimball Richmond] noticed the Navy's error as they were about to land and ordered the boats to be taken back to the correct beach. On the way back the craft carrying Lt. Funcheon's 4th section, and the craft with Lt. Cunningham's 5th section, were swamped and started to sink. The personnel were picked up by a control boat and taken to another ship. The time was now 0700 hours when Capt. Richmond contacted Lt. Col. [Charles] Horner, the battalion CO, and told him the situation. [Horner] then ordered K Company to take over I Company's mission.

By the time Company I's four remaining LCAs came ashore at about 8:00 A.M., about ninety minutes late, most of the 16th Infantry's follow-on waves had already landed.

Company L had a similarly grueling journey from *Empire Anvil*, losing one of its six LCAs several miles offshore due to swamping. The remaining five had a difficult time making headway in the heavy sea and arrived at the beach at 7:00 A.M.—thirty minutes late. The company landed farther east on Omaha Beach than any other unit on D-Day and had the misfortune of disembarking directly opposite a German strongpoint atop a 130-foot bluff with a perfect field of fire.

3rd Battalion, 16th Infantry, 1st Division
D-Day After Action Report, June 23, 1944

The [Company L] assault landing craft touched down in front of several rows of underwater obstacles. The personnel waded and struggled ashore by crossing 200 yards of open beach under intense enemy fire: machine gun, rifle, mortar, artillery, and antitank weapons. Many men were hit and injured while still in the water. The company gained the comparative shelter of a vertical cliff where section leaders attempted to reorganize their men amid much confusion caused by enemy fire upon the beach. The company losses at this stage were high. . . . Company aidmen distinguished themselves by treating wounded while exposed to enemy fire.

PFC John Sweeney
Company L, 16th Infantry, 1st Division

All of a sudden the British coxswain said we were going into the beach. We landed on the sand and started running out, Lt. [Jimmie] Monteith leading the way. I and others got out of the landing craft and started running toward the cliff. I must have run 20 or 30 yards. All of a sudden I got hit by machine gun fire coming from the left-front. I was turned completely around, the bazooka that I had been carrying was full of holes, the life belt I had been wearing was taken right off me. I laid there on the sand, but I thought to myself: I can't lay here on the beach. People were falling all around me, so I got up and started running toward the cliff. Somehow I made it. I didn't realize that I was hit in the arm and leg until later. The carnage and destruction were unbelievable—bodies in the water, destroyed landing craft, confusion.

Company L's bewildered survivors piled up against the cliff, took several deep breaths, and analyzed their surroundings. They were alone on one of the most secluded sectors of Omaha Beach. The cliff, about twelve to fifteen feet high, provided a false sense of security because no German rifle or machine gun fire could reach any American positioned behind it. However, a few well-aimed grenades or mortar shells could wreak havoc, and at

"The carnage and destruction were unbelievable." Troops from the 3rd Battalion, 16th Infantry, pile up against the cliffs on Omaha's eastern extremity shortly after H-Hour. In a short time, the rising tide will reach the base of the cliffs in this sector. U.S. ARMY SIGNAL CORPS, NATIONAL ARCHIVES.

high tide—now little more than two hours away—there would be no beach here save for a band of rocks only a few feet wide. If follow-on waves deposited even more men on this sector, overcrowding would result, and if the Germans discerned that, the results could be catastrophic.

The only alternative was to move inland. But how? Climbing the cliff would be difficult—and in direct line of sight of an enemy strongpoint, suicidal. A shift to the right, or west, offered the only hope, for in that direction, the cliffs gave way to a less lofty earthen embankment. On top of that embankment, however, the enemy had placed coils of barbed wire, all under the direct observation of that strongpoint. Whatever Company L decided to do promised to be hazardous.

TO MOVE EVER FORWARD

About 400 yards to the right of the unfortunate Company L, a jumble of fifteen LCVPs crunched haphazardly ashore directly in front of the Colleville draw. Much to the consternation of embarked soldiers who knew precisely where they were supposed to land, navy coxswains had dropped them far to

H-Hour: Colleville Draw

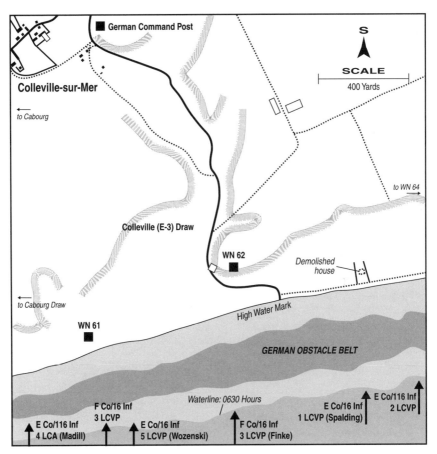

German Command Post

Colleville-sur-Mer

to Cabourg

S

SCALE

400 Yards

to WN 64

Colleville (E-3) Draw

WN 62

Demolished house

to Cabourg Draw

WN 61

High Water Mark

GERMAN OBSTACLE BELT

Waterline: 0630 Hours

E Co/116 Inf
2 LCVP

E Co/16 Inf
1 LCVP (Spalding)

F Co/16 Inf
3 LCVP (Finke)

E Co/16 Inf
5 LCVP (Wozenski)

F Co/16 Inf
3 LCVP

E Co/116 Inf
4 LCA (Madill)

the east of their targets. Companies E and F of the 16th Infantry constituted the bulk of this cluttered wave, but also included were four utterly lost craft belonging to Company E of the 29th Division's 116th Infantry—nearly two miles distant from the sector assigned to them by the Omaha plan.

Capt. Edward Wozenski
Commander, Company E, 16th Infantry, 1st Division

Nearing the shore, to a point where it was possible to easily recognize landmarks, it became obvious that the company was being landed approximately 1,000 yards left of the scheduled landing point. How anyone who had been briefed could make such an error, I will never know, for the lone house which so prominently marked [the St. Laurent draw] was in flames, and clearly showed its distinctive outline.

1st Sgt. L. Fitzsimmons
Company E, 16th Infantry, 1st Division, July 1944

The men kept yelling at the coxswain: "You're going left!" He ignored them and kept on the same course. We landed far left—near the 3rd Battalion's sector. The only boats [we] could then see were numbers 2 and 3, which were a little to our right.

That all was not well was immediately obvious to the beleaguered and seasick infantrymen plodding down LCVP ramps into the rolling surf. It was bad enough to land on the wrong beach. It was infinitely worse to rush ashore opposite two dominating strongpoints filled to capacity with German troops who were thought to have been of such poor quality that the navy and air force would have driven most of them away.

PFC Paul McCormick
Company E, 16th Infantry, 1st Division

One of our BAR men named Murphy was standing up against one of the posts that were sticking in the beach. He was firing at a pillbox when, all at once, he practically disappeared with the post. A German mine was on top of the post and it exploded. . . . My best friend, [PFC] Donald Freidinger [was killed]. On board ship the night of June 5, Donald and I said to one another if one of us didn't survive the landing, we promised to visit the other's family. I fulfilled that promise in 1946.

Company F, 16th Infantry, 1st Division
U.S. Army Historical Division, interview with various Company F soldiers, July 4, 1944

The 5th section was commanded by Lt. Otto Clemens and his assistant T/Sgt. Raymond Strojny. . . . Lt. Clemens said, "Take her in! Let's get the hell off this ship!" Moving toward the shore the boat received enemy machine gun fire directly on the ramp. When the boat landed the enemy machine gun continued to fire, but the ramp could not be opened. When the ramp did get down, the machine gunner was out of ammunition or changing his barrel. Most of the men got off the boat in good shape before the gun again opened up.

Capt. Edward Wozenski
Commander, Company E, 16th Infantry, 1st Division
The boats were hurriedly emptied, the men jumping into water shoulder-high under intense machine gun and antitank fire. No sooner was the last man out than the boat received two direct hits from an antitank gun, and was believed to have burned and blown up. Now all the men in the company could be seen wading ashore into the field of intense fire from machine guns, rifles, antitank guns, and mortars. Due to the heavy sea, the strong cross-current, and the loads that the men were carrying, no one could run. It was just a slow, methodical march with absolutely no cover up to the enemy's commanding positions. Men fell, left and right, and the water reddened with their blood. A few men hit underwater mines of some sort and were blown out of the sea. The others staggered on to the obstacle-covered, yet completely exposed beach. . . . Men were falling on all sides, but the survivors still moved forward and eventually worked to a pile of [shingle] at the high water mark. This offered momentary protection against the murderous fire of close-in enemy guns, but his mortars were still raising hell.

For the lost men of Company E, 116th Infantry, all was confusion. Where they were, God only knew, but they certainly were nowhere near any fellow Twenty-Niners. Whatever beach sector this was, its German defenders were currently displaying a ferocity that no one had foreseen. But on the positive side, numerous nearby GIs wore the legendary Red One patch on their shoulders, and if anyone would know what to do, it would be them.

Company E, 116th Infantry, 29th Division
U.S. Army Historical Division, interview with various Company E soldiers, September 1944
The company CO, Capt. Lawrence Madill, was wounded in the trip across the beach. He found that PFC Walter Masterly was the only remaining man of the mortar squad, and although he had the mortar, he had no ammunition. Masterly volunteered to go back to the beach and salvage some ammunition, but the Captain told him to set up his mortar while he went for the ammunition. He picked up the ammunition, but on his return trip he was hit twice by machine gun bursts and went down. His last words were: "Senior non-com, take the men off the beach!"

Sgt. Walter Smith
Company E, 116th Infantry, 29th Division

I remember debarking from the landing craft and trying to take shelter from the enemy fire behind one of their obstacles. Capt. Madill came up behind me and others, ordering all who could move to get up the beach. I looked up at him, and his left arm appeared to be almost blown off.

Meanwhile, a single boat team from Company E of the 1st Division's 16th Infantry, under the command of Lt. John Spalding, somehow separated from the outfit's other five craft and landed alone halfway between the St. Laurent and Colleville draws. Although Spalding's team attracted heavy fire traversing the beach to the shingle, it had by chance stumbled into a vulnerable seam in the enemy's Omaha Beach defenses. Spalding and his resolute senior NCO, T/Sgt. Phillip Streczyk, would soon exploit their favorable position to the fullest.

Company E, 16th Infantry, 1st Division
U.S. Army Historical Division, interview with various Company E soldiers, July 4, 1944

Streczyk's section, which was to contribute one of the most intrepid actions of the day, came in exactly where Company F was supposed to land. (The place of landing was identified by Streczyk's surviving members and by Streczyk during the interview [in July 1944].) Streczyk got 32 men onto the sands, took 12 casualties mostly from bullet fire in getting across the beach, and continued onward immediately with 20 men.

2nd Lt. John Spalding
Company E, 16th Infantry, 1st Division, February 1945

Sgt. Streczyk and the medic, Pvt. George Bowen, were carrying an 18-foot ladder which was to be used for crossing the antitank ditch or for any other purpose that might arise. They were struggling with it in the water just about the time I was having my worst trouble staying afloat. As the ladder came by I grabbed it. Streczyk yelled and said, "Lieutenant, we don't need any help," but, hell, I was busy trying to get help, not give it. I told them to leave the thing, so it was abandoned in the water. . . . I had swallowed about half the ocean and felt like I was going to choke. . . . Our first casualty came at the water's edge. Pvt. William Roper, rifleman, was hit in the foot by small arms fire just as he hit the beach. He kept trying to get his leggings off, but couldn't reach the lacing, so I helped him get it off. . . . By this time I noticed a number of my men on the beach, all standing up and moving across the sand. They were too waterlogged to run, but they went as fast as they could. It looked as if they were walking in the face of a real strong wind. We moved across the [shingle] to a house which was straight inland. The first place we stopped was at a demolished building; there was some brush around. We halted there by a minefield at the first slope.

And so the invasion had begun, but no one could say that it had begun well. The air force and navy seemed not to have affected the enemy at all. Most outfits had come ashore late and in the wrong place. With shocking ease, the enemy's nearly invisible resistance nests were cutting down Americans all across the beach—men with names like Wilczek, Hoback, Sullivan, Di Paola, Schenk, and Stevens, who spun onto the sand to die. If fate spared them scant moments for final reflection, they surely thought of home: Canarsie, or Bedford, or Farmville, or Hell's Kitchen, or anyplace where someone would grieve. They must have thought what a waste it was—they could have done anything, anything at all . . . if only . . . And then the surging tide enveloped their bodies in the frothy surf, and the relentless breakers lifted them and tumbled them forward, ever forward, to deposit them ultimately in neat lines at the high-water mark—a place they were not able to reach in life, but where they would soon answer final roll call.

CHAPTER 8

Clear the Way

THE TIME IS SHORT

April 9, 1944, was a day that Gen. Leonard Gerow would remember for the rest of his life, for it was on that date that the Germans dropped the proverbial monkey wrench right into the well-oiled machine of Operation Neptune. Freshly developed air photographs of the Calvados coast delivered to V Corps headquarters on April 9 revealed that the enemy was energetically erecting formidable obstacles all over Omaha Beach. Gerow would rather have received intelligence of a fresh German battalion in the beach defenses than this piece of alarming news. Could it be that the secret had been revealed and the Germans had somehow learned where the Allies would invade? The contemplative Gerow seriously doubted that possibility. Ever since Rommel had arrived in France in early 1944, the enemy had been constructing beach obstacles all over the French and Belgian coastlines. It was entirely plausible that sooner or later the Germans would turn their attention to Calvados and install obstacles there. No reason to panic . . . yet.

Nevertheless, the enemy's coastal obstacles would force already frazzled V Corps invasion planners back to their desks to rethink several elements of the Neptune plan. In an era of almost unimaginably advanced war weapons, Rommel's odd assortment of beach impediments seemed comically archaic, like contraptions that might have been placed outside a medieval castle to deter an attacking enemy. According to Rommel's scheme, every beach on which the Allies could conceivably land would be lined with hundreds of these obstacles, most of which would be topped with mines. Their specific points of placement would be critical, for as the tide rose, they were supposed to be submerged and nearly invisible to Allied naval crews bringing landing craft ashore.

If a steady stream of troops and equipment was to go ashore on D-Day, beach obstacles could not be allowed to get in the way. Gerow fully appreciated that carnage would most likely result if landing craft were forced to move shoreward directly through obstacle belts at high tide, or even half-high tide. Vessels' bottoms could be staved in, or even worse, mines could blow those vessels and their occupants to bits. A lot of men could die before a single GI set foot on Omaha Beach.

Gerow's staff had to solve the beach obstacle quandary—and quickly. How would passages through the obstacles be cleared? Where could army or navy units be found to do it? What if the plan failed to work? Rommel's simple, inanimate beach obstacles were indeed worth more than a battalion of troops, for almost every element of the Neptune plan utterly depended on a safe passage to the beach for landing craft of all sizes. Without that, the fulfillment of other V Corps objectives could not occur.

Good generals think ahead. They anticipate what the enemy might do and prepare sensible counterstrategies—and Gerow had done exactly that. Even before the Germans had placed a single barrier on Omaha Beach, Gerow had directed his staff to ponder the potential problem posed by beach obstacles and prepare a makeshift plan that could be put into effect should the need arise. The plan was completed by March 31 and submitted to higher headquarters for approval. Its conclusion: The job would be exceedingly difficult, but it could be done. But there was still hope that the enemy would fail to construct any obstacles on Omaha, and the scheme would not be needed.

As the Americans were deliberating, however, the Germans were working. Gerow was perhaps less surprised than most when he examined the April 9 air photo for the first time. Still, he was probably the most anxious man in V Corps, for he fully understood that the current breaching plan, although undeniably thorough, was not entirely realistic and would have to be extensively revised based on the new photographic evidence. The entire Omaha assault relied on this plan's successful execution, but the troops and equipment required by the plan were not currently available, and even worse, tests at the Assault Training Center had not yet determined the most effective means of clearing the beach of obstacles. Assuming adequate troops could be assembled in time, how could they gain the necessary level of expertise in the next few weeks if the trainers themselves were still learning? This was war on the fly—and Gerow knew it. Nevertheless, there was no alternative except to keep planning.

Maj. Gen. Leonard T. Gerow
Commander, V Corps, letter to Brig. Gen. William Kean, U.S. First Army, April 10, 1944

I am rather disturbed about the progress being made on training in connection with the removal of underwater obstacles. The time is short. . . . To cite specific matters of concern to me, I find that the engineer battalion specially trained in the U.S. for work of this character has not arrived in the U.K. Furthermore, no information is available as to its state of training or equipment. Another matter of concern is the availability of Dozer tanks. Based on prior information, I have set up 12 of these tanks for the very necessary task of opening up beach exits. I now find that number is to be reduced to a total of eight.

Brig. Gen. William Kean
Chief of Staff, U.S. First Army, letter to Maj. Gen. Leonard Gerow, April 13, 1944

I have your letter of 10 April with reference to underwater obstacles, and can assure you that we are as disturbed as you are about the progress we have made. We are endeavoring to hold a field test of technique and tactics as proposed by you, VII Corps, and the Navy on the idea of using Division and Corps engineers instead of Army[-level] engineers. . . . I realize that this whole subject has been worked out far too late. However, you can rest assured that I will push it to the limit, and we will do the best we can with the time available.

Propelled by the urgency of the situation, and armed with improved intelligence, V Corps prepared a new breaching plan by April 29. Despite its challenging logistical and personnel requirements, the plan was straightforward: Just a few minutes after first-wave tank and infantry units landed on Omaha Beach shortly after low tide, about 1,000 specially trained demolition engineers and sailors would follow. If the invasion schedule could be adhered to, and the Germans did not add too many new obstacles to the beach, every enemy impediment on the beach would be on dry sand, well ahead of the waterline. Then the demolition teams would jump to their task, wiring the obstacles with explosives and blowing them up. Sixteen tanks, modified with frontal bulldozer blades, would land at H-Hour from

LCT(A)s to assist in obstacle clearance. If the plan worked, the end result would be several gaping corridors, clearly marked so that later waves of landing craft could reach shore, even at high tide, without fear of being destroyed by submerged obstacles.

Headquarters, V Corps
Plan to breach beach obstacles, April 29, 1944

It was agreed that the plan must provide initially for 16 gaps, each gap not less than 50 yards wide. . . . U.S. Navy representatives stated that a flotilla of 36 LCMs could and would be made available. The 36 LCMs will be towed behind the 16 LCT(A)s and the 16 LCTs carrying DD tanks.

In the detailed organization for breaching the 16 initial gaps required, 24 teams will be organized on the basis of three teams to each two gaps. . . . The assault would be concurrent with the commencement of breaching operations. In this case the present assault waves of infantry, DD tanks, M4 tanks, and tank dozers would touch down at H-Hour with substantially the present naval and air support. The assaulting infantry would advance under cover of tank and Navy fire, and the demolition parties would land at H+5 minutes to attack the obstacles with tank and armored dozers and with explosives to open sufficient initial gaps for the oncoming waves of landing craft before the rising tide drowned out the obstacles.

In conclusion, it is further stated that the breaching of obstacles is a difficult task at best, and it must be undertaken only under the most favorable circumstances, which, in the case of present obstacles, is when they are dry.

The planners feared time more than they did the Germans. H-Hour on June 6 was 6:30 A.M., more than an hour after low tide, when the demolition teams would land on Omaha Beach. At that point, the tide would be rising rapidly. Although the obstacles would still be dry, the troops would have to carry out their demolitions swiftly, for the tide rose in Normandy at an astonishingly rapid rate. Within thirty minutes of landing, the surf would be lapping around the bases of any obstacles the Americans had not yet demolished. Rising at a rate of about one foot every ten minutes, the tide would completely cover most obstacles by 8:00 A.M.

The fulfillment of such a mission would be difficult and dangerous, even if the Germans had abandoned Omaha Beach. It would be virtually impossible if the demolitioneers were forced to work under enemy fire. No single element of the assault depended more on a successful preinvasion air and naval bombardment than did the obstacle clearance plan, for if the

Germans could not be driven from their pillboxes, or at least forced to keep their heads down while clearance work was under way, those unfortunate men working to clear the beach would have very short life expectancies.

Col. R. K. McDonough
Chief of engineers, V Corps, March 29, 1944
Army objections raised [concerning the demolition plan] included the following: Insufficient time for certainty of success. Insufficient men to allow for casualties, with resulting chance of failure. Air and naval bombardment would not furnish sufficient covering fire for parties. . . . The effectiveness of demolition parties, both Army and Navy, working in water under heavy fire is doubted.

D-Day changed the rules of amphibious warfare. According to American doctrine as practiced in the Pacific and Mediterranean, the U.S. Navy bore much of the responsibility for clearance of beach obstacles, and in mid-1943, the navy established a school at Fort Pierce, Florida, to teach demolition techniques to classes of volunteer sailors. Trained in groups of six—the capacity of the navy's standard rubber boat—graduates emerged as Naval Combat Demolition Unit (NCDU) teams. However, the enormity of the D-Day operation made it obvious to Neptune planners that the army would have to become involved in beach demolitions. The army had plenty of engineers committed to demolition work, and in fact, one of the demonstration outfits at the Assault Training Center, the 146th Engineer Battalion, had become expert in the type of demolition work the Omaha invasion required.

Altogether, twenty-one U.S. Navy NCDUs and the army's 146th and 299th Engineer Battalions would carry out the Omaha Beach clearance plan. The 299th, composed mainly of men from western New York, was among the last of many hundreds of army units to be assigned to Operation Neptune. After working with the navy at Fort Pierce, it departed New York on April 6 for an eleven-day Atlantic crossing to Britain and commenced training with V Corps on April 24, only six weeks before D-Day. For a job as difficult as the sappers would face on Omaha Beach, there was much to learn in a very short time. For members of the 299th, who held such recent memories of Broadway, it was a harsh immersion into war.

Operation Neptune
Omaha Beach Engineer Plan, May 24, 1944
[Sixteen] gap assault teams will land from LCMs at H+3 minutes [6:33 A.M.], prepare and mark a 50-yard gap from the low water line to the high water line. Upon completion of the initial gap at each band, they will widen and extend the gap to

clear the beach of all obstacles. [Eight] gap support and [two] command teams will land as directed, not to exceed H+8 minutes [6:38 A.M.] and assist the assault teams as directed.

Headquarters, 1st Infantry Division
Special Engineer Task Force Plan, May 22, 1944
Fundamentally each gap assault team consists of one Naval Combat Demolition team reinforced by Army personnel [nine sailors, five soldiers]; and one Army team [of twenty-five enlisted men, two medics, and one officer], subdivided into two mine crews and two demolition crews [forty-two men total]. . . . Tankdozers will land at H-Hour [from LCT(A)s] and proceed against obstacles, removing them by crushing, pushing, and towing or any combination thereof. First priority will be given to wooden obstacles.

Bigot-Neptune Omaha Beach Map
Notes, May 22, 1944
Underwater obstacles will be encountered from approximately 275 yards from back of beach. A number of gaps will be cleared in these obstacles. The seaward limits of these gaps will be marked by Dan buoys with green flags, and range markers on the beach will mark the approximate center of the gaps.

Maj. Milton Jewett
Commander, 299th Engineer Combat Battalion
Each demolition man had about five or six fuses assembled with their cap sticks around the outside of his helmet—one is sufficient to blow a hand off, but if it blew around his helmet, [he] would only get a headache. He carried 40 pounds—compound C-2 (plastic), and tetrytol (similar to TNT, but more powerful)—in a bag over his shoulder, [plus] rifle or carbine. Some carried bangalore torpedoes. All carried reels of primacord, which is nothing more than a cord of wrapped TNT. Some carried cans of purple smoke to warn infantry that [explosions] were going to take place.

2nd Lt. Wesley Ross
Commander, Team 8, 146th Engineer Combat Battalion
The wooden obstacles and Element C were to be demolished by 2.5-pound blocks of Composition C-2 plastic explosive, encased in a denim sack—a "Hagensen Pack," after its designer U.S. Navy Lt. (jg) Carl Hagensen. . . . For the heavy steel hedgehogs, 15-pound tetrytol satchel charges were to be the explosive of choice. . . . Tetrytol and C-2 were the selected explosives because they are more powerful than TNT, are quite stable, and are not normally detonated by small arms.

If the twenty-four demolition teams were to fulfill their essential D-Day mission, the navy would have to transport them to Omaha Beach on time and on target, for the invasion schedule was so unforgiving that lateness or imprecision in beaching to any appreciable degree would make the demolition job almost unachievable. However, the demolition teams' cross-Channel trip on June 5 was hardly conducive to orderliness. Unlike first-wave infantrymen, who crossed the Channel on relatively luxurious troopships, GIs and sailors assigned to demolition teams experienced almost unimaginably grueling journeys aboard open-decked LCTs, crowded with troops and tanks, and rolling and pitching violently in the rough weather. On LCTs, the simplest acts, such as sleeping and eating, were extraordinarily difficult. To be carried directly into battle by these primitive means was brutal for the engineers and NCDU men who were so vital to the invasion's success.

Ens. Victor Hicken
Officer-in-command, LCT(A)-2227, Gunfire Support Group, Force O
Heads [latrines] failed on some of the smaller boats, and holes had to be cut into the decks so that men could relieve themselves on some of the LCTs. Fresh water supplies fell low. Sleeping, or attempting to sleep, on the open, cold decks of the smaller landing craft in a gale added further miseries. And what was to come next was even worse. . . . The fleet, again under way, began to run foul of the weather with heavy seas making maneuvering difficult and dangerous. The waves were wine-dark and their tips were whipped into white curls by the strong cross-wind.

299th Engineer Combat Battalion
U.S. Army Historical Division, interview with Teams 13 and 14,
July 15, 1944
Part of the LCT's sides washed away. Men sick, waves washed over deck, stove went out, nothing to eat. Explosives wet, could not be dried out. Gap Assault Team 14, the same.

BLOWIN' UP A STORM

The trip to Normandy was only a beginning. At 3:00 A.M. on D-Day, several miles off the French coast, the demolition teams were required to depart their cramped LCTs for even more cramped fifty-foot LCMs, which prior to embarkation the men had loaded with the explosives that would be required on the beach. Each LCT towed one LCM, and when the GIs and sailors accomplished the transfer between the two craft, each proceeded shoreward under its own power to meet its fate on Omaha Beach. Given

H-Hour: Actions of U.S. Demolition Teams

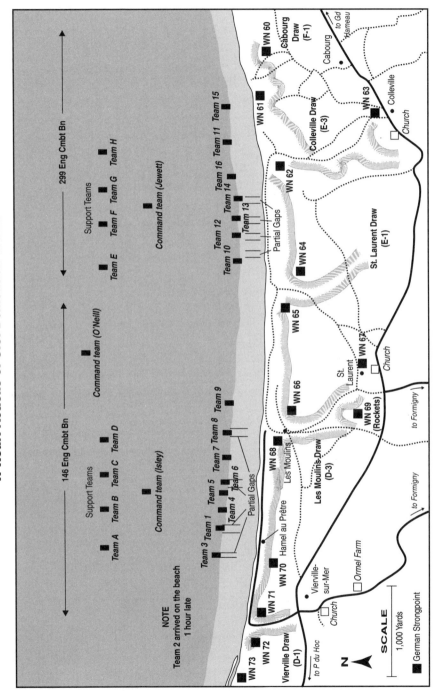

NOTE
Team 2 arrived on the beach
1 hour late

146 Eng Cmbt Bn

299 Eng Cmbt Bn

Support Teams

Team A   Team B   Team C   Team D

Command team (Isley)

Command team (O'Neill)

Support Teams

Team E   Team F   Team G   Team H

Command team (Jewett)

Team 3 Team 1

Team 5

Team 7 Team 8 Team 9

Team 4

Team 6

Partial Gaps

Team 10

Team 12

Team 13

Team 14

Team 16 Team 11 Team 15

Partial Gaps

WN 60

Cabourg
Draw
(F-1)

WN 61

Colleville Draw
(E-3)

WN 63

Colleville

Church

to Gd
Hameau

Cabourg

WN 62

WN 64

St. Laurent Draw
(E-1)

WN 65

WN 67

Church

WN 66

St.
Laurent

St. Laurent

WN 69
(Rockets)

to Formigny

WN 68

Les Moulins

Les Moulins Draw
(D-3)

Hamel au Prêtre

WN 70

to Formigny

Vierville-
sur-Mer

Ormel Farm

Church

WN 71

WN 72

Vierville Draw
(D-1)

WN 73

to P du Hoc

SCALE

N

1,000 Yards

■ German Strongpoint

that worn-out men carried out this procedure in the darkness and heavy seas, it is remarkable that any LCM made it to the beach on time. But of the twenty-four LCMs carrying the demolitionists shoreward, all save two did exactly that.

By 8:00, assuming the operation worked smoothly, there would be sixteen breaches through the obstacle belt at approximately 200-yard intervals. But the operation went awry from the start, despite the demolition teams' timely arrival on the beach. Normandy's notorious coastal crosscurrent pushed LCMs far to the east, in some cases by almost a mile. Drifting smoke from grass fires did not help. Consequently, the navy set down most of the demolition teams on the eastern half of the beach, leaving the western side comparatively empty. Seven 299th Engineer Battalion teams landed on Omaha's far eastern extremity, although the plan called for just three in that sector. In contrast, on the opposite end of the beach, none of the three 146th Engineer teams assigned to clear the obstacles opposite the Vierville draw landed anywhere near it.

Compared with the events the demolitionists were about to endure, landing off-target would be remembered as trivial. Determined to blow breaches on whatever beach sectors they currently occupied, the GIs and sailors burst out of their LCMs into the surf. The array of obstacles that the teams had trained so vigorously to raze lay dead ahead. Burdened with blocks of C-2 explosives, fuses, blasting caps, and much more, the men could do little more than plod toward their objectives, roughly forty yards distant.

2nd Lt. Wesley Ross
Commander, Team 8, 146th Engineer Combat Battalion

Our LCM crew was very professional and operated as if this were just a routine landing exercise. Some of them had made landings in Africa and Sicily, so they were no neophytes. Our coxswain had promised me an easy wade ashore, and he gunned his Gray Marine diesels, driving the LCM hard aground before dropping the ramp—he was a real pro! The water came only up to our knees. . . . Running in multiple short dashes and hitting the ground often denied the enemy gunners an easy target. Bullets knocked splinters from the wooden obstacles overhead after I had hit the ground—or so I heard later! I ran the ring main clockwise around the wooden obstacles, and Sgt. [William] Garland ran his around counter-clockwise. We square-knotted the ring mains together where we met. . . . Twenty minutes after landing, Team 8 with its attached NCDUs had a 50-yard section of the wooden obstacles—consisting of posts and ramps—ready to blow. Garland and I then tied 45-second detonators to opposite ends of the ring main and each tossed out a purple smoke canister as a warning signal to the infantry, and moved a short distance inland. The blast made quite a mass of kindling and poles, but a number of obstacles were not destroyed in this initial effort.

299th Engineer Combat Battalion
U.S. Army Historical Division, interview with various 299th Demolition Teams, July 15, 1944

Team 11: No infantry ahead of team. Casualties in group—over half.

Team 12: Craft came in with its machine gun blazing away at shore installations. . . . As soon as ramp down, [enemy] machine guns opened up. First group got off. Ten men tried to get the pre-loaded rubber boat off the LCM but couldn't move it.

Team 13: Eight Navy men got off the LCM with the loaded rubber boat. Artillery shell exploded [the boat] and set off the primacord. Three later found dead. Many infantry unloaded just as the charges about to be blown. A tankdozer tried to haul out obstacles, [but] infantry took cover behind it and prevented it from maneuvering.

Team 14: Shell hit the LCM and blew up the loaded rubber boat. Naval demolition crew members killed. Infantry moving in, and its wounded, prevented blowing the charges.

Team 15: Mortar scored direct hit on the rubber boat loaded with explosives. Three men killed and several wounded.

Team 16: LCM blown up by direct hit just after men got out. Too many wounded in and behind obstacles to blow them.

146th Engineer Combat Battalion
U.S. Army Historical Division, interview with 1st Lt. Ben Bartholomew, Team 7, June 30, 1944

The team touched down at H+7 [6:37 A.M.] on the left flank of Easy Red. Timing was good, but the team was supposed to land on the right flank of Easy Green, about 300 yards east. Obstacles encountered began with band posts, mixed in with log ramps; then consecutive bands of log ramps; then post and log ramps, immediately followed by hedgehogs. . . . The tide was exactly as expected, about 110 feet from the first obstacles at 0637. . . . The team used tetrytol and was ready to fire by 0655. At that time a vessel loaded with infantry came crashing in, smashing through the timbers and setting off about seven mines on the posts. This boat was followed by other craft with infantry, and it was impossible to fire the charges on the first tide. The shell fire was very hot. The infantry was pinned down in the obstacle area and the team, finding it obvious that the gap could not be blown, helped to carry injured men off the beach and keep them out of the oncoming tide.

"We will do the best we can in the time available." Demolition Team 8,
146th Engineer Combat Battalion, in England prior to D-Day. The CO,
2nd Lt. Wesley Ross, is lying in front of his team with his legs crossed.
Courtesy Wesley Ross.

299th Engineer Combat Battalion
U.S. Army Historical Division, interview with 2nd Lt. Phil Wood, Team 14, July 14, 1944

The ramp dropped and Lt. Wood and his men got their rubber boat into the water
and dropped in amid the hail of machine gun bullets. There was no one on the
beach at the time, but other small craft filled with infantry were nearby. The men,
overburdened, dropped their bangalore torpedoes and made their way toward the
obstacles. As he went with them, Lt. Wood looked over his shoulder and saw an
88 shell hit squarely in the center of the LCM where the Navy demolition crew
was trying to launch its rubber boat, filled with explosives. The ammunition in the
rubber boat was detonated, and the fire enveloped the LCM. The coxswain was
blasted off the vessel, and the lieutenant in charge managed to dive off, but the
Navy demolition crew members were believed to have been killed by the blast.

PFC Chuck Hurlbut
299th Engineer Combat Battalion, Team 15

Everything's nice and quiet, then all of a sudden, "ping, ping, brrrrr" on the ramp,
we could hear the machine guns hitting. Something's going wrong. We dropped

the ramp. To my knowledge, we all got off the craft OK. But thereafter it was devastation. Jesus, guys started dropping and screaming all around you. Somehow the rubber raft got off, and it was right behind me. I grabbed the tow rope, and I said, "Hey, I'll get it in there where we can use it." I threw it over my shoulder and started pulling. All of a sudden I feel it get heavier. I look around, there's three bodies of guys who were thrown in. Two were face down, I don't know who they were. One was face up. I knew who he was [PFC Charles Burton]. So I kept pulling. And then all of a sudden, "Boom!" A mortar came over and it hit the raft. . . . I was knocked head over heels. I guess I blacked out. When I came to I was on my hands and knees. I was spitting blood. . . . I sat back down, and I pulled my rope in, and all I got was a big piece of tattered rubber. That was the raft. The three guys: gone.

146th Engineer Combat Battalion
U.S. Army Historical Division, interview with Sgt. Homer Jackson, Team C, June 30, 1944
Team C was supposed to land on Dog Red. Actually it landed on the beach beyond Fox Red at 0715 with the 299th Engineers. Reason for the variation is not known, but the difficulty may have been caused by ignorance of the physical characteristics of the beach. . . . At touch down time, the tide was very near the obstacles. Machine gun fire was heavy. . . . Team members tied on charges, but there was no chance to blow a gap because of the infantry in the vicinity. It was impossible to get them clear of the area. Mines were blasting landing craft, although the obstacles themselves were not serious. As the tide came in, team members were pinned to the beach by fire, but they aided the wounded.

Ens. Lawrence Karnowski
U.S. Navy, Commander NCDU-45, Team 10
Lt. Gregory [of the 146th Engineer Battalion] and his men pulled off the rubber boat, then headed for the dune lines and their obstacles. We disembarked as two 88 shells dropped near our LCM, and [we] got busy tying charges to the obstacles. . . . The first [detonation], fired at 0650, went magnificently. Machine gun fire erupted, keeping us on our bellies. Chief Conrad C. Willis, couldn't resign himself to crawling and placing charges . . . so he took off with a roll of primacord and placed several charges, but machine gun fire cut him down, the only man I lost that day and best one I had.

The casualties among the demolition teams within the first thirty minutes of the invasion were so great that no historical account of their work can ever be complete. However, survivors' narratives and unit reports agree that the combined army-navy teams managed to fulfill at least a small portion of their overall beach clearance mission. Of the sixteen fifty-yard breaches the mission called for, the demolitionists probably finished six and partially completed several more before the tide rose to a level at which work was impossible. The cost in casualties among the gap teams to achieve even that limited end was more than one-third of the roughly 1,000 soldiers and sailors who landed among the first waves. Given the enemy's brutal reaction to the invasion, the leaders of the demolition force presumably considered even a single breach through the obstacles an outstanding exploit.

On one fact all accounts would agree: Most of the gaps that were blown through the German obstacles on D-Day morning were on the eastern half of the beach, generally in the Easy Red sector between the St. Laurent and Colleville exits. Omaha's western side, the 116th Infantry's sector, probably had only two breaches, neither of which was anywhere near the westernmost draw at Vierville—a failure that would later prevent landing craft from coming ashore in this sector.

But even the limited success of the obstacle clearance mission had a decidedly positive impact on the landing, for when the fog of war cleared and observers weighed the outcome of the invasion's first hour, those beach sectors where soldiers and sailors had managed to breach gaps strongly hinted at the locations of vulnerable seams in the enemy's defenses.

146th Engineer Combat Battalion
U.S. Army Historical Division, interview with Sgt. William Garland,
Team 8, June 30, 1944
The operation was nothing like what had been expected. The men thought the infantry would be ahead of them, but the beach was innocent of footprints.

Rear Adm. John Hall
U.S. Navy, Commander, Force O
How do we get such truly brave and fearless men?

CASTLES ON THEIR COLLARS

To overcome the enemy's positional advantage on Omaha Beach, General Gerow intended to commit in the early hours of the invasion several engineer units apart from those attached to the obstacle clearance mission. Gerow reasoned that the Germans could not fail to grasp the importance of the beach exits, and he therefore assigned four engineer battalions—one per draw—the responsibility of opening up those exits as early as possible on D-Day. The Germans were celebrated for their military ingenuity, and the American engineers were prepared to contend with almost anything the enemy might concoct to block passage up the narrow draws. From air photographs, the Yanks were already aware of the enemy's minefields, antitank ditches, concrete walls, and barbed wire. However, there might be much more the enemy had in store about which the invasion planners didn't know.

Probably the most formidable barrier on Omaha Beach was the massive concrete wall the Germans had erected across the mouth of the Vierville draw. No American vehicle could leave the beach via this exit unless this wall was obliterated, a task that the Neptune invasion plan assigned to the 29th Division's 121st Engineer Combat Battalion. An enormous amount of explosives would be required for this task, but if the Germans had reinforced the wall with steel rods prior to pouring the concrete—and it was unknown whether they had—the 121st's engineers worried that even a prodigious explosion might fail to do the job.

To accomplish the tasks of opening up the four beach exits as quickly as possible, the engineers needed to work unhindered by enemy fire. In this respect, the Neptune plan was reassuring: The preinvasion naval bombardment in conjunction with the assault by the first waves of tanks and infantry should enable the engineers to enter the draws and commence their work sometime early in the morning. D-Day planners were so confident of this assumption, and so eager to open up the beach exits early, that they scheduled the leading elements of all four engineer battalions to land less than one hour after the first wave. If the enemy was still active in the draws—well, that's why the army designated these outfits engineer *combat* battalions.

Lt. Col. Robert Ploger
Commander, 121st Engineer Combat Battalion, 29th Division

I suppose that it goes without saying that the engineers, without their support equipment, were on the beach too soon. A lot of my men became involved in engaging the Nazi infantry as riflemen. . . . As to our landing plan, Company C was supposed to be landed to the right of Company B, in front of the concrete wall. The Company C commander, Capt. [Svend] Holmstrup, sought to be the first man of his company ashore but met a bullet in the forehead just as he was about to step down the ramp. I landed at 7:10 A.M. in a boat with the Company B contingent under Capt. [Edward] Humphrey, but we landed over a mile east of our planned site. I was first off, followed by my S-2, Capt. Humphrey, my radio operator, and then the other 40 engineers. I dropped into eight feet of water, but my life belt saved me. I ran about 150 yards and rested behind a German hedgehog. I noticed the obstacles had not been blown, and I considered, but then dropped, the notion that the 121st should take over the job. I ran another 150 yards forward and dropped into a shell hole. Suddenly my left ankle felt as if it had been whacked by a baseball bat. I had been wounded. I looked back and I was amazed that I couldn't see any members of my team.

Pvt. A. Cvitanovitch
Company C, 112th Engineer Combat Battalion, attached to 29th Division
Most of the boys were so sick they didn't care what was going on. When we got about 300 yards off the beach you couldn't see what was happening on it because it was full of smoke, but you could hear all kinds of weapons firing and some of our boys said, "The 29th is on the ball; they are really going to town!" Then about five minutes later we got our first burst of machine gun fire. . . . It wasn't the 29th making the firing on the beach, but the Germans firing at us. A few minutes later we stopped and as the ramp went down all of us got panicky. The boys who were sick weren't sick anymore. I saw two men getting hit in the barge, and I know that five men got wounded in the water and two killed from my barge. There were many more floating dead from the 116th who had landed before us.

Lt. Col. William Gara
Commander, 1st Engineer Combat Battalion, 1st Division
Our mission on D-Day was to open the E-1 exit road. We had to clear four lanes, each eight yards wide, completely free of any obstacles, minefields, antitank ditches, and walls from the high water line right up to the exit road and up to Transit Area 3. The toughest part of our assignment was filling a 15-foot-wide antitank ditch. . . . I was fortunate in having an engineer battalion that had quite a bit of combat experience. [However], we didn't land anywhere near where we were supposed to, and as a result there was mass confusion, a long time getting things organized, and I would say at least a three-hour delay in getting started on our assigned missions. . . . It was a shame that the aerial bombardment that had been promised just didn't do the job. Essentially, Omaha Beach was unscarred.

In addition to their essential role in the invasion's spearhead, engineers would be responsible for managing the beachhead. Omaha Beach was not New York harbor by any stretch of the imagination, but if the army was to wage a campaign of immense proportions on the European continent in 1944, the inflow of supplies over the beach for the next several months would have to rival the constant energy of the New York waterfront. To fulfill this ambitious role, the army created units called Engineer Special Brigades (ESB), two of which would be allocated to the Omaha invasion under the overall command of Brig. Gen. William Hoge, who in 1942 had been the chief engineer of the renowned 1,500-mile Alaska-Canada highway. With 9,000 soldiers on its rolls, an ESB was nearly the size of a combat division—and much more diverse. An ESB consisted of more than 50 different units, ranging in size from engineer battalions of more than 800 men to a bomb disposal squad of only 7. The varied military specialists among ESB personnel included surgeons, military policemen, chemical decontaminators, signalmen, photographers, firefighters, navy beachmasters, military stevedores, and drivers for the army's legendary DUKW (pronounced "duck") amphibious truck. In the event ESB personnel failed to notice that there was a war on, they would be reminded of that fact when they observed their graves registration personnel at work.

Operation Neptune
Engineer Special Brigade Mission, May 1944
Establish and operate all shore installations necessary for debarkation, supply, evacuation, and local security in order to insure the continuous movement of personnel, vehicles, and supplies across the beaches.

Col. Paul Thompson
Commander, 6th Engineer Special Brigade
A unit getting a new commander shortly before battle is to be joined pretty obviously is a unit with problems. "They are not 'problems,'" General Hoge told me emphatically. "They are 'challenges.'" Hoge told me that when I reported to him on March 6, 1944, to take command of the 6th Engineer Special Brigade. He observed that it took more skill to manage an ESB than it did to lead an infantry division. An ESB has to come out smoking at the bell, has to participate crucially in the fight for the first 1,000 yards, and then has to stay the course for weeks and weeks. . . . Three engineer combat battalions formed the solid foundation of an ESB. Was ever before such sheer engineer power packed into a single military unit?

Fortified with the same innocent confidence that every GI and sailor possessed on the morning of June 6, the leading elements of the two ESBs—5th on the east, 6th on the west—stormed ashore less than an hour after the first waves had hit the beach. After the men had taken just a few awkward strides in the surf, confidence vanished. For the moment, rifles and grenades would be needed more than mine detectors and shovels.

149th Engineer Combat Battalion, 6th ESB
U.S. Army Historical Division, interview with Lieutenants Whipple and Thorson, June 16, 1944

The operation was not like the exercises. In the exercises, which went smoothly, there was no thought of being under fire, and the men did not even carry their weapons. But when the engineers landed on Omaha Beach, it was under heavy artillery, mortar, automatic weapon, and small arms fire. This battalion suffered about eight percent casualties, including key men such as the CO [Lt. Col. James Taylor], the executive officer, and the Company B CO.

6th Naval Beach Battalion, 5th ESB
U.S. Army Historical Division, interview with Cmdr. Eugene Carusi, USN, June 16, 1944

[The 6th Naval Beach Battalion's job] was to mark hazards to navigation, determine landing points, evacuate casualties, direct landing and retraction, control boat traffic, and maintain ship-to-shore communication. . . . Cmdr. Carusi landed with the first platoon of Company C, 37th Engineer Battalion from an LCT on the middle of Easy Red at H+65 [7:35 A.M.]. Groups ashore lost all equipment. There was intense fire. The landings were made in water about four feet deep with 75 yards of water to cross before water was only knee-deep, after which there was a deep runnel which added to the landing difficulty. The groups dug in. . . . Personnel continued to land and there were many casualties.

37th Engineer Combat Battalion, 5th ESB
U.S. Army Historical Division, interview with Captain Howard, Company C, June 22, 1944

The mission of Company C was to establish road exits E-1 and E-3 after they had been opened up by Companies A and B, and to maintain dump areas and traffic circulation behind the beach. Its secondary mission, but possibly its most important one, was the operation and establishment of transit areas. . . . The H+80 [7:50 A.M.] platoon actually was the first to land and may have been the first engineer unit landed on the beach. It came in about H+45 [7:15 A.M.] while the infantry was still milling about the beach and the assault waves were piling up on each other. There was a tremendous amount of confusion. Lt. Ross, leading the unit, saw that it was impossible to do any of the assigned work and led his platoon to the beach where he organized an impromptu company of infantry.

CHAPTER 9

Bullets like Rain

ONLY AN 88 COULD BE THAT MEAN

If ever a military design demanded flexibility, it was the plan to storm Omaha Beach. As the invasion unfolded at H-Hour on June 6, even the greenest private could see things were going wrong. No one had seen a single bomber; most troops had landed far off target; the Germans were clearly not second-rate—and there were many more of them on the beach than intelligence had indicated. According to the dictates of the invasion plan, wave after wave of landing craft were charging shoreward behind the first, packed with troops blissfully unaware of the fate that awaited them on shore.

Unhappily for the Americans, there was little anyone could do to alter the plan. It would be hours before the top brass could order any appreciable modification to the invasion scheme, and even then their choices would be limited. Leaders on the beach would have to sort out the mess and determine a logical course of action to remedy the invasion's faulty start, assuming they lived long enough. Until then, Bradley, Gerow, and Huebner, seemingly helpless on their command ships offshore, would simply have to wait, doing little except to offer steadfast encouragement that adherence to the plan still promised success.

7:15 A.M.: Hamel au Prêtre and the Vierville Draw

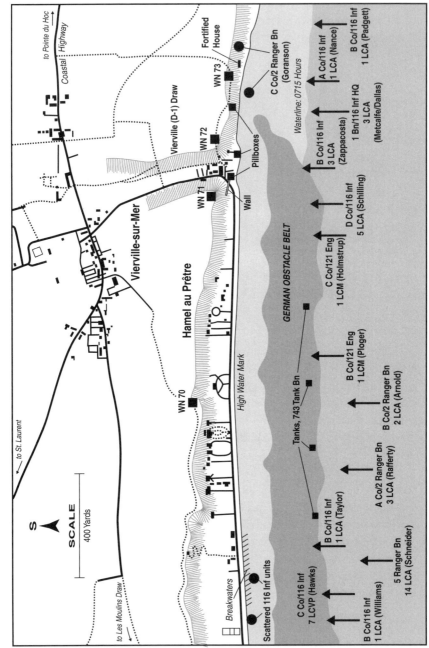

S

SCALE

400 Yards

→ to St. Laurent

to Pointe du Hoc →

Coastal Highway

Fortified House

WN 73

C Co/2 Ranger Bn (Goranson)

A Co/116 Inf 1 LCA (Nance)

B Co/116 Inf 1 LCA (Padgett)

Vierville (D-1) Draw

WN 72

Pillboxes

Waterline: 0715 Hours

B Co/116 Inf 3 LCA (Zappacosta)

1 Bn/116 Inf HQ 3 LCA (Metcalfe/Dallas)

WN 71

Wall

D Co/116 Inf 5 LCA (Schilling)

Vierville-sur-Mer

GERMAN OBSTACLE BELT

C Co/121 Eng 1 LCM (Holmstrup)

Hamel au Prêtre

B Co/121 Eng 1 LCM (Ploger)

High Water Mark

Tanks, 743 Tank Bn

B Co/2 Ranger Bn 2 LCA (Arnold)

WN 70

A Co/2 Ranger Bn 3 LCA (Rafferty)

B Co/116 Inf 1 LCA (Taylor)

C Co/116 Inf 7 LCVP (Hawks)

5 Ranger Bn 14 LCA (Schneider)

Breakwaters

B Co/116 Inf 1 LCA (Williams)

Scattered 116 Inf units

to Les Moulins Draw →

A military adage dictates: Do not reinforce failure. But if failure was not to be reinforced, were there any successes on Omaha Beach that could be? Apparently there were none, at least from the perspective of anyone observing the initial landings from offshore at 7:00 A.M. By the end of the invasion's first hour, however, a trickle of information filtering back from the beach began to hint at a vital detail: The apparently impregnable enemy defenses had several soft spots. Later this trickle would turn into a flood of indisputable evidence of the enemy's weaknesses and would instigate a fundamental and spontaneous change in the method by which the Americans planned to win the battle. In its simplest terms, this evidence proclaimed: Attack up the bluffs, not through the draws.

On the tidal flat in front of the Vierville draw, the Virginians from the 116th Infantry's Company A had been slaughtered at H-Hour by an unseen enemy entrenched on the heights just beyond the beach. According to the invasion timetable, thirty minutes later two more Stonewall Brigade companies, B and D, would land in quick succession from twelve British LCAs on that same fatal sector, followed by three more LCAs carrying 1st Battalion headquarters and medical personnel. Only when those incoming troops and naval crews spotted the open beach and bodies of Company A men floating in the surf did they foresee what was about to occur. By then it was too late to stop it.

Pvt. Robert Sales
Company B, 116th Infantry, 29th Division

I was the radio operator for Capt. Ettore Zappacosta [CO, Company B]. About 1,000 yards off the beach, the only words he spoke were, "Sales, step up there and see what's going on on the beach." I looked over. I couldn't tell anything. I said, "Company A—I can't see 'em. It looks like bodies laying on the beach, but I can't tell." Shortly thereafter the British coxswain said, "I cannot go in any further. I'm going to drop the ramp." There was no argument about it. . . . When the ramp went down, mortar shells were hitting on both sides of us. Machine guns were all over top of us, just like you were in a bees' nest. The captain was the first man to get off the boat, and he was hit on the ramp and fell into the water. Sgt. [Richard] Wright was next off, followed by the first-aid man [T/5 Trent Kincer]. I was fourth off the boat. The sea was rough, the ramp banged up and down, and I caught my heel and went over the side into the water. When I got up, Capt. Zappacosta was up and calling to me, "I'm hit!" He went down and I did not see him come up. . . . To this day I have found no one who got off that boat alive but me, and I have looked everywhere.

HQ Company, 1st Battalion, 116th Infantry, 29th Division
U.S. Army Historical Division, interview with Sergeants Nowlin, Bower, Bilinski, September 1944

Nowlin, with the communications platoon, saw his first men jump off with full loads. They came up with them and started on, still carrying their equipment. Some of them were hit as they plunged into the crossfire which was sweeping the sandbar and the water next to the beach, others toiled on carrying their equipment. It startled Nowlin to see them going forward feeling the fire and still straining under their burdens. Back of these first files, however, the movement had flagged right at the ramp. Lt. Col. [Bernard] McQuade, CO of the 58th Field Artillery Battalion, who had come in on the same boat, was hit as he stepped from the boat. He died in the water. Capt. Robert Ware [1st Battalion surgeon] was hit between the eyes as he made the sand. Lt. James Limber, battalion S-2, was wounded in both legs while making his way through the water; he crawled onto the beach and a shell fragment hit him between the eyes.

Pvt. George Kobe
Company D, 116th Infantry, 29th Division

I was with the mortar platoon, and I was in the landing craft with Capt. Walter Schilling [CO, Company D]. Suddenly I heard a German 88 whiz through the craft, ripping off the ramp and blowing off both steel doors of the LCA. The right door hit Capt. Schilling in the head, killing him instantly. The left door hit our platoon sergeant, John Stinnett, and he was blinded in one eye. Only an 88 could be that mean. There was no panic. How we made it through to the seawall, I'll never know. It was the worst fire I was ever subjected to in all of my time in combat.

Sgt. Robert Slaughter
Company D, 116th Infantry, 29th Division

I didn't care what the Germans had to offer, I needed to get to dry land. . . . About 150 yards from shore I raised my head despite the warning from someone to "keep your head down!" I could see the craft to our right taking a terrific licking from small arms. Tracer bullets were bouncing and skipping off the ramp and sides, as they zeroed in on the boat, which touched down a few minutes before we did. We then knew that this was not going to be a walk-in.

The veteran Royal Navy LCA crews were trained to search for soft spots in the enemy's coastal defenses when bringing their embarked troops ashore, and some who witnessed what was happening to their brethren in nearby landing craft attempted to do exactly that. A group of three Com-

"The worst fire I was ever subjected to." View of the western half of Omaha Beach from the bluffs adjacent to the Vierville draw. In the invasion's first ninety minutes, the 116th Infantry and Rangers suffered severe losses in this area. Photo is from a prewar French postcard. COURTESY MARYLAND NATIONAL GUARD.

pany B LCAs under the command of Sub-Lt. T. E. Arlidge, a tough ex-policeman from London's East End, swung more than 1,000 yards to the east, searching for a safer sector on which to disembark the Yanks. This astute course of action—one that would be imitated by many following waves—saved this little group of Stonewallers from the carnage their comrades were being subjected to in front of the Vierville draw.

One mile to the east, follow-on waves of Stonewallers from Major Bingham's 2nd Battalion prepared to join the inferno in front of the Les Moulins draw. Like all members of the highly trained but green 116th Infantry, these men had never seen combat, but for many, their abrupt introduction to it on D-Day would be all they would ever see.

1st Lt. Edward McNabb
Company H, 116th Infantry, 29th Division, July 1944
I could see pretty clearly that there was a hell of a lot of fire in the area in front of us. We had a young naval officer in our boat who was in command of our boat division. He was doing well, and when we got close inshore he suddenly passed word up asking if I recognized the beach. I wasn't too sure to begin with, and when he asked that, I wasn't sure of anything. The bluffs were covered with

smoke and the lower part of a draw mouth was visible. This could be any one of three places. My company CO [Capt. George Boyd] looked it over for a while and then told the naval officer, "Take us on in. There's a fight there anyway." By the time we were around 300 to 400 yards offshore, the smoke had cleared and we recognized the Les Moulins draw. We weren't drawing any fire yet, but there was plenty on the beach: small arms, with tracers in plenty, and high explosive bursts were all over it.

It was a sickening feeling to come into that beach when we saw it. I don't know whether anyone was actually afraid. We'd built up a feeling of spirit that drowned that. Capt. Boyd, the naval crew, and I could see what was about and what it meant. We kept the men's heads down so that they wouldn't see it and lose heart. The tanks were still in the water's edge, some still firing, and some were on fire. Men from the assault companies were taking shelter around these tanks and in the water. The majority of these were wounded and many dead were floating in with the tide.

We ran our boat in alongside a burning LCT at about H+35 [7:05 A.M.] and floundered through 75 yards of water, which was about chest-deep at first. . . . [We] stopped temporarily in the supposed cover of the beach obstacles and waited to see how the men with the heavy weapons came out of the water. The mortar squad was unable to carry the waterlogged equipment so they dragged it to the water's edge and were attempting to pick it up when a shell hit and knocked out all but three men. We looked for the craters that the Air Corps and Navy had promised us. There were none. I ran into a burst of machine gun fire at about the center of the beach and was hit in a couple of places in the left shoulder. Lt. Tomasi, our battalion surgeon, was close by and ran over and cut off my equipment under fire and sent me back to the water's edge if I could make it. I didn't make it, but the tide came up, and I washed ashore in front of the three-story house on Easy Green.

Maj. Sidney Bingham
Commander, 2nd Battalion, 116th Infantry, 29th Division, January 1947
On the way in the beach was obscured by smoke and dust, and it wasn't until we got within 1,000 yards of the shore that I could see anything. I noticed explosions and thought that they were from the engineers blowing up the beach obstacles. For some reason I thought all was well until after struggling ashore through shoulder-deep water, I paused for a breather behind a steel tetrahedron obstacle and noticed sand kicking up at my feet. It then occurred to me that I was getting shot at and that machine gun bullets were kicking up that sand. From then on there was no doubt in my mind. I was scared, exhausted. The fancy assault jacket issued for the operation was well loaded and soaked up a good deal of water and weighed a ton.

I finally crossed the beach and got to the shingle along the beach road where about 100 men from F Company were seeking what little shelter that was afforded by the road. The only officer I could find was Lt. [Theodore] Lamb, who was painfully wounded and very dazed.

WHAT DO YOU DO IN THE INFANTRY?

Meanwhile, on Omaha's far eastern end, members of the 1st Division's beleaguered 16th Infantry struggled to find a chink in the enemy's armor. They would not find it in the wide mouth of the Colleville draw, where Germans had set up nearly invulnerable and invisible firing positions on the lengthy bluffs curving up both sides of the draw—perfect terrain for a devastating crossfire. With the height advantage the Germans possessed, their line of sight was so dominating that no American could move anywhere opposite the draw's mouth without being detected—and in all probability, shot.

Company H, 16th Infantry, 1st Division
U.S. Army Historical Division, interview with Sgt. R. Hopes, June 12, 1944
The company reached the shore at approximately 0727 hours. They were immediately hit by machine gun fire and heavy casualties ensued. They hit the beach too far left of where they were to land. . . . The tide was rising at this time and many of the wounded, who probably could have been saved, were drowned. The situation on the beach was critical, and at times looked very black. One of the company machine guns set up on the left and started firing at the pillbox and open emplacements that were on the left flank. Enemy mortar fire was dropping on the beach, but the enemy either was scared or was hit, because it wasn't very effective and, after a time, ceased. There was machine gun fire coming from the extreme left. This sector was supposed to be taken up by the 3rd Battalion.

Capt. Lawrence Deery
Chaplain, 16th Infantry, 1st Division
[In the LCA,] I was eating an apple. "Lunch was in the bags"—that is, Army, Vomit. "Doc" [Maj. Charles] Tegtmeyer told me to throw the goddamned apple away. . . . Then I saw the British Army [probably Royal Navy] officer reading. I thought he must have been a priest. I thought he was reading his office. I discussed this with Tegtmeyer. I moved forward with difficulty and looked over his shoulder and read: "*Si quid forte jocosius hoc mihi juris cum venia dabis dixero.*" [Translation: "*If I perchance will have said something in too joking a fashion, you will rightly grant me this indulgence.*"] I was amazed, and so would you be. A look at the top of the book confirmed my suspicions: it was Horace.

7:00 A.M.: Colleville Draw

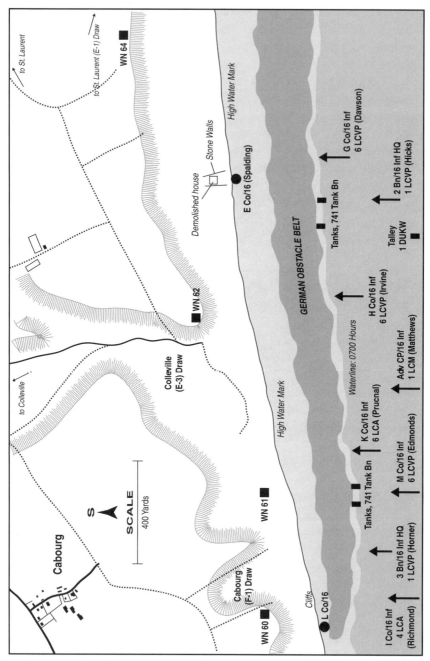

Cabourg

Cabourg
(F-1) Draw

WN 60

WN 61

Colleville
(E-3) Draw

WN 62

WN 64

to Colleville

to St. Laurent

to St. Laurent (E-1) Draw

Demolished house

Stone Walls

High Water Mark

High Water Mark

High Water Mark

Waterline: 0700 Hours

GERMAN OBSTACLE BELT

Cliffs

L Co/16

E Co/16 (Spalding)

SCALE

400 Yards

I Co/16 Inf
4 LCA
(Richmond)

3 Bn/16 Inf HQ
1 LCVP (Horner)

Tanks, 741 Tank Bn

M Co/16 Inf
6 LCVP (Edmonds)

K Co/16 Inf
6 LCA (Prucnal)

Adv CP/16 Inf
1 LCM (Matthews)

H Co/16 Inf
6 LCVP (Irvine)

Talley
1 DUKW

Tanks, 741 Tank Bn

G Co/16 Inf
6 LCVP (Dawson)

2 Bn/16 Inf HQ
1 LCVP (Hicks)

Able Seaman Wally Fraser
550 Assault Flotilla, Royal Navy Volunteer Reserve
At about 0400 hours on 6 June, we were lowered [from *Empire Anvil*] and within less than an hour the other seaman and I were taking turns on the one hand pump supplied on these craft to stop us sinking. The Americans were straddled across their seats in the well deck; most were seasick and they still had to get ashore and fight after sitting in nearly two feet of sea water for the journey to the beach. On the way we were almost lifted out of the water by getting too close to some of the larger naval ships firing broadsides onto the mainland. The beach was strewn with metal structures housing fused shells in the tidal areas, debris from landing craft which had fouled them, and also bodies of young Americans who would never see their homeland again floating with the Combined Ops sailors who had endeavored to get them to the beach.

1st Lt. William Joseph
HQ Company, 3rd Battalion, 16th Infantry, 1st Division
The day after the invasion one of my men came to me and asked what in the hell I was laughing at after I had jumped off the LCVP into the water. I thought and thought at what I could laugh at when machine gun bullets were flying all around, and artillery shells were falling. Then I remembered that I had laughed at one of my corporals, Johnson, who was over six feet tall. I had jumped into the water and waded toward shore. About 50 feet from the boat, I turned around to see how many of my men had been hit and if they had all gotten off the craft. Corporal Johnson was throwing equipment left in the bottom of the boat over the side, and the air was full of this equipment. Then he picked up Corporal Opitz, who was deathly seasick, off the bottom of the boat and pitched him bodily into the water. It struck me so funny that I remembered I almost drowned from laughing so hard.

Capt. Lawrence Bour
HQ Company, 2nd Battalion, 16th Infantry, 1st Division
Our LCVP [ramp] went down and I found myself under machine gun fire, and no sign of any friendly troops on the beach in front of me. I took shelter in knee-deep water behind a post used as an obstacle. After a few seconds I realized that my best move was straight ahead to the shingle embankment. . . . The living lay sprawled from the shingle to a yard or two from the water's edge; the dead floated in the shallows just beyond. I spied a friend from A Company lying prone on the sand. I stopped and chatted for a minute. He shook my hand, still prone, and congratulated me on my captaincy, which I had gotten the day we were shut up in the marshaling area. It seemed an odd place for felicities.

Capt. Fred Hall
HQ Company, 2nd Battalion, 16th Infantry, 1st Division
The beach was in a state of confusion. . . . We were under small arms and artillery and mortar fire. It was apparent that the naval and air bombardment preceding the landing had had little effect. Once ashore, it was a matter of survival, but I was so busy trying to round up unit commanders to organize their men to move along and eventually off the beach, there wasn't much time to think except to do what had to be done.

An advance party from the 16th Infantry's headquarters led by Lt. Col. John Matthews, the regiment's second-in-command, approached the Colleville draw in an LCM around 7:25 A.M. The team's job was to set up a command post and organize the 16th Infantry's beachhead. As the LCM scraped bottom and its crew prepared to drop the ramp, Matthews shouted, "This is it; good luck!"

Advance CP, 16th Infantry, 1st Division
HQ Company, 16th Infantry, Morning Report for June 6, 1944
The Advance CP group in the LCM moved toward the beach in a rough sea, and upon nearing the beach encountered a considerable volume of artillery and machine gun fire. The tide was at low ebb, and to reach the beach it was necessary to traverse a wide stretch of water, making way through various lines of beach obstacles fitted with mines. . . . As the men hit the water approximately waist-deep, machine gun fire swept the section, and a bullet tearing through Master Sergeant Carpino's gas mask struck Lt. Col. Matthews in the head. Not knowing he was dead, Sgt. Carpino, with much difficulty, got his body to shore only to learn that he had been killed instantly. No actual CP functioning was possible. The only interest on the crowded beach was to disperse the men and obtain as much cover as possible.

Col. Benjamin Talley, one of General Gerow's most trusted V Corps engineers and a renowned veteran of the Aleutian Islands campaign in the Pacific, observed the 16th Infantry beach sector from a DUKW cruising about a quarter mile offshore. Talley's seemingly straightforward job was to report to Gerow periodically by radio on the events he could perceive on the beach, but as the 16th's landing progressed, Talley could convey no good news to his boss.

Col. Benjamin Talley
Deputy chief of staff for plans, V Corps

I explained to my men briefly what I thought they would be going into and endeavored to describe to them the best I could the situation they would meet, in order to lessen the shock they might experience when first under fire. I reminded them that I was no braver than they, and that it is not a question of whether a man is afraid—but it is how he acts when afraid. I knew these men well and concluded my remarks with a simple statement: "Good luck, and God bless you." To my surprise, as one man they said, "And you, Colonel." From that moment we were as one, and acted and thought as one. . . . The tide was well out and hundreds of men were in the water mostly clinging to the obstacles, which had not been breached; and hundreds of helmets appeared to be floating in the water alongside the obstacles. Actually they were the heads of men clinging to the obstacles for protection. . . . [Four tanks] were moving in single file parallel to the beach. Suddenly one of them burst into flames. An instant later, a second, and then the third was afire. The fourth one backed up and returned to the water's edge. . . . I actually saw the steam—not smoke—from the machine gun that was firing at our DUKW from the top of the hill behind the beach. The Germans identified my DUKW as an important target because it had two antennae prominently sticking up.

No historical account can with honesty classify any outfit that landed on Omaha Beach on the morning of June 6 as lucky. Some units, however, may be defined as less unfortunate than others. Among those that may be consigned to that category are Lt. John Spalding's boat team from Company E and Capt. Joseph Dawson's Company G, both of the 16th Infantry. Spalding's team had come ashore shortly after H-Hour halfway between the St. Laurent and Colleville draws, virtually alone. About twenty minutes later, Dawson's company followed in its wake. Although both groups met heavy fire crossing the tidal flat, they managed to reach the line of shingle at the high-water mark relatively intact. Here they had by chance stumbled into a position where they were separated from German strongpoints by a greater distance than any other 1st Division units that had yet landed—more than 500 yards. Additionally, Spalding's and Dawson's men were partially shielded from enemy observation by three decrepit stone cottages situated just beyond the shingle, wrapped on two sides by sturdy stone walls several feet high. From this place, Spalding and Dawson were among the first Americans on Omaha Beach to arrive at the unanticipated conclusion that the only way off the beach would be over the bluffs, not straight through the beach exits as the invasion plan had specified.

Dawson was a native of Waco, Texas, and a 1933 graduate of Baylor University. The unnamed U.S. Army historical officer who interviewed him in August 1944 noted in his report of Company G's D-Day activities, "This man is an unusually accurate witness."

Company G, 16th Infantry, 1st Division
U.S. Army Historical Division, interview with Capt. Joseph Dawson,
August 22, 1944

The water was still quite clear when G hit the beach. The company was supposed to land at H+30 [7:00 A.M.], and did so at the designated spot. . . . The men had to walk across the sands; they could not sprint because of the weight of ammo, demolitions, etc. It was the feeling of the men that their losses would have been cut in half had their loads been cut likewise. When the ramps went down, some of the men couldn't move ashore, but stumbled and fell in the water. They had become so cramped because of crowding that their muscles would not respond. . . . It even seemed to some of the leaders that they were glad of the chance to assault, so miserable had they felt on the in-journey. Except for the wounded and perhaps a few stragglers, the men streamed on up to the shingle. The light machine guns and mortars were all with Dawson; he put up the machine guns on top of the shingle, and the mortars at the base of it. . . . The company profited by the fact that there was a small defilade directly ahead, and this was what helped most in getting the advance going.

As John Paul Jones had asserted: They "had not yet begun to fight."

PRAISE THE LORD

In the meantime, on the opposite extremity of Omaha Beach, someone made a decision that would have an impact on the invasion far out of proportion to that decision's simplicity. Sometime around 7:20 A.M., an unidentified individual—possibly a naval officer aboard a control vessel close offshore—reached the entirely sensible conclusion that any further landings opposite the Vierville draw would be suicidal. All or parts of three companies had been slaughtered there within the invasion's first forty minutes. Furthermore, no demolition engineers had shown up in that sector to blast paths through the German beach obstacles. Accordingly, as the fast-rising tide covered up those obstacles, any attempt to bring more troops to shore there in the face of an undaunted enemy could result in the invaders' total annihilation.

Hitler's Atlantic Wall. U.S. first-wave troops land at low tide on Omaha Beach amid a thick belt of German beach obstacles. This photo was probably taken about 7:15 A.M. on the morning of D-Day. U.S. ARMY SIGNAL CORPS, NATIONAL ARCHIVES.

Ens. Victor Hicken
Officer-in-command, LCT(A)-2227, Force O, Gunfire Support Group
We managed to pull LCT(A)-2227 off the beach [from a position directly opposite the Vierville draw] at about 6:50 A.M. Coming out we were hailed by a control vessel and asked if we had any casualties. We had none. Then they told us that Dog Green was being closed to further landings.

The 29th Division's Company C, 116th Infantry was the first intact unit to benefit from the change of plan. Its commander, Capt. Berthier Hawks, probably would have suffered a crisis of confidence had he known that four of his fellow 116th company commanders had already been killed. Ignorant of this alarming development, Hawks—nicknamed "Old BB Eyes" by his men—led his 194 troops ashore at about 7:25 A.M. in seven U.S. Navy LCVPs drawn from the transport *Thurston*. Logically, there was only one direction for the diverted troops to go, and that was east. Prudently following the lead of Sub-Lieutenant Arlidge's Royal Navy LCAs, which carried parts of Company B, the American coxswains headed for shore about 1,000 yards east of the Vierville draw on a sector Neptune plans specified as Dog White.

This zone was situated squarely between the Vierville and Les Moulins draws, directly opposite some of Omaha Beach's most forbidding bluffs. However, as Dawson and Spalding had just learned by chance in the 1st Division sector, landing as far as possible from the draws offered the GIs not only relative safety once they crossed the beach, but also a possible secure avenue of advance later on. True, the bluffs appeared impenetrable, but if the Germans thought so too, their defenses would be much weaker there than they were in and around the draws. An ascent of the bluffs would surely be difficult, but there was no other way.

Company C beached in an orderly formation on a frontage no more than 100 yards wide—a rarity on D-Day. The Fates would be more compassionate to Bertie Hawks's men than they had been to any other GIs so far on D-Day.

Capt. Berthier Hawks
Commander, Company C, 116th Infantry, 29th Division, June 1944

Everything went according to plan until we neared the landing beaches. We could see artillery fire landing on the beach that we were to land on, Dog Green, so . . . we shifted over to a section of the beach that looked a bit better and started in. The LCVPs moved along very nicely until we got to landing obstacles along the beach. Then the trouble started. . . . Our craft was having a great deal of difficulty wedging its way in. Finally we heard the command "Ramps Down!" given. I was closest to the front and rushed out first into the water. It was over my head. Finally I got back in the craft, and it moved in closer. We could get out in three feet of water. There was spasmodic machine gun fire. A lot of rifle fire was coming from the high ground in front of us, and a lot of artillery fire. The men had a very heavy load, and some experienced difficulty in crossing the beach as fast as they would have liked. . . . We landed with 194 men and officers, and I estimate that we lost about 20 men in crossing the beach.

Company C, 116th Infantry, 29th Division
U.S. Army Historical Division, interview with T/Sgt. Weldon Huffer, March 1945

As the boat neared the beaching point, the surf made it rise and plunge more violently. It was still underway, and at the top of one of those surging risings when the men felt the bottom of the boat strike some underwater projection. The craft teetered uncertainly; then turned on its side, spilled men and equipment into four or five feet of water. "All the special stuff, like flamethrowers, demolition charges, bangalores, and mortars were lost when we went into the drink," said Huffer. Amid the confusion, the men struggled for footing, surged their way through the rough water to the beach. Huffer and Sgts. Dopolski and Palembas were all insistent that no other troops were on the beach when they touched down. . . . The water-soaked men scurried across the beach to the low, timber seawall.

Sgt. John Polyniak
Company C, 116th Infantry, 29th Division
With all the training and expectations, we all felt proud of the job we were to do. My thoughts were back home—of the past, and what the folks there were doing. . . . We were fortunate as we had but one injury [in the boat team] on the landing, a gunshot wound to one of the fellows in the knee.

Irony is a feature in all battles, and Omaha Beach was no exception. And now, shortly after 7:30, one of the most notable ironies of the Omaha Beach invasion was about to take place. Gerow's V Corps included two elite Ranger battalions, the 2nd and 5th, both of which were rigorously trained in the style of the legendary British commandos to carry out special combat missions. To support the main Omaha landings, Gerow's invasion planners had a few such missions in mind, and they split up the Ranger force into three groups for that purpose: Force A comprised three companies (D, E, F) from the 2nd Rangers; Force B consisted only of Captain Goranson's Company C, 2nd Rangers; and Force C included the entire 5th Ranger Battalion of more than 500 men, as well as the two remaining 2nd Ranger companies (A and B). Forces A and B would focus entirely on achieving the special missions for which they had trained so hard in the past months: Rudder's Force A at Pointe du Hoc, four miles west of Omaha, and Goranson's Force B at Pointe de la Percée.

The planners consigned Force C to a support role, with a combat mission that varied depending on whether Rudder's Rangers fulfilled their mission at Pointe du Hoc. Under the command of Lt. Col. Max Schneider, Force C would load up in twenty Royal Navy LCAs by 5:00 A.M. and head for the coast halfway between Omaha Beach and Pointe du Hoc. Here the LCAs would circle well offshore and wait for a crucial radio message from Rudder. The phrase "Praise the Lord" would indicate that the Pointe du Hoc mission had succeeded. "Tilt" would signify that it had failed. If Force C did not receive a message by H+30, or 7:00, Schneider must consider Rudder's mission a failure.

One way or another, the plan dictated that Force C reach Pointe du Hoc by nightfall. Above all, the Force C Rangers yearned for a "Praise the Lord" signal. If Rudder sent a "Tilt" message, or no message at all, Force C would land on Omaha Beach near the Vierville draw and then swiftly march four miles westward, through countryside likely swarming with Germans, to reach Pointe du Hoc by land.

The last thing Force C's Rangers wanted to do was fight their way off Omaha Beach. But at 7:30 on Omaha Beach, the men Gerow needed above all to salvage the rapidly deteriorating situation were high-quality infantry reinforcements—and he was about to get them.

Capt. John Raaen
Commander, HQ Company, 5th Ranger Battalion, Ranger Force C
Ranger Force C lay off Pointe du Hoc and Pointe de la Percée for better than 45 minutes. We circled and circled, praying for the message from Force A that they had landed successfully. The message never came. Our radio was at my feet in the forward part of an LCA. We did hear two messages. One was a beachmaster on Dog White saying the troops were landing without resistance. Another one had the word "Charlie" in it, but we couldn't make it out. We were supposed to wait until 0700. If we did not receive the success signal by that hour, we must land on Dog Green behind the 116th. Schneider waited until 0710 before ordering us to divert.

A disappointed Schneider ordered his nineteen LCAs (one of his original twenty had swamped five miles offshore) to head east to Omaha Beach. Opposite Dog Green beach, they turned ninety degrees to the right and headed to the beach in three waves: first, Companies A and B, 2nd Rangers, in five LCAs, followed by two waves of seven LCAs each conveying the 5th Rangers. Whether the first wave of Rangers ever received word that Dog Green had been closed has never been established, but the disaster that had earlier unfolded in front of the Vierville draw was evident to all and sufficiently daunting to drive the wave well east of that beach exit.

It was not far enough. At about 7:35, the first wave's five LCAs slammed through the rolling surf amid the outer belts of German beach obstacles, now mostly submerged. They had the misfortune of touching down directly opposite an active and nearly invisible German *Widerstandsnest* atop the bluffs behind a few smoldering beach villas. When the British seamen dropped their ramps, the German machine gunners could hardly miss.

Companies A and B, 2nd Ranger Battalion
U.S. Army Historical Division, interview with various Company A and B Rangers, July 1944
As [a Company A LCA] reached the underwater obstacles, the coxswain started to maneuver through, but Lt. Edlin didn't like the look of the mines fixed to the

[obstacles] and [requested] him to drop the ramps 80 yards out. The water was waist-deep, and Edlin could see the splash from crisscross fire directly in front of the craft. Edlin dove in to avoid the bullets. Three Rangers were hit as soon as they got into the water. A few took momentary shelter behind the beach obstacles, then pushed on to the sand. . . . The next craft in line [from Company B] was blown up about 300 yards from shore by an explosion that seemed to be underneath the craft, and was therefore attributed to a mine, perhaps on an outer obstacle. The coxswain was killed and the platoon leader and another Ranger wounded. Sgt. Maj. Manning Rubenstein yelled "Abandon Ship!" and the men went over the side. Rubenstein, swimming, noticed for the first time that they were under fire. He and Sgt. Fyda saw five men killed in the water. Many wounded reached the sand; then went back into the water to avoid grazing fire and to float in with the tide.

Capt. Edgar Arnold
Commander, Company B, 2nd Ranger Battalion, Ranger Force C
After reaching the edge of the water and while running across the beach, I suddenly found myself on the sand as if knocked down by some unknown force. My first thought was: I have had it. I immediately felt my body: no blood, no pain. I realized that my carbine had been knocked out of my hands and was about ten feet away. . . . The thing that struck me was the complete chaos on the beach. Dead men seemed to be everywhere. I began to get visions of being pushed back into the sea.

1st Lt. Robert Edlin
Company A, 2nd Ranger Battalion, Ranger Force C
Sgt. Klaus, one of the section sergeants, was showing me pictures of his wife and children on the way in. He was hit and about to give up to the tide near the water's edge when I reminded him of our conversation. It brought him back. . . . Another man was hit through the spine. I crawled to him, and he was crying. He told me, "I'm not gold-bricking, Lieutenant. My legs won't move. Help me get up so I can get one of the bastards!"

There can hardly have been many soldiers in the U.S. Army with more combat experience than Max Schneider. As a member of the renowned Darby's Rangers, he had participated in the North Africa, Sicily, Salerno, and Anzio invasions, and fully understood the enemy's military proficiency. From one of the 5th Ranger landing craft a few hundred yards offshore, Schneider observed a display of that proficiency against the five 2nd Ranger LCAs that had just touched down opposite the enemy strongpoint.

He is reported to have blurted out, "I'm not going to waste my battalion on that beach!"

Schneider conferred with the British wave leader, and both agreed that it would be prudent to redirect the 5th Rangers' fourteen remaining LCAs eastward by about a half mile. Using hand signals, the Royal Navy officers swung their waves off to the left. This turned out to be the right thing to do. In two waves of seven LCAs each, the 5th Rangers landed at about 7:50 close to the point where Hawks's Stonewallers had gone ashore about twenty minutes previously.

On this beach sector, a series of fifteen breakwaters, fifty-five feet long and fifty-five feet apart, jutted seaward from a low wooden seawall at the high-water mark. Constructed with huge boulders and wooden posts and rails, the breakwaters had been installed by the locals years before to prevent beach erosion. Those Rangers who had managed to cross the beach safely fell prone in the breakwaters' alcoves, for here they would be comparatively secure from enemy small-arms fire originating from the flanks. High-angle mortar fire would be an entirely different matter, but the enemy had not yet figured that out. This would be an excellent spot for the Rangers to catch their breath and ponder their next move.

T/Sgt. Herbert Epstein
HQ Company, 5th Ranger Battalion, Ranger Force C

I was shoulder-to-shoulder with Colonel Schneider in the lead boat and clearly saw what was happening to Companies A and B near the Vierville draw. It was Schneider who ordered the flotilla commander to turn left and run parallel to the beach until he saw a clearer spot. He then ordered the flotilla commander to get us in—and fast. I have always felt that Schneider was the unsung hero of Omaha Beach. He was certainly my hero, and I credit him with saving my life and countless others by his savvy and decisiveness.

Capt. John Raaen
Commander, HQ Company, 5th Ranger Battalion, Ranger Force C

Waves lashed at us, throwing the boat right and left, pitching, tossing, smashing into the German obstacles. At one point we were crashing down on a pole-type obstacle with a teller mine wired to it. Too bad—this is it! But another wave grabbed us, throwing us to the left, and we were past the mine and a few moments later, the rest of the obstacles. Suddenly the coxswain gunned the engine and we hit the bottom with a jolt. The ramp dropped and [Maj. Richard] Sullivan dashed out to the left. I was second and chose the right, shouting, "Headquarters! Over here!" The water wasn't as high as my boots. Our coxswain had done well by us. Ten

The breakwaters on the Dog White sector of Omaha Beach. The 5th Ranger Battalion landed in this area at about 7:50 A.M. and began its ascent of the bluff shortly thereafter. COURTESY MARYLAND NATIONAL GUARD.

yards of shallow water amid the damnedest racket in the world. You could hear the bullets screaming by. . . . Ahead was the seawall. It was packed with men two- and three-deep. They couldn't dig in because the rocks [of the shingle] were six to eight inches in diameter, layered deeply. As I dropped down into the shelter of the seawall and breakwater, I looked back. My men were coming up, dropping to the right and left of me. Artillery was falling at the water's edge, but only small arms from our right were hitting near the seawall. Bodies were strewn all over the beach.

Cpl. John Burke
Company A, 5th Ranger Battalion, Ranger Force C
We were lying against a seawall off the beach, and one fellow who always boasted he would bayonet a Kraut was very quiet. Someone yelled, "Hey, how many Krauts are you going to bayonet?" The reply was: "Boy, do I wish I was back in England!"

1st Lt. Charles Parker
Commander, Company A, 5th Ranger Battalion, Ranger Force C
The coxswain of our boat put us off in about waist-deep water [on the far left of Schneider's force]. . . . We were virtually untouched in the landing on Dog White

by virtue of Schneider's decision. Smoke was covering the whole area. That meant that the Germans couldn't put too much direct fire on us.

Capt. John Raaen
Commander, HQ Company, 5th Ranger Battalion, Ranger Force C
This was our Ranger chaplain, Father Lacy. . . . Old, probably in his late thirties or early forties. Short, he couldn't have been over 5'6". Fat, at least 30 pounds over-weight. Thick glasses. . . . He was assigned to my boat, so I checked him and his equipment out a dozen times as we went through our boat drills. The next time I saw him, I was kneeling on Omaha Beach right next to the seawall, looking back at my LCA as my men still poured out of it and began running toward me and the safety of the wall. There was Father Lacy, the last man out. He was no more than ten feet clear of the boat when a German shell hit the fantail of the LCA. . . . I looked away and did not see Father Lacy again until much later. Others saw him, and like minstrels sang his praises. Lacy didn't cross the beach like we heroes did. He stayed down there at the water's edge pulling the wounded forward ahead of the advancing tide. He comforted the dying; calmly said prayers for the dead. . . . Father Lacy stayed behind at the water's edge, doing the work for which God had chosen him.

LOUSY CIVILIAN IDEAS
One of the riskiest elements of the Omaha invasion plan was V Corps' intention to use comparatively large and vulnerable landing craft known as LCIs (landing craft, infantry) to land troops only an hour after the first wave had hit the beach. This decision was based on two assumptions, nei-ther of which came true: first, that there would be an adequate number of clearly marked gaps through the enemy's beach obstacles, which by then would be partially submerged by the rising tide; second, that enemy machine gun and rifle fire would for the most part have been neutralized. Even if only one of these two conditions had been achieved, any attempt to beach a 380-ton, 160-foot LCI at such an early hour in the invasion would have been treacherous. When both conditions were unfulfilled, the task of bringing a fully laden LCI safely to shore at such an early hour became nearly impossible.

Those with sarcastic tongues labeled LCIs "lousy civilian ideas," and at first glance that seemed an apt description. According to A. J. Liebling, a reporter for *The New Yorker* who was aboard one of the first LCIs to land on Omaha Beach, "The crews probably would have found it more comfort-able sailing on the *Santa Maria*." However, LCIs were very good at the task for which they were designed: conveying a large body of troops—typ-

7:30–8:30 A.M.: LCI First Tide Landings

SCALE

1000 Yards

■ German Strongpoint

NOTES

LCIs 91+92 destroyed on beach

LCI-85 sunk returning to sea

LCI SCHEDULED TO LAND ON FIRST TIDE

NAME	BRANCH	TIME	SECTOR	TROOPS
LCI-88	U.S. COAST GUARD	7:35 AM	EASY RED	CO. B, 37TH ENGINEERS
LCI-493	U.S. NAVY	7:35 AM	FOX GREEN	CO. A, 37TH ENGINEERS
LCI-90	U.S. COAST GUARD	7:40 AM	EASY GREEN	CO. A, 149TH ENGINEERS, CO. B, 7TH BEACH BN.
LCI-91	U.S. COAST GUARD	7:40 AM	DOG WHITE	CO. B, 147TH ENGINEERS, HQ 116TH INF.
LCI-94	U.S. COAST GUARD	7:40 AM	DOG RED	CO. B, 104TH MED. BN., 29TH MP PLAT.
LCI-92	U.S. COAST GUARD	8:10 AM	DOG WHITE	CO. C, 147TH ENGINEERS, CO. A, 7TH BEACH BN.
LCI-83	U.S. COAST GUARD	8:30 AM	FOX GREEN	CO. B, 20TH ENGINEERS
LCI-85	U.S. COAST GUARD	8:30 AM	EASY RED	CO. A, 1ST MED. BN.
LCI-89	U.S. COAST GUARD	8:30 AM	EASY RED	HQ, 1ST ENGINEERS

1899-35-5

*"Lousy Civilian Ideas." U.S. Coast Guard LCI-83 lands on the western edge
of Omaha Beach, near the F-1 draw, at about 8:30 A.M., carrying Company B,
20th Engineers. The intake/exhaust ducts of two 741st Tank Battalion Shermans
are visible in the left-center. These are probably the two tanks that Lieutenant
Monteith would later recruit to help subdue a nearby enemy strongpoint.*
U.S. ARMY SIGNAL CORPS, NATIONAL ARCHIVES.

ically 200 men—to a specific point on a beach and landing them there in a
compact mass.

For a vessel that was more than thirty times the weight and four times
the length of an LCVP, the LCI's draft of less than five feet was little more
than twice that of an LCVP. An LCI could therefore set down only a short
distance off a beach, right up in the shallow surf, and deposit its occupants
in water generally no deeper than chest-high. Smaller landing craft could
do better—but not by much.

The Neptune plan dictated that nine heavily laden LCIs, mostly
manned by the U.S. Coast Guard, land on Omaha Beach within the invasion's first two hours. In theory, this scheme was sound, assuming the
enemy would be disorganized by the preinvasion bombardment and the
first wave's assault. No commander could deny the obvious military advantages of landing units intact rather than broken up among a half dozen
small landing craft. The first hour of the Omaha invasion had proved how
unit integrity could evaporate instantly when LCAs or LCVPs landed rifle

companies dispersed across a wide front. Undeniably, however, bringing in LCIs so early entailed great risk. If the German defenders were still active, a large, unarmored LCI would attract enemy attention and become an easy target. A well-aimed enemy shell could penetrate its hull like the proverbial knife through butter, and no one wanted to contemplate the consequences of a direct hit on a vessel packed tightly with 200 GIs, a twenty-four-man crew, and tons of explosives. Furthermore, LCIs attempting to land on sectors containing undemolished beach obstacles faced immense danger from mines, which could blow through the vessels' unprotected bottoms and sink them in an instant. Maneuvering between the obstacles would not be easy, as an LCI was hardly as nimble as an LCVP.

The time had come to determine whether the risk was worth it.

Lt. (jg) Arend Vyn
USCG, Officer-in-command, LCI-91, Action Report, June 10, 1944

Upon approach to Dog White beach it became evident that proposed markers for a cleared channel through the underwater obstructions had not been placed. A small break in the Element C was blocked by what appeared to be a sunken DUKW. A beaching was made between units of Element C at the scheduled time, H+70. . . . Troops disembarked reluctantly over both ramps in the face of heavy enemy machine gun and rifle fire. . . . The ship was swinging with the tide toward the stakes on the port bow, so the ship was retracted. While doing so a teller mine was exploded at the port bow injuring a few soldiers but not causing fatal damage to the ship. . . . [At about 8:00 A.M.] a second beaching was made about 100 yards west of the original one in an effort to get in beyond the obstructions. A portion of the remaining troops had disembarked over the port ramp when what appeared to be an 88 struck the center of the well deck and exploded in the fuel tanks below. A blast of flame immediately followed and within seconds the entire well deck was a mass of flames. Water pressure was inadequate to fight the flames. . . . Because the fire could not be gotten under control to enable the ship to retract, the order was given to abandon ship.

Capt. Robert Walker
Assistant S-3, 116th Infantry, 29th Division, aboard LCI-91

The skipper of LCI-91 was a Coast Guardsman from Boston. He told me he had entered the Coast Guard expecting he would spend the war guarding the Atlantic coast. Instead, he said, he was now on his third amphibious invasion. . . . I took a look toward the shore, and my heart took a nosedive. I couldn't believe how peaceful, how untouched, and how tranquil the scene was. The terrain was green. All buildings and houses were intact. "Where," I yelled to no one in particular, "is the damned Air Corps?" We began to have casualties from small arms fire on the front deck. . . . I heard a blast and saw that a man wearing a flamethrower had been hit and his fuel tank was on fire. Several men standing nearby had burns. The man with the flamethrower was screaming in agony. He went over the starboard side and dived into the sea. I could see that even the soles of his boots were on fire.

Motor Machinist Mate 1st Class Clifford Lewis
USCG, LCI-94, Diary, June 6, 1944

Tracer shells began skipping out over the water towards us. They exploded very close and shrapnel clattered against the ship. At 0745 we were called to man our beaching stations. I made a dash for the engine room hatch and could feel and hear shrapnel and machine gun bullets careening by. I took my place at the throttles beside Sorensen. Hass stood by the clutches. We crunched on the beach at 0747 amid loud explosions which made the ship shudder. We disembarked our troops and started out when the Skipper noticed we had fouled an LCVP with a line. . . . At that moment three shells burst into the pilot house and exploded, killing three of my shipmates and wounding two, including an officer.

Photographer's Mate 3rd Class Seth Shepard
USCG, LCI-92, June 25, 1944

Ahead of us everywhere were small landing craft and now the beach itself was plainly visible, even with the smoke. Suddenly I realized that we were in for a tough time as I made out shattered Higgins boats [LCVPs] on the beach and men running to take cover. I could see a few houses in the lee of the hill, wrecked and on fire. My heartbeat multiplied when I looked over the starboard bow, near the beach, and saw the Coast Guard manned LCI-91 enveloped in flames and smoke. She was the first LCI to hit that sector of the beach and we were scheduled as the second. Below us, in the pilot house, Edward E. Pryzbos, quartermaster first class, USCG, at the steering controls, gave one look at the "91," and yelled to our two waiting pharmacist's mates: "Looks as if we're going to have a rough landing." [At about 8:10 A.M.] a terrifying blast lifted the whole ship upward with a sudden lurch from the bow. A sheet of flame and steel shot out from the forward hold. The ship quivered as if it were pulling apart and the concussion threw the three of us in the conn backward and down hard. The heat was like the midst of a blast furnace. . . . Forty-one soldiers in the forward troop compartment were trapped in a fiery furnace, most of them being killed instantly. . . . The scene was extreme confusion. The piles of K-rations and gear for the soldiers were littered over the well deck. Flames and dense smoke were pouring from the hatch, [and] the ramps were damaged making both impossible to lower. Everywhere were faces blackened from the smoke and fire. . . . I saw Army officers pleading with their men to get off

"Looks as if we're going to have a rough landing!" A U.S. Coast Guard crew takes cover from enemy fire behind their LCI's pilothouse. Two DD tanks are visible on the beach beyond the German beach obstacles.
U.S. ARMY SIGNAL CORPS, NATIONAL ARCHIVES.

as quickly as possible. Some soldiers were jumping overboard and others hid or let themselves down a chain up forward of the damaged ramp. The cries of some of the helpless soldiers in the deep water were pitiful.

THE TIMES THAT TRY MEN'S SOULS

As the invasion's first hour passed into history, there was probably not a single GI on the beach whose D-Day experiences matched the expectations of training. Second-wave infantrymen landing an hour or more after the assault troops had confidently expected their role to be mopping up a few dazed German survivors and then pressing inland to prepare for the expected enemy counterattack. Between 7:30 and 8:00 A.M. the invasion timetable called for two 800-man reserve infantry battalions, one from the 1st Division, the other from the 29th Division, to land from LCVPs on their respective beach sectors for just that purpose.

Given that the navy had deposited more than 6,000 troops on Omaha Beach within the invasion's first sixty minutes, one would expect the beach to be congested. Indeed, in several locations the beach was jammed with humanity, but the Germans were working furiously to depopulate those places faster than the Americans could reinforce them. In the invasion's early stage, however, extended stretches of the Omaha beachfront were only sparsely occupied by troops, the most notable being the sector between the Les Moulins and St. Laurent draws. Squarely in the middle of this three-quarter-mile bluff line was the hypothetical boundary separating 1st Division troops on the east and 29th Division soldiers to the west. It was toward this beach that the 29th Division's 3rd Battalion, 116th Infantry, hurtled at 7:30 A.M.

PFC Norman Grossman
Company L, 116th Infantry, 29th Division
I had a very fatalistic opinion on the subject of combat. I figured if I was going to get it, I was going to get it, and there was nothing I or anyone else could do about it. However, I had a sort of premonition that I was coming back. . . . As we neared the shore I heard the clatter of machine guns and the explosions of artillery and mortar fire. Before I knew it I heard someone yell, "The ramp is down! Everyone out!" We dashed into waist-deep water and ran the 300 yards to clear the beach. I remember a burst of machine gun fire landed about ten yards from me, but I kept going, for we had instructions to get off the beaches as fast as we could. At the end of the beach was a sand dune covered with rocks, behind which we took refuge. . . . I asked my platoon sergeant what to do, and I could see by his face he did not know. I then got the funniest feeling I have ever experienced. I felt like the young soldier who said, "A guy could get killed here!" I wanted to run—I didn't know where—but I wanted to get out of there. I finally controlled myself and set about the task of figuring how to push on.

Lt. Col. Lawrence Meeks
Commander, 3rd Battalion, 116th Infantry, 29th Division
I had my hand on Capt. [Philip] Gaffney's shoulder when there was an incredibly loud explosion, blowing the ramp off the landing craft. [Gaffney was commander of Company D, 81st Chemical Mortar Battalion, attached to the 116th Infantry on D-Day. The explosion was caused by a mine attached to an underwater obstacle.]

Capt. Gaffney and some of his men who were up front on the craft were killed. The captain's head slumped on my shoulder, and I noticed he had blood oozing from his nose and mouth. I could see he was dead. This was our first battle casualty, and the first person I saw killed. Water gushed into the landing craft, sinking it in shoulder-deep water. We shed our equipment—about 60 pounds—and keeping low in the water, waded ashore. It was probably fate that saved us because if we hadn't sunk we would have touched down in front of a machine gun emplacement and probably would have been killed. We picked our way through the obstacles. I tried to warn the men that tracer bullets were grazing the beach about a foot above the ground. I gave the order to get across as fast as possible and not to bunch up.

Company K, 116th Infantry, 29th Division
U.S. Army Historical Division, interview with various Company K soldiers, September 1944

The company was to come in as part of the reserve [3rd] battalion. . . . The sections were landed very near together on a piece of beach which had no other personnel on it at that time. The [shingle] was very low, and with small arms fire continually firing above it, there was no desire on the part of the men to move to either flank to contact other boat sections. Besides, the sections had been instructed that they were to move to the battalion assembly area as boat sections rather than organize as a company.

Sgt. Felix Branham
Company K, 116th Infantry, 29th Division

We had a little Italian fellow named Gino Ferrari in our company, who was 20 years old. He would turn 21 on June 20, and we used to joke with him, "Ferrari, you'll never live to be a man [of 21] because the moment you hit the beach you're going to get your heinie shot off." Lo and behold, he was the first man I saw killed on Omaha Beach. I was behind him on the beach, and I said, "Gino, move on up!" I knew he was hesitant, and I moved ahead of him. I looked back and he'd gotten hit right in the forehead. His face was full of blood. Later, I saw the tide washing his body up toward the shingle.

Company M, 116th Infantry, 29th Division
U.S. Army Historical Division, interview with various Company M soldiers, September 1944

Company M came ashore on new beach where there had been no prior landings. The beach was perfectly clean of craters, and the obstacles had not been removed. . . . [Sgt. Bruce Heisley declared,] "All of the men seemed shakier and weaker than usual. Sea-sickness was getting some, but fear was getting most of us.

7:40 A.M.: St. Laurent Draw

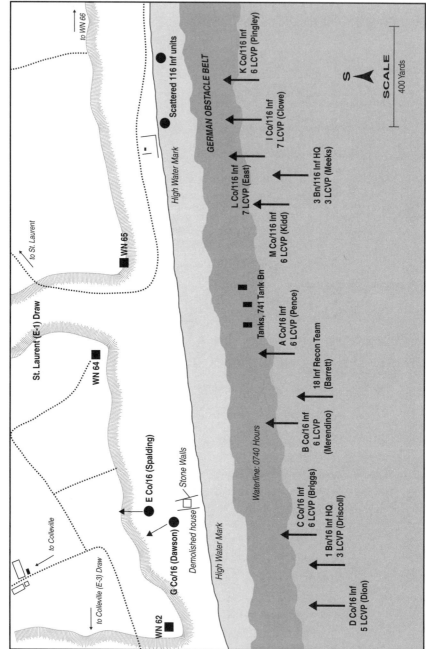

The burdens that we could ordinarily carry, we had to drag. But we dragged it. Not one thing was left on the beach." Then they went forward as a body, making for the shingle. [According to PFC Hugo de Santis,] "Everything was carried to that point. We all felt we were carrying too much equipment and even before we started, the men had gone silent from nervous fatigue. But they strained to get every last thing off the beach." On that run to the shingle "the company learned with surprise how much small arms fire a man can run through without getting hit. The enemy was simply throwing lead," [said S/Sgt. Thomas Turner]. There was not a single straggler. A few men were hit during the passage. Others were so weak from fear that they crawled across the beach. But their leaders yelled at them to come on. Within ten minutes, they too had crossed the 100 yards of sand.

2nd Lt. Donald Anderson
Company L, 116th Infantry, 29th Division
Morale was terrific. . . . The ramp of our LCVP hung up, and the Navy crewman pulled his pistol to shoot the ramp cable in half. This cable was approximately three-eighths of an inch in diameter and to shoot it in that confined space had everyone looking for a corner to hide in. About that time the ramp finally came down, and I stepped off—right over my head.

Like their 29th Division cousins to the west, the 1st Division's reserve battalion, the 1st of the 16th Infantry, landed amid beach conditions completely at variance with what it had been led to expect by the Neptune plan. Conveyed to shore by twenty-six LCVPs manned by U.S. Coast Guard personnel from the transport *Samuel Chase*, the battalion touched down largely intact between the St. Laurent and Colleville beach exits. The German defenses at both draws appeared far from neutralized, however, and their vigorous fire had obviously prevented earlier waves from leaving the beach by those routes. Someone was going to have to hastily figure out a way off the beach.

1st Lt. William Dillon
Executive Officer, Company A, 16th Infantry, 1st Division
We were to land on a high ebbing tide at 7:30 A.M.—for once the LCVP was on course. I looked over the ramp and could see the little valley which was to be on our right, but I could also see that the engineers hadn't been there to blow the teller mine ramps about [400] yards from the beach. By now we were getting all kinds of fire. I didn't look back, but there wasn't a footprint in the sand, nor a dead man on the beach, and we were supposed to be the second wave. Where was the first wave of troops?

"It was like going into a new world." First Division troops, probably from Company C, 16th Infantry, land on Omaha Beach from a U.S. Coast Guard LCVP at about 8:00 A.M. Demolition engineers are visible working on German obstacles, and a Sherman tank can be seen on the beach. U.S. COAST GUARD.

HQ Company, 1st Battalion, 16th Infantry, 1st Division
U.S. Army Historical Division, interview with various HQ Company soldiers, June 23, 1944

The forward CP group of the 1st Battalion, 16th Infantry, landed on the left side of Easy Red, Omaha Beach. The machine gun and rifle fire was terrific, and men were being hit from the front and flanks as they left the LCVPs. Men who were carrying the heavier loads of equipment, such as wire and radios, seemed to be the ones who were hit more often because they could not move as fast as the rest. Upon reaching the beach it was found that there were many men from the first assault unit still lying there. Some were going back into the water to get wounded men, ammunition, and equipment.

Quartermaster 2nd Class Robert Adams
Coxswain, USCG, LCVP Boat Division, USS Samuel Chase

As we approached the beach sometime [around 8:00 A.M.], I was standing to steer the boat, and the officer was standing as well to keep posted on where we were going. Everybody else was down. When we got in fairly close to the beach, I could see a haze and smell the cordite odor of gunpowder. It was like going into a new world. We could hear the chatter of machine gun fire and then the sound of mortars. . . . As I looked around me I could see the bodies of dead soldiers floating; they were probably from the army's amphibious DUKWs. The men were floating with their rumps sticking out of the water. Their life belts were around their waists, not their chests. . . . When our LCVP's ramp opened, our brave group from Big Red One bounded out onto Omaha Beach. I recall that I looked to my left and two soldiers were holding up another one in between them and yelling words of encouragement to him.

1st Lt. Lawrence Beach
Company B, 16th Infantry, 1st Division, July 4, 1944
Boats were lowered from the [*Samuel Chase*] at 0555 hours on 6 June. The landing craft put the company ashore on Easy Red beach at 0755 amid heavy artillery and small arms fire. Practically all the preceding waves were still pinned down on the beach. . . . The company moved up to the wire and section leaders did an excellent job of hasty reorganization.

A 1st Division reserve regiment, the 18th Infantry, was scheduled to land shortly before noon to support its 16th Infantry comrades. A three-man 18th Infantry reconnaissance team had orders to land several hours early with the 16th and locate suitable inland assembly areas for the 18th. But when this team came ashore within the invasion's first hour, its members immediately realized that the enemy's blistering fire would prevent them from moving inland anytime soon. Given the impossibility of fulfilling its assigned mission, the team therefore began to tackle other tasks of much greater immediacy.

1st Lt. John Foley
HQ Company, 18th Infantry, 1st Division, June 15, 1944
As Pvt. [Carlton] Barrett, Lt. [John] Foley, and Pvt. [William] Carter made the beach, they realized that the mission could not be accomplished until the enemy machine guns, mortars, and artillery observers were cleared from the high ground overlooking the beach. . . . Pvt. Barrett and Lt. Foley started to work dragging soldiers from the surf who were in danger of drowning, and assisting them to the meager security that the beach offered. . . . When Lt. Foley was wounded, Pvt. Barrett skillfully bandaged his wounds and probably saved his life, as the shrapnel wounds were above the left eye, and he was bleeding profusely. . . . Pvt. Barrett then waded out to contact landing boats to get litters to evacuate the casualties,

"No sacrifice too great." Cpl. Carlton Barrett (center) of the 18th Infantry, 1st Division, is awarded the Medal of Honor for his heroic actions at Omaha Beach. The officer to the left is Gen. Joseph Stilwell. The officer to the right is unidentified. U.S. ARMY SIGNAL CORPS, NATIONAL ARCHIVES.

then he assisted in carrying the wounded to the boats. As the last of the wounded were being removed from the beach, Lt. Foley noticed [18th Infantry] craft coming in to land. He called Pvt. Barrett and sent him to contact the boats that were about to beach. Pvt. Barrett was instrumental in furnishing information in regard to the situation. He kept up this work on the beach until he became a casualty, suffering wounds in the left foot, both legs, and hips. Pvt. Barrett is small in stature—about 5'4" in height, weighing 125 pounds. He truly exemplified the saying [the 1st Division's motto]: "No sacrifice too great. No mission too difficult. Duty first." His dauntless, daring courage shown on that bloody beach was a boost to the morale of all soldiers who witnessed his deeds.

Private Barrett, a native New Yorker, would be awarded the Medal of Honor on October 2, 1944—the only one of three soldiers who were awarded the Medal of Honor for action on Omaha Beach to survive the day.

Many members of the 5th Engineer Special Brigade also accompanied the 16th Infantry ashore, fully expecting to immediately begin their job of preparing the beach for the massive influx of men and matériel that would soon arrive, according to the directives of the strict invasion timetable.

T/Sgt. James Montague
HQ Company, 37th Engineer Combat Battalion, 5th Engineer Special Brigade, July 1944
The low silhouette of the shoreline came into view, and as we drew closer, all field glasses were scanning the picture anxiously. . . . Sgt. Moffatt turned toward me, pointed to the shore, and formed the words "E-1." I looked toward the indicated position, but before I could orient myself the whine of machine gun slugs sent us all flying for the doubtful protection of the sides of the craft. Our coxswain crouched low in his cockpit and kept to his course. Sgt. Gibbons was watching him closely and said afterward that the fear of God was plain in his eyes, but he kept us going. Other craft were banging our sides and knocking us about. Suddenly we broached on a stake, and towering above us were stakes and "Element C" with teller mines swaying precariously and threatening to topple into the boat any minute. The machine guns continued to whine overhead, and men called to the coxswain to drop the ramp. The coxswain was still doggedly trying to remove the craft from the stake when I heard Col. [Lionel] Smith [CO, 37th Engineer Battalion] order the ramp dropped. The water poured into the bow, and men began shedding equipment before they dropped off into neck-deep water. These were veterans of the Fighting 1st, men who had landed in Sicily and Africa. . . . Sgt. Moffatt turned to look back at the craft and said that the coxswain was hanging from his cockpit out over the side of the boat. I was amazed to find the beach black with the first waves. We had been expecting to find the beach free of small arms fire, and here were the assault waves crowded on the shingle behind the low mounds of dirt in front of the lateral beach road. Mortar shells were bursting in the shingle, sending shrapnel and rock flying over the crowds of men. . . . An infantryman passed me with a .30 caliber machine gun and hurriedly set up behind the low bank. He fired one burst, a mortar shell exploded, and he held up his right hand minus two fingers.

By 8:00 A.M., a crisis was unquestionably at hand. The arrival of the reserve infantry units had created dangerous congestion behind the shingle along much of its four-mile length on Omaha Beach, and a far greater number of fresh GIs scheduled to swarm ashore in the next few hours would make that congestion appreciably worse. Furthermore, the tide was rising rapidly, and fairly soon the beach would be narrowed to less than ten yards wide—hardly room enough for the thousands of men pinned behind the shingle. Once the Germans trained their mortars on those inviting targets, they could hardly miss, and it was hard to imagine that anyone could survive.

In truth, Omaha Beach was a balloon ready to burst. If it did, an already broken invasion plan would blow apart completely. Surely this was not what General Marshall had envisioned when he promised West Point's graduating Class of 1942 a "Great Offensive" in France. But soldiers know that plans alone do not guarantee victory—if they did, every battle would be easy. Rather, success depends on the soldiers' ability to react to circumstances. On Omaha, there were a number of capable American leaders who grasped that concept and who knew that there was a solution to their predicament that was becoming clearer by the minute: Get off the beach— and do so by attacking up the bluffs, not through the draws. In the current dilemma, that was the only conceivable course of action. Evidence, however, did not guarantee action; and if someone did not take action soon, well . . . Generals Gerow and Bradley would have to make some difficult decisions that could set the Allied war effort back months.

CHAPTER 10

Move or Die

A GENERAL NAMED DUTCH

At 7:30 A.M., the U.S. Navy's LCVP 71 neared Omaha Beach after a grueling two-hour journey from the transport *Charles Carroll*. An observant enemy soldier might have been puzzled by the sight of this solitary vessel. On a day when British and American craft maneuvered in packs, LCVP 71 was notable because it sailed alone. But even the most perceptive German defender could not have discerned that Number 71 was conveying a very unusual group of American soldiers. Surely no landing craft on D-Day had a higher percentage of officers aboard. Of the twenty-six U.S. Army troops transported by LCVP 71 toward the shoreline, twelve were officers, including one general, one colonel, and five majors. Eleven of the fourteen enlisted men hauled heavy backpack radios, which would be critical on the beach if American commanders were to comprehend events that were taking place beyond their lines of sight. If the enemy had indeed figured out how significant LCVP 71 was and destroyed it, the history of the Omaha Beach landing unquestionably would have been considerably different.

The Germans did not notice LCVP 71, but even so, its essential role in the invasion nearly came to an abrupt and violent end as it plunged into the surf about fifty yards off Omaha Beach. The enemy's beach obstacles in this sector had not been cleared, and by 7:30, the swiftly rising tide had

7:30 A.M.: Brig. Gen. Norman Cota Lands

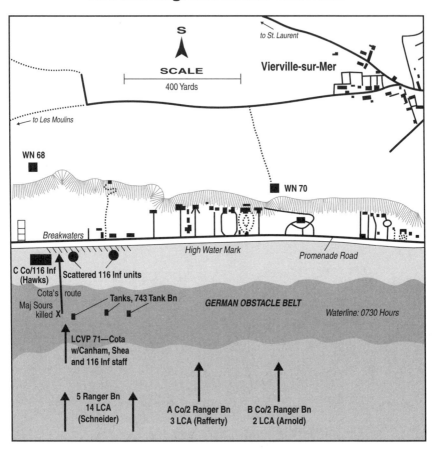

nearly covered them. As many of these obstacles were topped with mines, a navy coxswain had to possess a steely nerve and a deft hand on the wheel to negotiate a safe passage to the beach. LCVP 71's coxswain, a sailor named Feliciano, gamely tried to do just that. He reduced speed sharply as he figured out a sensible path to bring his vessel between the menacing obstacles, but the sea had other ideas. Lofty breakers, originating in the surf just seaward of the obstacles, rolled inexorably shoreward and threatened to heave the LCVP forward in spurts with them. Even worse, Calvados's notorious crosscurrent dragged the landing craft to the left, and at the slow speed the situation currently demanded, it was extraordinarily difficult for Feliciano to control his vessel.

At one point, as Coxswain Feliciano delicately guided LCVP 71 past a wooden pole that was obviously capped with a mine, the waves and current smacked the vessel into the pole once . . . twice . . . three times, with so much force that the third blow toppled the mine from its shaft and sent it splashing into the sea. The craft's occupants could do nothing except to prepare themselves for the mine's detonation, which at a distance of just a few feet would certainly be ruinous. One anonymous soldier, voicing the thoughts of all, blurted, "Kiss everything goodbye!" But the mine did not detonate, and Feliciano, now safely through the obstacles, raced LCVP 71 the few remaining yards to the beach and ordered the ramp dropped.

The passengers scrambled to disembark into the surf. Among them were Col. Charles Canham, commander of the 29th Division's 116th Infantry; three 116th staff officers, Majors Thomas Howie, Asbury Jackson, and John Sours; the regimental surgeon, Maj. Robert Buckley; and a general by the name of Norman Cota.

1st Lt. Jack Shea
Aide-de-camp to Brigadier General Cota, 29th Division, November 1944
Moderate small arms fire was directed at the craft as the ramp was lowered. . . . The first cover available was the partial screen provided by a DD tank of C Company, 743rd Tank Battalion, which had landed at H-6 minutes [6:24 A.M.]. There were about 18 of these tanks standing just above the waterline on Dog beach. They were faced toward the mainland at an interval of 70–100 yards, and about 25 yards from the seawall. They were firing at enemy positions to their immediate front. . . . Small arms fire from the flanks, which wounded one of the group seeking cover behind the tank, caused the group to rush forward to the cover of the low, timber seawall approximately 900 yards east of the Vierville exit. This wooden seawall was about four or five feet high. . . . All of the troops who had

landed up to this time [7:30] were crowded against the seawall, sprawled there seeking protection from enemy rifle and machine gun fire that came from foxholes and fire trenches on the crest of the bluffs that rose behind the beach.

Maj. Robert Buckley
Surgeon, 116th Infantry, 29th Division

When I got up onto the sand, where there were a lot of spider-like obstacles made of about eight-foot lengths of railroad rails crossed on each other at their centers, I flattened out on the sand behind one of them to catch my breath a little and saw Maj. Sours behind another off to my right a short distance. He saw me looking, and grinning back he called over, "How're you doing, Doc?". . . . After we'd rested on the sand for not more than a minute or two, there was an extra-heavy spattering of [bullets] in the water, in a runnel, just in front of us. I think Maj. Sours was almost immediately behind me—I'm not sure—as he started getting up at the same time I did. Everybody ran in individually and got [to the shingle] the best way he could. . . . I ran up to where Maj. Jackson was, and just as he was asking if I'd seen Tom Howie, up he ran, all hunched over, and sat down to do as we were doing, loosening our web equipment and other gear so we could get around better. While the three of us were catching our breath, we saw two men who seemed to need help out in the water, so with an enlisted man who was sitting next to me, I ran back out to them. The enlisted man began helping one of them, a soldier with a wounded leg, and I went over to the other one, who was lying face down in the water about the middle of the runnel. I could tell from his uniform that he was one of our officers, and when I lifted him partly up, I saw it was Maj. Sours. He was already dead when I found him.

Maj. Thomas Howie
S-3, 116th Infantry, 29th Division, June 9, 1944

It was the consensus of all officers and men questioned that prior to H-Hour there was positively no evidence of friendly aerial bombardment of the beaches. There were no craters along the water's edge, no demolition of beach installations, and also very little evidence of naval gunfire.

Brig. Gen. Norman D. Cota, a 1917 West Point graduate and now the second-in-command of the 29th Division, was probably the oldest soldier to land on Omaha Beach on the morning of D-Day. Known to his friends as "Dutch," Cota had reached his fifty-first birthday just six days previously, hardly qualifying him as elderly by civilian standards. But warfare is a young man's game, and amid the carnage of Omaha Beach, the middle-aged Cota was unquestionably out of place.

Cota survived the treacherous journey across the beach and reached the meager cover of the shingle on the sector distinguished by its fifteen breakwaters projecting seaward from the timber seawall. Here Cota observed GIs lying prone, piled up in heaps along the shingle and behind the wall. Few of them dared to move, and even worse, Cota could perceive no imminent effort on their part to do so. As a general, Cota had been privy to the high-level councils that had planned the Omaha Beach landing, and more than any other leader in this sector he recognized that the invasion could succeed only if its strict timetables were adhered to and its objectives accomplished in a timely manner. Cota's first glimpse of the paralysis behind the shingle convinced him that the invasion was dangerously out of kilter, and unless urgent action was initiated immediately, many of the men pinned behind the seawall would eventually be killed and the invasion would end in disaster.

Instances of generals being precisely in the right place at the right time are a rarity in military history, but this was undeniably one of those cases. Few general officers in the American Army knew more about inspiring soldiers to fight than Cota, and now that wisdom began to pay off. In the simple world of Willie and Joe, U.S. Army generals were a majestic but rare species, and their infrequent encounters with enlisted men were more likely to produce apprehension than enthusiasm. But Cota was an exception. Already a legend within the 29th Division due to his affability and habitual participation with the troops in field exercises, Cota was a bona fide friend of the common soldier and familiar to virtually all members of the division, down to the most humble private. Cota preferred to lead rather than push, inspire rather than intimidate. And above all, he was fearless.

Such was the type of general the prostrate troops on Omaha Beach needed—and they needed him immediately. Only a few minutes before Cota reached the seawall, the 116th Infantry's Company C under Captain Hawks had landed in this same sector, and it had so far avoided the slaughter that many other 116th units had suffered in the invasion's first hour. Also, following Cota's arrival, Colonel Schneider's 5th Rangers stormed ashore relatively intact in the same area, near where Cota was prowling the seawall to see what he could do to get things moving. To the astonishment of the prone riflemen, Cota walked upright, unflinchingly, daring the enemy to bring him down. Perched atop his stodgy, unmilitary body was a helmet with a single star and the yin-yang blue and gray symbol of the 29th

Division. Cota drew stares from unbelieving GIs as he earnestly waved his Colt pistol in the air, offering frequent shouts of advice and encouragement in his harsh workingman's accent. Cota had to give these men his undivided attention, for to him they represented the only visible means of salvaging what had been up until then a ruinous invasion.

1st Lt. Jack Shea
Aide-de-camp to Brigadier General Cota, 29th Division, November 1944
In each of the bays formed by [the breakwaters], an average of 80–100 troops had gathered. Members of all units were hopelessly jumbled. . . . First-aid men of all units were the most active members of the group that huddled against the seawall. With the limited medical facilities available to them, they did not hesitate to treat the most severe casualties. . . . Col. Canham and Gen. Cota conferred. . . . They realized that the enemy was aware of the concentration of troops in the lee of the seawall and that further high-trajectory [fire] could be expected. It was necessary to get off the beach immediately.

1st Lt. Robert Bedell
Company C, 116th Infantry, 29th Division, March 1945
[Cota] was waving that .45 pistol of his around, not too excited or loud, just telling me: "Well, lieutenant, we've got to get them off the beach. We've got to get them moving."

Sgt. Francis Huesser
Company C, 116th Infantry, 29th Division, March 1945
Cota came up to us . . . and said we had to get off the beach. . . . I guess all of us figured that if he could go wandering around like that, we could too.

T/5 Tom Herring
Company C, 5th Ranger Battalion
Before Cota reached Schneider, a flurry of artillery fire caused him to hit the dirt. I was lying to the left of PFC William Stump, also C Company. Stump asked me for a match, saying his were wet. "Mine too," I said. Stump reached across my back and punched a soldier next to me and asked, "Hey, Buddy, you got a light?" As the soldier rolled onto his left side, the star on his jacket epaulet was visible to both Stump and me. Stump said—"Sorry, sir!" Cota reached into his jacket, pulled out a Zippo, flicked it, held it for Stump to light up and said, "That's OK, son, we're all here for the same reason."

Maj. Richard Sullivan
Executive Officer, 5th Ranger Battalion
The activities of Gen. Cota seemed to be stupid at the time, but it was actually nothing but sheer heroism and the dedication of a professional soldier and fine officer. . . . I remember his aide-de-camp [Lieutenant Shea] being a nervous wreck trying to get the general to stop his activities.

Capt. John Raaen
Commander, HQ Company, 5th Ranger Battalion
As I got ready to move out, I saw, or had pointed out to me, a man casually wandering down the beach toward us. It was clear that he was someone with authority, for he was shouting orders and encouragement to the troops huddled against the seawall or burrowing into the edge of the embankment. By the time he got to our vicinity, I realized that he was quite high-ranking, a colonel or general officer. I jumped up, ran over to him, saluted and reported: "Captain Raaen, 5th Ranger Infantry Battalion, sir!"

"Raaen . . . you must be Jack Raaen's son. I'm General Cota. What's the situation here?"

"Sir, the 5th Rangers have landed intact . . . " He asked where Colonel Schneider was located. . . . He started toward Schneider, then turned to the troops in my vicinity and said, "You men are Rangers! I know you won't let me down!" When Cota reached Schneider, Sergeant Jim Graves observed that Schneider jumped up at attention and saluted the general. Cota meticulously returned the salute. Graves thought it foolish for anyone to expose himself so unnecessarily to that dreadful small arms fire coming in from our right. Cota asked: "Are you Colonel Schneider of the Rangers?"

"Yes, sir!," Schneider replied.

Cota then told him, "Colonel, you are going to have to lead the way. We are bogged down. We've got to get these men off this goddamned beach." After Cota finished speaking with Colonel Schneider, he turned toward the men nearby and said, "Rangers! Lead the way!"

Brig. Gen. Norman Cota
Letter to J. C. Raaen (Capt. John Raaen's father), March 24, 1949
I well remember the day your boy speaks of. I remember him now, as well as the Executive [Major Sullivan]. I was glad to see them at that particular time, for they were badly needed. The 5th Rangers were a wonderful outfit. . . . Give my best to Johnny when you see him. It was lads like him who our nation can thank for the beachhead it won on D-Day in Normandy. Believe me, they were the only reason that enabled an old crock like myself to shake fear loose and "roll on."

GUESTS OF THE THIRD REICH

When historians later sifted through the reports of the morning battle on Omaha Beach, they discovered an essential truth: The fighting on a given half of the beach generally paralleled the fighting on the opposite half, sometimes nearly identically. Such was the case when the command elements of the 1st Division's 16th Infantry, led by Col. George Taylor and his staff, came ashore on Omaha's eastern side about forty minutes after Cota's LCVP had touched down about two miles to the west. A near-fatal encounter with a German mine had sent Dutch Cota an immediate message that all was not well on the beach. And now, as Taylor's craft approached the coast, his suspicions intensified that the invasion was not proceeding as planned.

Capt. Lawrence Deery
Chaplain, 16th Infantry, 1st Division
Sergeant Ken Finn remarked as the tide crept up to the shale, "Looks like we'll be guests of the 3rd Reich!"

Headquarters, 16th Infantry, 1st Division
U.S. Army Historical Division, interview with Col. George Taylor,
June 21, 1944
Col. Taylor came in with the Rear CP with essential regimental staff and personnel. The rest was with Lt. Col. John Matthews [XO, 16th Infantry]. The coxswain went into Exit E-3 and was fired on. Col. Taylor had the coxswain pull out and get in at a more favorable spot. The tide was one-half in. [Taylor's group was] fired on while wading up to their necks. "It was a helpless feeling wading while shot at," [said Taylor]. The shore battalion and engineers were behind the [shingle] and there was little firing from our troops. There was a state of confusion. The troops were lined up on the beach like cans in a store room. There was nothing official from anybody. All were interested in holing-in and keeping out of the fire. Taylor moved to Exit E-3 and found that [Matthews's Advance CP] had been hit. The men were all intermingled on the beach. They couldn't get anywhere until we stopped the fire from the strongpoints.

Capt. William Friedman
HQ Company, 16th Infantry, 1st Division
Col. Taylor, then commanding officer of the 16th, looked around and in a great stentorian voice screamed, "Get the hell off the beach! If you stay on, you're dead or about to die!" It worked, and people got themselves organized in small groups.

"If you stay on the beach, you're dead or about to die!" Col. George Taylor, CO, 16th Infantry, 1st Division, urged GIs to move inland from the deadly eastern sector of Omaha Beach on the morning of D-Day. Portrait by Sgt. William Fraccio of the 16th Infantry, 1944.
COURTESY DAVID ALLENDER.

Col. George Taylor
Commander, 16th Infantry, 1st Division, Distinguished Service Cross Citation, June 14, 1944
Col. George A. Taylor, in command of the 16th RCT, landed during the most crucial, threatening period of the operation. Thousands of leaderless men lay huddled on the seven-yard beachhead, their organization disastrously cut down by fire. The exits were blocked, supporting weapons had not or could not be landed or were already destroyed, and the attack was arrested. Without hesitation, unmindful of the snipers and machine gun fire directed at him, Taylor moved up and down the beach, continuously exposing himself to the murderous fire. He found officers and gathered groups of men together for them to lead. He found, led, and drove men into the action. Calmly and cooly he assigned objectives to these newly organized groups. He converted a bewildered mob into a coordinated fighting force.

Taylor was not the only soldier to attract attention on this deadly beach sector. While the vast majority of GIs taking cover behind the shingle saw little immediate hope of carrying out the jobs for which they were trained, a radio operator from 16th Infantry headquarters named John Pinder toiled desperately in the surf amid the enemy's lethal fire to salvage the communications equipment he knew would soon be essential to his chief, Colonel Taylor. Veterans of the 1st Division had witnessed many astonishing acts of fearlessness in North Africa and Sicily, but those who witnessed Pinder's feats on Omaha Beach would never forget them.

Sgt. Robert Michaud
HQ Company, 16th Infantry, 1st Division, November 4, 1944
While participating in the invasion of France in the vicinity of Colleville-sur-Mer on 6 June 1944, I personally witnessed the following actions by T/5 John J. Pinder, Jr., HQ Company, 16th Infantry. While leaving the assault boat on which he had come in, Corporal Pinder was struck by a shellburst. [Soldiers holding T/5 rank were addressed as "corporal."] Although the side of his face was left hanging and he could only see from one eye, he held his hanging flesh with one hand and with the other gripped the radio and dragged it to shore. When he reached the shore, Corporal Pinder refused medical treatment, and before he could be stopped, ran back into the heavily mined water to rescue more floating equipment. He continued this work, rescuing much needed equipment in a very calm manner, seeming to disregard the intense fire all about him. Corporal Pinder made several trips to salvage communications supplies, and on one of these, while returning to shore, he was struck by a machine gun strafing the area. Despite his serious and painful wounds, he managed to struggle ashore with the load he was carrying. Even in this condition, he did not stop, but continued to help in setting up communications, exposing himself on the beach without any fear of the constant fire, until he was hit again and killed.

Pinder, a native of Pittsburgh, would be awarded the Medal of Honor posthumously on January 4, 1945.

ANGELS ON THEIR SHOULDERS

Colonel Taylor could not have known when he came ashore that several small bands of his intrepid warriors were vigorously fighting back, and in fact, a few of them had on their own initiative battled their way off the beach. Lieutenant Spalding's solitary Company E boat team did so first. It had traversed the tidal flat midway between the St. Laurent and Colleville exits by 7:00 A.M., and shortly thereafter Sgt. Curt Colwell used a bangalore torpedo to blast a narrow gap through the enemy wire beyond the shin-

"Disregarding the intense fire all around him." Cpl. John Pinder of HQ Company, 16th Infantry, 1st Division, was awarded the Medal of Honor posthumously for his actions on Omaha Beach.

U.S. ARMY SIGNAL CORPS, NATIONAL ARCHIVES.

gle. One by one the thirty-two GIs ascended the little rocky embankment, rushed across a narrow dirt road paralleling the beach, and passed through the gap to the comparative safety of tall brush grass and the walls of a ruined stone cottage at the foot of the bluffs. Deterred by an apparent minefield to their front, the team slipped to its left. Spalding's redoubtable platoon sergeant, Phillip Streczyk, and PFC Richard Gallagher had located what seemed to be a reasonably sheltered passage up the slope, and the team began its ascent.

The bluffs in this sector are among the most moderate on Omaha Beach, but the climb was anything but easy. About 400 yards to Spalding's left, the aperture of a large enemy concrete pillbox pointed directly at the path the team would follow to the bluff crest, and from commanding positions at or near the crest itself, enemy machine gunners prepared to zero in on the unsuspecting GIs. Even worse, the enemy had suspected that invaders might use this route up the bluffs and had planted mines all over the slope. However, Spalding's team was able to take advantage of the bluff's furrowed surface, for its dips and folds offered decent cover from enemy fire emanating from both the front and flanks.

2nd Lt. John Spalding
Company E, 16th Infantry, 1st Division, February 9, 1945

Sgt. [Fred] Bisco kept saying, "Lieutenant, watch out for the damn mines." They were a little box-type mine, and it seems that the place was infested with them, but I didn't see them. We lost no men coming through them, although H Company coming along the same trail a few hours later lost several men. The Lord was with us and we had an angel on each shoulder on that trip. Trying to get the machine gun above us, Sgt. [Hubert] Blades fired his bazooka and missed. He was shot in the left arm almost immediately. PFC [Raymond] Curley was shot down next. Sgt. [Grant] Phelps, who had picked up PFC [Virgil] Tilley's BAR on the beach, moved into position to fire and was hit in both legs. . . . We decided to rush the machine gun, about 15 yards away. . . . As we rushed it, the lone German operating the gun threw up his hands and yelled "*Kamerad!*" We would have killed him, but we needed prisoners for interrogation, so I ordered the men not to shoot him. He was Polish.

The enemy soldier must have been amazed to be addressed in fluent Polish by Streczyk. Despite his wounding of three Americans, the Pole claimed that threats from his German superiors forced him to shoot—and that he had purposely tried to miss. The contemptuous Streczyk sent him down the bluff to the beach under guard. The prisoner provided valuable intelligence that sixteen Germans currently occupied a strongpoint overlooking the St. Laurent draw about 700 yards to Spalding's right. If the Americans could wipe them out, the fire on the landing beaches would be considerably reduced.

2nd Lt. John Spalding
Company E, 16th Infantry, 1st Division, February 9, 1945

At this point, Lt. [Kenneth] Bleau of G Company came up and contacted me. He had come up our trail. His company had landed in the second wave behind us. Just a few minutes later Capt. Dawson of G Company came along. . . . Dawson said that he was going into Colleville and told us to go in to the right [toward the strongpoint]. . . . This was about 0800.

Unaware of Spalding's movement, Company G—reduced from 190 men to about 150 by casualties on the beach—had blasted its own lanes through the enemy wire. Strung out over a considerable distance, and diverging slightly from the route Spalding's GIs had taken only minutes before, Dawson's men began their ascent of the bluffs under heavy fire as their Company E brethren fought their way to the crest.

"The Lord was with us and we had an angel on each shoulder on that trip." At right, Lt. John Spalding of Company E, 16th Infantry, 1st Division, was one of the first men to penetrate the German Omaha Beach defenses on D-Day. Pictured with Spalding, as the lieutenant was recovering from his wounds in early 1945, is a Medical Corps officer. COURTESY DAVID ALLENDER.

Company G, 16th Infantry, 1st Division
U.S. Army Historical Division, interview with Capt. Joseph Dawson, August 22, 1944

A minefield lay behind the wire. There were two dead Americans lying in the mined area; they had been blown up. [One was probably PFC Lewis Ramundo of Company E, who had been killed moving past the ruined cottage with Spalding.] The men of G went through the field over the bodies of the two dead men, figuring that this was their safest route. They then continued on through the [ruins] and proceeded up the draw. Dawson was out ahead of them . . . with PFC Frank Baldridge to see if he could clear the way for his men. They got halfway up the draw. Dawson then found himself caught between the fire of his own men and fire from an enemy machine gun at the head of the draw. . . . [He] crawled on another 75 yards. He moved to any cover he could find. The draw was V-shaped, the ruins being at the bottom of the V. There was a promontory at the top near the left-hand angle of the V. He crawled on behind this . . . and was within ten yards [of an enemy machine gun nest] when the Germans saw him, swung the machine gun around and fired wildly. He heaved a fragmentation grenade; it exploded between them and killed two men.

Parts of two lost boat teams from the 29th Division's Company E, 116th Infantry, joined Spalding's and Dawson's audacious scramble up the bluff. They would remain with their newfound friends from the Fighting First until June 8.

Pvt. Charles Neighbor
Company E, 116th Infantry, 29th Division
We soon discovered that we were not alone on the beach. As we were beginning to size up the situation, a couple of men with 1st Division patches appeared. We found that several boats of F [probably G] and E Companies of the 16th Regiment had landed in the vicinity. The men attacked the machine gun nest with hand grenades and, with the aid of our mortar, crippled it badly. We were glad to see them, not only because of what they had done, but because they were experienced combat troops, seasoned in North Africa, and their experience would be valuable in leading us in our first assault.

Capt. Edward Wozenski
Commander, Company E, 16th Infantry, 1st Division
In climbing the bluff [later in the day after moving west along the beach with the main body of Company E], I met Sgt. Streczyk coming down to post me on the situation. He stepped on a teller mine right in front of my nose. I asked him what in hell he was doing since we both saw the mine clearly. He answered: "Well, it didn't go off when I stepped on it while going up the bluff." . . . If Streczyk did not earn a Medal of Honor, no one ever did. Thousands of men were on the beach being killed like flies. To lift your head over the [shingle] was to invite quick death. Yet Streczyk led a small group up the bluffs, cleared out enemy pillboxes, released a flare indicating his breakthrough, which I and others followed.

Company A reached the shingle about 300 yards to the east of the St. Laurent draw at a spot where no troops had yet blown any gaps through the enemy wire. Active German strongpoints on the bluff directly in front and on the opposite side of the draw made this sector exceptionally treacherous. Furthermore, to reach the foot of the bluff, the Americans would somehow have to traverse a wide antitank ditch filled with water.

8:15 A.M.: Spalding and Dawson Move Inland

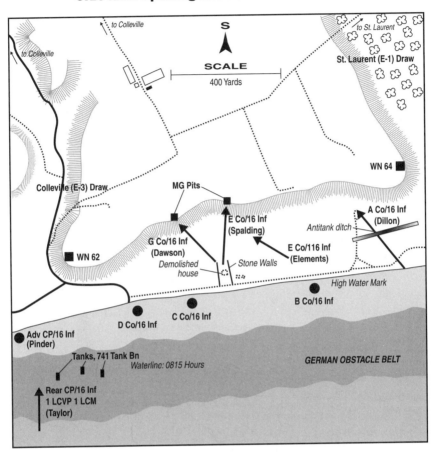

PFC Leroy Herman
Company A, 16th Infantry, 1st Division

Capt. [James] Pence [CO Company A] stood up in the beach area and yelled, "Come on, you bastards, let's go! If we're gonna die, we might as well die a little further inland!" He was hit twice, but not seriously. . . . [Later] Lt. Mack joined me and asked me if I had a cigarette. [There was no "Lt. Mack" in Company A. Herman presumably meant Lt. Atwood McElyea, a member of Company A.] I did have a carton in my pack wrapped in waxed paper and told him to get some out of my pack. We couldn't stand up because the bullets were coming over us so fast and thick. Lt. [McElyea] said, "You know, Herman—I think they are shooting at us for real!" With that remark, he raised his head up out of the hole to look around and was hit right between the eyes with a bullet.

1st Lt. William Dillon
Executive Officer, Company A, 16th Infantry, 1st Division

As we got to the top of the [shingle], there was a big concertina barbed wire entanglement. Where did the Navy go? Our one bangalore torpedo wouldn't go through. Soon some more men came up and we got two more torpedoes from them. We slid all three under the barbed wire, pulled the fuse and jumped behind a sand dune. It went off and made a hole big enough to drive a truck through. . . . As we went through the gap we came to bulrushes, waded through them and came to a wide canal or tank ditch. I stepped into the water and went in over my head. That's when I found out what the CO_2 [carbon dioxide] tubes in my [life belt] were for! I pulled both triggers and up I popped! I paddled across and started up the hill. I looked at the ground and could see both types of foot mines: one looked like a horse chestnut. . . , the other had three metal prongs sticking out of the ground and would pop up face-high and go off. Off to my right Lt. McElyea of Asheville, N.C., Sgt. Pat Ford of Brooklyn, N.Y., Sgt. Benn, and Babcock the aid man kept going a few steps at a time until Ford stepped on one of the horse chestnuts. It blew Ford's leg off, threw him into the air and he came down on his shoulder on another one that tore up his arm. . . . This is also where McElyea had some of his brains shot out. I thought he was dead, but years later Capt. [Polydore] Dion [CO Company D] said he got home and lived in Asheville, and had married one of the nurses from Lyme Regis [England]. . . . We slid left and stayed close to the ground. . . . I studied the ground and saw a faint path zigzagging to the left up the hill, so I walked up the path very carefully.

Capt. Albert Smith
HQ Company, 1st Battalion, 16th Infantry, 1st Division, June 1944

The only thing that got us off the beach was experience under fire, not assault training.

Company C had the good fortune of arriving at the shingle line in the same locale where Dawson's Company G had begun its audacious ascent of the bluff. Consequently, gaps through the enemy's wire barrier already existed, and imprecise paths through the minefields on the slope had been exposed. Once Company C reached the crest, it followed in G's wake toward Colleville.

1st Battalion, 16th Infantry, 1st Division
D-Day After-Action Report, July 4, 1944
A Company was on the right, C Company on the left, and B Company followed C Company up the cliffs. By 0930, the battalion was at the top of the cliffs. From the top of the cliffs, the battalion attacked straight inland.

The GIs had made it up the bluff—but plenty of dangerous work remained to be done.

SO MUCH OWED TO SO FEW

Shortly after Spalding's team reached the bluff crest, another group of 16th Infantry GIs fought its way off the beach from a sector so remote that it had not even figured in the Omaha assault plan. This party, composed mostly of members of Company L and other 3rd Battalion units, fought an isolated, all-day battle that is often overlooked in D-Day lore but had a decisive impact on the final American victory. Like almost everyone else on Omaha, Company L was brought ashore far to the east of its designated landing point. But unlike the others, it was deposited on a shoreline so unsuited for military operations that the unit could easily have become paralyzed indefinitely had not its leaders offered extraordinary motivation to get their men moving. General Eisenhower himself was said to have been so impressed with the audacity of this action that one of only two Medals of Honor the army awarded to 16th Infantry troops on D-Day went to a Company L officer, Lt. Jimmie Monteith.

Having lost one of its six boat teams several miles offshore, Company L touched down beyond Omaha's eastern limit in a sector where the high-water line is marked not by shingle, but by a low, rocky cliff line. Although the depleted company was relatively secure in the lee of the cliff, the only way off the beach was to slip right toward an area where the cliffs yielded to an earthen embankment about six feet high. If the company could scale this modest barrier, it could then move inland through the narrow Cabourg (F-1) draw. This draw bore no resemblance to Omaha's four others. It was nothing more than a semicircular indentation in the coastal bluffs, almost a natural amphitheater, through which a rough track ascended to the inland plateau.

The major impediment to Company L's progress was not the terrain, but a powerful German strongpoint situated on the bluffs just east of the draw. This was one of the most dominant positions on the whole Calvados coast. From it, the entire crescent of Omaha Beach was clearly visible, and a German with a pair of binoculars could see anything that moved for miles along the coastline. Any American movement over the embankment below the strongpoint would be blocked by barbed wire, and attempts to blast through that wire would be made under direct enemy observation. The strongpoint sat on such commanding ground that even if the assaulting soldiers managed to penetrate the wire, they could attack the enemy position only by moving inland through the draw and approaching it from the rear—under constant enemy fire.

Company L, 16th Infantry, 1st Division
After-Action Report, June 1944
The assault on the beach strongpoints was begun immediately, and the company began to push inland from the beach around the west edge of the cliff. The company CO, Capt. John Armellino, was seriously wounded when he repeatedly exposed himself to [enemy fire] to direct tank fire in support of his company's advance. . . . The 2nd assault section under Lt. Jimmie Monteith was ordered to push up a small draw and engage pillboxes on the left strongpoint. The 3rd section was to advance on the right of the 2nd, with the 5th following.

Sgt. Hugh Martin
Company L, 16th Infantry, 1st Division, March 20, 1945
When the troops were pinned down I saw Lt. Monteith go to the same place where [Captain Armellino] was struck down. He went right through the thick fire to the [741st Tank Battalion] tanks and got them into action. . . . He paid no attention to the shells and machine gun fire when he went to the wire and afterwards led us through the minefields.

Monteith and others vaulted the embankment, inserted bangalore torpedoes under the wire, and blew lanes through which the GIs could pass and then move up the draw's steep slope. The two 741st tanks on the beach that Monteith had contacted, as well as the destroyer USS *Doyle*, fired at the German strongpoint and at least intermittently stifled enemy resistance.

Company L, 16th Infantry, 1st Division
U.S. Army Historical Division, interview with various Company L soldiers,
June 1944

The sections attacking the strongpoint had come up the hill under bullet and rifle grenade fire. The men had moved along in squad column and were taking advantage of the shrubbery within the draw so that the enemy fire did them little hurt. They could see the Germans moving around in position on the top of the hill and the BAR men . . . were spraying the ground steadily. The BAR fire was extremely effective, and they saw some of the enemy fall. . . . [Lieutenant Monteith's] section phoned Lt. Robert Cutler [now replacing Armellino as CO of Company L] that it was ready to close on the position if the naval fire [from the *Doyle*] could be lifted. Just then Cutler saw purple smoke rising from the strongpoint and told [Monteith] that part of [Company L] was already closing in. . . . [Lt. Kenneth Klenk's] section moved into the outlying trenches of the strongpoint and began mopping up with grenades and satchel charges. About four or five of the enemy were knocked out during the close fighting before the remainder surrendered. The Americans lost only one. He is supposed to have been killed by a mine. In [Monteith's] section, four men were wounded, but they were treated on the ground and remained to fight. . . . At 0900 Lt. Cutler called to [the 3rd] Battalion and told them that the enemy had been subdued in the strongpoint.

741st Tank Battalion
Unit Journal, June 6, 1944

0830 hours—One DD tank from C Company, under the command of Sgt. [George] Geddes, claims credit for knocking out two French 75mm guns [operated by Germans] on the hill to the left of E-3 [Colleville] exit.

USS *Doyle*
Cmdr. James Marshall, War Diary, 1100 hours, June 6, 1944

Stopped 800 yards off beach Easy Red. Observed enemy machine gun emplacement on side of steep hill at west end of beach Fox Red, enfilading landing beach. Fired two half salvos [from 5-inch guns]. Target destroyed. Shifted fire to casemate at top of hill, fired two half salvos, target destroyed. Army troops begin slow advance up hill from beach.

Company L had achieved a notable victory. With the German position at the Cabourg draw neutralized, enemy fire directed against other 1st Division troops on Omaha's eastern extremity would be nearly eradicated.

9:00 A.M.: The Eastern Flank Secured

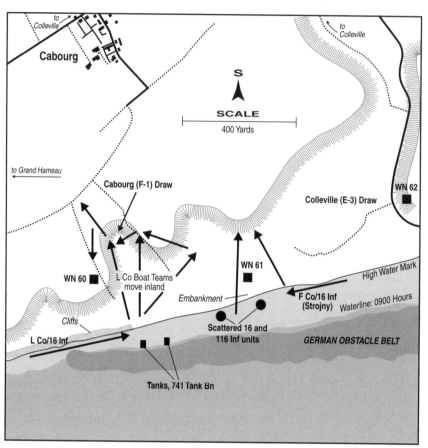

Colonel Taylor must have been pleased when he later learned of the 16th's two penetrations of the enemy defenses, but he could not rest until his regiment had cleared the St. Laurent and Colleville beach exits for vehicular movement as Neptune invasion orders demanded. When Taylor landed at 8:15 A.M., however, he immediately discerned that the 16th was no closer to fulfilling that mission than it had been at H-Hour. Even worse, German mortar and artillery barrages were still slaughtering his men behind the shingle at the mouth of the Colleville draw. To steer clear of this killing ground, the pinned GIs would have to move, yet movement seemed nearly impossible given the enemy's two intact strongpoints on either side of the draw. Somehow those two positions would have to be overcome.

On the eastern side of the mouth of the Colleville exit, the Germans had constructed a strongpoint, designated WN61, consisting of a mammoth concrete pillbox housing a deadly 88, several protected positions for lesser weapons, and the ubiquitous barbed wire and minefields. This was one of the enemy's rare defensive works that was not positioned on high ground. For some unknown reason, the Germans had placed it on a piece of grassy flatland only about forty yards from the high-water mark, and as such it was easy for the Americans to spot and was to some extent vulnerable to naval fire.

GIs with combat experience, of whom there were many in the 16th Infantry, saw that the German strongpoint could be attacked directly if a suitable weapon was available, assuming someone would have the nerve to crawl just beyond the shingle to do the deed. The 16th Infantry's Company F had landed at H-Hour in this sector, along with a mix of several other units. The right weapon was indeed available, as was the right man.

S/Sgt. Frank Strojny
Company F, 16th Infantry, 1st Division
I saw that our sector of the beach was too vulnerable to enemy fire, so I gave the word for all to move to the left to get behind hills for protection. . . . I was doing this because all my superiors were dead or wounded. Someone had to take over— I had lots of combat experience; all relied on me. . . . I saw an enemy gun knocking three of our tanks out in a matter of minutes. That was the end of our tank support. I spotted the gun emplacement, called for a bazooka team. None were available, as they were dead or wounded. So I went searching for a bazooka on the beach, knowing that that gun had to be knocked out to make our sector a success. I found a bazooka and ammunition, came back to the original position, then figured a way to best fire at the gun emplacement.

Company F, 16th Infantry, 1st Division
After-Action Report, June 1944

[Sergeant Strojny] took up the bazooka, but it was pierced through the tube by shell fragments. The enemy gun continued firing, which made Strojny mad. He decided to try the bazooka anyway, so he loaded a round and fired. The first two rounds missed, [but] the next two were direct hits. Nevertheless the gun continued to fire. Strojny yelled for more ammunition, but there was none. He then went down to the beach and returned with six rounds he had found. He fired all six from the same position, all rounds hitting the target—the last one causing the [enemy's] ammunition to explode. A number of dead were seen, and only one German was seen to escape. Strojny fired at the German with an M1, but was wounded by a sniper. The bullet entered [Strojny's] helmet over his left eye, going through the helmet and leaving a large hole in the rear of it. Despite this, Strojny was only superficially wounded.

Sergeant Strojny's feat gave the men pinned behind the shingle the opportunity to move off the deadly beach. But even this was not easy.

Company F, 16th Infantry, 1st Division
After-Action Report, June 1944

Seeing the pillbox in flames, Strojny urged his men forward. He got up, but no one followed. He did see a good spot to the left, so he urged his men to it. His men followed him, but the men from [Company E] 116th Infantry [29th Division], who were nearby, did not. Sgt. Strojny had his men pick up two BARs the 116th had abandoned. He worked to the left to the point where his unit was to cross, but as there was wire he could not get through. Strojny got a man from the 116th to blow a hole through the wire. The BAR men were placed on the right to fire into a wooded area. Pvt. Charles Rocheford had his hand blown off by a mine as he came into position. Strojny ran through the gap and cleared the minefield. He motioned for the others to follow. Five men from Strojny's section and an officer and a squad from the 116th followed. They received machine gun fire from their right flank. The entire group headed to this [enemy] fire, and seven Germans were killed.

After more than two calamitous hours, the exploits of Strojny, Monteith, Spalding, Dawson, and their comrades had given the 16th Infantry its first successes of D-Day. But even these accomplishments did little to lessen the steady, precise, and lethal pounding the GIs were receiving from German howitzers and mortars, verifying Colonel Taylor's stern warning that if the men valued their lives, they must immediately leave the beach. If the men wished to heed their colonel's counsel, at least they could now focus on following in the footsteps of the audacious trailblazers who had already forged ahead.

DUCKS IN A SHOOTING GALLERY

Meanwhile, four miles to the west—about as far as one could travel and still be considered on Omaha Beach—Captain Goranson's Company C, 2nd Ranger Battalion, had also initiated a move inland. Goranson's outfit had suffered dreadful casualties crossing the tidal flat, but three Rangers, Lt. William Moody, Sgt. Julius Belcher, and PFC Otto Stephens, had moved 300 yards west and managed to climb the nearly sheer cliff face on the sector known as Charlie.

The ascent of the cliff in Goranson's sector would not be easy, and those Rangers still capable of accomplishing it—at this point less than half of Company C's original complement of sixty-five—slipped westward along the cliff base to follow the first three men up. As later events would prove, this was precisely the right thing to do, for this movement neatly sidestepped a powerful German defensive position sited at the clifftop almost directly opposite Company C's landing point and enabled the Rangers to make the strenuous climb with little interference from enemy fire.

Even so, this enemy strongpoint would eventually have to be dealt with, and doing so would be a tough job. The position featured labyrinthine zigzag trenches, heavily fortified fighting positions and dugouts, and a brilliantly camouflaged concrete pillbox sited in the rising folds of the bluff. The pillbox's aperture faced east, making it nearly invisible when viewed from the sea, and its field of fire straight down the length of the beach was a machine gunner's dream. With virtual impunity, enemy troops occupying this position were massacring 29th Division GIs in front of the Vierville draw. Goranson's Rangers were familiar with the strongpoint, for it was distinguished by a large manor house solidly constructed with stone, improbably tucked into a small nook in the cliff face and visible from several miles out to sea. Allied intelligence officers had assigned it an ominous label: the "fortified house." An even stronger defensive site was a sturdy stone barn situated just beyond the house on a spine of high ground that marked one of Omaha's highest spots.

Moody and Stephens cautiously patrolled eastward along the cliff edge toward the house and discovered to their surprise that the enemy, perhaps focused on the landings in front of the Vierville draw, did not vigorously resist their advance. Meanwhile, more Rangers climbed the cliff behind them, urged on by shouts from the crest: "Come on up! It's all clear!" Goranson reached the top by about 7:15 A.M., and after a few moments to ponder the situation, made a fateful decision. Instead of proceeding westward to eliminate the formidable German strongpoint at Pointe de la Percée, he would attack in the opposite direction—toward the fortified house. With the disaster that was unfolding in front of the Vierville draw, Goranson felt he had no other choice.

As Moody and six Rangers secured the area around the house—now shattered by naval fire—he reported back to Goranson that he had heard German troops in the trench lines on the far side of the building. The Rangers moved past the house warily, for they knew that the enemy, although currently nowhere to be seen, lurked somewhere in the dugouts and trenches marking this strongpoint. Goranson's meager force, however, could do little more than probe the enemy position and hope for the best. Lieutenant Salomon, who had managed to climb the cliff despite a wound he suffered on the beach, was one of the first Rangers to enter the maze of trenches on the far side of the house.

1st Lt. Sidney Salomon
Company C, 2nd Ranger Battalion
I ran a short distance ahead and jumped into a shell-hole or depression in the ground. As I peered ahead, it became apparent that there was a trench running perpendicular from the cliff inland. Just then, Lt. Bill Moody jumped into the shell-hole on my right. He had been at the fortified house with a couple of his men. I told Bill about the trench that I had just spotted. He pushed up with his arms and looked over the edge of the shell-hole. Just then I felt him slump over on my right side. I looked and saw that he had been instantly killed [by a sniper's bullet]. I ran back to the edge of the cliff and called down to Capt. Goranson [now back on the beach] that Bill had just been killed. I then told Pvt. Stephens to follow me, and we ran ahead to the trench and jumped in. I cautioned Otto, and we started inland. A dugout was spotted ahead on the left, so I took one of my white phosphorus grenades and lobbed it in. We waited, then advanced to the doorway. No one was there. . . . Another trench branched off to the right—that created a dilemma. But we went ahead, and to the left was an 80mm mortar position, but no personnel. . . . We slowly continued ahead where the trench curved to the left. As I rounded the curve, a German soldier was approaching. All three of us were startled. I recovered first and grabbed him, and we took his weapon. He was much smaller than either of us, and quite subdued. I suggested that we send him down to the CO on the beach. . . . I remained on top for the rest of the day, as the enemy was apparently driven back

9:00 A.M.: C Company, 2nd Rangers, Moves Inland

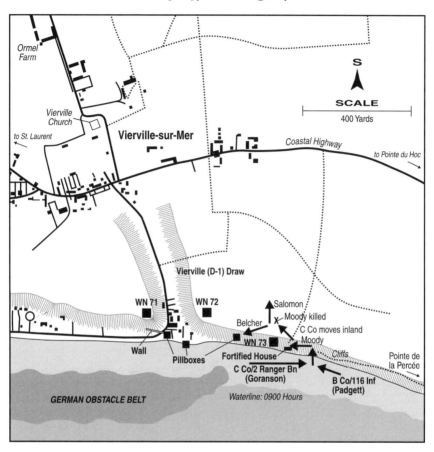

inland. We had so few men it seemed futile to advance and that it would be more advantageous to retain possession of this hard-earned and costly ground.

As Salomon reconnoitered inland, Sergeant Belcher, accompanied by Sgt. George Morrow and PFC Floyd Crego, endeavored to infiltrate the enemy trenches by creeping eastward along the cliff edge past the house. If the Rangers had harbored any hopes that the Germans had withdrawn from their strongpoint, those hopes soon vanished.

Company C, 2nd Ranger Battalion
U.S. Army Historical Division, interview with various Company C Rangers, July 1944
Separated from the Rangers by the house and barn, the enemy was not very much in evidence until some move was made to pass the house. . . . The Germans grenaded [Belcher's] party, and the Rangers threw the grenades back. Belcher inched up to the trench-edge, stuck his rifle over and was confronted with a German rifle right at his own head. Both guns misfired. The German ducked into a dugout in this mortar position. Belcher and one rifleman entered the trenches and shot three Germans near the mortar emplacement.

Company C, 2nd Ranger Battalion
Company C History, "Roughing It with Charlie," 1945
On the other side of the house, T/Sgt. George Morrow of South Bend, Indiana, and Sgt. Belcher spotted a machine gun nest housed in a pillbox, which was spraying the beach unmercifully with lead. This nest was one of [those] causing C Company a lot of casualties on the beach. Sgt. Belcher kicked the door of the pillbox open and threw in a white phosphorus grenade. As soon as the phosphorus began to burn on the Jerry skins, they abandoned the gun and ran out the door, screaming to the high heavens and Hitler to help them out. Later Sgt. Belcher put it: "Just like shooting ducks in a shooting gallery."

On the beach, Cpl. Randall Rinker, a medic, worked furiously to treat those Rangers who had been wounded during the landing, dragging as many as he could from the beach to the cliff base. Would help ever come? Goranson tried vainly to contact 29th Division troops in front of the Vierville draw, but from his perspective, the invasion in that sector had been a disaster, and he glumly wondered whether his outfit was now all alone in France. The only 29th Division unit Goranson had managed to contact was a single boat team from the 116th Infantry's Company B, which had been separated from its comrades and landed in the Rangers' sector.

Company B, 116th Infantry, 29th Division
U.S. Army Historical Division, interview with S/Sgt. Odell Padgett,
September 1944

The beach was strewn with heavy boulders and could be traversed only with extreme difficulty. . . . Padgett and Lt. Leo Pingenot picked their way over the boulders and got to the cliff [base]. They looked back and saw that most of their men were still immersed in water. Padgett yelled back: "Are you hit?" For that moment, both men believed that their boat team had been destroyed. The men yelled back that they were OK and only seeking cover. . . . By coaxing and encouragement Padgett and Pingenot got them coming forward again, and they crossed the beach with the loss of one killed and three wounded. This group joined a group of Rangers and fought with them all day long, helping them destroy the German positions around the fortified house and in the emplacements at the top of the cliff.

Goranson did not yet realize that his decision to turn east rather than attack Pointe de la Percée would contribute significantly to the Americans' eventual victory on Omaha Beach. With a little help from the 29th Division, only sixty-five Rangers, over half of whom the enemy had felled within minutes of the landing, had reduced a seemingly unassailable enemy resistance nest that at H-Hour had inflicted a large part of the carnage on American troops on Omaha's western sector. Anyone who ever may have doubted the usefulness of the Rangers' rigorous commando-style training needed only to learn of this action to be reassured that it all was worthwhile.

ON THE UPWARD TRAIL

Meanwhile, General Cota was struggling to solve the predicament faced by 29th Division troops pinned at the seawall about 500 yards west of the Les Moulins beach exit. Prior to Cota's appearance, the 116th Infantry's Company C and a few boat teams from Company B had landed there, mercifully spared the fate their Stonewaller comrades had suffered from the enemy's heavy firepower at the Vierville exit—where B and C were originally supposed to have come ashore. Nevertheless, it would not be painless for this group to move inland, for beyond the seawall and paved promenade road paralleling the beach, the Germans had deployed two belts of barbed wire: one on the beach side of the road, and another much more formidable band on the opposite side. These could be traversed only if the GIs could snip them with wire cutters or blow them with bangalore torpedoes—under enemy fire.

Even if the GIs could penetrate the wire barrier, they would have to cross about 150 yards of open ground separating the beach from the bluff. Assuming they survived the enemy fire and minefields, their progression to the foot of the bluffs would yield the even tougher problem of ascending the slope, which on this beach sector was particularly steep and almost entirely devoid of cover. One factor that worked to the Americans' advantage, however, was the intermittent shrouds of smoke still emanating from burning bluff grass, providing concealment for the dangerous tasks the infantrymen would undertake to follow Cota's advice and leave the beach as swiftly as possible.

1st Lt. Jack Shea
Aide-de-camp to Brigadier General Cota, 29th Division, November 1944
Cota had found a section of the seawall that had a low mound of earth some five yards beyond it. He directed the placing of a Browning Automatic Rifle there, after having crawled forward to reconnoiter the firing position. He instructed the operator to fire at any enemy he could see on the bluffs. This was to provide covering fire for the men who would then attempt to get off the beach.

Company C, 116th Infantry, 29th Division
U.S. Army Historical Division, interview with various Company C soldiers, September 1944
To the right of the company was a gap in the seawall. Pvt. Ingram E. Lambert led off by crawling through this gap, then raised up, jumped a strand of barbed wire, crossed a road, and stopped at a barbed wire entanglement on the far side. The wire was of the double-apron type and had to be blown. Pvt. Lambert set a bangalore torpedo, but was killed by machine gun fire before he could set it off. Lt. Stanley H. Schwartz followed and set off the charge. . . . After a first group had made the dash across the road and through the wire, intense artillery and machine gun fire was laid down on this point.

1st Lt. Jack Shea
Aide-de-camp to Brigadier General Cota, 29th Division, November 1944
The first soldier to go through the gap was hit by a heavy burst of machine gun fire and died in a few minutes. "Medico!" he yelled when hit. "Medico! I'm hit! Help me!" He moaned, cried for a few minutes. He finally died after sobbing "Mama" several times.

Interviews with other Company C survivors specify that two members of the outfit were killed by machine gun fire while crossing the promenade road: Privates Ralph Hubbard and George Losey. The first soldier through the gap was in all probability one of these two.

Having blown at least one additional gap in the barbed wire at another location, the bulk of Company C and a single Company B boat team under the command of Lt. Walter Taylor successfully crossed the promenade and entered the grassy flatland between the bluff and the beach. Luckily for the GIs, here they stumbled onto a network of German communication trenches dug into the sandy soil, which allowed their cautious progression toward the foot of the bluffs to be virtually undetectable by the enemy. Lacking a formal attack plan, small groups of men moved forward stealthily on their own initiative. Up until now, the invasion had been a mess. All plans had already been discarded—and who had time to formulate any new ones? If, as General Cota had said, it was imperative to get off the beach immediately, any route would do. Angling to their right, the Stonewallers headed toward the foot of the bluff where a promising course to the top beckoned, seemingly sheltered from enemy fire.

Lt. Col. Robert Ploger
Commander, 121st Engineer Combat Battalion, 29th Division
While I was walking west along the beach looking for some of my engineers, I ran into Gen. Cota. He said, "Ploger, bring me some bangalore torpedoes so we can blow this wire." I went off to look for some. A little later I ran into Gen. Cota again, and this time he asked me to find him some minefield marking tape, which came in long rolls of white cloth. He wanted it to mark lanes through minefields beyond the wire and up the bluff. I immediately went off on another search.

Sgt. John Polyniak
Company C, 116th Infantry, 29th Division
Our boat team made it to the seawall with no casualties. We hardly hesitated when we reached the wall. I was carrying a bangalore torpedo, and I reached over the wall, placed it under the enemy wire, and blew it with my igniter. The team made it through the gap safely, moved ahead until we reached the bluff, and climbed to the top.

Company C, 116th Infantry, 29th Division
U.S. Army Historical Division, interview with various Company C soldiers, March 25, 1945
[Company C] slipped through the wire, down a slight bank and into a series of shallow communication trenches that ran diagonally to the right between the promenade and the foot of the bluffs. [This was about 8:05 A.M.] The men worked

through the maze of communication trenches, successively gained the concealment of some tall grass, and then some clumps of bushes near the foot of the bluff.
[The column] snaked its way along the base of the bluff in a westerly direction,
then started to ascend the bluff to the right. The lead element of this single column
that went up to the flat land that stretched out near Vierville was Lt. [Robert]
Bedell and the men of his Number 1 assault section. During this entire phase of
confusion that preceded and immediately followed the breaching of the wire, the
men noted that soldiers from many other units were mixed in with the C Company
column that made its way through the wire and up the bluff. . . . Bedell followed
a dim trail up and to the right, across the face of the bluff. Little fire was being
directed at the column here, for they were in sharp defilade to direct fire. . . . The
main hindrance to the progress of the column was the fear of anti-personnel
mines. Slowly, [the column] worked forward, the men searching the ground
before placing their feet for each successive step.

Capt. Berthier Hawks
Commander, Company C, 116th Infantry, 29th Division, July 1944
One thing happened then that I don't exactly understand. The grass caught on fire
on the seaward edge of the high ground and gave us concealment from fire from
German positions. We crossed about 125 yards of low ground before coming to
the 90-foot [actually about 115 feet] cliff. We scaled the cliff without too much
difficulty.

1st Lt. Jack Shea
Aide-de-camp to Brigadier General Cota, 29th Division, November 1944
[Our] CP was scattered and forced to displace forward hurriedly when five or six
rounds of extremely well-placed light mortar fire fell in [our] midst. . . . The fragments of these mortar shells killed two enlisted men within three feet of Gen.
Cota, seriously wounded his radio operator, T/3 C. A. Wilson, threw him 20 or 30
feet up the bluff, and [me] 75 feet below.

RANGERS LED THE WAY

U.S. Army Rangers had always thought of themselves as something special, and on D-Day they proved it. At the cliffs on Omaha's western
extremity, Captain Goranson's men had revealed what a small Ranger force
could accomplish despite appalling casualties, treacherous terrain, and
sturdy enemy defenses. Shortly after 8:00 A.M., midway between the
Vierville and Les Moulins draws, the 2nd Rangers' Companies A and B
were about to prove the point again. Like Goranson's outfit, A and B lost
more than half their men crossing the beach, and of the two companies' six

8:30 A.M.: Rangers and Stonewallers Move Up the Bluff

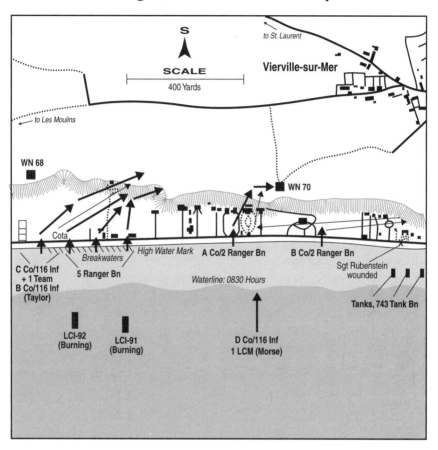

officers, five became casualties only moments after exiting their landing craft. As the stunned survivors reached the shingle, they needed only to glance straight ahead at the bluff crest to see the German *Widerstandsnest* responsible for the carnage still spitting out its destruction. Such a formidable position could hardly be seized by those few fortunate Rangers who had so far escaped German fire. They would nevertheless try.

In Company A, no officers remained unwounded, but Lt. Robert Edlin, a platoon leader, urged his surviving NCOs to press on up the bluff with all available Rangers in tow. Luckily for the Rangers the enemy had inexplicably failed to deploy barbed wire along the promenade road on parts of this sector, which greatly eased the problem of getting the Rangers off the beach. Nevertheless, under a heavy fire, the men had to scramble up the shingle embankment (there was no seawall here) dash across the road, and move past some beach villas before reaching the foot of the bluff. If those tasks were not difficult enough, the Rangers then had to ascend the bluff—which in this location was among Omaha's steepest—and attack an enemy in an obviously advantageous defensive position. Drifting smoke, as well as the buildings and their surrounding stone walls, offered some cover, but the task seemed almost impossible.

Company A, 2nd Ranger Battalion
U.S. Army Historical Division, interview with various Company A Rangers, July 1944

Put in charge of the company, Sgt. [Theodore] James had only one idea as he saw wounded men being killed by fire searching the shingle: get the men off the shingle before mortars and artillery registered in. . . . When Sgt. John White got to the shingle, he could hear Sgt. James and other non-coms yelling to men still on the sand to hurry along. Four or five Rangers were near White, behind the shingle. Four others, who must have gone on their own without waiting for anybody, had crossed the shingle and promenade road and were behind a low [stone] wall just beyond, fronting a villa and wired with a single-apron barbed wire. Sgt. White yelled at the Rangers near him to cross the road, but they couldn't hear him in the noise. He decided that if he went across himself, they would follow—and some did. Two were hit in this crossing. . . . White was under the impression that his party was completely isolated, and that the rest of the company must have been wiped out on the beach. The picture changed suddenly: Sgt. [William] Courtney came down the steep slope just behind the house and told them that he and [Sgt. Garfield] Ray had got up to the top. Ray was still up there, and Courtney offered to show White the best way up.

1st Lt. Robert Edlin
Company A, 2nd Ranger Battalion

It seemed to me that most of the Rangers reacted as they had been trained: non-coms took over quickly; the wounded retained fairly good control of themselves. . . . I remember Sgt. Courtney of Cleveland, Ohio, stood on top of the ridge and called, "Come on! The S.O.B.s are cleaned out!" He was fired on by a machine gun. He knocked it out and then stood up and repeated his words.

Company A, 2nd Ranger Battalion
U.S. Army Historical Division, interview with various Company A Rangers, July 1944

Sgt. White found Ray standing in the open and waving his BAR, with two or three enemy machine gun positions in plain sight at the crest, 20 yards further on. No Germans were visible for the moment. . . . White and Ray started to the left to investigate what looked like another machine gun post and drew no fire until Ray was directly in front of it. The enemy fire was wild. White fired into this position from the front, and Ray, getting behind the position, shot a German as he left his gun and ran out the entrance. . . . Working in twos or threes, the Rangers [who included Courtney, Sgt. Gabby Hart, and PFC Bill Dreher] went along the trench system and cleaned it out. Several enemy were killed and six taken prisoner, for the loss of one Ranger killed and two wounded.

Nearly sixty years after D-Day, Edlin remembered these Rangers as "the bravest men I ever saw."

Meanwhile, the 2nd Rangers' Company B, under Capt. Edgar Arnold, had landed from two LCAs nearly a quarter of a mile to the right of Company A. Unhappily for Arnold, a gap of nearly 300 yards separated his two LCAs as they beached. In this sector, the shingle embankment gave way to a ten-foot masonry seawall sloping at a forty-five-degree angle from the promenade road down to the beach. This sturdy barrier provided sanctuary from enemy small-arms fire, but Arnold had no desire to remain there. First he gathered the survivors of his two scattered boat teams as best he could; then he ordered his men to ascend the sharply inclined seawall, cross the promenade road, and move toward the heavily defended Vierville draw on their right. However, the countless dead Americans on the tidal flat in front of that draw, as well as the noticeable lack of live ones, clearly indicated that the 29th Division had made no progress in capturing that position. The Company B Rangers therefore turned back eastward, to the point where their Company A brethren had just climbed the bluffs.

In the meantime, a lone LCM touched down on the beach behind the Rangers and disgorged a lost boat team from the 116th Infantry's Company D into the surf. This team, led by Lt. Verne Morse, was almost an hour late in reaching the beach because its Royal Navy LCA had swamped several miles offshore, forcing the GIs—minus their mortars and machine guns— to transfer to a passing LCM heading shoreward. When the astonished Morse finally made it to dry land, he could find no trace of his company, nor any 116th outfit for that matter. But he and his thirty men were promptly recruited by a 2nd Rangers headquarters group to assist in the assault up the bluffs. The Stonewallers obliged.

Company B, 2nd Ranger Battalion
U.S. Army Historical Division, interview with various Company B Rangers, July 1944

The plan had been for Company B of the 2nd [Ranger] Battalion to serve as flank and point protection for the 5th Battalion in its march inland through the Vierville exit. Not knowing that Col. Schneider had deliberately turned away from that area because of enemy fire at the exit, Capt. Arnold told his men they would work down along the foot of the bluff to D-1 [Vierville draw] and go through as planned. [Actually, to his left, the 5th Rangers and A Company of the 2nd were going straight up the bluff at that very moment.] Sgt. Maj. [Manning] Rubenstein and a BAR man were sent ahead to reconnoiter the route. . . . Word was sent back to Capt. Arnold that the route was practicable, and the rest of the group came down. . . . Arnold told Rubenstein to contact three DD tanks standing on the tidal flat and ask them to lead the group up to the exit, just beyond the seawall. Rubenstein got a boost over the stone wall south of the road and started to the seawall. A bullet struck his throat and came out his face. . . . Rubenstein lay on the road about an hour before he decided he wasn't dying. Then he yelled to one of the tanks just behind the seawall for a cigarette. The tanker unbuttoned [his hatch] and threw him a pack. After sitting on the road a while, Rubenstein decided to go back to the house where B Company had started and walked down the road. Arnold [had] led his men back by the same path they had used before . . . found where A Company had gone up the bluff, and joined them on the top.

Company D, 116th Infantry, 29th Division
U.S. Army Historical Division, interview with 1st Lt. Verne Morse, March 25, 1945

Morse and his men hurried to the inner edge of the beach as soon as their craft was landed. . . . Morse met a Ranger lieutenant [probably 1st Lt. Gerald Heaney,

HQ Company, 2nd Rangers] who had some of his men gathered about him. He was organizing the Rangers, giving them directions on the way in which they were to ascend the bluff. The Ranger lieutenant saw Morse and asked him where he was going.

"Gruchy," replied Morse. "I'm supposed to be supporting C Company [116th Infantry], and they're going to go there too."

"Well starting now, you're supporting me," said the Ranger officer as he smiled. "We'll both go to Gruchy."

Morse agreed . . .

When the group of Rangers and Morse's heavy weapons men reached the crest of the bluff, they found that two of the five-man covering force that had been sent ahead had been killed by fire that came from their right flank. . . . Morse and the Ranger lieutenant discussed the situation briefly. They finally agreed that they should move toward this opposition to the right. . . . Veering sharply to the right, this combined group moved in on the weapon pits and machine gun nests that had been dug-in and camouflaged on the crest of the bluff. . . . The group worked around these positions, moving in on the Germans from the right rear. Morse said that they had killed a few Germans there "just by shooting," when a Ranger yelled to Morse for a hand grenade. He said that he had just seen one of the enemy scoot into a dugout near the end of one of the communications trenches. Morse gave him a grenade. He threw it in and a German came stumbling out with his hands up.

"Cover me, lieutenant!" yelled the Ranger. "I'll move around behind him and take away his side arms." As the Ranger started to circle the enemy soldier, he suddenly stopped, pointed to Morse's rear. Morse turned quickly to see two [enemy] soldiers standing less than five feet from him, with their hands raised. . . . Morse gingerly disarmed them and herded them back to the east where the remainder of the PWs had been gathered.

About 500 yards farther east, Colonel Schneider's 5th Ranger Battalion had assembled behind the shingle in the cramped alcoves between the fifteen timber and stone breakwaters protruding from the seawall. Thanks to a combination of luck and Schneider's foresight, roughly 450 Rangers from this outfit had landed in a compact mass in an area that was, at least for the moment, relatively secure from enemy fire. Before any action could be taken, however, the Rangers would have to reorient themselves, for they were on an unfamiliar beach sector far from their designated landing point. Should they head straight up the bluff from here? As leaders pondered their next move, the Rangers took in their surroundings.

"The bravest men I ever saw." Eight members of the 5th Rangers were awarded the Distinguished Service Cross for valor on June 6 and 7. From left, they are Lt. Col. Max Schneider, Capt. George Whittington, 1st Lt. Charles "Ace" Parker, 1st Lt. Francis Dawson, Sgt. Willie Moody, T/5 Howard McKissick, PFC Denzil Johnson, and T/3 Alexander Barber (a medic). U.S. ARMY SIGNAL CORPS, NATIONAL ARCHIVES.

Capt. John Raaen
Commander, HQ Company, 5th Ranger Battalion

Not ten yards to my right, a grizzled old engineer sergeant set a heavy machine gun tripod down in a gap in the stone breakwater. He then ambled back to my left. A moment later he returned with a heavy, water-cooled machine gun. A thin lieutenant in a green sweater was carrying boxes of ammunition and cooling water for him. Together they very calmly set up their machine gun in that exposed gap in the breakwater. The sergeant very methodically began to traverse and search the hill to our right where the firefight appeared to be. The lieutenant, and I'll always remember the disdain he showed, turned around, standing on the breakwater with his hands on his hips and spat out something to the effect, "And you call yourselves soldiers!"

A short distance to the Rangers' left, General Cota had just successfully exhorted the 116th Infantry's Company C to leave the beach and press ahead up the bluffs, and he now turned his attention to Schneider's men.

When he encountered the Rangers, Cota must have had the immense satisfaction of knowing that at last something in this chaotic landing had turned in their favor. Schneider's elite Rangers, who would have landed several miles down the coast at Pointe du Hoc had the invasion plan worked out, were precisely what Cota needed at that time and place to revive the invasion, and he promptly employed the same sort of encouragement he had just used on Company C to get them moving.

5th Ranger Battalion
U.S. Army Historical Division, interview with various 5th Rangers,
July 1944
Capt. [Edward] Luther, of E Company was giving orders to his two platoon leaders, when an officer walked along behind his men and started urging them to get up and cross the wall. Looking over his shoulder, Luther put up a warning hand and said: "Hey Bud! Take it easy—don't get excited. This is my outfit—I'll take care of it!" The officer called out, "Well, you've got to get over that wall!" Luther hollered back, "Quit bothering my men; you'll disorganize them. The Colonel's over there if you want to see him, but quit bothering me." Just then the platoon leaders started the men across the wall. A big grin came over the officer's face, and he started walking down the beach again. As he turned, Capt. Luther saw the star on his shoulder for the first time, and took off over the wall hoping that Gen. Cota wouldn't remember him.

The Rangers' immediate predicament was blasting lanes through the enemy barbed wire on the far side of the promenade road beyond the seawall. As other units had already demonstrated, bangalore torpedoes would do the job nicely, and the 5th Rangers swiftly prepared to make use of them. Within ten minutes of Schneider giving the order to move inland, the 5th blew four breaches through the wire on its front, and the Rangers rose up, hopped over the low seawall, dashed across the road, and filed through the narrow gaps to the flat grassland beyond.

Capt. John Raaen
Commander, HQ Company, 5th Ranger Battalion
By now [about 8:15 A.M.], Col. Schneider had given the word to advance. The gap in the wire was to our left . . . and I drifted [that way] with the company, leaving the engineer lieutenant with his hands still on hips looking disgusted. (I heard he was killed a half-hour or so later.) In the process I picked up half of headquarters that had landed in Schneider's boat, among them my second-in-command, Lt. Howard Van Riper and Sgt. [James] Graves. Graves, like the rest of us, was con-

fused by having landed on the wrong beach. He asked me: "Captain, do you know the way to the rendezvous point?"

"Yes, Sergeant, I believe I do."

Graves looked relieved as he said, "Then I will try to follow you."

We found the gap. A line company was passing through. Some Heine was firing from the right along the beach road. There was a shattered stone building, probably a pillbox, just across the road. C Company was moving through now. I tagged on, rushing across the road. There, lying stomach-down and trousers down on a stone slab on the left of a ruined pillbox was little [PFC] Tony Vulle [a member of Company C and a former Golden Gloves boxer from New York City]. Tony, though the smallest man in the battalion, insisted on carrying the heaviest load, the 81mm mortar baseplate. Vulle was now having general repairs done to his gluteus maximus [buttocks] while the battalion moved by. He hadn't crossed the road fast enough.

We trotted down a little path and then the column stopped and hit the dirt. I wasn't too comfortable there in the open, so I shifted my men to the left into a small gully or ditch. The column moved again, stopped, moved. There was heavy brush at the base of the hill and a flagstone path leading through it. Starting up the hill, there were about six stone steps straight up, and then a path leading up and right. The column stopped as I reached the last step. I sat down and looked back toward the beach. Men were still coming through the gap in the wire.

Like the 116th's Company C, the 5th Rangers went up the bluff diagonally to their right, on a northeast-southwest axis. Although on the bluff the Rangers were in large measure immune from enemy fire, their route of ascent took them directly into the dense smoke clouds that had been emanating from grass fires on the bluff since H-Hour. What had a moment ago been a blessing was unexpectedly transformed into a curse, as the smoke accentuated the disorder triggered by the hasty movement up the slope. Strung out in a column of vast length, the Rangers plunged into the billowing, choking haze, hoping that it would all be sorted out at the crest. The smoke, too, was a symbolic divider: Below it was the amphibious war for which the Rangers had trained so long, but which had persisted only a few hours; above it would be an entirely different war—one of hedgerows, labyrinthine sunken lanes, and ancient French villages.

Capt. John Raaen
Commander, HQ Company, 5th Ranger Battalion
The advance had slowed to a crawl. Climb a few steps, stop and wait. Climb some more, stop. . . . By now the smoke was so bad that we found ourselves gasping for

breath, gulping in smoke. I couldn't see ahead through the tears. Some of the men nearby had been asking if they could put on their gas masks, but I had decided to tough it out. Now even I gave in and passed the word for gas masks. My mask wouldn't come out of the carrier; it was jammed somehow. I put my helmet between my knees and then yanked hard. The mask came out, but so did the maps and the D [ration] bars I had secured in the carrier. Fortunately I was able to retrieve everything but the orange that disappeared downhill. I finally got the mask on, put on my helmet and took a deep breath—and almost smothered. . . . I had forgotten to take the covering plug out of the canister. I yanked off the mask, and with that my helmet came off and started to roll down the steep hill. Sgt. Graves grabbed it. Now I was choking in the smoke. I finally got the mask and helmet back on, yanked the tab, breathed in some dank, smokeless air, took three steps and was out of the smoke. I was so furious, I kept the mask on another 50 feet just to spite myself.

We saw our first German, a dead one. He was lying in a little hollow just below the crest. We'd never seen a dead man before. He was sort of greenish-yellow, looked like wax. Of course, he was a booby-trapped dummy! It wasn't till much later that we realized our wax man was really a dead man. In the hollow we paused for breath before crossing a tiny stone wall into the hedgerow country.

THEY HAD NOT YET BEGUN TO FIGHT

About 800 yards eastward, Maj. Sidney Bingham of the 29th Division had already learned the hard lesson that any outfit unlucky enough to have landed directly opposite a nest of German strongpoints stood little chance of accomplishing its D-Day mission. Most of Bingham's 2nd Battalion, 116th Infantry, had touched down near the mouth of the Les Moulins draw, which was covered by intricate enemy defensive works. Here the Germans had constructed sturdy fighting positions both on the bluffs and on the low ground just beyond the shingle. In the invasion's first hour, enemy troops occupying these strongpoints had inflicted dreadful casualties on Bingham's men, leaving most of the survivors paralyzed behind the shingle.

The most notable of the enemy resistance nests on the flatland was the three-story house with its distinctive mansard roof and tower, situated on the eastern side of the draw's mouth only a stone's throw from the shingle. The Germans had erected a machine gun nest in a corner of the ground floor, expertly disguised as a harmless appendage to the house. An obvious target of American naval and tank fire, the house had suffered considerable damage, but the Germans within its ground-floor resistance nest were evidently unhurt and still shooting with abandon at the prostrate Americans only a few dozen yards away.

If the GIs were to get off the beach, Bingham concluded that seizing the house would be a first step. He collected as many willing and able-bodied men as he could find and organized a desperate frontal attack over the shingle.

Maj. Sidney Bingham
Commander, 2nd Battalion, 116th Infantry, 29th Division
An impression that overcame me at this juncture was one of complete futility. Here I was, the battalion commander, unable for the most part to influence the situation or do what I knew had to be done. Another impression that I had, as I am sure others did as well, was the profound shock of seeing dead and wounded comrades in substantial numbers—and being unable to help in any way.

Capt. Richard Bush
S-2, 111th Field Artillery Battalion, 29th Division, September 1944
[The men] were beat up and shocked. Many of them had forgotten that they had firearms to use. Others who had lost their arms didn't seem to see that there were weapons lying all around and that it was their duty to pick them up.

2nd Battalion, 116th Infantry, 29th Division
U.S. Army Historical Division, interview with Maj. Sidney Bingham,
June 1944
At the patch of shingle, Bingham found cover behind the [seawall]. Here he found Lt. Theodore Lamb's section of F Company. The lieutenant was wounded and the section was doing nothing. Some of Bingham's headquarters group had come up. High explosive shells were falling all around; machine gun and rifle fire were catching his men. The major got as many headquarters and F Company men "as I could jar loose," and moved toward a three-story house. He [found] the executive officer of F Company—Lt. [Ernest] Wise (killed shortly afterward). They went toward the house. With the aid of Maj. [Fred] McManaway [Bingham's executive officer] of Roanoke, Virginia, the major got about 50 men across the wire and seawall toward the three-story house. . . .

[Bingham] discovered that no one had weapons that would function. . . . He got men into dugouts and [they] began to clean weapons. He went to the three-story house and stationed men in the upper stories. They had difficulty in getting up since the stairs had been destroyed. They picked out targets, but the rifles wouldn't fire. This was about 0800. He went back from the house to a dugout to

[try] the radios. However, every time the aerial went up, it drew fire. He got ten men, including Sgt. Beverly, HQ Company, Sgts. [Sager] Ream and [Edward] Ward, both of F Company. They went east of the big house through wire, which had to be cut with wire cutters, to the top of the east side of the Les Moulins exit. Machine gun fire killed Ward. [Bingham] sent men around the machine gun, but their guns still wouldn't shoot, so they came back to the big house.

111th Field Artillery Battalion, 29th Division
U.S. Army Historical Division, interview with Capt. Richard Bush, September 1944
Capt. Richard Bush, artillery S-2 who was aiding battery recon officers in seeking gun positions, was with Bingham at this time. Bingham's radio was out. He tried to use Bush's, but it wouldn't work. Bingham then started doing personal work with small groups of riflemen. . . . He got them cleaning their weapons, and if they were empty-handed, he showed them where they could pick up arms.

Col. Paul Thompson, commander of the 6th Engineer Special Brigade, had landed in this sector at about 7:40 A.M., expecting to supervise all the diverse construction tasks that Neptune plans had assigned to him. However, instead of preparing the beach for vehicular movement and the off-loading of supplies, Thompson found himself involved in Bingham's attack on the Les Moulins draw.

Col. Paul Thompson
Commander, 6th Special Engineer Brigade, Distinguished Service Cross Citation, June 1944
The attack on a vital beach exit (D-3) was being held up by heavy enemy machine gun fire. Upon discovering the situation and ascertaining that the assault units were pinned to the beach and were not pressing the attack, Col. Thompson called for volunteers to assist in wiping out the machine guns. Several infantrymen volunteered. With complete disregard for his own safety, Col. Thompson, while under heavy enemy fire, blew a gap in the wire entanglements. He then fearlessly led his party through the gap and was rushing to assault the enemy machine guns when he was seriously wounded by enemy fire from another emplacement.

Maj. Sidney Bingham
Commander, 2nd Battalion, 116th Infantry, 29th Division
The ground floor of this [three-story] house had a sort of loading dock arrangement that was fortified, something like a pillbox. I crawled up into that place

under the porch, and here in the sand was Col. Paul Thompson, bleeding like a
stuck pig. In fact, he was in deep shock. I thought he was a goner: he had a hole in
his neck and another hole in his shoulder. My motor officer, Jim Bagley—we
called him "Bucket Head" because it was alleged he could wear the helmet without a liner—was acting as a Florence Nightingale to Thompson. When I got there
Bagley had a handful of blood and sand and sulfa tablets. He was [putting] them
in Thompson's mouth, and Thompson chewed up the sand and blood and tablets.
Bagley almost strangled him by putting a first-aid pack around Thompson's
neck. . . . He indicated that he had another wound, a hole in the shoulder, and
pointed to the first-aid pack on Bagley's belt. Bagley said, "To hell with you, you
son-of-a-bitch, I might need it later on today for myself."

Col. Paul Thompson
Commander, 6th Engineer Special Brigade
A couple of weeks later, General Bradley came through the hospital, and he said:
"Thompson, I want to know just what happened." So I described it as best I could,
and then I ended by saying, "So you see, General, there I was with all my responsibilities going out there and doing the job of a sergeant." Instead of being indignant, General Bradley said to me, "Well, Thompson, thank the Lord there were
several colonels doing the jobs of sergeants that day."

If any segment of the enemy's coastal defenses could be described as
vulnerable, it was the 1,200-yard tract of bluff between the Les Moulins
and St. Laurent draws. The crest top featured trenches and *Schützenlöcher*
(foxholes), but few permanent fighting positions fortified with concrete.
From the American perspective, the midpoint of the bluff line here was the
boundary between the 1st Division's 16th Infantry and the 29th Division's
116th Infantry, but the tendency of assault units to land far eastward of
their designated landing points in the invasion's opening phase caused this
entire sector to become *de facto* 116th territory. That regiment's 3rd Battalion had landed here at 7:30 A.M., and thanks to the paucity of enemy
emplacements to its immediate front, it had crossed the beach and reached
the line of shingle relatively intact. But like so many other troops on D-
Day, the Stonewallers were thoroughly bewildered: This was definitely not
their assigned beach sector—and where was the 2nd Battalion, through
which the 3rd was supposed to pass? Enemy mortar and artillery shells
were whizzing over the crest and bursting on the beach with increasing frequency, and it didn't take the troops long to reach the conclusion that the
most sensible thing to do was to ascend the bluff directly, leaving the congested and treacherous beach behind.

"I was doing the job of a sergeant." Col. Paul Thompson, commander of the 6th Engineer Special Brigade, was badly wounded at the mouth of the Les Moulins draw. (Photo taken later in 1944 after Thompson had been promoted to brigadier general). U.S. ARMY SIGNAL CORPS, NATIONAL ARCHIVES.

Company L, 116th Infantry, 29th Division
U.S. Army Historical Division, interview with various Company L soldiers, September 20, 1944

On getting to the [shingle], they found it already clogged with infantry. They were men from G Company [116th]. They had been there for some time and seemed to be in good condition. Lt. Donald Anderson of L Company came up and asked: "Who in hell are you?" They replied that they were from the 2nd Battalion [116th]. He then turned to [Sgt. Joseph] Daya and said, "Get the team on its way. We sure as hell are not staying here. This beach has too many people." There was a single apron of wire ahead of the company. At Anderson's order, Daya moved on and started cutting it, lying on his back as he did so. A man from the 2nd Battalion came in on the right of him and tried to do likewise. But before he could find a low spot and partial cover, his clothing got hung in the wire, and the enemy machine guns cut him apart. Daya had found partial cover among some boulders and completed his work. Anderson then led the team right on through the gap and up the hill. Near the crest he came to a dip, which was brush-covered and partially defiladed to bullet fire. They stopped there for a few moments to gather themselves before going on. The [enemy] artillery found them there, and two men were wounded. Daya yelled, "Get the hell out of here!" They moved on up.

Capt. Carroll Smith
S-3, 3rd Battalion, 116th Infantry, 29th Division

[I] started up the bluff with a boat team from L Company to make a brief reconnaissance and see what could be done toward coordinating the efforts of the teams in the attack on St. Laurent. However, as we came up the shelf about halfway up the bluff, a gun suddenly fired from the left so close that the blast was deafening. After careful examination, the muzzle of what appeared to be an 88 was discovered protruding from a small niche in the bluff, so mounted that it could fire only straight up the beach to the west. The amazing thing about this was the excellent camouflage. A whole boat team of approximately 30 men had just crawled up this bluff only about 50 yards to the right of this emplacement and didn't see it. Looking in the direction of fire, it was obvious this gunner had waited for a remunerative target, as an LCI which was just touching down [probably LCI-92] burst into flames on the forward deck. . . . Realizing that something had to be done about this gun quick, the S-2 sergeant, who was an exiled German of the Jewish faith and particularly anxious to defeat the Nazis, was sent back to direct the fire of an immobilized tank of the 743rd Tank Battalion on the gun emplacement. The sergeant had hardly uttered the words "Yes, Sir," and raised up enough to turn around, when he was shot by a burst of machine gun fire apparently coming from the embrasure of the emplacement. . . . [I] crawled back down the bluff to the tank, got the attention of the crew by pounding on the turret with a rifle butt, and directed a dozen tank rounds at the emplacement. However, the 75mm tank fire made no impression on the concrete, and realizing it had been discovered, the enemy crew continued to fire up the beach at a rapid rate. Finally . . . the position was neutralized by placing demolition charges around the embrasure and blasting it in. It was later discovered that the only entrance to this position was through a tunnel over 200 yards to the rear.

PFC Norman Grossman
Company L, 116th Infantry, 29th Division

The [bluff] was booby-trapped with anti-personnel mines. The fellows at the top yelled a warning to us as we approached. We went up the hill single file, for we knew if the man in front of us didn't get blown up, we wouldn't either. I didn't see anyone hit a mine, but I heard that one of my best friends hit one as he neared the top and was blown all the way down to the bottom of the hill. . . . While we were

8:30 A.M.: 3rd Battalion, 116th Infantry, Moves Inland

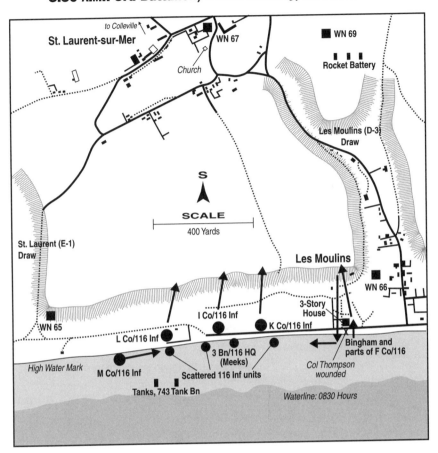

pinned down here, the Jerries started to shell the beach with rockets. What an eerie sound! I thanked God I was off the beach.

Sgt. Felix Branham
Company K, 116th Infantry, 29th Division

I carried an M-1 rifle—and I never fired it until after I got up the bluff. I didn't know what to fire at. I couldn't see any Germans. They were too well hidden. But they were firing at us!

Lt. Col. Lawrence Eugene Meeks
Commander, 3rd Battalion, 116th Infantry, 29th Division

[My command group] stayed at the [shingle] until late afternoon, when conditions improved somewhat. We began moving down the beach, getting the company commanders together and organizing.

Company I, 116th Infantry, 29th Division
U.S. Army Historical Division, interview with various Company I soldiers, September 1944

Sgt. Vincent Corsini found on landing that his group was badly mixed with Company G [116th]. G made no attempt to move off the beach, but the 1st Sergeant of Company K was seen moving up and down the beach trying to get men off the beach. Capt. William Pingley [CO Company K] was kneeling on the beach, smoking his pipe and looking to the front. . . . The third section was the first [Company I boat team] to leave the beach. As G Company had not moved forward or breached the wire, it was necessary for this group to do it. The [shingle] varied in height from two to five feet along this portion of the beach, but the wire on the top consisted only of two strands. T/Sgt. Clyde Sale cut this wire with cutters and in less than ten minutes from the time the high water mark was reached the men were leading out. Sgt. Mabrom Hudnell and a scout, PFC Finley Whitlock, led the column single file through a minefield and up the hill.

Altogether the enemy had put incalculable labor, time, and resources into the Atlantic Wall, and the Americans had taken only two hours to get through it. True, the invasion plan was in tatters, unimaginable casualties had been suffered, the beach exits were not in American hands, and much more intense fighting lay ahead. But unless German reinforcements arrived soon to counterattack and cordon off the American penetrations of the bluffs, the enemy's coastal strongpoints would be surrounded and wiped out one after another.

CHAPTER 11

Everyone
an Infantryman

THE GRAVENESS OF THE HOUR

By 9:00 A.M., the Americans were barely winning the battle of Omaha Beach, but not even their most perceptive generals would appreciate that truth until the afternoon. This pronounced lag between reality and perception persisted all day. By noon, it had reached such critical proportions that General Bradley recalled in his autobiography, "I reluctantly contemplated the diversion of Omaha follow-up forces to Utah and the British beaches." Bradley, as well as Generals Gerow and Huebner, was completely ignorant of the decidedly positive news that by 9:00, the GIs had penetrated the German coastal defenses in at least seven places and had neutralized five of the enemy's twelve coastal strongpoints.

That there was much to be negative about was obvious to anyone within eyesight of Omaha Beach throughout D-Day. Starting shortly after H-Hour and continuing for several hours thereafter, the alarming messages received at V Corps headquarters aboard *Ancon* would have shaken the resolve of even the most steely general. Amid the cacophony of bad news, Gerow did not receive even a scrap of positive intelligence until shortly before 11:00 A.M., when Colonel Talley radioed from his DUKW: "Men advancing up slope behind Easy Red. Men believed ours on skyline Easy Fox. House at Exit E-3 silent. Destroyer shelling Les Moulins. Things look better." Gerow could not have known then that 16th Infantry GIs, led by

Spalding's Company E boat team, had in fact first ascended the slope behind Easy Red almost four hours previously, and a steady stream of 1st Division men had been climbing it and trudging inland ever since.

Anonymous V Corps staff officer
Letter to U.S. Army Historian Gordon Harrison, January 7, 1948

Early reports received by Gen. Gerow on the command ship *Ancon* were meager and unsatisfactory. At approximately 10:00 A.M., Gen. [William] Kean, Chief of Staff of the First Army, and Gen. [Truman] Thorson, G-3 of the First Army, arrived from the USS *Augusta*, command ship of Gen. Bradley, to inquire concerning the situation. As information was meager, these two officers, accompanied by Col. [Henry] Matchett [V Corps Chief of Staff] departed for the beach in order to secure first-hand information.

Lt. Col. Robert Pratt
Assistant G-3, V Corps

Col. Talley, who had directed the staff effort during the planning, had a force of three radio-equipped DUKWs from which he was to report activities on the beach. The fragmentary messages we got from him told only of confusion and lack of advance. It became so bad that Gerow finally dispatched the Chief of Staff, Col. Matchett, in an LCT to see what was going on. Henry came back to the *Ancon* after several hours, white and shaken by what he had seen. He told a story of confusion, heroism, and valor, of men [taking action] because they had to—and of a plan that the elements, the enemy, and fate had pushed astray.

The invasion plan had been based on several assumptions that had failed to materialize: that the Army Air Force would pummel the beaches; the German defenders were few and second-rate; enemy beach obstacles would be cleared; landing waves would land on time and on target; and DD tanks would surprise and overwhelm enemy defenses. Omaha Beach landing diagrams starkly display the invasion planners' belief that those assumptions would be valid. One entry in the 16th Infantry's plan called for eight LCTs to convey six Piper Cub aircraft, sixty-seven jeeps, and one command car to Fox Green beach at H+220 (10:10 A.M.).

Piper Cubs, jeeps, and command cars would not be useful items on Omaha Beach for some time to come.

Maj. Gen. Clarence Huebner
Commanding General, 1st Division

As far as the 116th and 16th and Rangers were concerned, I had no control.

Maj. Carl Plitt
S-3, 16th Infantry, 1st Division, July 1944

The most outstanding criticism of all may be directed toward the tactical phase. The loading and landing tables were completed without a complete knowledge of the tactical situation. . . . The build-up was entirely too fast and once started into shore, the Navy had no means of controlling or turning back craft from the beach. Needless to say this caused too many troops and vehicles to be brought to shore during a critical stage prior to the time the beach was clear of fire. . . . Summing it all up, the plan for Operation Neptune was a good one, but it didn't work! It was the individual courage and heroism of the American soldier that won the [battle] on 6 June 1944.

Lt. Col. Thornton Mullins
Commander, 111th Field Artillery Battalion, 29th Division, 0900 hours, June 6, 1944

To hell with our artillery mission. We've got to be infantrymen now! [Mullins's resolution cost him his life. Leading a tank against an enemy machine gun nest near Les Moulins, he was wounded in the abdomen by a sniper's bullet and died that afternoon.]

THE LEGION OF LOST SOULS

In the U.S. Army in World War II, the most steadfast supporter of the frontline soldier was artillery. On Omaha Beach, however, he would have to live without it. The confident invasion plan assumed that two or three hours after the initial assault wave had landed, the GIs would have the beach secured and be pushing inland. Planners speculated that the infantrymen would need their artillery when the Germans launched their customarily prompt counterattacks, and the landing schedule therefore called for two field artillery battalions, the 7th (of the 1st Division) and the 111th (of the 29th Division), to land at about 8:15 A.M., less than two hours after H-Hour. Each battalion fielded a complement of twelve 105-millimeter howitzers, which would be transported to the beach by DUKW amphibious trucks launched from LSTs seven miles offshore. In the heavy seas off Omaha on D-Day, this was an excessively lengthy journey for the overloaded DUKWs, each of which was burdened by the weight of its howitzer, fourteen crewmen, fifty shells, dozens of sandbags, and much other equipment.

The DUKWs had trouble staying afloat from the moment they drove into the sea through the LSTs' open bow doors. The artillerymen had anticipated this problem and knew its cause. When they witnessed the first

"I can still hear those men calling for help over the noise." A U.S. Army amphibious truck, the legendary DUKW, is pictured. Not a single one of the 13 DUKWs of the 29th Division's 111th Field Artillery Battalion made it to the beach. U.S. NAVY, NATIONAL ARCHIVES.

DUKW sink on the journey to the beach, they immediately heaved the sandbags overboard. When that action did not help, almost everything else in the vessel, including ammunition, followed the sandbags into the rolling sea. Soon nothing but the howitzers and their crews remained. But even that drastic weight reduction for the most part did not work. The outcome was a disaster: Not a single DUKW of the 111th Field Artillery made it ashore, and only six of the 7th Field Artillery did so.

Cpl. Clarence Hintze
Battalion Clerk, HQ Battery, 111th Field Artillery Battalion, 29th Division
The CP/Fire Direction DUKW [which did not carry a howitzer] was scheduled to land at H+105 [8:15 A.M.]. Dawn was just breaking as our vehicle, which was the last loaded and first unloaded, slowly backed down the ramp [of LST-310]. I was seated on the back seat, and when the dual rear wheels slid off the ramp, the water rose over the end of the seat before the stern finally raised it above the water. We all knew the water conditions and that the 111th's DUKWs were overloaded, but

we in the CP vehicle were OK as we moved toward our rendezvous area. It was soon apparent that we were slowly sinking due to malfunctioning pumps. A British boat, similar to our PT boats, leading a wave of landing craft to its assigned beach, stopped and picked us up before our DUKW sank.

M/Sgt. John Hickman
121st Engineer Combat Battalion, 29th Division
In the hold of the LST I was on were the DUKWs of the 111th Field Artillery. As each one left, and as they were lining up [in the water] to go ashore, I saw them sink. I can still hear those men calling for help over the noise.

The personnel of several other outfits scheduled to land within the invasion's first two hours discovered with dismay that the specialized heavy weapons they were trained to operate would be extraordinarily difficult to deploy on the beach due to the enemy's intense fire. The 81st Chemical Mortar Battalion, an outfit the army originally had envisioned as a deliverer of gas shells but which now functioned for the most part as a conventional heavy mortar unit, was scheduled to land almost in its entirety by 7:30 A.M. But even under peaceful conditions, the manhandling of the mortars, each of which weighed 330 pounds, was grueling work. The only way to move them was to break them down into three parts and fasten them to simple two-wheeled handcarts, which the men would haul like beasts of burden off the landing craft and across the beach. The 81st's GIs needed only one close-up glimpse of the beach to know that it could not be done.

81st Chemical Mortar Battalion
Battalion History, 1945
Company A, in support of 2nd Battalion, 16th Infantry, landed at Easy Red Beach. Several mortars and carts were carried away by the heavy seas. After a hard struggle, the equipment was rescued, and the company remained on the beach the entire morning, subjected to devastating machine gun fire which made it impossible to move. The company commander, Capt. [Thomas] Moundres, was severely wounded while making his way through the surf to the beach. [He died later that day.] . . . The wave containing C Company's [eight] LCVPs bore in toward [Fox Green] beach on schedule, but since the infantry was still pinned down within a few yards of the water, the control boat moved them back to sea. [They did not land until 3:00 P.M.] . . . At 0720 D Company's craft beached on Easy Green in support of the 3rd Battalion, 116th Infantry, under an incessant hail of machine gun, mortar, and artillery fire. Of necessity the boat teams were landed in water up

to their waists, and the precaution that had been taken to attach inflated life belts to the carts proved a wise one. Machine gun bullets ripped into the belts on several of the carts, however, deflating them and causing the carts to sink.

Three antiaircraft artillery (AAA) battalions found themselves in the same predicament. According to the Neptune plan, at 7:00 A.M.—only thirty minutes after the initial assault troops had taken their first steps in France—the 397th AAA Battalion would land from eighteen LCVPs, after which the unfortunate members of the unit would face the backbreaking task of manhandling thirty-six heavy machine guns from their landing craft to the high-water line. Here they would set up their weapons at intervals of 150 yards, spread over a front of more than three miles, and wait for the Luftwaffe. But reality did not bear the slightest resemblance to the plan.

397th Antiaircraft Artillery Battalion
D-Day After-Action Report, June 14, 1944
At 0645 we saw the beach clearly and headed toward that point on its outline which each man had memorized. Few of us realized that the enemy still held complete control of the high ground immediately south of the beach because we were intent on recognizing our landing terrain features. On the beach hugging the ground behind the first protecting rise of ground of sand was the assault wave of infantry intently watching us approach. We learned why they were watching shortly after this, for between 0700 and 0715 the battalion landed. As the ramps would drop and the men would start pouring out, an 88 shell, a mortar shell, or crossfire from machine guns would burst at the open ramp. The toll of life was appalling, men bleeding and drowning everywhere. The enemy would force a group of us down prone in the water and then would spray the cluster with machine guns. Men blown out of LCVPs by artillery fire and still in confusion as they splashed and flailed the water would be showered with the deadly fire of those machine guns.

Starting at about 8:30 A.M., two more AAA battalions, the 197th and 467th, were conveyed to the beach in eighteen LCTs, one battalion attached to the 16th Infantry, the other to the 116th. The 197th and 467th operated heavy machine guns and small-caliber antiaircraft guns mounted on armored half-tracks, and if the invasion went smoothly, these vehicles would drive inland through the beach exits as the gunners prepared to execute the job for which they had trained so long and hard. Had the enemy air force put in an appearance, the concentration of American antiaircraft fire would have been deadly, but two hours into the landings the least of Gerow's worries was the Luftwaffe.

197th Antiaircraft Artillery Battalion
Battalion History, 1945

[The 197th] learned that half-in, half-out of the water were hundreds of obstacles—pilings, hedgehogs, tetrahedra, most of them mined. They learned that the passages through these obstacles were narrow and too often clogged with wrecked landing craft. They learned that they must debark with all their vehicles in deep water—that many of their vehicles drowned out. They learned that maybe you didn't make it in your first try, and so you tried again. And they learned that if an 88 round landed in your LCT, you didn't make it at all. They learned that if you reached the beach, you were pinned down at the water's edge. . . . All this they learned at a price: 1 officer, 4 enlisted men killed; 1 officer, 11 enlisted men seriously wounded; 14 halftracks, 3 jeeps, 1 trailer lost.

In the event German tanks counterattacked the American beachhead on D-Day or shortly thereafter, General Huebner considered it vital to land specialized antitank units soon after H-Hour. In the first two days of its July 1943 invasion of Sicily, the Fighting First had experienced some harrowing moments fighting Axis tanks, and Huebner aimed to be better prepared this time. The 16th and 116th Infantry each had a company dedicated to this type of warfare, each of which contained 165 men and nine 57-millimeter guns, and the plan called for each company to land on its respective sector at around 8:30 A.M. from two LCTs. However, weighty guns towed by trucks were utterly useless weapons on Omaha Beach that morning, for the enemy's heavy firepower made it impossible for their drivers to drag the guns off their landing craft. Without their cherished weapons, the unhappy members of the antitank outfits would instead have to fight as riflemen.

Lt. Forest Ferguson of the 116th's Antitank Company was one of those men. For natives of Florida who were football devotees, Forest Ferguson was a celebrated name. As an All-American receiver on the University of Florida football team from 1939 to 1941, "Fergie" Ferguson's prowess on the gridiron outshone anyone who had previously caught footballs for the Gators. But now Ferguson was a member of a different team, the Stonewall Brigade, and when he scrambled out of his landing craft into the surf, he saw immediately that many of his comrades were dead. He crossed the beach to find various 116th units scattered behind the shingle.

Waiting for the Luftwaffe. Members of an antiaircraft artillery (AAA) battalion aboard U.S. Navy landing craft prior to D-Day. Several heavy machine guns mounted on armored half-tracks are visible. U.S. ARMY SIGNAL CORPS, NATIONAL ARCHIVES.

2nd Lt. Forest Ferguson
Antitank Company, 116th Infantry, 29th Division, Distinguished Service Cross Citation, June 1944

Lt. Ferguson reached the shore to find the assault infantry pinned down in front of skillfully placed obstacles, receiving a withering fire with many casualties being inflicted. With utter disregard for his personal safety, Lt. Ferguson, with three men he had encouraged to assist him, bravely moved forward under fire with a bangalore torpedo to the obstacles holding up large numbers of infantry. This involved a great risk of life. He exploded the torpedo with a hand grenade. It blew a gap in the obstacles. He gallantly rose from his position, shouting, "Let's go, men!" By this heroic example, he inspired and heartened those about him to charge through the opening. This touched off the slowed-down attack with an impetus that enabled the troops to carry the enemy-held positions behind the obstacles. [Later] Lt. Ferguson received a head wound.

Capt. Joseph Shelley
Medical officer, Company B, 104th Medical Battalion, 29th Division
I met Lt. Forest Ferguson aboard the *Empire Javelin* on June 5. He was very unhappy about being transferred from an assault platoon of the 116th Infantry in the first wave to a supporting unit in a later wave. I remember telling him that it might save his life. We played cribbage all night. No one could sleep. I found out after the war that he was shot in the head on D-Day and spent ten years in a Veterans Administration hospital, finally dying in 1954 from complications of his wound. I never saw him again.

The Omaha landing plan relied on U.S. Army tanks to help win the battle of the beach. The V Corps planning staff had hoped that the 112 Shermans scheduled to land within minutes of H-Hour would overawe and demoralize the enemy's coastal defenders, causing them to offer feeble resistance, flee, or surrender. That hope was swiftly shattered: Many tanks never made it to the beach; many more that did were promptly knocked out by enemy antitank guns sited in nearly invisible firing positions. With no beach exit yet open, this deplorable state of affairs showed no sign of improvement. The tankers must have been among the first soldiers to grasp the truth of Cota's and Taylor's warnings that those who wished to live must leave the beach immediately, and when they observed the infantry moving inland up the steep bluffs, they surely felt a pang of envy that their tanks could not follow. Until the infantry opened the draws, the tankers could do little except drive up and down the beach, keeping a sharp lookout for well-camouflaged German strongpoints and blasting away at those they could see. But the enemy would also make every effort to blast them, and on an open beach the tanks were at a severe disadvantage because there was no place to hide—a problem that would worsen as the rising tide narrowed the width of the beach to only a few yards. This type of warfare was certainly not what the tankers had expected when they joined the army's celebrated armored forces. Maybe the infantry wouldn't have been so bad after all.

743rd Tank Battalion
Unit History, "Move Out, Verify," 1945
In the D-Day plan, Lt. Col. [John] Upham [CO, 743rd] was to follow his assault tanks in at H+90 [8:00 A.M.]. But from H-20 [6:10 A.M.] Col. Upham's calm, crisp voice was directing operations of his battalion by radio from an LCT a few hundred yards offshore. . . . He saw his men hurt, some of their tanks knocked out,

destroyed. He watched while his tanks assembled and then found themselves bot-tlenecked in a bad situation on the beach. . . . When the LCT swung into the beach at last, the Colonel was first over the side. He waded ashore in the face of enemy fire. His one concern was to get to his tanks. He reached the first of these vehicles and personally guided them across the fire-swept beach. . . . Sometime during that hectic morning, a German sniper took careful aim upon the slim figure of an American tank colonel walking in the water on the beach beside his tanks. The sniper squeezed off his shot and probably never knew he had hit his target. The slug shattered the Colonel's right shoulder, but he refused medical attention, kept on with his work. . . . His clothes were wet, his one arm dangled uselessly, but he remained cool and calm as his men always knew him. "You couldn't get the Colonel excited—not even then," Cpl. [William] Beckett said of that moment. [Upham was evacuated about 2:00 P.M.]

Lt. Col. Robert Skaggs
Commander, 741st Tank Battalion, approximately 0900 hours,
June 6, 1944
The government paid five billion dollars for this hour. Get the hell in there and start fighting!

Capt. William King
S-3, 741st Tank Battalion, letter to U.S. Army Historian, August 11, 1945
At about 10:00 A.M., I was despatched by Col. George Taylor, CO of the 16th Infantry, to round up every available tank that could move and launch an assault on Exit E-3. When I reached the last tank on the beach that belonged to my outfit, I found the tank and crew intact with the exception of the tank commander [S/Sgt. Walter Skiba], who had been hit by a piece of shrapnel. So I took command of the tank, backed away from the shingle and started for the E-3 exit myself. So much wreckage was littering the beach, both human and matériel, that it was necessary for the driver to weave in and out of the debris. After proceeding down the beach toward E-3 for about 200 yards, we took a rather wide sweep to the left, or toward the water's edge, to avoid a cluster of vehicles and wounded men. A teller mine, probably washed off a beach obstacle, ended the trip. The mine blew the center bogie assembly off and broke the track in two.

WE'RE GOING IN
To the generals on the distant command ships who were receiving a suc-cession of incomplete and gloomy radio messages from the beach, there was only one sensible course of action: go ashore and clarify the situation

personally. Only then could useful remedial measures be evaluated and orders issued to put them into effect—if it was not already too late.

Brig. Gen. Willard Wyman, second-in-command of the 1st Division, was accustomed to war's chaos. In the spring of 1942, serving as one of Gen. "Vinegar Joe" Stilwell's staff officers, he had taken part in heavy fighting alongside Chinese troops against the onrushing Japanese invaders of Burma. The enemy had speedily broken the front wide open, and Stilwell, Wyman, and a small command group barely escaped with their lives, retreating 400 miles through immense jungles and mountain ranges to refuge in India. If he had survived that close call in Burma, Wyman could survive Omaha Beach.

Boarding a Coast Guard LCVP from *Samuel Chase* early on D-Day, Wyman headed shoreward with a small command party. Don Whitehead, a well-known Associated Press reporter, accompanied the group. Wyman did not plan on setting up a command post on the beach too early; if the invasion was working, Colonel Taylor of the 16th should have everything under control. About 8:00 A.M. Wyman instructed the coxswain to pull up beside PC-553, the Easy Red control vessel that was anchored about one and a half miles offshore. This ship had been observing the landings and monitoring radio transmissions since H-Hour, and it took Wyman only a few minutes to discern the unadulterated story of the invasion so far. He returned to the LCVP and immediately declared, "We're going in!"

Wyman's group arrived on the beach at 8:39 A.M. between the St. Laurent and Colleville draws—and was shelled within moments of its arrival at the shingle. Luckily Wyman had a functional radio, and his first message to Huebner aboard *Ancon* at 9:00 was the laconic: "Beach slow." This was probably the least pessimistic report Huebner had received on D-Day so far.

Don Whitehead
Reporter, Associated Press, 1947

I lay on the beach wanting to burrow into the gravel. And I thought: "This time we have failed! God, we have failed! Nothing has moved from this beach and soon, over that bluff, will come the Germans. They'll come swarming down on us. . . ."

"We've got to get these men off the beach," Wyman said. "This is murder!" Wyman studied the situation for a few minutes—and then with absolute disregard for his own life and safety, he stood up to expose himself to the enemy's fire. Calmly, he began moving lost units to their proper positions, organizing leadership for leaderless troops. He began to bring order out of confusion and to give direction to this vast collection of inert manpower waiting only to be told what to do, where to go.

"This time we have failed! God, we have failed!" First Division troops and engineers take cover behind the shingle embankment near the E-1 draw at about 9:00 A.M. on D-Day. COURTESY CORNELIUS RYAN COLLECTION, OHIO UNIVERSITY.

The general speedily deduced that the invasion had broken down. To Wyman, the essential problem was plain: Even if some small groups had already penetrated the bluffs, the draws must be opened as soon as possible, or the ever-increasing congestion on the beach would lead to disaster. On the 16th Infantry's sector alone, he could tally more than 100 bulldozers, tractors, half-tracks, DUKWs, and tanks trapped on the beach like caged animals. As an unyielding enemy still held the draws, they had no place to go—and their cage was shrinking dramatically as the tide rose. In large measure, the German fire was too hot for their drivers to carry out their assigned work. Since his 9:00 message to *Ancon*, Wyman had gained a more thorough perception of the problem, and his next communication at 9:50 was more to the point: "The beach has too many vehicles. Send combat troops."

Wyman transmitted his next message to Huebner at 10:10: "Reinforce 2nd Battalion, 16th Infantry at once." According to the invasion scheme, the 2nd Battalion's foremost mission was to seize the St. Laurent draw, after which 1st Division engineers would clear it so that vehicles could start moving inland. The abundant vehicles trapped on the beach were sufficient proof for Wyman that this task had not yet been fulfilled, nor could he observe any troops with an intention of fulfilling it. But thanks to Wyman and Huebner, those troops would appear before long.

But where was the 2nd Battalion? The grisly scenes that greeted Wyman on the beach hinted at its fate, and the hundreds of dazed men pinned behind the shingle for hundreds of yards eastward no doubt yielded further evidence. Since, as Whitehead would report, Wyman moved constantly, appraising the situation and coaxing GIs to move ahead, he was certainly aware that a 2nd Battalion boat team from Company E under Spalding, as well as most of Company G under Dawson, had already advanced up the bluffs midway between the St. Laurent and Colleville exits and were moving inland. That was assuredly good news. But if the Germans in the St. Laurent draw were not wiped out soon, the slaughter that Wyman observed on the beach when he landed could only worsen.

Wyman probably did not realize that Spalding's group had already materially contributed to rectifying the lamentable state of affairs. Down to twenty-one men after reaching the top of the bluff, the team turned right, or west, cautiously following an enemy trench system parallel to the crest, which conveniently led the troops directly to one of the hated strongpoints overlooking the St. Laurent draw.

2nd Lt. John Spalding
Company E, 16th Infantry, 1st Division, February 9, 1945
We were now in hedgerow and orchard country. . . . We now found a construction shack near the strongpoint overlooking the E-1 draw. . . . Sgt. Kenneth Peterson fired his bazooka into the [shack], but no one came out. We were about to go on when I spied a piece of stovepipe about 70 yards away sticking out of the ground. I formed my section in a semi-circular defensive position. We were now getting small arms fire again. Sgt. Streczyk and I now went forward to investigate. We discovered an underground dugout. There was an 81mm mortar, a position for a 75mm [gun], and construction for a pillbox. All this overlooked the E-1 draw. The dugout was of cement, had radios, excellent sleeping facilities, dogs. We started to drop a grenade into the ventilator, but Streczyk said, "Hold on a minute," and fired three shots down the steps into the dugout. He then yelled in Polish and German for them to come out. Four men, disarmed, came out. They brought out two or three wounded. I yelled for [Sgt. Clarence] Colson to bring five or six men. We began to get small arms fire from the right (west). I yelled for [PFC Edwin] Paisecki and [PFC Alexander] Sakowski to move forward to the edge of the draw. A firefight took place. The Navy now began to place time fire in the draw. This was about 1000.

Their job done, Spalding's team turned south toward Colleville in the wake of Captain Dawson's Company G. Spalding's day was far from over, but thanks to his small band of intrepid GIs, an entire enemy strongpoint was no more.

General Wyman was cheered by the sight of numerous Germans streaming down the bluff with their hands over their heads. But his goal of opening the St. Laurent exit could not be realized until the Fighting First captured the enemy strongpoint on the draw's west side. The exit road that Wyman coveted passed directly in front of this strongpoint, and no American engineer would be able to get anywhere near that road to prepare it for vehicular movement unless the Germans were driven away or killed. This time, however, the task would require many more than twenty GIs, for the defenses—including a large concrete pillbox housing an antitank gun—were much sturdier than the ones Spalding had just neutralized.

If Wyman wanted reinforcements, he would soon have them in abundance: More than 3,000 fresh infantrymen would land just east of the St. Laurent draw within the next ninety minutes. Their timely arrival would hearten Wyman, relieve pressure on the 16th Infantry, and revitalize the entire invasion. But this was not the way these new troops had expected to enter the battle. The original plan had assumed that just the 16th and 116th Regiments would secure the beach while three reserve infantry regiments, totaling more than 10,000 men, waited patiently offshore for that task to be fulfilled. The reserves would then land on a beach devoid of enemy fire, march intact up the draws, and push on by dark to inland objectives up to five miles away. When that plan dissolved only moments after H-Hour, it was obvious to all that the reserves would now be involved in toe-to-toe fighting on, and just beyond, the beach, a profound change of plan that would in all probability trigger confusion and uncertainty. Seizure of their original inland objectives would have to come later.

DEAD CORPSMEN CAN'T SAVE LIVES

Wyman's entreaty for help to open the St. Laurent draw would yield him the 750 men of the 2nd Battalion, 18th Infantry, a 1st Division outfit that landed comparatively intact across a wide front to the west of the St. Laurent exit at about 10:30 from LCI-489 and eighteen LCVPs drawn from the transport *Anne Arundel*. By this time of day Omaha Beach appeared wholly different than it had at H-Hour. At 10:00 the tide had risen to its highest point, and it would stay that way until 1:00 P.M. The beach had disappeared almost entirely. All that remained between the lapping waves and the shingle was a strip of sand a few yards wide.

The invasion planners understood that for reinforcements to land at high water, the enemy's plentiful beach obstacles would have to be cleared by demolition engineers in the invasion's first hour. Failure to do so could result in the destruction of many landing craft as they prepared to beach. Happily for Wyman, the beach sectors near the St. Laurent draw where reinforcements were landing—and would continue to land for several hours—had been reasonably cleared by engineers. Navy coxswains could bring their landing craft ashore here with a decent chance of avoiding destruction from a German obstacle, or a mine on top of an obstacle. But the few obstacles that had survived the engineers' demolition work were particularly treacherous because they were submerged at this tidal stage and therefore invisible.

2nd Battalion, 18th Infantry, 1st Division
U.S. Army Historical Division, interview with various 2nd Battalion soldiers, July 1944

After passing the Line of Departure, our boat wave circled for a time, not heading beachward. The battalion CO [Lt. Col. John Williamson] found a naval officer who said that his boat group CO was missing, and that he was in command, but he didn't know where to land. [Williamson] made radio contact with shore and instructions were made to land on the right side of the Ruquet River [a tiny stream flowing down the E-1 draw]. . . . After an interval, [the naval officer] still didn't move in. . . . [He] said that no channels were marked, and it was therefore unsafe to go in. [Williamson] ordered him to take in the boats regardless. The boats moved in column, landing at high tide, 45 minutes late [10:30 A.M.]. Most boats hit underwater obstacles, but none were damaged.

Pharmacist's Mate 1st Class James Argo
LCI-489, embarking HQ Company, 2nd Battalion, 18th Infantry, 1st Division

Suddenly all hell broke out. Lt. [Harry] Montgomery [LCI-489 CO] yelled, "Get off the bridge!" and we abandoned the bridge immediately. The German bunkers that were supposed to have been blasted out in an air raid weren't. Fire started coming from everywhere. . . . Wood timbers and cross ties and barbed wire were attached to mines. One of the first things I remember seeing just before all hell broke out was a couple of dead men draped over these obstacles in the shallow water. . . . I was told that the Germans wouldn't aim fire directly at men in the Red Cross helmets. A few hours into battle, I took my helmet off because I was certain they were aiming right at that Red Cross. I guess the Germans figured for every hospital corpsman they took out, the more overall casualties there would be. Dead corpsmen can't save lives.

10:00 A.M.: St. Laurent Draw

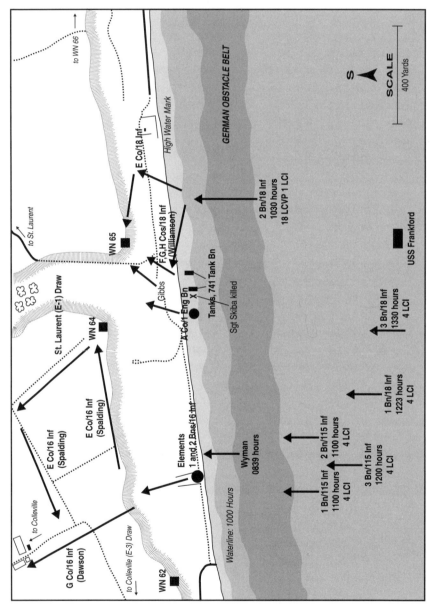

to WN 66

to St. Laurent

E Co/18 Inf

High Water Mark

GERMAN OBSTACLE BELT

WN 65

2 Bn/18 Inf
1030 hours
18 LCVP 1 LCI

F,G,H Cos/18 Inf
(Williamson)

Gibbs

A Co/1 Eng Bn

Tanks, 741 Tank Bn

Sgt Skiba killed

USS Frankford

St. Laurent (E-1) Draw

WN 64

E Co/16 Inf
(Spalding)

E Co/16 Inf
(Spalding)

3 Bn/18 Inf
1330 hours
4 LCI

1 Bn/18 Inf
1223 hours
4 LCI

Elements
1 and 2 Bns/16 Inf

Wyman
0839 hours

2 Bn/115 Inf
1100 hours
4 LCI

3 Bn/115 Inf
1200 hours
4 LCI

1 Bn/115 Inf
1100 hours
4 LCI

Waterline: 1000 Hours

to Colleville

G Co/16 Inf
(Dawson)

to Colleville (E-3) Draw

WN 62

S

SCALE

400 Yards

The 2nd Battalion's pressing challenge was to subjugate the vexing enemy strongpoint on the west side of the St. Laurent draw. No one in the 2nd could have predicted that the battalion's first action in France would be to launch an assault from the water's edge directly against an entrenched enemy on the bluff. That was surely the 16th's job. But according to Williamson's hasty orders, that is precisely what the battalion had to do. With help from some unanticipated sources, it succeeded.

2nd Battalion, 18th Infantry, 1st Division
U.S. Army Historical Division, interview with various 2nd Battalion soldiers, July 1944
The beach shingle was full of tanks, vehicles, tractors, bulldozers, and troops. The assault troops had not touched down at this particular point, and the high ground immediately in front of the beach was still held by Germans who had all troops on the beach pinned down. [Williamson] ordered E Company to advance on the right flank and the rest of the battalion to go around the left to get behind the opposition and clean it out. . . . [With] the help of a tank at the water's edge, a pillbox covering the right (west) side of the valley was captured with 15 to 20 Germans.

The 2nd Battalion's attack on the German *Widerstandsnest* was supported by Lt. Col. George Gibbs, the commander of the 1st Division's 7th Field Artillery Battalion. Like Thornton Mullins of the 111th Field Artillery, Gibbs knew that for the moment, everyone on Omaha Beach must temporarily disregard his military specialty, grab a rifle and a few grenades, and try his hand at infantry tactics. At this endeavor, Gibbs proceeded to prove that he was particularly capable.

Lt. Col. George Gibbs
Commander, 7th Field Artillery Battalion, 1st Division, Distinguished Service Cross Citation, June 30, 1944
Displaying superb courage, Lt. Col. Gibbs left his place of comparative safety, and under the intense direct fire of the still intact fortifications overlooking Exit E-1, moved down several hundred yards of exposed beach to where his unit was supposed to land. [Refusing] cover in his movements, although a constant target for the deadly accurate fire of the numerous snipers, Gibbs was a vital factor in the reorganization of the confused, hurt men huddled on the beach, and was an inspiration to them in his calm, steady assurance. . . . Finding a small breach [through wire], which led through a heavily strewn minefield, Gibbs and a comrade officer [Capt. Robert Woodward] gathered a few men and led them across the field on a magnificent frontal assault against two enemy gun emplacements. With complete

disregard for his own safety, Gibbs entered the maze of underground tunnels and fortifications, and led his desperately fighting group in the neutralization of the fantastically resisting enemy. Gibbs was among the first to reach the enemy-dominated ridge line [west of the E-1 draw], and was highly instrumental in opening the way inland from the beach to the incoming troops.

PFC Alfred Alvarez
Battery C, 7th Field Artillery Battalion, 1st Division
Someone pointed out Col. Gibbs, our battalion commander, standing up, probably trying to inspire the troops. Another soldier said that the colonel was a Regular Army officer, so this apparently must have explained his actions.

Williamson's 2nd Battalion was also offered considerable assistance by the destroyer USS *Frankford*, plus a few Shermans from the 741st Tank Battalion and 467th AAA Battalion half-tracks that had survived the carnage on the beach.

USS *Frankford*
Lt. Cmdr. James Semmes, War Diary, 1021 hours, June 6, 1944
Fire was commenced [at St. Laurent draw]. . . . Troops on Easy Red were being held up by a mortar battery located on ridge by River Ruquet. After close observation the exact location of the battery was noted at 1032. At 1036 commenced firing on the battery using direct fire, range about 1,200 yards. On the fifth salvo a direct hit was obtained, a large cloud of green smoke was noted and the mortar battery ceased firing. Our troops then advanced, and a number of German troops were seen to surrender.

Cpl. Steven Hoffer
Company A, 741st Tank Battalion, June 1944
From our defiladed position [behind the shingle] S/Sgt. [Walter] Skiba's tank fired on several machine gun nests from which fire was visible, then picked up a log emplacement and fired several rounds of 75mm, located at extreme top of hill on our right. A captain from the 16th Infantry came to the tank and directed fire on a concealed 88mm gun. Later this captain and a lieutenant colonel [probably Gibbs] went up to the same position and captured 21 prisoners. In the meantime, the captain directed fire on two other targets, which were knocked out, and the infantry was then able to advance. The enemy during this time was laying down heavy mortar fire around us, and several holes were noticed in and around our [intake and exhaust] stacks. One shell landed quite close to the tank, and S/Sgt. Skiba was killed almost instantly (approximate time, 1045 hours). The crew assisted in taking S/Sgt. Skiba out of the tank and calling the medics to his aid.

S/Sgt. Thomas Fair
Company A, 741st Tank Battalion, June 1944

I noticed the tide was closing in on us, and we had no exit to escape from in case we had to move, for there was a hill in front of us, [also] a good tank obstacle, and casualties were piling up all around us. I started down the beach to look for our platoon leader, who was Lt. [Gaetera] Barcelona. The going was slow, for we had to weave in and out among bodies, sometimes stop until the medics cleared them from our path.

467th Antiaircraft Artillery Battalion
Battalion History, 1945

An M15 halftrack was used to neutralize this 88mm gun [in the E-1 draw], and approximately 35 rounds of 37mm ammunition were fired to accomplish this mission. This action led the way to the opening of Exit E-1. M15 and M16 halftracks were also used to neutralize enemy sniper positions and communications trenches.

Col. Benjamin Talley
Deputy Chief of Staff, V Corps, letter to U.S. Army Historian G. Harrison, February 18, 1948

It is suggested that the official history give credit to fire from destroyers in breaking the stalemate in front of E-1, inasmuch as I observed destroyers keeping up a heavy fire at point blank range on the trenches on the military crest immediately west of the exit and on the emplacements until they were silenced.

Shortly before noon, the German strongpoint was finally cleared out, and Wyman at last had the draw he considered one of the keys to the battle. Wyman ordered Williamson's battalion to slide east several hundred yards along the beach, move up the bluff via the path forged by Spalding and Dawson that morning, and assume the mission of the 16th Infantry's mauled 2nd Battalion by pushing inland to and beyond Colleville-sur-Mer. Meanwhile, 1st Division engineers immediately jumped to the task of preparing the St. Laurent exit road for vehicles, a job that was complicated by the fact that the work had to be performed under enemy mortar fire. But when lanes through the shingle were finally bulldozed, mines swept, and road surfaces smoothed out, the pressure that had been building to almost a bursting point on the beach would finally begin to be relieved.

1st Engineer Combat Battalion, 1st Division
Battalion History, "Eight Stars to Victory," 1947

Slowly the enemy was driven back, and elements of Company A cleared a lane leading to exit road E-1. A bulldozer was secured to fill an antitank ditch. Upon landing, Company C immediately went to work on exit road E-1 and opened a vehicle transit area just east of St. Laurent-sur-Mer. By 3 o'clock in the afternoon, the road and vehicle transit area were opened and ready for use. Until noon the following day, all the task force tanks, vehicles, and supporting weapons that were unloaded traveled over this one beach exit road.

741st Tank Battalion
Unit Journal, 1700 hours, June 6, 1944
Ordered by Headquarters, 16th Infantry combat team to move all [tanks] through Exit E-1 to assemble in area 500 yards east of St. Laurent-sur-Mer. Complied with.

CITIZENS OF DEATH'S GRAY LAND
As Williamson's troops battled for the St. Laurent draw, Wyman cheerfully received 2,500 reinforcements from the 29th Division's 115th Infantry. Until February 1941, when the entire Maryland National Guard was called to active service by presidential order, the 115th had been known as the 1st Maryland. Now, forty months later, the regiment was composed mostly of draftees, but the bulk of its senior officers and NCOs were Maryland guardsmen who had learned the rudiments of war while holding down civilian jobs in peacetime. More than three years of active service, however, had blurred the distinctions among citizen-soldiers, professionals, and conscripts. All, regardless of their military origins, were equally focused on the coming task and shared the trait of being new to combat. But those lucky enough to survive D-Day would consider themselves veterans by the following dawn.

PFC William Wilch
Company E, 115th Infantry, 29th Division
I want to go on record that our company commander, Capt. [Waldo] Schmitt, Lt. [Richard] Donnelly, Lt. [Kermit] Miller, and the rest of the platoon leaders who I served with were the bravest, most honest, caring, capable, yet humble men I have ever met—or even heard about. They were the best example of the flower of our generation. [All three were later killed.] I feel lucky that I had such fine officers to lead us. They were as physically conditioned as any that ever served. We were known as "Colonel Warfield's Singing Battalion." We could march or run with any unit in the Army or Marines.

Luckily for Wyman, the story of the 115th on D-Day demonstrated at least some flexibility in the V Corps' invasion plan. The Neptune scheme had originally assigned the 115th to Force B, a large follow-up convoy

"A magnificent display of courage." The German pillbox at the mouth of the E-1 draw held up the 1st Division advance in this sector until noon. The pillbox was finally seized by direct assault, supported by fire from the USS Frankford. *Later in the day, General Wyman used it as a command post. (Photo taken on June 7.)*
U.S. ARMY SIGNAL CORPS, NATIONAL ARCHIVES.

whose landing craft would disembark their troops on Omaha Beach on the evening of D-Day and the following morning. However, at the urging of 29th Division commander Maj. Gen. Charles Gerhardt, who was convinced that the original invasion plan did not provide adequate infantry on the beach should the enemy resist the initial assault waves, Gerow won approval from Bradley to allow the bulk of the 115th to sail with Force O's assault convoys so that the regiment could be committed to the beach, if needed, on the morning of D-Day. When the enemy immediately displayed the resolute resistance to the invasion that Gerhardt feared, it became obvious to Gerow that the 115th was indeed needed, and he decided only minutes after H-Hour to commit the regiment to the beach starting at H+4 hours (10:30 A.M.).

Headquarters, V Corps
USS Ancon, G-3 Message Journal, 0632 hours, June 6, 1944
Land 115th RCT [Regimental Combat Team] at H plus 4 hours unless otherwise directed.

Headquarters, 1st Infantry Division
USS Ancon, *G-3 Message Journal, 1131 hours, June 6, 1944*
From Commanding General 1st Division [Huebner] to General Cota. Use 115th Infantry to clear high ground southwest of beach Easy Red in 16th Infantry sector. Coordinate with CO CT [Combat Team] 16 [Colonel Taylor], CT 18 [Col. George Smith], and General Wyman.

Headquarters, 1st Infantry Division
USS Ancon, *G-3 Message Journal, 1146 hours, June 6, 1944*
From Commanding General 1st Division to all control vessels. Rush all infantry elements to beach.

The bulk of the 115th, about 2,500 men, was conveyed to Normandy in twelve U.S. Navy LCIs. Another 700 men of the 115th, in company with the regiment's vehicles and heavy guns, followed later as part of Force B. The LCI skippers held orders to land the regiment in two waves astride the mouth of the Les Moulins draw, but when they approached the beach, they saw that the Germans in that sector had not yet been subdued, nor had their beach obstacles been cleared. A landing on that beach appeared suicidal. The skippers therefore turned their LCIs back to sea to try their luck on a different sector. The beach between the St. Laurent and Colleville draws, about one mile to the east, looked promising, although neither control vessels nor signalers from shore could confirm that this beach was indeed safe. However, the 115th's scheduled landing time of 10:30 had already passed—so this sector would have to do.

The first wave of eight LCIs, carrying the 115th's 1st and 2nd Battalions and liaison teams from the 110th Field Artillery, touched down shortly before 11:00. Four LCIs of the second wave, conveying the 3rd Battalion, landed an hour later. In this area, the Germans were still active, and it was obviously not a safe place for the navy to linger. Sailors hurriedly lowered their LCIs' port and starboard gangways, and the GIs streamed down them into the water. The tide was high, and the troops needed to plod only about thirty yards to reach the shingle.

So far, so good—but what next? This was not the sector on which the 115th had expected to land. Intermittent enemy barrages were already causing casualties, and there would be many more if the men did not quickly adhere to the army's fundamental tenet: Don't bunch up. The 115th's commander, Col. Eugene Slappey, could offer no immediate guidance, for the LCI on which he was embarked had struck an underwater obstacle, forcing its skipper to retract for another landing attempt. Instead of being among the first members of the regiment's initial wave to disembark on Omaha, Slappey was one of the last. Slappey's temporary absence, however, did not deter the 1st and 2nd Battalions from moving forward on their own initiative within fifteen minutes of their landings. The 3rd Battalion would follow once the last four LCIs came ashore. In this sector, plenty of gaps had already been blown in the enemy's barbed wire courtesy of the 16th Infantry, and German small-arms fire was scattered and inaccurate. It didn't take a military genius to figure out that moving beyond the shingle to the bluff was the right thing to do.

Lt. (jg) Douglas Wright
Officer-in-Command, LCI-408, carrying Company G and 115th Regimental HQ, Action Report, June 16, 1944

As we approached the beach there were many craft seen milling about, apparently undecided as to what to do or lacking the proper signal from shore. We found our way through these craft and grounded on the beach at 1103, failing to make a satisfactory beaching. The bow was quite a distance from shore, while the stern rested on a bar seaward of one of the deep runnels which was under the bow. Some Element C [obstacles], wreckage, and stakes had scraped the length of the hull as we came in. . . . We came in again, to the west of our first position and at 1143 dropped stern anchor again for a second beaching. At 1146 soldiers and equipment started ashore. The water was deep for a short distance off the bow, and two lines were led out from the ship, one from each ramp. The soldiers were very heavily loaded, and such equipment as they could not carry on their backs (reels of wire, radios, signaling equipment) was buoyed up by having spare lifebelts attached. At 1201, SC2c [ship's cook, 2nd Class] R. J. Aubin was at his station as pointer on Number 2 gun, and was killed instantly when a fragment from either an 88 or mortar shell struck him in the back. All soldiers and gear made the beach without casualty.

Lt. Col. John Cooper
Commander, 110th Field Artillery Battalion, 29th Division

I was on LCI-411 with Company B of the 115th, which still had many members from Hagerstown, Maryland, from the old National Guard days. Captain [LeRoy] Weddle, the company commander, divided the men into two groups: one group would go down the left ramp; the other the right ramp. I proceeded down the right ramp. We got down almost to the foot of the ramp when a sound like a riveting machine went off over our heads. We looked up and saw little pieces of paint coming off the LCI. It was a machine gun firing from somewhere off to our right—just missing our heads. We hastily retreated up the right ramp and proceeded down the left ramp instead, which was somewhat protected from fire coming from the right.

Ens. J. J. Terranella
Executive, LCI-554, Carrying Company D and 1st Battalion HQ, Action Report, June 20, 1944

Just as we dropped anchor, we experienced that natural fear because now we realized that not all the gunfire was coming from our units. The enemy was dropping shells all around us, and mines had exploded under landing craft near us. The sight of so many dead bodies and damaged craft made us feel as if we were lucky so far. We wondered how long it would be before we were hit, and I'm positive everyone prayed terrifically while we were under fire.

Sgt. Charles Zarfass
Company A, 115th Infantry, 29th Division, 1945

As I took my first step onto the Continent, I saw the whole company, lying as if frozen, in one big square. To the right and left of me there were tanks at the water's edge, to be used as a covering force for the assaulting infantry.

Ens. Harold Clark
Executive, LCI-555, Carrying Company M and 3rd Battalion HQ, Action Report, June 12, 1944

A floating body was seen off the port bow as we started for the coast. . . . As the last four men to leave the ship were proceeding down the starboard ramp, the pressure of the current tended to bend the ramp at the highest mast point, twisting the ramp off its housing. The men on the ramp at the time jumped into the water, which at this point was approximately five feet. Robert G. Starkey, S1c [seaman 1st class], whose duty it was to assist the soldiers off the ramp, lowered himself into the water, and by virtue of his hold on the anchor line, greatly assisted the remaining four men ashore. . . . It is the opinion of this writer that had it not been for the assistance of this seaman, the safety of these men and equipment would have been more seriously endangered.

Cpl. Walter Eckert
HQ Company, 3rd Battalion, 115th Infantry, 29th Division

I would have qualified for the most scared guy on that beach. We had orders not to dig in on the beach. Well, everybody had a shovel, and most everyone started to dig in. A boy by the name of Benny Beale from Frederick [Maryland] hollered, "Eckert, you so-and-so, stop filling up my foxhole with sand!"

Lt. Cmdr. Lindsay Henry
Commander, LCI Group 34, letter to his wife, June 7, 1944
We were in the center of the attack, and it was a shambles. I wasn't touched and feel fine. I had a good sleep and am eating well. We will never again have to land under fire, so don't worry about me. My deliverance is certainly due to the prayers of many of you at home. . . . This is the end of Germany and Japan. It won't take the armies long now. When I saw the 115th Infantry charge up the hill from the beach, I knew nothing could stop them. The old colonel [Slappey] led them. I hope he is all right. When he left my ship I wished him good luck, and he said: "If I can't do more, I can show these men how an officer can die!"

The 115th Infantry would follow its 1st Division predecessors up the bluff and through the door the enemy had left open in its defenses between the St. Laurent and Colleville draws. But as the GIs dashed over the shingle embankment toward the foot of the bluff, their leaders grasped the immediate predicament: The bluff's heavy brush and furrowed surface would channel the ascent into two or at most three discernible paths. No unit of the 115th's size had yet attempted to climb the bluff on D-Day, and it was obvious that to do so would be as difficult as rushing an entire football team through a narrow doorway. Getting 2,500 men to the top was going to take some time.

With the invasion plan in tatters, precisely what the 115th was supposed to accomplish once it reached the crest was so far unspecified, but a chance encounter between General Wyman and Colonel Slappey provided clarification. The village of St. Laurent would be the 115th's immediate objective, a task that guaranteed a battle, since the Germans, at last report, firmly held that place. Each 115th outfit would have to turn nearly ninety degrees to its right once it reached the top of the bluff and then proceed cross-country, through very difficult terrain, to reach St. Laurent.

In their long, snakelike columns, the GIs of the 115th ascended the bluff cautiously: 1st Battalion on the left, 2nd Battalion on a separate trail to the right. The 3rd Battalion would follow behind the 2nd. The troops promptly passed wounded soldiers with their feet blown off lying adjacent to the paths up the bluff, confirming what the men already suspected: This place was mined.

Lt. Col. John Cooper
Commander, 110th Field Artillery Battalion, 29th Division
We found a hole in the wire, and the whole company [B, 115th] filtered through. About a dozen men remained on the shingle. As we started up the bluff, we turned

"I would have qualified for the most scared guy on that beach." High tide rises on Omaha at about 11:30 A.M. near the E-3 draw. Vehicles of several kinds are scattered on the shingle. The 29th Division's 115th Infantry has just landed; LCI-553, which carried Company H and 2nd Battalion HQ, is visible in the background, at left. U.S. ARMY SIGNAL CORPS, NATIONAL ARCHIVES.

and yelled at them to get up and move forward. Two or three did, but most stayed. Then a heavy artillery or mortar shell hit behind the shingle. You could see the men being blown up in the air. It was a hell of a mess. That was the last thing I saw of the beach.

Cpl. Walter Eckert
HQ Company, 3rd Battalion, 115th Infantry, 29th Division

There was a path up over the cliff. I remember about halfway up, there was a fellow sitting there with a tourniquet up around his knee. There wasn't anything at all below [the tourniquet]. He was calmly smoking a cigarette. He said, "Watch it—there are some personnel mines here." I don't know whether he was doped up, but it didn't seem to bother him. But I was scared to death.

After its successful battle against the enemy strongpoint at the St. Laurent draw, the 18th Infantry's 2nd Battalion followed the 115th up the bluff. Later, the 18th's 1st and 3rd Battalions, conveyed by nine U.S. Navy LCIs, landed on the same beach sector and ascended the bluff by the same steep paths littered with mine casualties. The landing of two infantry regiments on the same sector over a two-and-a-half-hour period, and their subsequent inland movement over the bluff's narrow trails, yielded considerable congestion and confusion. But by midafternoon, more than 5,000 1st and 29th Division infantrymen had successfully scaled the bluff with little hindrance from the enemy. A slender gap in the enemy defenses that the Germans had probably considered inconsequential before D-Day had cracked wide open, and the Americans were pouring through it. Nothing short of a panzer division could plug that hole now.

2nd Battalion, 18th Infantry, 1st Division
U.S. Army Historical Division, interview with various 2nd Battalion soldiers, July 1944
The battalion went a few hundred yards left [east of the St. Laurent draw], started up over a minefield, where two narrow paths were found. These were jammed with troops of another unit [probably 3rd Battalion, 115th Infantry]. There were more than half a dozen men lying near the paths with their legs blown off. The battalion's companies passed the other troops, reached the crest top, and bore left to reach the assembly area near Colleville, F Company in the lead.

Capt. Edward McGregor
S-3, 1st Battalion, 18th Infantry, 1st Division, July 8, 1944
The 1st Battalion started disembarking at 1223, a few hundred yards east of Ruquet River. A gloomy sight presented itself. The landing itself was most hazardous. The gaps blown by the engineers in the underwater obstacles were few and narrow. The beach was under heavy shell fire, plunging machine gun fire, and a murderous sniper fire. The companies threaded their way straight uphill, through minefields. Our equipment was intact, and control okay. Our assembly areas were from 500 to 1,000 yards inland.

Capt. J. F. Gurka
S-1, 3rd Battalion, 18th Infantry, 1st Division, July 8, 1944
The 3rd Battalion was supposed to land at 1015. We landed between 1300–1400 on D-Day. Mines and underwater obstacles prevented LCIs of the 3rd Battalion from coming in. Most of the personnel landed in small craft. The LCI carrying the 3rd Battalion CP group and L Company hit two mines about 150 yards offshore and could get no closer. These men came ashore on lifelines. The whole landing was under artillery and mortar fire. The beach was accurately covered by this fire. Eight men from L Company were wounded when the LCI hit the underwater

"A gloomy sight presented itself." U.S. Navy LCIs 490 and 496, carrying elements of the 1st Division's 18th Infantry, approach Omaha Beach near the E-1 draw at about noon. Smoke produced by the fight around the German strongpoint at the mouth of the draw is visible. U.S. ARMY SIGNAL CORPS, NATIONAL ARCHIVES.

mines. After landing, the 3rd Battalion had to go through a mine belt. There were no regularly cleared paths. Capt. [Frank] Fitch, CO of L Company, was the first wounded by mines and was later killed by shell fragments.

COHORTS OF THE DAMNED

As American troops tramped up the hill, German prisoners came down—perchance, in the grand scheme of the war, a symbolic reflection of each nation's current fortunes. For the enemy captives, the war was over. A transport would deliver them to the United States, where they would thankfully sit out the demise of Nazi Germany under conditions that could only be described as serene compared with what they would have coped with on the western front for the next eleven months. But presently, their captors had to interrogate them, right on that chaotic hillside while the shock of battle still swirled in their heads. Capt. Fred Gercke, in charge of a U.S. Army prisoner interrogation team attached to 16th Infantry headquarters, came ashore with Colonel Taylor at about 8:20 A.M. and was one of the first Americans to cross-examine German prisoners on D-Day. His very first question led to an astonishing discovery.

Capt. Fred Gercke
Commander, POW Interrogation Team 24, June 27, 1944
A narrow path through some minefields was at last cleared for us, and we filed up
the rising ground for a few hundred yards up to where a fairly steep bluff offered
pretty good cover against low-angle fire, and established the [16th] Regimental CP
and aid station. In order to keep contact in the terrific confusion at the beach, I kept
within view of our CO, Col. Taylor, at all times. . . . Just when I started filing up
the path toward the proposed CP, I saw the first batch of prisoners coming down
the hill, a sorry looking lot, carrying their own wounded. I stopped them and
declared that spot off the path on the hillside the PW enclosure and went to work.
The first thing I did was to ask one of the prisoners for his paybook, and I could
not believe my eyes when I saw that he was from the 3rd Company, 914th Infantry,
352nd Division. [Gercke probably failed to remember the proper company and
regimental numbers. He probably meant 8th Company, 916th Regiment, as indicated by the 16th Infantry Unit Journal entry.] This regiment and division were
supposed to be about 50 miles south from us, and the only thing our order of battle
had told us that we would run into at the beach would be the 726th Infantry of the
716th Infantry Division. I checked with several other prisoners, but they were all
from the same unit and then sent our discovery up to the S-2 [intelligence officer]
on the hill. I found out that this 352nd Division had their units emplaced in various
field fortifications along the coast for a number of weeks already, which accounted
partly for the terrific fire we encountered during the initial stages of the landing. . . . They all talk freely. (I have had to shut some of them up for talking too
damned much.) The officers I had (highest rank, captain) also talked fairly freely
when engaged in conversation, but did not respond so well to direct questioning.

On the opposite half of Omaha Beach, Lt. Jack Shea, Cota's aide-de-
camp, learned as he climbed the bluff off the beach that some German captives did not survive long enough to reach the interrogation stage.

1st Lt. Jack Shea
Aide-de-camp to Brigadier General Cota, 29th Division, November 1944
From a point just below the crest, the attention of the troops was drawn to a single
American rifleman who walked along the promenade directly below them. Before
him marched five German prisoners who had been stripped of their weapons and
who held their hands above their heads. Inasmuch as they were the first Germans
who the men had seen, they caused particular interest. As they reached a point
about 800 yards east of the Vierville exit on the promenade, the two leading prisoners crumpled under a burst of machine gun fire that was obviously of German

"They all talk freely." German prisoners gather near the mouth of the E-1 draw on June 7. The presence of German troops from the 352nd Division on Omaha Beach was a shock to U.S. intelligence officers on D-Day.
U.S. NAVY, NATIONAL ARCHIVES.

origin. Their captor dove toward the protecting cover of the seawall, while two of the remaining three sank to their knees. They seemed to be pleading with the operator of the machine gun, situated on the bluffs to the east, not to shoot them. The next burst caught the first kneeling German full in the chest, and as he crumpled the remaining two took to the cover of the seawall with their captor.

The battle of the beach was over. The battle of the beachhead was about to begin.

CHAPTER 12

Beyond the Beach

HOW YOU TELL THE MEN FROM THE BOYS

For all the Germans' reputed military prowess, the Atlantic Wall turned out to be a wretched failure. Supported by a naval bombardment of only forty minutes, and lacking the promised support from the Eighth Air Force, the Americans had managed to infiltrate large bodies of troops between the Germans' celebrated coastal defenses in only a few hours. If, as Rommel had emphasized, the German Army's fundamental goal must be to push enemy invasion forces back into the sea, the Allies would have to be contained within slender beachheads for a much longer period than that to permit sizable reinforcements to reach the battle zone and counterattack.

The Germans on Omaha Beach could not win—yet they could still obstruct the invasion by such a considerable degree that the inevitable American victory would be marginal at best. If the surviving German strongpoints could hold out another day, and the tempo of artillery and mortar fire on the beach could be sharply intensified, the beachhead could become so lethal that the Americans might have to call off, or at least delay, later waves of reinforcements. Meanwhile, if the 352nd Division's limited local reserves could be committed to Omaha, they might be able to contain the Americans' many inland penetrations and deny them the critical coastal villages controlling the beach exits. American troops could continue to advance up the bluffs, and might eventually seize the draws, but if the Germans could hold on to the coastal highway to which all five beach exits joined, the American beachhead would be effectively contained.

But for how long? If a panzer division did not show up within the next day or two, the 352nd Division would certainly dissolve under the weight of the Americans' vast numerical superiority. Much to Rommel's distress, the German high command in its remote headquarters was far less capable of discerning the realities of the Omaha landing than the American generals on their command ships off the beach. This severe intelligence lag caused the German high command to perceive the fight for Omaha Beach much more favorably than the actual situation warranted. Consequently, German commanders failed to grasp the vast scale of the American invasion and the magnitude of the early penetrations of the beach defenses. No panzer division would arrive in time to seize the initiative from the Americans, nor would anything more than a single reserve infantry battalion from the 352nd Division reinforce the German defenders of Omaha Beach before evening. If, as Nathan Bedford Forrest had declared, success in war can be defined simply as "getting there first with the most," the Germans had virtually no chance of achieving that success.

Oberstleutnant Fritz Ziegelmann
Assistant chief of staff, 352nd Infantry Division

[Shortly after 8:00 A.M.] I succeeded in establishing telephone communication with the troops in WN 74 (Pointe de la Percée). The commander, whom I knew personally, described the situation in detail: "At the water's edge at low tide near St. Laurent and Vierville the enemy is in search of cover behind the coastal zone obstacles. A great many motor vehicles—and among these ten tanks—stand burning at the beach. The obstacle demolition squads have given up their activity. Debarkation from the landing boats has ceased; the boats keep further seawards. The fire of our strongpoints and artillery was well placed and has inflicted considerable casualties upon the enemy. A great many wounded and dead lie on the beach. Some of our strongpoints have ceased firing; they do not answer any longer when rung up on the telephone. Immediately east of this strongpoint, one group of enemy commandos has landed and attacked WN 74 from the south, but after being repelled with casualties it was withdrawn toward Gruchy. . . ." The regimental commander [Oberst Ernst Goth of the 916th Regiment], who also had listened to this conversation, reported further that up till then we had succeeded in frustrating an enemy landing on a wide front. . . . Countermeasures were being taken against the weak enemy, who had infiltrated at two places. The 916th Regiment, however, had to report that the casualties on our side were successively ris-

ing in number because of the continuous fire of the naval artillery and of the landing boats, so that reinforcements had to be asked for.

The Germans would continue to lob artillery and mortar shells onto the
beach for the rest of the day. This bombardment, in conjunction with fire
from snipers and machine gunners housed in the five or six surviving
strongpoints on the bluffs, would make life treacherous for any American
who lingered on the beach. But by 10:00 A.M., the crucial struggle had
shifted inland. Having penetrated the beach defenses at several points, the
Americans could now focus their efforts on seizing the modest Norman villages astride the coastal highway. With these villages firmly in American
hands, German counterattacks aimed at rescuing their beleaguered coastal
strongpoints could be blocked. Then the Americans could move down the
draws in reverse, surround and capture those strongpoints, and finally open
up the coveted roads leading off the beach. By now the invasion timetable
could not be salvaged—but once the draws were opened, the American
horde would storm off the beach like a football team on the opening kickoff.

The landing now evolved into four distinct minibattles centered upon
the villages the Americans yearned to liberate—from west to east, Vierville-
sur-Mer, St. Laurent-sur-Mer, Colleville-sur-Mer, and Le Grand Hameau.
Of these, Vierville was the first to fall.

With General Cota's encouragement, the 116th Infantry's Company C
was the first intact unit to ascend the bluffs on Omaha's western side. Midway between the Vierville and St. Laurent draws, Company C topped the
crest into a verdant but deadly pastureland. The first men to the top saw a
rectangular grassy field about ten acres in size, bordered by two of Normandy's legendary hedgerows—a terrain feature the company would come
to know intimately in the weeks ahead. About 275 yards due south along
the hedgerows, a narrow dirt road approached Vierville from the east. If the
object was to seize Vierville, following that road west would be the way to
do it.

Company C, 116th Infantry, 29th Division
U.S. Army Historical Division, interview with various Company C soldiers,
March 25, 1945

[1st Lt. Robert] Bedell, and the men in his section, were positive that their elements were the first to reach the rim of the bluff in this sector. They saw no other
troops when they got up there. They admitted that troops from Ranger units . . .
were scattered in with the C Company column that was winding up and over the
crest of the bluff, but were satisfied that it was elements of C that first got over the

crest. Machine gun fire from the right and left front struck at the lead elements as they came over the rim. This machine gun fire pinned the column down. And it was here, again, the men remarked that General Cota came into the picture to prompt their advance. Several of the group recalled Cota saying, "Now, let's see what you're made of. This is how ya tell the men from the boys." . . . Cota asked for some volunteers to "go get that guy over to the left." Three Rangers said they'd go, started moving along a low hedge and ditch that ran to the south. By this route they were able to flank the enemy machine gun from the right. . . . As proof of the success of their mission, one of the [Rangers] strode along carrying the MG42 [German machine gun]. Several belts of German ammunition were draped around his neck and shoulders.

Led by Bedell's boat team and strung out in a long, jumbled column, Company C filed across the field cautiously—there were *Achtung! Minen* signposts here—and arrived at the dirt road. Here they turned right: Vierville was dead ahead. Bedell's point men discovered to their surprise that the enemy did not offer resistance from the buildings on Vierville's eastern outskirt. The Stonewallers entered the village around 10:00 A.M.— no Germans. A couple of quaint Norman houses lining the narrow main street had been damaged by naval fire, and in front of a cobbler shop, two dead horses were still tethered to a German supply wagon filled with military provisions. These spoils of war were free for the taking, but there was no time for that. Only 200 yards ahead was the junction of the coastal highway and the road leading down the Vierville draw to the beach. Bedell's scouts advanced stealthily toward that junction—still no resistance. Nervous locals, too frightened to greet their liberators, peered out of windows at the passing column. With the critical junction under Bedell's control, all Germans still manning the strongpoints at the foot of the draw were now surrounded. The V Corps had just liberated its first village in World War II. Hundreds more would follow in the next eleven months.

Company C, 116th Infantry, 29th Division
U.S. Army Historical Division, interview with various Company C soldiers, September 1944
While in the town, the men encountered Brig. Gen. Norman D. Cota, who was calmly twirling his pistol on his finger. He said to them, "Where the hell have you been, boys?"

The main body of Colonel Schneider's 5th Ranger Battalion reached the bluff crest only a short time after Company C had filed off toward

10:00 A.M.–1:00 P.M.: Vierville-sur-Mer

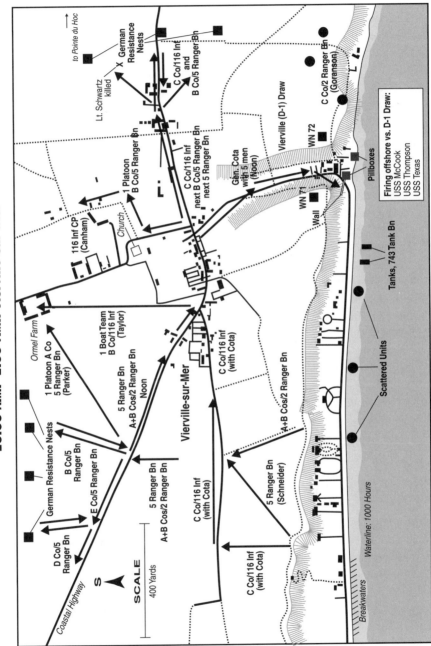

to Pointe du Hoc →

X German Resistance Nests

C Co/116 Inf and B Co/5 Ranger Bn

Lt. Schwartz killed

1 Platoon B Co/5 Ranger Bn

116 Inf CP (Canham)

Church

C Co/116 Inf next B Co/5 Ranger Bn next 5 Ranger Bn

Gen. Cota with 5 men (Noon)

Vierville (D-1) Draw

WN 72

C Co/2 Ranger Bn (Goranson)

WN 71

Wall

Pillboxes

Firing offshore vs. D-1 Draw:
USS McCook
USS Thompson
USS Texas

Ormel Farm

1 Platoon A Co 5 Ranger Bn (Parker)

1 Boat Team B Co/116 Inf (Taylor)

5 Ranger Bn A+B Cos/2 Ranger Bn Noon

German Resistance Nests

B Co/5 Ranger Bn

E Co/5 Ranger Bn

D Co/5 Ranger Bn

5 Ranger Bn A+B Cos/2 Ranger Bn

C Co/116 Inf (with Cota)

Vierville-sur-Mer

C Co/116 Inf (with Cota)

A+B Cos/2 Ranger Bn

5 Ranger Bn (Schneider)

C Co/116 Inf (with Cota)

Coastal Highway

N
S

SCALE

400 Yards

Tanks, 743 Tank Bn

Scattered Units

Waterline: 1000 Hours

Breakwaters

Vierville. Schneider and his force of more than 400 men were focused solely on their primary mission: get to Pointe du Hoc posthaste, four miles westward, and join forces with their brother Rangers who had landed there early that morning under Colonel Rudder. Surely Rudder's Rangers needed help by now, and Schneider's men could not let them down. Unlike Cota, who viewed the capture of Vierville as a necessary first step in opening the beach exit road, Schneider considered Vierville an obstacle to his speedy advance to rescue Rudder. He hoped to avoid enemy resistance by bypassing Vierville around its southern periphery and then head to Pointe du Hoc by any open route.

5th Ranger Battalion
U.S. Army Historical Division, interview with various 5th Rangers, July 1944

When Col. Schneider reached the bluff top, considerable confusion prevailed. The first Ranger units had come up into the fields more or less disorganized and were milling about. Only one platoon of A Company [under Lt. Charles Parker] had gone straight off inland without hesitation. Col. Schneider decided to reorganize and proceed as a battalion. . . . Runners were sent out to locate units; officers came in and reported. B and C Companies seemed to be the only ones with their units all accounted for at the moment, and B was ordered to lead off finding its own route to the assembly point [a road junction southwest of Vierville]. Vierville was to be avoided. . . . The remnants of A and B Companies, 2nd Rangers [which had reached the bluff crest about 450 yards to the west of Schneider after neutralizing a German strongpoint there], were coming in from the west and were fitted into the column. . . . At least a half-hour was taken up in making these arrangements. There were no signs of the enemy to the south or west. . . . B Company's 1st Platoon started off as point, Lt. Bernard M. Pepper in command.

Although the enemy did not contest the 116th Infantry's movement through Vierville, unhappily for Schneider the Germans fiercely resisted the Rangers' attempt to move around the town to the south. Aside from the platoon under Lieutenant Parker, which had reached the bluff first and had marched inland without learning of Schneider's reorganization order, none of the Rangers succeeded in making it to the assembly area. After several hours of fruitless fighting south of the coastal highway, Schneider realized that his men would not get to Pointe du Hoc by that route. Instead, they would have to go directly through Vierville and follow the coastal highway westward.

But that course was no better. The 116th Infantry's Company C, with Bedell's boat team in the lead and supported by a Company D team under Lieutenant Morse, tried it around 11:00 and advanced only about a third of a mile out of town before being stopped by German fire, which killed three Stonewallers who had sought shelter in a roadside ditch. Bedell retreated and then moved south into the pastures to flank the enemy's defenses. That didn't work either and resulted in the deaths of two more men—including Lt. Stanley Schwartz, the officer who had blown Company C's first gap in the enemy wire back on the beach.

By noon, the Stonewallers battling with the enemy west of Vierville were joined by the 5th Rangers' Company B, commanded by Capt. George Whittington, with Pepper's 1st Platoon in the lead. The Rangers' presence helped, but they still could not crack open the enemy defenses.

Company C, 116th Infantry, 29th Division
U.S. Army Historical Division, interview with various Company C soldiers,
March 25, 1945

Cota had seen the column stop [west of Vierville] and was on his way to see what the delay was. "They told him that the bodies in the [ditch] had been hit and killed by sniper fire," described Morse. "But Cota stood there with his .45 still in his hand. He told us that we had to get something off the road to maneuver against the source of the enemy fire that was holding us up." . . . It was at this point that the typical Normandy hedgerow first presented itself as a problem. Bedell and Lt. Schwartz had their men strung along the hedgerow that ran south from the farm buildings, but every move they made to cross this hedgerow and continue on toward the west was met with heavy small arms and automatic fire from a range of 200–300 yards. The enemy guns were evidently well-camouflaged, and the riflemen found it impossible to determine an enemy location by muzzle blast or smoke. The Germans were using smokeless powder.

5th Ranger Battalion
U.S. Army Historical Division, interview with various 5th Rangers,
July 1944

Company B now started west down the highway toward Vierville. . . . Not a shot was fired in the village, and there were no signs of enemy or friendly forces. Pushing through on the highway to Pointe du Hoc, the point was half a mile beyond Vierville at noon. Here the enemy had prepared positions on the side of the road and fired on the main body after the scouts had gone past. Pepper sent his platoon into a large field south of the road to go after a machine gun position. He had lost two men killed. Up the road from Vierville, alone and smoking a cigar, came Gen. Cota, who [the Rangers] had last seen at the top of the bluff when the Rangers were reorganizing. The General asked what was holding them up. "Snipers," said Pepper. "Snipers? There aren't any snipers here!" A shot came close to the General. "Well, maybe there are," and he walked off.

SUPPOSE YOU GO FIND OUT

By the time the rest of the 5th Rangers could disengage from their abortive maneuver around Vierville and move directly through the town to the west, it was too late. The ever aggressive Cota had departed Vierville by noon to open up the beach exit, and the senior commander remaining on the scene, the 116th's Col. Charles Canham, was sufficiently impressed by the enemy's resistance south and west of town to abandon the attempt to achieve his regiment's ambitious D-Day objectives. At this point, Canham could account for only a tiny fraction of his regiment, and by any angle from which he analyzed the situation, it seemed impossible to accomplish much more than he already had done. Given the supreme significance of a secure beachhead to the high command's subsequent plans for the Normandy campaign, it seemed best to dig in right here, at least until the fate of the missing parts of the Stonewall Brigade could be clarified.

But the situation did not clarify anytime soon, and Canham began to worry that even his tiny Vierville enclave could easily fall to what some American generals euphemistically referred to as "enemy enthusiasm." If the Stonewallers could not be found, the Rangers would do just as well, since they were attached to the 116th and fully subject to Canham's orders. As Ranger platoons moved through Vierville, fully expecting that Schneider would lead them on to Pointe du Hoc, the testy Canham appropriated them with crisp orders that no one dared question: The Rangers must immediately deploy into this crazy quilt of fields and hedgerows the locals called *le bocage* to defend the newly won ground to the last. If Rudder's men at Pointe du Hoc could not hold on, that would be unfortunate; but if Vierville was in German hands at nightfall, it would be a disaster that even Eisenhower would notice. Some indignant Rangers did not agree—but orders were orders.

Maj. Thomas Howie
S-3, 116th Infantry, 29th Division, June 9, 1944
Communications were completely out except for the radio of Lt. Jones, 743rd Tank Battalion liaison officer. In the meantime, the [116th headquarters] group had become separated from liaison officers and radio teams of the 1st U.S.

Infantry Division and the 16th Infantry. . . . A platoon of Rangers [2nd Platoon, Company B, led by Lt. Matthew Gregory] was contacted while attempting to rejoin the 2nd Ranger Battalion [at Pointe du Hoc]. Col. Canham impressed this group as security for the CP and immediately sent a patrol south to Louvières in an effort to contact our 2nd Battalion. [The patrol] reported back no friendly units south of Louvières and the countryside infested with Germans.

Capt. Berthier Hawks
Commander, Company C, 116th Infantry, 29th Division, July 1944
We tried to crack the [enemy line west of Vierville], but finally gave it up and decided to dig in. We sent out patrols to find the rest of the battalion. My communications sergeant, S/Sgt. Edwin Herring, found the regimental S-3, Maj. Thomas Howie, and he gave him the location of the regimental CP, the remnants of G Company, and a few heavy weapons. The rest of the regiment's location was unknown. On the way back, Sgt. Herring ran into Lt. Col. [John] Metcalfe [CO 1st Battalion], the rest of the battalion staff, part of HQ Company, and about fifteen men from A Company and guided them into our position. Later, part of the 58th Armored Field Artillery Battalion caught up with us. They gave us a concentration of fire on the German position, and again we attacked, but with no success. It was decided then that we would dig in for the night.

PFC Carl Weast
Company B, 5th Ranger Battalion
Next to an orchard was an unimproved road that we started to explore when we saw a G.I. looking out from a hedgerow extending east from the road. He asked who we were and who was in charge, then told us that he was part of the group that had established the command post of the 116th. Others of the command group came out and identified themselves, including Col. Canham. Col. Canham impressed our platoon as his CP guard when he discovered that his men were still back on the beach.

1st Sgt. Avery Thornhill
Company B, 5th Ranger Battalion
[West of Vierville,] we lost our first two men killed in action. One, a very fine boy, who never smoked, drank, and never missed going to Mass when he could help it. The other, a happy-go-lucky soldier, and if I may say so, a very good one. . . . This soldier was one of a group of six of us who ran together from the start at Camp Forrest, Tennessee. One of this group had been pinned down in front of a hedgerow, and it was believed he was hit, as we could hear someone moaning. This boy jumped up and said, "They can't do that to [name deleted in original].

He leaped to the top of the hedgerow and was immediately hit in the heart. Needless to say he died immediately. After giving his life for his friend, it was life given up for nothing, as we were able to relieve the men on the other side without casualty, and his friend was not hurt. A German who had been hit by a hand grenade was doing the moaning.

While Canham worried about Vierville, Cota worried about the Vierville draw. Cota reasoned that any success achieved by the 116th Infantry and the Rangers would be of no consequence unless tanks and vehicles laden with supplies could soon leave the beach and move inland through the draw. But from his perspective in Vierville, Cota saw no indicators that such a movement was imminent. The enemy still controlled the draw at beach level, a detail that was unmistakably corroborated by a ferocious naval barrage directed against the draw's mouth starting shortly after noon. If the navy was working so hard to clear the enemy from the beach exit, Cota resolved to contribute. At about 12:30, he and a band of five faithful followers started down the draw's blacktopped road toward the beach.

1st Lt. John MacAllister
S-1, 121st Engineer Combat Battalion, 29th Division
I proceeded into Vierville to the intersection with the road up from the beach exit. I remember just how lonely I felt. Some time later Gen. Cota and an infantry rifleman came up. He said, "Good morning, lieutenant. Where's the rest of the invading army?" He then noticed the castle on my collar [the U.S. Army Engineer branch symbol], and his next question was, "Why has the beach exit not been opened?" When I replied that I didn't know, he said, "Well suppose you go find out." I started down the road to the beach, and he called out, "Wait, we'll go with you." By that time Maj. [Allan] Olson, our battalion's executive officer, had joined the group, and we all started back to the beach.

1st Lt. Jack Shea
Aide-de-camp to Brigadier General Cota, 29th Division, November 1944
For the past 25 to 30 minutes a naval cruiser [actually the destroyers *McCook* and *Thompson*, and later the battleship *Texas*] had been firing on the fortifications at the mouth of the exit. . . . Gen. Cota, his aide [Lieutenant Shea], Maj. Olson, and Lt. MacAllister (the latter two officers of the 121st Engineer Battalion) joined with two enlisted men to make up a patrol that entered the exit from the rear to ascertain why no traffic had been cleared through it. As the patrol entered the rear

of the exit, the naval fire ceased. The concussion from the bursts of these guns had seemed to make the pavement of the street in Vierville actually raise beneath our feet in a bucking sensation, and had knocked several of the regimental group off their feet as they passed the crossroad above the exit.

"I hope to hell they cut out that firing," said Maj. Olson.

"That firing probably made them duck back into their holes," warned Gen. Cota.

Cota underestimated the naval fire's effect. Instead of forcing the Germans to "duck back into their holes," it caused many of them to come out—with their hands over their heads. In addition to the fire of the two destroyers, evidently the earth-shattering blast of just six rounds from *Texas*'s 14-inch guns fired from a distance of two miles—point-blank range for a battleship—was sufficient to convince most beach defenders that Hitler was hardly worth such suffering.

Lt. (jg) Coit Coker
Action Report, U.S. Navy Shore Fire Control Party 3, June 1944

On the plateau was a field of grass with numerous foxholes containing Germans. It was decided about noon to bring naval fire on this field by spotting in deflection from well to the right crossing D-1 Exit (to avoid hitting ourselves), which was then not yet clear. The destroyer *McCook* furnished this fire. As fire traversed the exit, *McCook* radioed us that a large party of Germans had emerged from the heavy concrete emplacements at the exit and were waving a white flag. We radioed to cease fire. The beach engineers took these Germans prisoner (30 in number) when fire was lifted. The total number of salvos: 4 (16 rounds). With Lt. [Donald] Vandervoort [of the 1st Battalion, 116th] spearheading, we took three more Germans prisoner by tossing hand grenades into foxholes.

USS *McCook*
Lt. Cmdr. Ralph Ramey, War Diary, 1217 hours, June 6, 1944

Commenced firing on numerous houses and emplacements in gully leading seaward from Vierville-sur-Mer church. Destroyed six houses (one three-story) and stone wall housing snipers and beach guns.

USS *Thompson*
Lt. Cmdr. Albert Gebelin, War Diary, 1223 hours, June 6, 1944

Commenced demolition of all houses and structures commanding Dog Green exit.

Headquarters, 1st Infantry Division
USS **Ancon,** *G-3 Message Journal, 1328 hours, June 6, 1944*
From Dog Green Control Vessel to Gen. Huebner: We can see POWs being taken
from pillbox that was blocking Exit Dog One.

No Omaha Beach invasion planner could have imagined that the first
American soldiers to pass through the Vierville draw would do so from
Vierville down to the sea. It was supposed to be the other way around. But
as long as the job got done, Cota's little band did not care how it was
accomplished. Surely there have not been many instances in history of a
general leading so small a force—in which officers outnumbered enlisted
men by two to one—to such a significant success.

1st Lt. Jack Shea
Aide-de-camp to Brigadier General Cota, 29th Division, November 1944
"Keep a sharp eye on those cliffs to your right," [said Cota]. There were a few
scattered rounds of small arms fired at the patrol, but a dozen rounds of carbine
and pistol fire sufficed to bring five Germans down from the caverns in the east
wall of the draw. They were stripped of their weapons as they reached the road
and herded before the patrol as it proceeded to the mouth of the draw. These prisoners sought the patrol's help in evacuating an alleged 12 "kamerades" whom they
said were wounded and lying in the caverns. Sensing a trap, Gen. Cota declined
the suggestion. [He reportedly asserted, "We're not going into caves!"] Later an
additional 54 prisoners were taken from the same cave. At the mouth of the exit
the patrol found that the antitank wall still stood. A concrete, covered emplacement, housing a 75mm high velocity antitank gun [actually an even more deadly
88] had been partially demolished near the western edge of the threshold. [This
emplacement had been disguised by the Germans, somewhat amateurishly, to
resemble a beach cottage. Today it is a monument to the National Guard of the
United States.]

1st Lt. John MacAllister
S-1, 121st Engineer Combat Battalion, 29th Division
On the way down Gen. Cota noticed two German soldiers on top of the cut, and
waving his .45 at them he said, "Come on down here, you sons-of-bitches!" They
did, and we took them with us back to the beach.

The center of the antitank wall had a small opening that permitted passage, one person at a time, down to the beach. As soon as Cota's group
passed through this gap, the German captives became frantic, yelling,

"*Minen! Minen!*" Cota declared, "OK, you go ahead," and in case none of them understood English, he reinforced this command with an authoritative gesture that they dared not challenge. One prisoner went first; the rest of the group trailed him, making sure to tread precisely in his footprints.

1st Lt. Jack Shea
Aide-de-camp to Brigadier General Cota, 29th Division, November 1944
Reaching the promenade, the patrol moved in an easterly direction. Bodies of riflemen, obviously of the 116th Infantry by the insignia they wore, were spread along the base of the concrete, inclined seawall. The first body lay about 40 yards east of the exit, and in any 100-yard sector from there down to Dog White beach there could be found 35 to 50 bodies.

Cota was almost back where he had started at 7:30 that morning. He now turned his attention to figuring out a way to demolish the wall blocking the mouth of the Vierville draw.

KILL-CRAZY

Of all the surviving American leaders who had landed on Omaha Beach by nightfall of D-Day, hardly any could claim that they had fully accomplished their missions as stipulated in invasion orders. One of those few who could make such a bold assertion was Lt. Charles Parker, commander of Company A, 5th Rangers. To the battalion officers, Parker was known as "Ace," a suggestion, perhaps, of the talent he applied to his job, but more likely a nickname derived from a well-known college football player of the mid-1930s. Company A had led the 5th Rangers off the beach and up the bluff that morning, and Parker and the 1st Platoon moved inland with such celerity that they missed Colonel Schneider's order for the battalion to hold up and reorganize beyond the crest before moving any farther south.

Parker and his thirty Rangers headed for the Ormel Farm (mistakenly labeled "Chateau de Vaumicel" on army maps), the 5th Rangers' prearranged rally point 400 yards due south of Vierville, where dispersed outfits could congregate prior to moving out toward a battalion assembly area southwest of Vierville—and then on to Pointe du Hoc. The fields and orchards through which Parker's Rangers moved were infested with Germans, and it took several hours for the frazzled GIs, now reduced to twenty-three in number, to reach the cover of Ormel's sturdy stone farm buildings and its large interior courtyard. Much to their surprise, they found twenty-five GIs already there, most of a boat team commanded by Lt. Walter Taylor of the 116th Infantry's Company B, which had been among the first groups of American troops to ascend the bluff between the Vierville and Les Moulins draws. Taylor's men had been battling the Germans for some time from within Ormel's walls—but they reported to a puzzled Parker, who was under the impression that he would arrive at the 5th Rangers' assembly area late, that they had not seen a single Ranger pass by Ormel.

Company B, 116th Infantry, 29th Division
U.S. Army Historical Division, interview with various Company B soldiers, September 1944

At the chateau [Ormel Farm] Taylor took two prisoners, a German doctor and an aid man. Having taken them, Taylor put them on a kind of parole and left his three wounded in their charge. . . . [Later] the Germans came on and attacked them [at the Ormel Farm], but the walls were slotted, and the enemy was driven back by well-placed rifle fire. A group of 15 men from the 2nd Rangers [actually Parker's twenty-three] then came in from the left and joined Taylor's force. . . . "He was an inspired leader throughout the day," said [S/Sgt. Frank] Price of [Taylor]. "He seemed to have no fear of anything, and no matter where he went, he was in the lead either of the march or of the fight. We followed him because there was nothing else to do."

Parker assumed that the rest of the 5th Rangers must have proceeded to the battalion assembly area by an easier route, so he and his men left Taylor with best wishes and cautiously set out for that point, about one mile distant, at 2:30 P.M. They immediately bumped into some Germans, who did not display much proclivity for a fight. Parker's men took twelve captives and pressed on. They arrived at the assembly area at about 4:30—still no sign of Schneider and the battalion. Were they ahead of their comrades or behind? Parker didn't know; regardless, his little group would carry on to Pointe du Hoc, now three miles distant.

If there were Germans prowling the countryside around Vierville, there certainly would be Germans around Pointe du Hoc as well. Consequently, getting through to Colonel Rudder's lines would be tricky, if not impossible. Nevertheless, Parker's tiny army would proceed. The Rangers followed a narrow country lane westward, paralleling the coast about one and a half miles inland. But with every step through the claustrophobic *bocage*, the Rangers' sense of isolation increased. Where was everybody? The Germans soon announced their presence, and after a harrowing fight at a farmhouse during which the Rangers barely escaped an enemy trap, the dog-tired GIs left their prisoners behind, backtracked a few hundred yards, scurried northward cross-country through the quilt of pastures bordered by hedgerows, and finally entered Rudder's lines at Pointe du Hoc shortly before dark.

Company A, 5th Ranger Battalion
U.S. Army Historical Division, interview with various Company A Rangers, July 1944

It was evident that the platoon had marched into a trap. It was no longer a question of getting further, but of getting out. . . . [S/Sgt. William] Kalar was one of the men who started over the wall to get to an enemy machine gun north of the road. As [S/Sgt. Clyde] Farrell covered him from the hedge, he left the wall and dashed for the hedgerow. A machine gun opened up, and Kalar could feel the bullets ripping into his pack. Then one hit his jaw. He threw himself under the hedgerow and felt the back of his head to see if the bullet had gone through. As he lay there, two enemy started to leave this hedgerow. Kalar killed both of them with his machine pistol and got back to the wall. Returning to Parker, he said: "Look what I got," pointing to his smashed jaw. And then suddenly Kalar went kill-crazy. He stood up and started walking straight down the road yelling, "I'm going to get that son-of-a-bitch!" The machine gun cut loose, and Kalar dropped out of sight. Then a machine pistol was heard firing. In a little while Kalar came walking back with two Germans, an extra machine pistol, and some ammunition strapped around his neck. Pointing at his jaw, he mumbled, "Look what I got!"

1st Lt. Charles Parker
Commander, Company A, 5th Ranger Battalion

When I first arrived at Pointe du Hoc that evening at 9:00, word was sent back to Colonel Rudder that we had arrived. His first question was: "Where the hell is the rest of the 5th Battalion?" I told him that since they weren't already there, they must be right behind me or coming on the main [coastal] road, and that they must have run into trouble in Vierville.

Rudder's hard-pressed force, which had suffered severe casualties, needed all the help it could get. It was isolated, with the sea to its back, and its climb up the cliffs at Pointe du Hoc and subsequent advance inland across the coastal highway had provoked a violent German reaction. Although the enemy's six heavy guns, the destruction of which was Rudder's main object, had been withdrawn from the coast prior to D-Day—a fact Allied intelligence had missed—a Ranger patrol had discovered them that morning in a field southwest of Pointe du Hoc, inexplicably lacking their crews, and destroyed them. Rudder's men had also set up defensive positions astride the coastal highway, effectively preventing German units deployed west of Pointe du Hoc from moving eastward in force against Canham's troops at Vierville. Throughout the night of June 6, and for part of the following day, Rudder's Rangers were under nearly incessant enemy attack, but they managed to hold out—assisted by Parker's small force—until relieved on June 8.

BIENVENUE À FRANCE

Meanwhile, on the opposite flank of Omaha Beach, the 16th Infantry was battling the enemy for possession of Colleville and Le Grand Hameau. The regiment that Eisenhower would soon designate his "Praetorian Guards" had seen many hard fights in its proud history, but the grizzled veterans of Arzew, Kasserine, Hill 523, and Troina could remember none that had begun as dreadfully as Omaha Beach. A lot of good men, including many of the old-timers from the 16th's days at Fort Jay in New York harbor, hadn't made it past the beach. Even if Colonel Taylor could manage to reverse the regiment's fortunes, the toll would unquestionably grow higher by nightfall.

The trauma of the beach would never be erased from the 16th's collective psyche; but the battle could still be won, and to do so, the regiment must take Colleville. There wasn't much to speak of in Colleville: an ancient church with its towering steeple, situated on the town's western fringe on a nose of high ground with a spectacular view of the sea; the walled-in farms; the public *lavoir* (laundry) pool; the sturdy stone *mairie* (town hall), located at the head of a picturesque dirt road leading down the draw to the beach a little under a mile to the north. The whole place featured only a couple dozen buildings and was only 650 yards from end to end. But those with a sense of the history of war must have realized that it has always been at such inconsequential places that soldiers clashed and changed the fate of the world.

The nature of the fighting in and around Colleville was wholly different than that at Vierville, which took place simultaneously three and a half miles to the west. While 116th Infantry troops and Rangers entered Vierville with not a single sign of the enemy on its streets or in its buildings, the Germans fiercely resisted every American attempt to move in Colleville throughout D-Day, and in fact held on to the eastern side of town until June 7. Furthermore, at about 9:00 A.M. the German high command committed a reserve infantry battalion (2nd, 915th Grenadier Regiment) of nearly 700 fresh troops from Bayeux to Colleville, and when it arrived around noon, its leaders were not focused simply on establishing a defensive perimeter to contain the Americans' inland penetrations. Rather, they aimed to do what German soldiers had always done in this war and the last: counterattack. Such a stratagem could drive the Americans back to the sea and rescue the beleaguered German troops still holding out in the coastal pillboxes. For the 16th Infantry, the Omaha battle was not about to get any easier.

After moving up the bluff between the St. Laurent and Colleville draws, Capt. Joseph Dawson's Company G led the way to Colleville astride a narrow dirt lane that meandered inland for about a half mile, joining the coastal highway just west of town. During the company's cautious approach to Colleville, Dawson was surprised by the greeting of an amiable French woman farmer standing off to the side of the path under an ancient tree: *"Bienvenue à France!"* ("Welcome to France!") This was more like what the GIs had expected in Normandy.

But the Germans in Colleville would see to it that the Americans enjoyed no more welcomes. On the town's western edge, Dawson's men collided with some sort of enemy encampment filled with grenadiers as angry as bees in an overturned hive. The enemy opened up with ripping bursts from machine guns and low-pitched bass gusts from mortars, and swiftly all became confusion—a condition worsened by Normandy's inscrutable hedgerows. But Dawson and many of his men had experienced what military pundits liked to call "the fog of war" before, and they returned the enemy's fire with equal ferocity. The fight took Company G two hours and cost it twelve casualties, but somehow the enemy was finally overcome.

Maj. William Washington
Executive, 2nd Battalion, 16th Infantry, 1st Division
I can remember talking to Joe [Dawson] about 10:00 A.M. up there at a little crossroads outside of Colleville, and he had been talking to a Frenchman. The Frenchman told him that there were 200 Germans in the village. All the information we had said there were about 30. . . . I said, "That guy's putting you on. He was sent out here to feed you a bunch of crap. Just take your company and go on in there and clean 'em out." So he did. But up until that point, he thought he was attacking 30, 40 men. [Instead,] he was attacking 200.

Dawson led the way east into Colleville, and there, just around a sharp bend on the main coastal road, was the church with its looming steeple. Were the Germans inside? Dawson and a patrol would find out.

Dawson and two Company G enlisted men warily entered the walled-in cemetery surrounding the church and headed for the doorway. They had only taken a few steps inside when three Germans from somewhere within opened fire, the blasts of their guns enormously amplified by the narrow, enclosed confines of the nave. They missed—but as one of Dawson's men plunged ahead, a fourth German in the steeple shot him dead from above. By revealing his position, however, that enemy soldier only brought on his own demise, as Dawson swiftly returned fire upward at the belfry—a spot from which the German could not escape. As for the remaining three Germans inside, Dawson would later recall somewhat euphemistically that the third member of his party "eliminated" them.

But unhappily for Dawson, the church was just a beginning. Most of Colleville and the key road leading down its draw to the beach lay farther to the east, and there would be much more bitter fighting ahead if Company G aimed to press onward.

Capt. Joseph Dawson
Commander, Company G, 16th Infantry, 1st Division
As I ran out of the church, a German shot at me. Fortunately, I turned and [saw] him, and I fired back—but not before he had fired another shot. I was carrying a carbine that I had picked up from the private who had lost his life in the church . . . and the bullet came through the stock of the carbine and shattered [it]; but one portion of the bullet went through my knee cap, and the other portion went through the soft part of my leg. . . . [It] caused me to be evacuated the next day.

Company G, 16th Infantry, 1st Division
D-Day After-Action Report, June 17, 1944
The 1st Section [with Dawson] reached the outskirts of the town at 1315 hours and occupied the church and house due south of the church at 687882 [map coordinate], where they became engaged with the enemy at point-blank range. Although three men were killed almost immediately and two seriously wounded, these buildings were occupied by our men and held. A heavy counterattack developed on all sides of the entire company at this time, but was beaten off successfully. . . . This engagement necessitated a consolidation of the company in an oval position as the enemy completely encircled us, and no front could be fixed. In order to contain the ground that had been gained, no further effort was made to advance, and the company dug in and awaited the 18th Infantry to pass through and relieve the pressure on us.

10:00 A.M.–7:00 P.M.: Colleville-sur-Mer

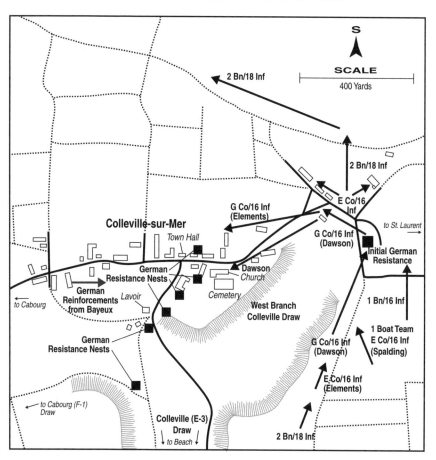

S

SCALE

400 Yards

2 Bn/18 Inf

2 Bn/18 Inf

E Co/16 Inf

to St. Laurent

G Co/16 Inf
(Elements)

G Co/16 Inf
(Dawson)

Initial German
Resistance

Colleville-sur-Mer

Town Hall

German
Resistance Nests

Dawson
Church

1 Bn/16 Inf

German
Reinforcements
from Bayeux

Lavoir

Cemetery

West Branch
Colleville Draw

1 Boat Team
E Co/16 Inf
(Spalding)

to Cabourg

G Co/16 Inf
(Dawson)

German
Resistance Nests

E Co/16 Inf
(Elements)

to Cabourg (F-1)
Draw

Colleville (E-3)
Draw
↓ to Beach ↓

2 Bn/18 Inf

Help came to Company G from many diverse sources over the next several hours, but Dawson likely was oblivious of this fact. The harried Fighting First staff officers who dispatched these reinforcements forward from the bluff crest committed them to Colleville's peripheries, rather than the town proper, for the entirely sensible reason that the obviously energetic enemy recurrently made attempts to surround Dawson's enclave in and around the church. If the Germans succeeded in this goal, they would surely smother Company G into annihilation—or captivity. Dawson, however, craved immediate and direct help.

Capt. Edward Wozenski
Commander, Company E, 16th Infantry, 1st Division, July 1944
Two skeleton sections of E Company moved on under Lt. Robert A. Hutch to take positions on the right of G Company. The situation at the time was extremely "touch-and-go," with the enemy in front [of], among, and behind the company. Still, Lt. Hutch led his men into this rather desperate situation, [and] by setting himself up and holding his ground, he eased the dangerous pressure on G Company's right and eventually established a battalion line.

2nd Lt. John Spalding
Company E, 16th Infantry, 1st Division
In the middle of the afternoon, Maj. Washington had sent my section on a mission [just west of Colleville]. We found ourselves very shortly surrounded. An hour or so later we had less than 100 rounds of ammo between us, and all efforts to make contact with our company had resulted in deaths [including, notably, Sgt. Fred Bisco, who had saved Spalding from stepping on mines as they had climbed the bluff earlier that morning]. Some men discussed surrender—which we quickly forgot about. We found a ditch, and single-file we crawled down this ditch, ran across a road and jumped into another ditch that enabled us to crawl to safety. As we crawled along, we passed a German machine gun with two dead Germans and one live German. Without saying a word, we exchanged the German's life for our own safety. I'm sure that I saw a twinkle in the German's eye as I crawled past him.

PFC Walter Bieder
Company E, 16th Infantry, 1st Division
[We] finally found the rest of our company—Capt. Wozenski and the rest of our outfit. Wozenski actually cried, "Where are my men? What did they promise us?" They were supposed to have bombed the whole beach area and they didn't do it. There were no craters at all there. D-Day night, out of 200 men, there were 60 of us left. Wozenski broke down, hollering, "Where's my men?" Sixty of us left.

1st Battalion, 16th Infantry, 1st Division
D-Day After-Action Report, July 4, 1944
1330 hours found Company C at the crossroads one-half mile west of Colleville-sur-Mer. B Company was on the right-rear of C Company, and A Company was on the right-rear of B Company. In the afternoon C Company cleared the woods and orchard, to the east of the crossroads, of snipers, riflemen, and machine guns. This area received intermittent mortar and artillery fire for the rest of the day and early evening hours. . . . Contact was maintained with the enemy continually from the time the battalion hit the beach. Prisoners captured during the first day's fighting totaled approximately 60. Casualties for the first day were four officers and 127 enlisted men. The CO of Company A, Capt. [James] Pence, was wounded on the beach and evacuated.

1st Lt. William Fulk
Assistant S-3, 18th Infantry, 1st Division, July 8, 1944
Lt. Brown, B Company, shot a woman sniper in the vicinity of Colleville. She was wearing the uniform of a German 2nd lieutenant. She was apparently acting as an artillery observer, and sniping in addition. She was wounded by a man in Brown's platoon. As Brown went up to check, she made a motion as though to throw a grenade. He shot and killed her. He didn't know it was a woman until her helmet fell off. Brown and his men stripped the upper portion of the body to confirm the fact it was a woman.

2nd Battalion, 18th Infantry, 1st Division
D-Day After-Action Report, July 1944
The battalion moved through the 16th—which had had heavy casualties—to the west edge of Colleville-sur-Mer by following sunken roads and hedge lines. The Germans had most of the gates and breaks in the hedges zeroed in with rifles and machine guns, and several of our men were lost as they advanced. At Colleville, the battalion veered south to the original assembly area, which was an original objective of the 2nd Battalion, 16th Infantry. F Company, still in the lead, drove off the enemy. . . . It might be well to bring out at this time that this fighting is much different than any encountered before by this division. The ground is covered with trees and hedgerows, making concealment excellent, but observation is practically non-existent. Fighting is at very close ranges, and this increases the difficulty.

In late afternoon, army and navy officers observing the beach from offshore came to the erroneous conclusion that the Germans were using Colleville's church steeple as an observation post to direct artillery fire against the beach. Three destroyers proceeded to bombard Colleville in what turned out to be the most severe of several serious "friendly fire" incidents on D-Day. Dawson could do nothing to stop it.

USS *Harding*
Cmdr. George Palmer, War Diary, 1854 hours, June 6, 1944
Received orders to . . . fire for two minutes on Colleville church, range 3,500 yards, which was complied with. At 1857 ceased fire; church badly battered. seventy-three rounds expended. At 1935 again received orders . . . to open fire again for two minutes on Colleville church and to spread fire around area. At 1937 opened fire again on same target, range at this time 3,800 yards, scoring numerous hits on church and area. Sixty rounds expended. It is believed that this church was being used as an observation post for mortar fire, since the beach at this time was being bombarded apparently from inland.

Maj. William Washington
Executive, 2nd Battalion, 16th Infantry, 1st Division
I actually thought it was pathetic that we captured a church steeple in Colleville-sur-Mer that gave us good observation of the enemy, only to have it shot down by the U.S. Navy. . . . The Navy Shore Fire Control Party had become casualties, their radios with the assault battalion had been damaged. Hence, the Navy had no clear picture of what was taking place ashore; nor did anyone else at that time. Someone apparently made the assumption that the enemy held the church steeple and was adjusting fire on the beach.

Capt. Joseph Dawson
Commander, Company G, 16th Infantry, 1st Division
At 4:00 [actually nearly 7:00] we were devastated with an artillery barrage from the Navy. It leveled the town, absolutely leveled it, and in doing so we suffered the worst casualties we had the whole day—not from the enemy, but from our own Navy. I was angered by it, angered beyond all measure, because I thought it was totally disgraceful. . . . And by that time I was frantically throwing up smoke bombs to alert them to the fact that we were in the town, but it was too late to prevent the barrage from occurring.

S/Sgt. Joseph Pilck
Company G, 16th Infantry, 1st Division
When we were near the Colleville church, the Navy opened up with their big guns and destroyed the church steeple. We lost quite a few of our soldiers from that bombardment.

Rear Adm. C. F. Bryant
Commander, Bombardment Group, Force O, July 2, 1944
We didn't know and had no way of knowing that the Army was held up. We
hadn't gotten the word. We had planned to sit offshore and wait for NSFCP [Naval
Shore Fire Control Parties] to contact us. It didn't work that way.

Adm. Harold Stark
Commander, U.S. Naval Forces Europe, Report on Neptune Naval gunfire
operations, 1945
Every firing ship was provided with an Army artillery officer, charged with maintaining up-to-date information about the position of Allied troops and with determining the desirability of firing at any given target. The organization worked as
follows: a) The Shore Fire Control Party made contact with his firing ship by radio
link and designated a target by reference to a grid; b) The Army liaison officer
decided whether it was safe to fire at that target; c) The ship itself controlled the
fire; d) The Shore Fire Control Party observed the fall of shot and corrected fire by
means of a clock code.

Board of Admiralty, Great Britain
"Comments on Naval Reports on Operation Neptune," July 1944
It must be appreciated that, once fighting is in progress on the beaches, seaborne
fire cannot effectively engage many beach defenses which are still active, owing to
the danger to our own troops, and that therefore these will have to be dealt with by
the normal Army methods for which their own supporting weapons are essential.

Despite the navy's well-intentioned but demoralizing barrage, Company G held on in Colleville for the rest of the day. However, due to a sizable enemy presence in Colleville's eastern fringe, as well as the
neighboring hamlet of Cabourg, Dawson could take no further offensive
action. Indeed, had it not been for the energetic exploits of the 16th
Infantry's 3rd Battalion, which in late afternoon had cut the coastal highway behind the Germans at Le Grand Hameau and threatened them with
encirclement, the enemy in all probability would have driven Dawson's
men out of Colleville.

THIS MAN WAS GOOD

Company L had led the 3rd Battalion off the beach through the Cabourg
draw well before noon and advanced astride a narrow dirt lane that forked a
few hundred yards inland. The right, or western, fork led to Cabourg, some
700 yards to the southwest; the eastern fork, heading off to the left, fol-

lowed the coast for about a half mile past the ruins of an ancient stone chapel and then turned inland to join the coastal highway at the village of Le Grand Hameau. Lt. Robert Cutler, who had taken command of Company L when the enemy felled Capt. John Armellino on the beach, set up a defensive perimeter around the split in the road and sent two patrols ahead to scout Cabourg and Le Grand Hameau.

The Cabourg patrol, consisting of PFC Lawrence Milander and Privates William Butt and Victor O'Dell, vanished, and nothing was heard from it until the next day—when it returned to the American lines with fifty-two German captives. The three GIs thereupon related their remarkable story. It turned out that as the men had cautiously approached Cabourg, which consisted only of about a dozen houses situated just north of the coast road, a concealed German shot Butt. As Milander and O'Dell hurriedly applied first aid to their wounded comrade, more enemy troops pounced out from beyond the hedgerows and took the men prisoner.

This new type of close-up warfare in the *bocage* would take a long time to get used to. The Germans, however, were obviously halfhearted soldiers, and Milander—who spoke German—worked on them that night, claiming that once the mighty American host got moving at dawn, the Germans would all die. Why not give up? They did. And the following morning, like a latter-day Sergeant York, Private First Class Milander marched them straight into captivity, adding yet another chapter to the lore of the Fighting First.

The four-man patrol to Le Grand Hameau, led by Sgt. Burton Davis, soon returned with valuable intelligence: The town was occupied by plenty of enemy troops. The GIs had gotten so close to the Germans, in fact, that Davis declared he could hear them laughing. Some even taunted the Americans by yelling out commands in English. The patrol agreed that the enemy troops must have been drunk.

If so, the alcohol triggered belligerence, for the enemy in Le Grand Hameau promptly launched a counterattack against Company L's perimeter near the head of the Cabourg draw. The American beachhead at Omaha was small, much smaller than General Gerow would have liked—and it certainly must not get any smaller. A retreat would put the Americans back on the beach, and that was a place to which the GIs did not want to return. The fighting turned very hot for a while, and as the troops had already realized, in the *bocage*, hardly anyone knew what was going on.

But at least one man did. Lt. Jimmie Monteith, who had guided Company L off the beach and up the draw that morning, appreciated the disas-

10:00 A.M.–4:00 P.M.: Cabourg

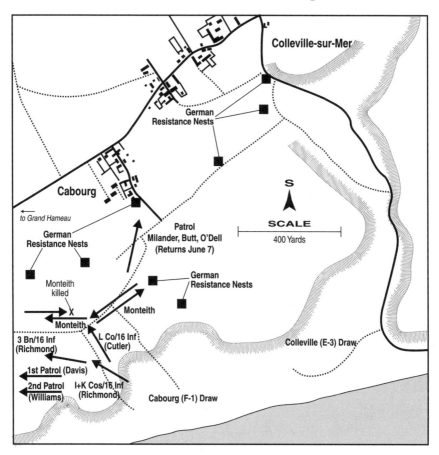

"This man was good." First Lt.
Jimmie Monteith of Company L,
16th Infantry, 1st Division, was
awarded the Medal of Honor
posthumously for valor on D-Day.
His platoon sergeant, T/Sgt.
John Worozbyt, said of him,
"He was a man I had the utmost
admiration and respect for."
U.S. Army Signal Corps,
National Archives.

trous consequences of a retreat and waged a one-man war to ensure that it
would not occur.

S/Sgt. Aaron Jones
Company L, 16th Infantry, 1st Division, March 20, 1945

In that sector the enemy was not fighting from fixed positions, but was moving
around in the hedgerows and setting up automatic weapons. A large group of
enemy started an attack on the position and set up machine guns on the flanks and
rear. The Germans yelled to us to surrender because we were surrounded. Lt.
Monteith did not answer, but moved toward the sound of voices and launched a
rifle grenade at them from 20 yards, knocking out the machine gun position. Even
with a large force the Germans couldn't break through our positions, so they set
up two machine guns and started spraying the hedgerow. Lt. Monteith got a squad
of riflemen to open up on the machine gun on the right flank. Under cover of the
fire he sneaked up on the gun and threw hand grenades, which knocked out the
position. He then came back and crossed a 200-yard stretch of open field under
fire to launch rifle grenades at the other machine gun position. He either killed the
crew or forced them to abandon the weapon. Back on the other flank, enemy riflemen opened up on us again and Lt. Monteith started across the open field to help

us fight them off, but was killed by the fire of a machine gun that had been brought to our rear.

Sgt. Hugh Martin
Company L, 16th Infantry, 1st Division, March 20, 1945
When [Lt. Monteith] knocked out the machine gun with the rifle grenade, he stood in full view at 40 yards, and the first shot fell short. The full fire of the gun was turned on him, but he held his position and fired the second grenade to knock out the position.

T/Sgt. John Worozbyt
Company L, 16th Infantry, 1st Division
Shortly before my platoon leader Lt. Monteith was killed, he expressed great concern for my safety and the safety of my men. When I made a report on the number of men wounded, I still had blood on my hands from administering first-aid to one of the casualties. It was then that Lt. Monteith, thinking it was my wound, cautioned me to be careful, and to see that the men were safe. He was a man I had the utmost admiration and respect for.

Lt. Gen. Walter Bedell Smith
Chief of Staff, Allied Expeditionary Force, November 20, 1944
Gen. Eisenhower: Please note that [for Lieutenant Monteith] the V Corps commander, Gen. Gerow, and the First Army commander, Gen. Hodges, and the 12th Army Group commander, Gen. Bradley, all recommend the Distinguished Service Cross [rather than the Medal of Honor]. I concur with them.

Gen. Dwight D. Eisenhower
Supreme Commander, Allied Expeditionary Force, November 20, 1944
Bedell: You are mistaken. Bradley recommends the Medal of Honor [for Lieutenant Monteith], and I must say that the thing looks like a Medal of Honor to me. This man was good.

After the enemy attack had been repulsed, Company L was reinforced by assorted 16th Infantry units that had come up the Cabourg draw under the direction of Capt. Kimball Richmond, the commander of Company I. The Germans were probably disorganized by their failed attack, so now was the time to return their belligerence in full with a determined advance on Le Grand Hameau. Thanks to Captain Richmond, the beachhead would soon be a little bigger.

3rd Battalion, 16th Infantry, 1st Division
D-Day After-Action Report, June 23, 1944

Capt. Richmond sent out a strong combat patrol under Lt. [Jack] Williams to take Le Grand Hameau, which was located about 1,500 yards inland and to the east. After a lapse of one hour, he followed the combat patrol up with the remainder of his combined force, which totaled 104 men—79 from L Company and the rest of Companies I and K. Lt. Williams outposted the main road with five riflemen and a light machine gun. After this had been done, a German scout car approached the town and was halted. Of its two occupants, one was taken prisoner and the other killed as he tried to escape. Pvt. [Charles] Hodge, who was manning a light machine gun, captured two staff cars and one scout car [of] the enemy. Valuable papers, maps, and a complete radio set were taken from these cars.

Capt. Kimball Richmond
Company I, 16th Infantry, 1st Division, Distinguished Service Cross Citation, July 1, 1944

Without hesitation, Captain Richmond pushed inland against the enemy. Completely disregarding his own safety, he led his men across open terrain and captured Le Grand Hameau and successfully defended it against superior forces until relieved. The personal bravery and determined leadership of Captain Richmond reflect great credit upon himself and were in keeping with the highest traditions of the Armed Forces of the United States.

THE PRESENT IS ALL YOU HAVE

By midafternoon, the surviving German beach defenders faced a bleak choice: either hang on and hope that reinforcements would rescue them, or flee as swiftly as possible to the south and yield the beachhead to the invaders. But with Vierville and Le Grand Hameau in American hands, and Colleville nearly so, both options appeared increasingly irrational. The Germans were dangerously close to being trapped. For the beach defenders to be rescued, reinforcements would have to punch through the American-held towns on the coastal highway—not a very plausible hope—or attack northward to the beach from the interior. The Norman road network leading inland from the coast, however, was entirely unfavorable to the Germans. Only three meandering roads headed south from the beach—two of which originated at points already controlled by the Americans. The third, still controlled by the Germans, connected St. Laurent with Formigny, two miles to the south, and it was on this road that the last slim German hope for success, but more likely survival, depended. If the Americans could speedily capture St. Laurent, or cut the road below it heading south, the trap would be closed, and the German coastal defenders' options reduced to two: surrender or die.

One of war's truest axioms is that a military force will fight with increased fervor to keep open an avenue of rescue or escape. Perhaps it was the enemy's devotion to this principle that repeatedly frustrated the American effort to seize St. Laurent, despite their vast numerical superiority. But at St. Laurent, at least part of the Americans' troubles stemmed from the fact that the unit originally assigned by invasion orders to seize the village, Major Bingham's 2nd Battalion, 116th Infantry, had been butchered on the beach. When the Americans managed to assemble substitute units to take over the job, the Germans were ready, and as a result, the battle for St. Laurent turned out to be one of the bitterest fights of the day. At St. Laurent, as in Colleville, the GIs succeeded in fighting their way in—but by nightfall, they had not forced the Germans out.

Actually, the Americans came close to capturing St. Laurent around noon, when Lt. Col. Lawrence Meeks's 3rd Battalion, 116th Infantry, initiated an energetic but disjointed advance inland from the bluff crest due north of the village. That the Germans inside St. Laurent would vigorously resist an attempt to take it became increasingly obvious the closer the Stonewallers approached the northern fringe of the village. Even worse, the fields north of St. Laurent were much more open than the standard Norman *bocage*, and given the enemy's lengthy fields of fire, any attempt by the 3rd Battalion to make a frontal attack there would surely result in a massacre worse than what had just occurred on the beach. But St. Laurent was not the responsibility of the 3rd Battalion. Rather, its invasion orders specified an advance on a southwesterly axis to an assembly area several miles inland—and no one had informed Meeks that his orders should be disregarded. Furthermore, the battalion had landed on a beach far to the east of its assigned sector. Now would be the time, therefore, to alter the 3rd Battalion's course of movement diagonally to the right. As a result, St. Laurent would be bypassed—but an even tougher obstacle lay ahead.

During Rommel's inspection of the German 352nd Division in May, several members of the division staff registered their concerns that the Atlantic Wall, as Rommel envisioned it, had no depth. Should the Allies crack the coastal defenses, nothing could stop them from pushing inland with impunity. D-Day proved that this judgment was in large measure accurate. However, in the middle sector of Omaha Beach, centered in and around St. Laurent, the German defense did in fact display some depth—a detail that the 29th Division learned with some difficulty on June 6. Situated about three-quarters of a mile inland from the high-water line, St. Laurent's sturdy stone edifices and tiny hedged-in orchards and pastures dominated the heads of Omaha's two middle beach exits, and as such, the village developed into a *de facto* German strongpoint on D-Day.

Additionally, about 400 yards west of the village on a commanding hill, the enemy had established *Widerstandsnest* 69, a backup defensive position that would block any American attempt to open the Les Moulins draw even if the Yanks managed to break through the German beach defenses at the draw's mouth. WN69 was so strong that it would be almost impossible to take it by a frontal attack. As the 29ers would soon learn, it would have to be flanked or bypassed.

Perhaps the real reason for the Germans' obvious fervor to defend this position was because it also was the site where they had positioned forty immobile *Nebelwerfer* (rocket) launchers. Each launcher could fire four 320-millimeter (nearly 13-inch) rockets, and on D-Day, these "Screaming Meemies," as GIs in the Mediterranean theater had aptly labeled them, would be something no American who fought near St. Laurent would ever forget. The rockets had a very short range and were highly inaccurate, but the hill on which their launchers were sited was only 1,200 yards from the beach, and in the crowded conditions prevailing behind the shingle for most of the day, the rockets could hardly miss. When they hit near or among the many groups of soldiers clustering behind the shingle, their huge blast effect was devastating. Unhappily for the GIs, Neptune invasion planners had only learned about the *Nebelwerfer* site two days before the invasion when they examined the last air photographs of Omaha Beach that had been taken prior to D-Day.

1st Lt. Jack Shea
Aide-de-camp to Brigadier General Cota, 29th Division, November 1944
Most of [the enemy fire] was landing on the sandy section of the beach, and occasionally a round would land in the midst of the troops huddled together in the lee of the wall on the shingle. Shell fragments of the *Nebelwerfers* resulted in unusually large chunks of shrapnel, the average size being about as large as the blade of an ordinary engineer shovel. One of these large fragments, striking a man in the small of his back, almost completely severed the upper portion of his body from his trunk.

When the 116th Infantry's 3rd Battalion shifted it axis of movement to the southwest around noon, thereby sidestepping St. Laurent on its left, it ran straight into the formidable WN69 and its Screaming Meemies. The German firepower that the 3rd Battalion had for the most part fortuitously missed on the beach would now be vigorously and efficiently displayed, proving that the beach was not the only place where the Yanks lost a lot of good men on D-Day. By nightfall, most of the battalion would still be fighting bitterly for that vital hill, and its journey to the assembly area would be indefinitely postponed.

Company L, 116th Infantry, 29th Division
U.S. Army Historical Division, interview with various Company L soldiers, September 20, 1944

[Lt. Donald] Anderson then oriented himself for the first time. He had started for the high ground knowing only that he was in the wrong place. On talking to his NCOs, he found that all were in agreement that the landing had been made far over to the left. He then decided that he would move against Les Moulins, the objective, regardless. The team followed along a hedgerow to the right, finally emerged onto open ground and drew fire from three places simultaneously. Part of the fire was coming from the direction of the beach, so Anderson decided that it was just as well to keep plugging ahead. Anderson, [Sgt. Joseph] Daya, and the two scouts led the team on. They kept low, got forward one more field, and there met a mortar section from Company I under Lt. [John] Davidson. At this time, both groups came under heavy fire. Anderson, still certain that the thing to do was keep moving ahead, walked up to the hedgerow and looked over to make a recon. A sniper drilled him through the head.

2nd Lt. Donald Anderson
Company L, 116th Infantry, 29th Division

I was shot in back of the neck with the bullet coming out my mouth. I had no pain; I was just stunned. I figured my brains were spilled all over my helmet, and this was the end—in 30 seconds or so, I would faint and be dead, so just relax and think a pleasant thought for 30 seconds. I thought about a girl I was dating in London. Thirty seconds went by and I didn't feel faint, so I felt I had it licked and wasn't going to die. While lying wounded, the second-in-command of my boat team, T/Sgt. [Albert] Odorizzi came up to take command and promptly decided he needed my wrist watch "just in case" and would return it the next time he saw me. I'm still looking for that watch.

Company I, 116th Infantry, 29th Division
U.S. Army Historical Division, interview with 2nd Lt. Norvin Nathan, July 2, 1945

At the top [of the bluff] Lt. Nathan saw a group of men ahead behind a hedgerow. They were three boat teams of I Company, 75 men. There was no enemy in sight.

Nathan went right with 10 to 15 men and a light machine gun. His team found a boat team commander from Company L who had been shot, Lt. [Donald] Anderson. They then worked up to the orchards [south of St. Laurent]. Nathan saw rocket positions [across the Les Moulins draw], and he ordered mortar fire against it. The Germans ran away back to a house. . . . He then went west to the D-3 [Les Moulins] draw. At the edge of the draw all the boat teams from Company I, with the company commander [Capt. Mifflin Clowe], caught up. Company K came up on the right. Germans were seen on the bluff across the draw, and machine guns opened up.

Company L, 116th Infantry, 29th Division
U.S. Army Historical Division, interview with Capt. Charles East,
June 29, 1945

Company L spent the afternoon trying to get past the crossroads [where the coastal highway and Les Moulins exit road joined] to reach the 3rd Battalion assembly area. The battalion was pretty well together, although companies were still operating by boat teams. Elements of all the companies were there. Enemy artillery fire was not the trouble. Rather, it was machine guns and snipers. The enemy controlled the high ground and swept all the approaches to the head of the Les Moulins draw. The 115th Infantry was on our [left] flank. One or two sections got past the draw and on to the assembly area, but the 3rd Battalion was largely stopped [at the head of the draw] for the night.

Capt. Maurice McGrath
Service Company, 116th Infantry, 29th Division, July 1944

When L Company, 116th Infantry, moved on toward Les Moulins in mid-afternoon, I was there to observe it. The artillery fire from the rear against the ground held by the company was terrific, and it seemed to me to be remarkable that they could hold their position at all.

PFC Norman Grossman
Company L, 116th Infantry, 29th Division

We were pinned down for about three hours [on the hill near WN 69]. I never thought we'd get out of this predicament, for the Germans seemed to have us. However, the order finally came to crawl off the top of the hill. Two hundred yards was a long way to crawl, especially with 20 pounds of equipment and a rifle. I think it took about 30 minutes for me to get beyond the edge of the hill so I could stand up without being hit. I remember that about 25 yards before I reached this point, I tried to get up on my hands and knees, but almost had the seat of my pants shot off.

In the meantime, a frustrated Major Bingham had abandoned his hope of breaking through the enemy defenses at the mouth of the Les Moulins draw. Instead, he tramped east along the beach, gathering as many of his 2nd Battalion GIs as he could, and climbed the bluff by the same paths the 3rd Battalion had used a few hours earlier. Bingham intended to move directly against St. Laurent from the north, but by the time he got there, the 29th Division's 115th Infantry was launching an attack against that town from the east. His men would join in that fight.

1st Lt. Robert Garcia
Executive, Company E, 116th Infantry, 29th Division
With [PFC Armand] Berthiaume and [T/4 Edward] Wilmoth in tow, I began the slow process of working inland. My objective was St. Laurent, a small village approximately 1,500 yards from the beach. It was so easy to get confused about direction, due to the ever-present hedgerows. At one point I came across a light machine gun section from a company unknown. They were set up to fire across the Les Moulins draw. They showed me the target. Right out in plain view was a group of German *Nebelwerfers*, firing toward the beach just as fast as they could load the tubes. The range was probably about 800 yards. But our machine guns weren't firing. I asked the non-com in charge what he was waiting for, and he replied that he "didn't want to give away our position." That was the first time I heard that line of reasoning, but not the last. I told him to start his guns firing, to watch the tracers, and to adjust his fire from the path of the tracers. The guns opened up at once. We could clearly see the tracers, and as the guns began to adjust their fire, we could see the Germans begin to move their guns. But not soon enough. All of a sudden there was a terrific explosion and a big ball of flame. We had hit either some of the ammo or some of the propellant.

But Garcia and the machine gunners had some help. In fact, the rocket launchers' smoky discharges and its missiles' distinctive screams were hard to miss, and most Americans within earshot or line of sight turned their heads to look. For the Allied sailors offshore who searched the coast intently through binoculars for targets, the enemy's *Nebelwerfers* were

Noon–9:00 P.M.: St. Laurent

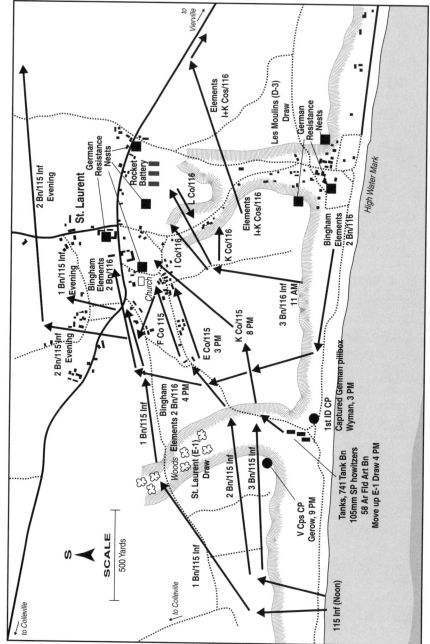

to Vierville

Elements
I+K Cos/116

2 Bn/115 Inf
Evening

German
Resistance
Nests

St. Laurent

Rocket
Battery

Les Moulins (D-3)
Draw

German
Resistance
Nests

L Co/116

1 Bn/115 Inf
Evening.

Bingham
Elements
2 Bn/116

I Co/116

K Co/116

Elements
I+K Cos/116

Bingham
Elements
2 Bn/115

High Water Mark

2 Bn/115 Inf
Evening

Church

F Co 115

E Co/115
3 PM

3 Bn/116 Inf
11 AM

K Co/115
8 PM

1 Bn/115 Inf

Bingham
Elements 2 Bn/116
4 PM

Woods

St. Laurent (E-1)
Draw

2 Bn/115 Inf

3 Bn/115 Inf

1st ID CP

Captured German pillbox
Wyman, 3 PM

Tanks, 741 Tank Bn
105mm SP howitzers
58 Ar Fld Art Bn
Move up E-1 Draw 4 PM

S

SCALE

500 Yards

V Cps CP
Gerow, 9 PM

1 Bn/115 Inf

to Colleville

to Colleville

115 Inf (Noon)

what they had been waiting for. Such an easy target could not survive for very long.

USS *Thompson*
Lt. Cmdr. Albert Gebelin, War Diary, 1155 hours, June 6, 1944
Rocket guns [German *Nebelwerfers*] observed firing on beachhead. . . . Shifted fire to the target immediately. 1213 hours ceased firing. Thirty rounds ammunition expended. Target completely silenced.

ARE YOU READY FOR IT?

For the 115th Infantry's 2nd Battalion, a frontal attack against St. Laurent, which the enemy surely had fortified in expectation of this moment, was not what the GIs would consider "mopping up." Such a phrase, or ones like it, had been uttered by staff officers too many times to remember at preinvasion briefings to describe the regiment's role in the assault, and the men had come to believe it. For the 115th, D-Day was supposed to consist of an unopposed landing followed by a hike of six miles to an inland objective. Then, as official orders stated, the regiment would "prepare to complete the mopping up of enemy resistance in the division zone." Not too bad, the GIs had reflected—and much less demanding than storming the beach at H-Hour. The hard part—the inevitable German counterattack—would come later. But who knew when, so why worry about it?

But the landing had not been unopposed, and there would be no march to the inland objective. Instead, for the 115th, there were pressing tasks immediately beyond the beach, and they would be much more difficult than just mopping up. Indeed, the simple act of climbing the mine-infested bluff had been treacherous enough. Now, after the troops had attained the plateau and shifted the axis of their march obliquely to the right, the 2nd Battalion's job would be to take St. Laurent. The 1st Battalion would cover the 2nd's left flank and maneuver around the south side of the village to envelop it; meanwhile, the 3rd Battalion would be in reserve on the right.

To carry out this attack, the 115th would have to cross the St. Laurent draw, the head of which featured such severely broken and wooded terrain that platoon leaders and company commanders would have been challenged even on a training exercise. When the somewhat jumbled 115th emerged from the low ground onto the draw's western rim, St. Laurent was a half mile ahead. A couple of isolated stone farm buildings stood in the intervening terrain, and a nearby field featured a German encampment with a few dozen undisturbed pup tents. Not much sign of the war from this perspective—but that would soon change.

At about 3:15 P.M., the 2nd Battalion commenced its attack, led by Companies E and F. The two outfits advanced cautiously astride what passed for St. Laurent's main street. A few hundred yards ahead was the village's squat Romanesque church, surrounded by a solid stone wall and an ornate wrought iron fence. Nearby was a stubby obelisk memorial to the locals who had died in World War I, but at the moment, the GIs needed no reminder that people die in war—and that in a year or two their own names might be carved into a similar memorial back in the States.

Although the area around the church consisted of only about six or seven buildings, it was an extraordinarily strong defensive position from which a small force could hold up an attacker many times its size. When Companies E and F approached within small-arms range, the Germans were ready to prove that point. And so the 115th Infantry's first offensive action of World War II would be to blast a determined enemy out of a house of God dating back several centuries. It didn't seem right, but a long time ago, someone had correctly categorized war as hell.

PFC William Wilch
Company E, 115th Infantry, 29th Division

Company E was the first American unit in St. Laurent-sur-Mer. Myself and [PFC] Burton Burfiend were scouts, and some French civilians showed us where the Krauts were. They were in a church and a big stone barn. The Krauts had machine guns in the steeple, and they sprayed everything that moved. We had a long fire-fight with the people in the steeple, but they were killing us. Lt. Col. [William] Warfield [CO, 2nd Battalion] was exposed all the time to enemy fire, but he made it. There were also some 1st Division people with us. We killed almost every Kraut that was in there.

115th Infantry, 29th Division
Regimental History, "The 115th Infantry Regiment in World War II," 1945

St. Laurent was a mass of tunneled emplacements, not only connected to each other, but also to strongpoints overlooking the beach. The German force holed up in the town was not large, but was strategically placed and difficult to locate. A sniper would fire from one spot and then show up at another a hundred yards away, having used the communications tunnels to advantage. . . . Fighting during the first few hours was rough, with few of the rules of warfare observed. German snipers seemed to like the targets offered by the Red Cross armbands of the medics, while few prisoners taken by our troops reached the collecting cages. . . . During the fighting for St. Laurent, members of the 2nd Battalion had as much difficulty dodging shells fired by the Navy into St. Laurent as they did from German snipers located in the town. At one stage of the battle inside St. Laurent, Lieutenant Colonel Warfield was seen sitting nonchalantly on the curb of the street with bullets whizzing around him. His feet were stretched out into the street, and the 2nd Battalion's commander was casually lobbing pebbles at a mongrel dog lounging nearby.

Pvt. William Phillips
Company E, 115th Infantry, 29th Division
It struck me as memorable that a man who was such an unmitigated son-of-a-bitch all the time we were in England could turn out to be such an excellent officer in combat—our battalion commander, Lt. Col. William Warfield, who was killed in action on June 10, 1944.

Capt. Maurice McGrath
Service Company, 116th Infantry, 29th Division, July 1944
With me [a few hundred yards to the west of St. Laurent] was a captain from the 293rd JASCO [Joint Assault Signal Company, a unit specializing in radio communication with Allied ships and aircraft]. He began to get suspicious about the church steeple in St. Laurent, as he figured the enemy must be producing this fire with the aid of a well-placed OP [observation post]. So he called for fire from the Navy, and as luck would have it the very first round hit the steeple and destroyed it. [The source of the fire was probably the destroyer USS *Thompson*.]

Capt. Robert Kaiser
Commander, Company F, 115th Infantry, 29th Division, 1945
T/5 Walter Brown and PFC Paul Shuman, my two company aid men, have really got what it takes. When we came through that minefield [on the bluff] they were right up front with us spotting and marking the mines with handkerchiefs and bandages. When I got hit [in St. Laurent] they came on the double under fire and helped me back.

The 115th Infantry suffered over 100 casualties on D-Day, and the vast majority of these came from Warfield's 2nd Battalion during its fight for St. Laurent. Of the twelve officers total in Companies E and F, six were wounded on June 6. But high casualties were not accompanied by success. When the 115th's commander, Colonel Slappey, ordered the 2nd Battalion to disengage from St. Laurent at about 8:15 P.M. and slip westward around the town's south side, the enemy had been driven from the village center around the church but still held on to several buildings 300 yards to the west at the junction of the Les Moulins exit road and the coastal highway. The road leading south from this junction to Formigny was the Germans' only remaining retreat artery, and they would therefore fight for it tenaciously. To clear St. Laurent once and for all, the 115th would have to attack yet again.

115th Infantry, 29th Division
Regimental History, "The 115th Infantry Regiment in World War II," 1945
When the 2nd Battalion headed away from the village, the 3rd Battalion under Major Victor Gillespie was ordered to enter and clear the town. Company K, with an attached tank [from the 741st Tank Battalion], headed into St. Laurent from the north. The men reached the center of the town without difficulty, but there the tank came under fire from a German antitank gun located to the south, and it was forced to withdraw. K Company suffered quite a few casualties, and the men retraced their steps northward. . . . Just before Company K was sent into St. Laurent late on Tuesday [June 6], Lt. Orlin DuVal went to the battalion chaplain, Capt. Eugene O'Grady, and told the Father that he had a feeling that he would not come out of St. Laurent alive. Father O'Grady asked the officer, "Are you ready for it?" Lieutenant DuVal replied that he was, to which Father O'Grady answered, "Well, then, go ahead." Lieutenant DuVal did go ahead with his company, and he was killed in St. Laurent on June 7. [The army listed DuVal, a native of Monroe, Michigan, as killed in action on June 7, but in all probability he was killed in Company K's evening attack on St. Laurent on June 6.]

741st Tank Battalion
Unit Journal, 2000 hours, June 6, 1944
One headquarters tank under the command of Cpl. [John] Resar cleared gun nests for units of the 29th Division in the vicinity of St. Laurent-sur-Mer.

1st Lt. Jack Shea
Aide-de-camp to Brigadier General Cota, 29th Division, November 1944
A sergeant of the 115th, 3rd Battalion, occupying the assistant driver's seat in the single tank that came down from [north of St. Laurent] was provided to assist in the direction of the tank's fire on the enemy stongpoint. This tank passed down between the narrowing of the road, caused by farm buildings built on either side, fired a few bursts of machine gun fire and after firing two rounds of 75mm ammunition, backed to its original starting position. Both the driver and the sergeant. . . stated that they were fired upon from the flank as they reached the crossroads.

They were not sure whether it had been an enemy bazooka or an antitank gun, but agreed that it was a high-velocity projectile that had been fired from their left flank and had missed them. . . . Mute evidence of the accuracy of the enemy's small arms fire lay in the grotesquely sprawled corpses of five riflemen, three on the southern edge of the road, and two in the northern gutter. They had been hit as they traveled that narrow section of road lying between the two walls of the extensive farm buildings on either side of the road.

Thanks to Lt. Col. John Cooper of the 110th Field Artillery Battalion, Gillespie's 3rd Battalion would have help from an unexpected source.

58th Armored Field Artillery Battalion
Battalion History, "The 58th Armored Field Artillery Battalion in World War II," 1945
By 1830 hours, the battalion had 11 of its guns [M-7 "Priest" 105-millimeter self-propelled howitzers] on shore and ready to fire, and under the able and courageous direction of the executive officer, Maj. Walter Paton, they moved off the beach in close support of the infantry. Looking back, it seems a miracle that any of the guns ever got ashore.

Lt. Col. John Cooper
Commander, 110th Field Artillery Battalion, 29th Division
At about 9:00 P.M., I remember a captain from the 115th Infantry asked me for help in the fighting in St. Laurent. There were two or three stone houses there, filled with Germans who were firing from the upper story windows. I called Lieutenant [John] Pollarine of Battery C, who had landed with the 115th's 3rd Battalion, and asked him to send up a couple of the 58th Armored Field Artillery's self-propelled 105mm howitzers [from Battery B]. One of my liaison officers with the 115th, Captain [Thomas] Cadwalader, had found these guns deployed on the plateau north of St. Laurent in the afternoon, and we figured they would be very useful in dislodging the Germans from the village. Pollarine sent the guns up, and they fired direct shots at the enemy-occupied houses from a couple of hundred yards away. The Germans began flying out of the windows right and left. We ended up capturing the buildings due to this devastating direct fire.

For the senior American commander on Omaha Beach, General Wyman, the chaos of the morning had crystallized into some semblance of order by late afternoon. Strong pockets of German resistance still survived in the Colleville and Les Moulins draws, but the Americans controlled

Vierville and Le Grand Hameau and were close to clearing the enemy out of Colleville and St. Laurent. As a result, Wyman realized that it was only a matter of time before the enemy's coastal resistance nests would wither and die. Furthermore, the enemy was obviously stretched to its limit: Even if the Germans could gather more reinforcements and fling them at the shallow American beachhead, they would in all probability not be able to break through to the beach. But as the day wore on, there would be no more significant enemy reinforcements. The enemy could not win.

Brig. Gen. Willard Wyman
Assistant Division Commander, 1st Division, Radio message, 1500 hours, June 6, 1944
To Gen. Huebner, pass to Gen. Gerow: 1st Division CP being set up at Exit E-1 at 679900 [map coordinate]. Gen. Cota states 29th Division CP being set up near Exit D-3 approximately 663900. Beach crust seems to be broken. Colleville taken. St. Laurent-sur-Mer partially occupied. 1st Battalion, 16th Infantry obliged to undertake mission of 2nd Battalion, 16th Infantry.

The human toll to reach this point had been appalling, but Wyman and other senior American commanders hardly had the time to ponder that disheartening thought. Historians could sort it out later; then the brave could be decorated, the dead honored, and soldiers could spin their yarns. But at least for now, things were beginning to look better.

CHAPTER 13

A Full Measure of Devotion

HANGING BREATHLESS ON THY FATE

Time was the issue now. Would there be enough of it before nightfall to land fresh troops and adequate supplies to sustain the offensive the next day? Could the five draws be opened in time to clear the beach of congestion and get the matériel to the troops who needed it? Could the lives of countless numbers of wounded men be saved? In short, despite its decidedly troubled start, could the invasion be salvaged?

In fact, what had come so far was only the beginning, a start that General Marshall hoped would lead to the Rhine and end in Berlin within the next year. On the other four D-Day beaches, the flood of men and matériel had already been unleashed. But on Omaha, there was still doubt. Unless the floodgates were opened, there could be no flood.

Omaha Beach unquestionably remained a dangerous place through nightfall. For the soldiers who landed or worked on the beach any time after midday, the increasing optimism of the generals was hard to fathom, given the gruesome sights that were visible in any direction one looked. Even worse, lethal enemy artillery fire fell on the beach all afternoon, and there didn't seem to be anything anyone could do to stop it. The Americans could only hope that the enemy's ammunition supply would soon run out.

The randomness of it all was startling: One second a buddy would be by a GI's side, and the next he would be lying on the sand oozing blood—or maybe even blown to bits. According to the standard GI philosophy, the only thing to do was to shake one's head and mutter that the poor guy's number must have come up.

Maj. Stanley Bach
HQ 1st Infantry Division, liaison officer with 29th Division, Diary,
June 6, 1944

1215 hours: Heavy mortar and 88 fire started on beach from east end to west end. Series of five shells in spots. Direct hit on Sherman tank, men out like rats—those alive.

1230 hours: LCT hit two mines and came on in; hit a third, disintegrated, and rear end sunk. At burst of shell, two Navy men went flying through the air into water. Never came up. . . .

1320 hours: Saw direct hit on beached LCM; flames everywhere; men burning alive. . . .

1400 hours: Fire on beach increasing. Aid man goes to help man who was machine gunned, but hit by bullet himself. Another aid man pulled him back to foxhole. . . .

1440 hours: More mortar fire, and more men hit. LCVPs unload five loads of men, they lie down on beach. Mortar fire kills five of them. The rest up and run for foxholes we left a couple of hours ago. . . .

1520 hours: Direct hit on truck's gasoline load. Canvas flames; another catches fire; then entire load goes up. Area 100 yards square: men's clothes on fire. Attempt to roll in sand to put out flames. Some successful. Others die in flames.

1540 hours: Infantry moving by us up path over crest and moving forward. We endeavor to move on. Machine gun holds us up for a few minutes, then lifts. We get to open field, follow path. See one man who had stepped on mine, no body from waist down, just entrails and chest organs.

1600 hours: We reach wood through field 500 yards from top of cliff we just came up. See man on knees; we think he is praying or scared. Roll him over and he is dead—died on his knees praying. . . .

P.S. I've seen movies, assault training demonstrations, and actual battle, but nothing can approach the scenes on the beach from 1130 to 1400 hours. Men being killed like flies from unseen gun positions: Navy can't hit 'em; Air cover can't see 'em; so infantry had to dig 'em out.

Col. Benjamin Talley
Deputy chief of staff for plans, V Corps

We walked up the beach only a few yards when a voice behind me called my name and said, "General Wyman is right over here. He would like to see you." . . . We were together only a few minutes when we heard an artillery shell coming. We lay flat. It struck nearby. We were shaken and for an instant seemed to be in darkness. Our ears were ringing, and we wondered if we would be deaf. Slowly our senses returned. Six of us were laying in a small group. . . . One of the soldiers cried out, and another whimpered softly to himself. General Wyman said, "We'd better be getting out of here. I am going this way." We told him that we were going up the beach toward the 29th Division, and we got up and ran. . . . On the other side of us another drama was being enacted. We thought we recognized a large man lying on the ground with his legs outstretched, except that his left leg bent up at an odd angle. His left arm was limp and twisted, and his face was cut and bleeding. Another soldier was kneeling over him trying to put a musette bag under his head. The soldier on the ground was heard to say, "It's my foot. I can't move it."

"Here, take this cigarette," his friend replied. "I've lit it for you. Open your lips."

Then we heard another shell coming. As it struck, the soldier on the ground raised his head a little. Then it fell back. The cigarette slid from his lips, and we saw it smoking on the ground.

The Americans desperately needed the five draws opened, and the engineers set out devotedly to get that job done before nightfall. With bull-dozers, shovels, and mine detectors, several engineer battalions had already combined their efforts to clear the St. Laurent draw, but with that village still partially occupied by the enemy, the E-1 exit for the moment was a dead end. The infantry would have to solve that problem later.

Col. Benjamin Talley
Deputy chief of staff for plans, V Corps, radio message, 1620 hours,
June 6, 1944

To Gen. Gerow: Situation improving. . . . Considerable rifle fire still exists [on] high ground [in] vicinity [of] Vierville. Very few tanks remain active. Will be several hours before exits are open for through traffic.

At Omaha's westernmost beach exit, the Vierville draw, the crux of the problem was the massive concrete wall the enemy had erected across the draw's mouth to block the movement of vehicles inland. At about 12:30 P.M., General Cota and his party of five had descended the draw from Vierville and in fact had moved through a narrow passageway in that wall to the beach. To Cota, the sight of burning vehicles and scores of American corpses on the sand at the foot of the draw was sufficient proof that most of the men assigned to blow this wall, and much of their equipment, had probably not survived the landing debacle. But there was a pressing need to demolish this barrier, and Cota set out eastward down the beach to find someone who could do the job.

1st Lt. Jack Shea
Aide-de-camp to Brigadier General Cota, 29th Division, November 1944
Cota turned to meet Col. [Lucius] Chase [executive officer of the 6th Engineer Special Brigade]. "Can you blow up that antitank wall at the exit?" Cota asked.

"We can, sir, just as soon as the infantry clean out those pillboxes around there," Col. Chase replied.

"We just came down through there. There's nothing to speak of there. Get to it!" Cota ordered.

Col. Chase then said that his men didn't have any TNT, for the Navy had failed to bring it in to them. Gen. Cota pointed to a bulldozer, which had about 20 cases of TNT lashed to its top. "Use that," he said, then turned and continued down the beach [to the east]. . . . Coming upon a second engineer bulldozer laden with cases of TNT, Cota went up to a group of troops who were huddled behind the seawall near it. "Who drives this thing?" he asked the group. No one answered. No one seemed to know. They just looked around at each other. "Well, can anyone drive the damn thing?" Again there was no answer. "They need the TNT down at the exit. I just came through there from the rear. Nothing but a few riflemen on the cliff, and they're being cleaned up. Hasn't anyone got guts enough to drive it down?"

A red-headed soldier came out of the group and said he'd get it down there. Cota slapped him on the back and sent him off with a hearty "That's the stuff!" Later, the general often remarked that he wished he had gotten the unidentified soldier's name. It was now about 1330 hours.

Cota continued on his way, assuming the engineers would get the job done somehow. They did. According to invasion orders, the unit responsible for blowing the wall was Company C, 121st Engineer Battalion, a component of the 29th Division. Most of the company, however, had been scattered eastward by errant landings. Even worse, the company commander, Capt. Svend Holmstrup, had been killed shortly after H-Hour exiting his landing craft. For the entire morning, enemy fire was far too hot to get anywhere near the wall, but later, as the enemy's rifle and machine gun fire subsided, many company members made their way slowly, inexorably westward to find the wall that orders demanded they destroy. A short time after Cota's departure, the 121st Engineers' commander, Lt. Col. Robert Ploger, arrived on the scene. Despite a painful wound to his left ankle, he gathered all available engineers—about twenty—and began to organize the effort to demolish the wall.

The object of the engineers' attention was about 125 feet long, 9 feet high, and 6 feet thick. To open the exit for American vehicles, Ploger's men needed only to blow a gap through its center wide enough to allow two lanes of traffic to pass. Even so, the job would be neither easy nor quick.

Lt. Col. Robert Ploger
Commander, 121st Engineer Combat Battalion, 29th Division
Word reached me that a C Company bulldozer was on the beach with its 1,000 pounds of TNT, and we scrambled to get it to the wall. I don't remember who the driver was. [Witnesses say it may have been PFC Joseph Drago or PFC Al Velleco.] In general, dozer operators were of a remarkably tough breed, and I've always marveled at the guts of that operator in driving onto a beach under fire with a load of enough TNT to blow the dozer into a hole in the ground. All it would have taken was one mortar round. I didn't know whether or not the wall was rein-

"They need TNT down at the exit." Offshore view of the Vierville exit at 3:00 P.M., just after U.S. engineers, supervised by Lieutenant Colonel Ploger, had demolished the concrete wall spanning the draw's mouth. The Vierville church steeple is visible in the background. The wall's destruction opened up the exit to vehicular traffic. U.S. NAVY, NATIONAL ARCHIVES.

forced with steel rods, but I had to assume it was. We therefore planned on using a lot of TNT to do the job. Sgt. Noel Dube of Company C did much of the work putting in the primers and fixing the leads. He also supervised the construction of a wooden platform to increase the effectiveness of the TNT by raising it off the road surface. Engineers from several different units participated in this task. When the charge was all in place, all personnel moved a safe distance away. After due warning, the detonation was accomplished at roughly 1500. I moved forward to inspect the results. The wall was demolished over the entire roadway; there was a dent in the pavement only about an inch and one-half in depth; there was a substantial amount of broken concrete lying all about, but no pieces were larger than one soldier could remove. I was astonished by how completely the wall was destroyed. It turned out that the Germans had not reinforced the wall with steel rods. That was a fatal mistake: the wall might have held together much more effectively had they done so. Also, the rods themselves might have been an obstacle that would have been tough for us to remove.

149th Engineer Combat Battalion, 6th Engineer Special Brigade
U.S. Army Historical Division, interview with adjutant, 149th Engineers, July 1944

Clearing up of the beach was expedited by the use of tank tractors. Wire was removed, and the wall blockade, which shellfire of the tanks could not tear down, was blown out. For most of the men it was the first time under fire. They conducted themselves well after the first shock, and applied themselves to the project of clearing the beach. . . . On D+1 a survey was made and 500 dead counted on Dog Green, White, Red, and Easy Green Beaches.

One draw over to the east, at Les Moulins, enemy fire was still too hot for engineers to work on opening the beach exit to traffic. In truth, German machine gun, mortar, and artillery fire here had been so severe all day that healthy American engineers at this locale were scarce. Les Moulins was a quaint village that in earlier and better days had been a quiet summer resort. The arrival of the *Boches*, however, led to hard times: The Germans leveled cottages that blocked fields of fire and converted others to fortified strongpoints. Several villas tucked into the draw's eastern wall were linked with tunnels and trenches and provided the perfect setting for the Germans to practice their bewildering tactic of firing from one position and swiftly scampering to another. That kind of maneuver was new to the Yanks, and it would take them weeks to get used to it.

In short, unless the GIs could root out almost every German from the cottages and dugouts scattered over the Les Moulins draw, it would be a dangerous task for American engineers to begin clearing the beach exit. By midafternoon, no one could guess how many enemy troops remained holed up in Les Moulins: It could be a squad of only 9 grenadiers—or a company of 150. Fortunately for the Americans, however, German resistance in Les Moulins subsided appreciably by evening, after 29th Division troops had moved in and around St. Laurent from the east—thereby cutting off whatever enemy troops still remained in the draw from their comrades further inland. By 7:00 P.M. opposition was limited to a rare burst from a machine gun and scattered shots from snipers, who promptly disappeared back into their hideaways. The engineers could finally get to work.

Capt. Maurice McGrath
Service Company, 116th Infantry, 29th Division, July 1944
At 2030 I decided I would try to go up the road and into Les Moulins [from St. Laurent]. By that time we were no longer attacking, and we had had no word that the [exit] road was open, but I thought I had better find out. I walked on into the village by myself and met no one until halfway through. I ran into some of my own vehicles coming up the hill. The drivers told me that they had been told that the last enemy positions in the village had been knocked out by naval shells late in the evening. [This was not true: Scattered German resistance continued in Les Moulins for two more days.] Being uncertain as to the state of things in our own sector, I directed the vehicles to move left [east, through the northern part of St. Laurent] toward the right flank of the 1st Division, where I felt they would be more secure. I then went on down to the beach. [McGrath probably saved the vehicles from destruction; had they driven straight south up the draw to the coast road, they would have run directly into a German resistance nest.]

Capt. William Callahan
Commander, Company F, 116th Infantry, 29th Division
An Engineer Special Brigade sergeant was hit early, in the face. It looked like one eye and part of the bone over the eye were gone. This NCO was continually exposed directing other engineer troops: replacing drivers on a bulldozer when they became casualties; helping the wounded—some far less hurt than he. . . . He continued to function and to be an inspiration to me and to those who were aware of him.

At the St. Laurent draw, about one mile to the east, the 1st Engineer Battalion had started to clear that beach exit shortly after midday. Troops from the 37th Engineers followed closely, and within a few hours, men and vehicles could proceed up the St. Laurent exit road in comparative safety.

True, the enemy still held parts of St. Laurent—so no one would be driving off the beach toward Paris anytime soon. But in spite of the chaos of the early morning hours, the engineers in this sector had fulfilled their mission and were the first to open up an exit road off Omaha Beach. As a result, tanks and self-propelled howitzers could make their way up to the plateau north of St. Laurent, and their presence there ultimately would lend considerable help to 29th Division efforts to clear the enemy out of St. Laurent for good.

T/Sgt. James Montague
HQ Company, 37th Engineer Combat Battalion, 5th Engineer Special Brigade, July 1944

On the beach, Capt. [Elbert] Scudero [CO, Company B], later joined by Lt. [Charles] Peckham, was following the 1st Engineers' mine detector crews up Exit E-1, and his own crews followed, widening the lane and clearing the road of mines. Borrowing a dozer from C Company, one of Capt. Scudero's men filled in the antitank ditch that ran across the road. Capt. Scudero returned to the beach, directing traffic, keeping the exit clear, and generally supervising the flow of men and vehicles from the beach up the exit road. . . . At 1700 the exit was operating fairly well, but sniper fire was still prevalent, and mortar and artillery fire on the junction of the lateral and exit road was periodic. . . . It may be safely said that Company B paved the way for the infantry to establish a foothold in this sector.

A mile to the east, at the Colleville draw, the situation was completely different. At almost one mile in length, the Colleville exit was Omaha's longest draw, and for engineers, the job of clearing it would have been difficult even if enemy resistance had been eliminated at H-Hour. But the Germans had not been eliminated; in fact, for most of the day, the enemy resisted with an unforeseen determination from commanding and nearly invisible fighting positions in and adjacent to the draw. When the Americans flanked the draw and fought their way into Colleville from the west, the Germans wisely countered this maneuver and held firm in the center of Colleville and the nearby hamlet of Cabourg until the morning of June 7, thereby denying the Americans control of the beach exit roads at the points where they joined the coastal highway about a mile south of the beach. Therefore, even if the Americans could break out from the beach, the Colleville draw would lead nowhere.

The GIs did not manage to eliminate German resistance at the draw's mouth until evening, at which point the engineers set out to fulfill their mission that had been so greatly delayed. Fortunately for the engineers, sunset in Normandy at this time of year did not occur until 10:10 P.M., and dusk's lingering light would enable them to work efficiently for nearly an hour after that. But there was no time for rest. Even after dark, the roar of bulldozers' engines and the shouts of engineers too jittery to do anything but keep working permeated the beachhead. Once the engineers could make up for all the lost time, maybe things would be all right after all.

T/Sgt. James Montague
HQ Company, 37th Engineer Combat Battalion, 5th Engineer Special Brigade, July 1944

Capt. [Louis] Drnovich, commanding A Company, landed with the reconnaissance section of the company at 0700. They made their way down the beach to E-3 [Colleville draw] but were unable to do much because of the small arms and mortar fire on the beach. The main body of the company landed at 0930, about two hours after their scheduled landing, aboard an LCT carrying two jeeps, a T-18 [tractor], and a D-8 [bulldozer]. . . . The company reached E-3 and an attempt was made to clear the exit. S/Sgt. Franks and Lt. McCain removed the tanks and half-tracks that were clogging the exit, driving them into a known minefield in order to open the road for traffic. Mine detector crews were sent up E-3, but were largely ineffective due to small arms fire from the high ground. Three 2 1/2-ton trucks were landed but were immediately demolished by 88 fire. Patrols were sent out from the beach in an attempt to locate, circle, and wipe out the 88s that were holding up the work. None of these patrols were successful. Capt. Drnovich attempted at various times to locate the spotter who was directing the fire, but snipers on the crest prevented this. The fire was unbelievably accurate. On two different occasions an attempt was made to land LCTs at the exit, but each time the ramp was dropped the shells landed squarely on the craft. Not a shell was wasted in getting range. Each shot was a direct hit. . . . [At dusk] Capt. Drnovich was still concerned because he was unable to locate the 88 that was causing so much havoc at the exit. Armed with a carbine and a few grenades, he set out, telling his platoon officers and first sergeant that he was going after the 88. He was found D+3 [June 9] a short way up the hill from the beach, shot through the head.

348th Engineer Combat Battalion, 5th Engineer Special Brigade
U.S. Army Historical Division, interview with Lieutenants Sidlowski, Selfe, and Walsh, June 30, 1944

Work on E-3 began about 2000 and, as the light began to fail, the [enemy] artillery let up and the work was speeded up. The road was open for tank traffic shortly after 0100 D+1 after being interrupted many times by artillery fire. A tank battalion went up after 0100 hours. [This was probably Company B, 745th Tank Battalion, consisting of seventeen Sherman tanks, which had landed on Omaha Beach at 4:30 P.M.] Work had been carried out by a D-8 and a T-18 which came in late D-Day. The last serious artillery barrage of the night was just before the tanks went over the road. [The Germans still controlled Colleville, at the head of the draw, so the exit road was not yet fully usable.]

The Cabourg (F-1) draw, on the eastern extremity of the beach, was small enough that it did not figure prominently in invasion plans. But when the other four draws on Omaha Beach proved so difficult to crack on D-Day, engineers applied themselves to the highly difficult task of opening this exit as soon as 1st Division infantrymen had seized it and moved beyond the beach. The chore was the responsibility of the 336th Engineer Battalion, but unhappily for that outfit's sappers, their first glance at the trail that the invasion plan had dictated they turn into a passable road was shocking. This trail climbed a precipitous slope and was barely wide enough for hikers. Another trail that the 336th was supposed to turn into a return road to the beach was almost as bad. American tanks and heavily loaded trucks could never travel on those routes no matter how much effort the 336th put into the job. The engineers would have to forge a completely new road that would ascend the draw on a gentler grade.

336th Engineer Combat Battalion, 5th Engineer Special Brigade
U.S. Army Historical Division, interview with Captain Lothspeech,
June 28, 1944

There was no attempt at company organization. C Company had the most men, A next, and then a platoon from B. . . . It was obvious that the F-1 road planned was not usable, and the alternate road was begun. This was not planned from an engineering standpoint; the logical route was taken. At the time it seemed quite obvious.

336th Engineer Combat Battalion, 5th Engineer Special Brigade
U.S. Army Historical Division, interview with Captain Hutchinson,
June 23, 1944

[The 336th] began clearing mines at 4:30 to 5:00 P.M. without mine detectors. The men probed for mines with bayonets. Later eleven detectors were salvaged and put to use. A minefield began 50 yards south of the shingle and ran to the top of the slope. The road developed was suggested in the battalion plan as a return road in the dump loop, but [this road] was found to be useless, and the new F-1 two-lane [road] was built as an alternate. The first roadway at F-1 was finished at 2030 on D-Day, one hour behind plan. Fourteen tanks passed over this road on the night of D-Day.

336th Engineer Combat Battalion, 5th Engineer Special Brigade
U.S. Army Historical Division, interview with Lt. Col. Paul Bennett, June 23, 1944

Two tanks blew their tracks on the way up the road. Work was hampered considerably by lack of mine detecting equipment. Out of 24 detectors we had planned to use, only seven were in workable order. The sweepers also ran into box mines, which the detectors couldn't pick up. Before going after the antitank mines, the sweepers had to probe for the box mines first [using bayonets]. . . . Of three dozers scheduled to come ashore D-Day, only one could be brought in. This was landed to the west of the 336th beach and made its way up the beach under fire. Other dozers came in later. Dozer operators worked up to 50 hours at a stretch, and their work was highly commended by Col. Bennett.

The Germans could not have imagined that the Cabourg draw, featuring nothing but a few narrow dirt trails leading steeply down to the sea, would ever become an American supply artery. But that is exactly what the 336th made it.

THE GENERAL THEY CALLED COACH

A writer in a May 1944 edition of the training pamphlet *Army Talks* declared, "This is a sergeant's war." The first few hours of combat on the second front proved the truth of this prophecy. When the enemy's fierce and unforeseen resistance on the beach caused the Omaha landing plan to disintegrate within minutes of H-Hour, most of the bewildered soldiers on the beach surely harbored a common thought: Now what? Nothing in the voluminous invasion plan could answer that question. Wyman, Cota, Taylor, Canham, Schneider, and other senior officers offered sensible remedies and provided inspiration to the inert body of troops clustered behind the shingle, but they could not be everywhere at once. As for Generals Huebner, Gerow, and Bradley, who monitored the invasion's progress from their command ships far out to sea, for all the good they were doing to put the invasion back into working order, they might as well have been on the moon.

With or without the encouragement of the top brass, the fighting men would have to look to their NCOs and junior officers to solve the tactical dilemmas of Omaha Beach. General Huebner, the commander of the 1st Division and the multitude of attached units assaulting Omaha on D-Day, had faith that his men would do exactly that. Huebner had been an enlisted man for six years, and later, as a company commander in World War I, he himself had demonstrated the initiative he hoped his men would display as the invasion degenerated into bedlam. Yes, it was a sergeant's war; but to Huebner, until the moment when someone would assume firm control of the battle, all those sergeants' actions would remain unsynchronized, bedlam would persist, and paralysis could easily set in. Huebner was the man to exert that control, but he could not possibly do so from *Ancon*. Due to communication breakdowns triggered by casualties and the general pandemonium on the beach, Huebner's perception of the battle was hours behind reality. Any order he issued onboard *Ancon* had a good chance of being pointless by the time the recipient received it. Huebner wasn't doing anyone any good where he was, so he decided to head for the beach, where he would prove that he was, indeed, as the men called him, "The Coach."

Force O, U.S. Navy
D-Day Action Report, Chronological Record of Events, June 6, 1944
1715 hours: Major General Huebner, CG 1st Infantry Division, and staff, left USS *Ancon* to establish headquarters in the beach.

Headquarters, 1st Infantry Division
G-3 Section, Record of 1st Division Operations, June 6, 1944
The Division command post group [including General Huebner] aboard the USS *Ancon* departed at 1700 for Easy Red Beach. The Assistant Division Commander [General Wyman] notified the Commanding General that the advance command post location was 676899 [a map coordinate, the site of an abandoned German pillbox near the mouth of the St. Laurent draw] with contact by phone with division artillery and the 116th Infantry, and by radio with the 18th Infantry. The Division Commander was requested [by General Wyman] to land the 26th Infantry as soon as possible. The group arrived on Beach Easy Red at 1900.

Lt. Col. Robert Pratt
Assistant G-3, V Corps
It seemed that all the elements were in a great mixup. We had selected one beach for a regiment [the 16th] of the 1st Division, and another for a regiment [the 116th] of the 29th Division, so that as they became reinforced, these would become divisional sectors. This was not to be until someone reorganized the mess. Gen. Huebner sensed this and took off for the beach with his staff during the late afternoon. Once ashore, things began to perk up, and some order was regained.

Ens. Richard Crook
Executive, PC-553, Force O
In the late afternoon, Maj. Gen. Clarence Huebner, the division commander, was on board briefly before heading ashore. [He] had come in from the *Ancon*. . . . General Huebner was eager to get ashore, but in the meantime, he had lost his pearl-handled pistol on board our ship. Maybe one of our boys took it; I don't know. There was a big furor about that. Fortunately, his mood had improved as the day had proceeded. He finally left in late afternoon—without the pistol—to take command of his men on the beach and begin the movement inland.

When Huebner and his staff arrived ashore, they went straight to the St. Laurent draw to locate the captured German pillbox Wyman was using as a temporary 1st Division command post. Given the enemy's constant bombardment of the beach, this pillbox was an eminently sensible place for a division headquarters, but it was not where Huebner's chief of staff, Col. Stanhope Mason, wanted it to be. Based on the 1st Division's experience in the Sicily invasion, Mason expected the Luftwaffe to begin bombing the invasion armada at nightfall, and if they did so, the beach would probably not be a place where division business could be conducted efficiently. Instead, with Huebner's approval, Mason chose a division command post more than a half mile beyond the bluff, in an orchard 400 yards east of St. Laurent. If the Luftwaffe did in fact put in an appearance that night, Mason reasoned that the orchard should be a safer and quieter place for Huebner to run the division.

Huebner's entourage trudged up the St. Laurent exit road to Mason's orchard sometime before 8:00 P.M. and set up the Fighting First's nerve center. Radio and telephone switchboard operators promptly endeavored to provide Huebner the secure communications he would need to make decisions and give his boss, General Gerow, an accurate depiction of the state of affairs on Omaha.

If Huebner wished to be kept abreast of the sergeants' war, this was the place to do it. German barrages frequently forced the staff to seek cover and, later, dig foxholes as deep as possible. Furthermore, when Huebner arrived, the GIs' attack on the enemy's nearby strongholds in and around St. Laurent was under way, and it sporadically triggered a cacophony of gunfire that was hardly conducive to the prudent deliberation required of a general to run a successful battle. It was not how the division staff had expected to enter Normandy, but this is where Coach had to be. This was an extraordinary day, and the men must see their general.

The ranking general on Omaha Beach prior to Huebner's arrival was not Wyman, but Maj. Gen. Charles Gerhardt, commander of the 29th Division. "Uncle Charlie," as he was known to the 29ers, had crossed the Channel with his staff aboard the destroyer escort *Maloy* and at the earliest opportunity had hitched a ride on a passing navy landing craft headed for the beach. He landed near the Vierville beach exit at 4:45 P.M. and immediately set up a division command post in an abandoned quarry near the east side of the draw about 200 yards beyond the beach.

Gerhardt was perhaps a little overeager to come ashore, for when he set up his command post, he held command authority over not a single 29th Division soldier on the beach aside from his staff. Unhappily for Uncle Charlie, all 29ers who landed on Omaha on D-Day were under Huebner's control, and this arrangement would persist until General Gerow of V Corps saw fit to terminate it and shift responsibility for 29th Division troops back to Gerhardt—an event that supposedly would occur sometime on June 7. Gerhardt could hardly wait.

Col. Benjamin Talley
Deputy chief of staff for plans, V Corps

General Gerhardt made me a bet that he would get ashore in Normandy before I did. I saw him at a V Corps briefing conducted by Gen. Gerow around 0930 on D+1. It was held in a gravel pit [the quarry] some 200 yards up the road from the German pillbox at the foot of the Vierville draw. He asked me when I landed. I told him a little after 1300. He said: "You win."

1st Lt. Tucker Irvin
G-2 Section, 29th Division Headquarters, June 17, 1944

We met no organized opposition as we moved up the Vierville exit and opened the first 29th Division CP in a quarry beyond the crest of the slope overlooking the beach. Although the advance echelon [General Cota and his staff] was supposed to set up in the woods on the other side of Vierville, regular headquarters had no communication with them, and so the temporary CP was set up in the quarry. About 10:00 P.M., radio contact with the advance echelon was established, and about 2:00 A.M. [June 7] Cota visited the quarry. It was decided to wait until [morning] to have the advance echelon join the regular headquarters' CP. This was done after daybreak.

Gerhardt may have been a general without a command, but that did not stop him from issuing orders. In preparation for Gerow's expected activation of the 29th Division on June 7, Gerhardt wished to establish stable communication with the 1st Division. But where was Huebner? No one knew, so Gerhardt sent one of his liaison officers, Capt. James Ballard, to find the 1st Division command post. Ballard's job would not be easy.

Capt. James Ballard
Liaison officer, G-3 Section, 29th Division Headquarters, July 1944
I asked for a volunteer to accompany me, and S/Sgt. Ted Josephs, Assistant Operations Sergeant, stepped up immediately. . . . The night was very dark. Vierville-sur-Mer was lighted up, however, for the most part by fires which were still burning. We sneaked up the road to Vierville and turned left at the little intersection which comprised the heart of the town. This put us on the road running east to St. Laurent. . . . In about one-half hour—it must have been nearly 10:00 P.M.— we had gone [about 800 yards], I guess. [It must have been well after 10:00 P.M., because darkness did not set in until about 11:00.] Then suddenly I saw a man lying prone so close I almost could have touched him. At once he jumped up and darted a few feet to the right. Immediately I heard a sharp whistle, and a volley of shots came in our direction. Almost at once three men came toward me. I was lying prone on the edge of the road. The color of the road was dark, however, while the men coming toward me were silhouetted against the sky. When I hit the road, I dropped my carbine, so I instinctively pulled my pistol and fired almost point-blank several times in rapid succession. Two men, shouting, fell to the ground. I don't know what happened to the third. It all happened so fast. I dashed to the right rear some distance and took cover in a field where I could gather my thoughts. I had lost Sgt. Josephs and thought him either killed or captured. . . . I worked as quickly as I could back to the quarry and there found that contact had been established with 1st Division elements via the beach. At dawn I commandeered a tank and set out on the St. Laurent highway to find Sgt. Josephs. When we had gone a mile or so, Sgt. Josephs jumped out of a ditch and hailed me. I was never so glad to see anyone in my life.

Gerhardt's enforcement of discipline within the 29th Division was legendary, and it took him only a short time to demonstrate that combat would not lessen his efforts to keep his Blue and Gray division a spit-and-polish outfit. According to division lore, as Uncle Charlie studied maps of Normandy while sitting on a box of C Rations in the quarry, he spied a soldier eating an orange and throwing the skin on the ground. This was too much for Gerhardt's fastidious disposition. He bolted toward the unfortunate GI and rebuked him for violating the 29th Division's strict code of hygiene.

In World War II, it was not the job of an American corps commander to lead from the front. But if General Gerow wished to follow Huebner and Gerhardt ashore on D-Day and establish V Corps headquarters within Omaha's slender beachhead, that was just what he would have to do. On the evening of June 6, there was virtually no place on Omaha Beach that was immune to German fire. Nevertheless, Gerow resolved to set up a V Corps command post on dry land before nightfall. Given the breakdown of American communications on D-Day, which had failed to provide the V Corps staff onboard *Ancon* with an accurate depiction of the battle, the only prudent course of action, according to Gerow, was to see the situation for himself and meet with his chief subordinates in person. The German strongpoint that Lieutenant Spalding's boat team had conquered early that morning on the bluff just east of the St. Laurent draw would do. The site featured a warren of trenches and dugouts, providing a comparatively safe place for staff officers to work—and sleep.

Lt. Col. Robert Pratt
Assistant G-3, V Corps

Gen. Gerow decided that the Corps should go in as soon as some clarity came out of the confusion. We left the *Ancon* by LCVP about 1900 and even this was difficult because of the high sea. The Admiral [Hall] had provided the ship's landing ladder so that the General would not have to use a cargo net to reach the LCVP. When about half of the party was onboard in the rearing and bouncing craft, an exceptional sea crashed the boat into the ladder, and the bottom was no more. . . . The balance of the party and the General now had to descend by cargo net. For some it was difficult. The passage to the beach was wet and uneventful, and we arrived on shore at 2030 after passing through the now-impotent obstacles and their entangled refuse. Gen. Gerow was proudly lifted ashore by a bulldozer commanded by none other than Col. Talley. He landed dryshod, the rest of us walked through knee-deep water and got thoroughly soaked in the process. . . . The Corps CP was a German slit trench running along the military crest of a ravine leading to the beach near St. Laurent. (It was still there 20 years later at the rear of the U.S. Cemetery.) The senior group resided in a log-lined dugout as far inland as one could go. The rest of us partook of the shelter of the trench. I set up the G-3 mapboard and attempted to get the situation plotted. With very little information that was accurate, this was difficult. Then the fun began as a sniper buried in a spider hole in the field to our front began shooting at the top of the board, which protruded above the lip of the trench. Some engineers with a mine detector routed him out and the excitement was over. His orders were to fire until his ammunition ran out and kill as many as possible.

For most of the day, persistent radio failures and the death or wounding of many members of naval fire control parties on the beach had deprived the navy of accurate knowledge of the invasion's progress. Naval support of the infantry on Omaha Beach was usually accurate and of profound value to the ground troops when active enemy positions were obvious, particularly in and around the beach-level openings of Omaha's five draws. But on a few occasions, naval fire was more of a hindrance than a help, and the arrival of the top brass ashore did not immediately clear up this problem. Lacking timely intelligence of the locations of American troops due to a near total inability to communicate with the spotters ashore, whose job was to maintain radio contact between fighting troops and supporting warships, the navy's gunfire support vessels occasionally relied on shipboard visual observation and hearsay evidence when considering bombardment targets. That evidence sometimes turned out to be inaccurate, and the unfortunate result was that American troops at times came under the fire of their own naval guns.

Cmdr. William Marshall
Commander, Destroyer Division 36, D-Day Action Report, June 1944
The support of destroyers during this phase was not utilized to over twenty percent of its possibilities. There was no communication with the beach, and on numerous occasions destroyers could not fire on targets which should have been fired on because they did not know the location of our own troops. . . . It was most galling and depressing to lie idly a few hundred yards off the beaches and watch our troops, tanks, and landing craft and motor vehicles being heavily shelled and not be able to fire a shot to help them.

Occasionally, however, destroyers opened fire even when solid evidence pinpointing enemy resistance nests was lacking. From offshore, sailors could see nothing beyond the bluffs except for the church steeples of Vierville, St. Laurent, and Colleville, and unless those sailors could contact U.S. Navy spotters in the frontlines by radio, any shooting at an inland target, given the situation's extraordinary fluidity, had a good chance of falling among American troops. In the early evening, a destroyer bombarded Colleville when troops from Dawson's Company G, 16th Infantry, actually occupied parts of that village. Similarly, more than four hours after the 116th Infantry and Rangers had first occupied Vierville, a naval bombardment shattered the Vierville church under the erroneous assumption that it contained an enemy observation post.

USS *Harding*
Cmdr. George Palmer, War Diary, 1350 hours, June 6, 1944
Received visual message from LCI-538. . . : "From info shore party: 'Believe church steeple to be enemy observation post. Can you blast it?'" We then asked, "Which church do you mean?" LCI replied, "Church at Vierville." We then asked LCI, "Don't you mean church at Colleville?" LCI replied, "Colonel Houston says not." [A Lt. Col. Earl Houston commanded the 348th Engineer Battalion, which landed in the afternoon to help open the Colleville draw.] We then asked LCI, "From what source did you obtain this information?" LCI replied, "From Colonel Houston." *Harding* then called Commander Force O Forward Observers [CFOFO] and reported the above requesting permission to open fire on church. CFOFO replied in about five minutes that permission to open fire on church for one minute was granted, further stating that fire had already been opened on the town and that no more than one minute's ammunition should be expended. At 1413 [we] opened fire at a range of 3,200 yards and completely demolished church, expending 40 rounds, every shell of which landed in the target. Major Reed of the Rangers later confirmed the fact that this target contained four enemy machine guns, which were completely demolished. [Rosters of the 2nd and 5th Ranger Battalions—the only Ranger units on Omaha Beach—do not reveal a Major Reed, nor was there a Major Reed in the 116th Infantry.]

Sometime around noon, sailors aboard a U.S. Navy destroyer spied a body of troops at the base of the cliff just west of the Vierville draw. Who were they? At a range of almost two miles, it was impossible to tell even with binoculars. But given the proximity of their position to enemy pillboxes in and around the Vierville draw, most of which were active, they had to be German.

They were not. A little after 7:00 A.M., three British LCAs had brought a command party from the 116th's 1st Battalion to the beach in this sector. The group, which included the battalion commander and his executive, Lt. Col. John Metcalfe and Maj. Thomas Dallas, had suffered heavy casualties moving across the beach to the base of the cliff. Here they remained pinned by German fire, seemingly originating from several directions simultaneously, for the rest of the morning and much of the afternoon.

1st Battalion, 116th Infantry, 29th Division
U.S. Army Historical Division, interview with Maj. Thomas Dallas, September 1944
In the late morning, the same destroyer which had caught the other groups farther to the right with its fire, began putting shells into Dallas's position and kept it up

until late afternoon. Dallas sent up orange smoke. The destroyer then fired several rounds in the direction of the smoke. The men made sets of signal flags from their handkerchiefs and wig-wagged to the destroyer: "We are Americans. Cease firing." [Lt. Robert Hackett, 1st Battalion signal officer, knew how to signal by semaphore, and he performed the signaling.] They got messages back on the ship's blinker: "Surrender to the Americans." This tragic comedy continued through most of the day with the result, according to Dallas, that he lost more men that afternoon to the destroyer than to the enemy.

Headquarters, 1st Infantry Division
USS **Ancon,** *G-3 Message Journal, 1448 hours, June 6, 1944*
From 1st Battalion, 116th: Navy shelling our beach Dog Green. Stop as soon as possible. We have troops on the beach.

Maj. Thomas Dallas
Executive, 1st Battalion, 116th Infantry, 29th Division, to Lt. Edward Gearing, 1300 hours, June 6, 1944
Goddamn it, tell those sons-of-bitches to stop the firing!

SOMETHING HAS GOT TO BREAK

Colonel Taylor's declaration that the Americans would triumph on Omaha Beach only by "throwing stuff onto the beaches until something breaks" had proved to be by far the most accurate of the Allies' many assessments of the invasion plan. By early evening of June 6, the Americans had indeed thrown a lot of "stuff" onto the beach, and the Germans undeniably had been broken. True, plenty of enemy indirect fire was still landing on the beach with powerful effect; but any enemy soldier who continued to resist the relentless expansion of the Omaha beachhead had a good chance of ending up a prisoner—or dead.

Any fears that General Huebner still harbored about the security of his beachhead were eased when he received news that the last of five U.S. Army infantry regiments scheduled to land on D-Day, the 1st Division's 26th Infantry, had commenced disembarking from twelve LCIs at the foot of the Colleville draw around 6:30 P.M. This intact body of nearly 2,500 fresh troops would not only clinch Huebner's victory on D-Day, but also allow the 1st Division to continue its offensive on June 7 without pause.

The 26th held orders to push southeast toward Bayeux after clearing the beach, but by the time the regiment landed, it was far too late for that. Besides, the mauling suffered by the 16th Infantry in the initial landing had

changed everything, forcing Gerow and Huebner on the night of June 6 to
swiftly devise a completely new scheme of operations for June 7. But first
the 26th would have to make it ashore—and more than the enemy's heavy
artillery fire made this task unexpectedly unpleasant. Perhaps the worst feature of the landing was the sight of hundreds of corpses in the surf and on
the beach, most of whom wore the Big Red One patch on their left shoulders. The many dead 1st Division men seemed to send a mute signal to
their 26th Infantry comrades: Don't underestimate the enemy—victory is
still a long way off.

Lt. Col. Derrill Daniel
Commander, 2nd Battalion, 26th Infantry, 1st Division
We were pretty relaxed because we knew we would not be in the assault wave.
Having been in the initial assaults at Oran [Algeria] and Gela [Sicily], my battalion was now in the reserve follow-up wave. It can be quite relaxing to know that
you won't be in one of the first boats to touch down on a defended shore. . . . I
recall the short boys with heavy machine guns and mortars (it's always the little
guy who carries these things) who clambered down the gangway from the LCI
into water up to their middles and walked over a sandbar toward the beach into
water over their heads. Most simply walked on toward shore without losing their
equipment. They obviously wanted to be on land. . . . I hurried my battalion off
the beach and deployed them to attack the place where we had been told to assemble [Colleville]—it was obviously still in the hands of the Germans. . . . Just after
the attack against the village had been laid on, orders were received to return to
the beach and proceed 1,500 yards to the west to the E-1 exit where further orders
would issue. It took quite a long time to call off the companies that had begun the
attack (radios of course didn't work at that particular moment). Finally at about
2300, the battalion went into assembly area about 1,000 yards off the beach up the
E-1 draw. There we were designated division reserve and even Corps had strings
on us as the only battalion not yet committed.

Col. John Seitz
Commander, 26th Infantry, 1st Division, June 16, 1944
The 26th Infantry Regiment landed on its assigned beaches on D-Day under
artillery and mortar fire. In view of the situation caused by the unusually heavy
resistance on the divisional beaches, the original plan as formulated by the 1st
Division was voided insofar as this regiment was concerned, and one battalion
[the 1st] was ordered to march directly east along the coast road to clean out
resistance at Colleville and Port-en-Bessin on the extreme left flank of the divisional zone of action. Another battalion of this regiment [the 3rd] was ordered to

the right flank of the divisional zone to plug what threatened to be a serious hole on that flank. The position occupied by this battalion effectively secured the only available exits off the beach. The remaining battalion [the 2nd] was ordered into divisional reserve prepared to move to any threatened point in the divisional zone. Midnight of D-Day found the regiment in position and well organized.

Capt. Robert Bridges
Commander, Company D, 26th Infantry, 1st Division, May 30, 1949
We landed very soon after 1800 near the boundary of Easy Red and Fox Green as nearly as I could tell. . . . I had set up machine guns and deployed the 1st Platoon, with which I had landed, to protect the rest of the company still landing. Sniper fire from the high ground to our front dictated this course. Lt. Col. Francis Murdock, my battalion commander, had landed on the same LCI and came up about this time with his sergeant-major and some others of his headquarters group. He told me that I was to take Company D to reinforce the 2nd Battalion, 16th Infantry, which had run into trouble at Colleville. . . . Lt. William Hume [executive, Company D] came up then with the last platoon, commanded by Lt. Walter Stevens. . . . I told him of our orders, and I turned to walk off. Just then heavy shelling of our area started, a fragment of the first shell wounding me. When the shelling ceased, Lt. Hume was dead, and several were wounded, including the battalion sergeant-major. I had been knocked into a burned-out basement, and finding myself unable to move, I called first for Lt. Hume, then for Lt. Stevens. [Stevens] told me that Bill was dead, so I told him what I knew of company strength in men and weapons, including ammunition, and the order that I had just received to go to Colleville, following the path that we were already straddling.

On D-Day, the sun was one of many critical factors that facilitated the American effort to rectify an invasion plan that had crumbled only moments after its commencement. The Americans took advantage of more than seventeen hours of daylight on June 6 to build up an immense force on Omaha Beach—the rough equivalent of more than two infantry divisions. In contrast, the German high command's strategic reserves in Normandy were few, and virtually none of those that were available could reach Omaha Beach by nightfall. To be sure, the German coastal defenders on Omaha Beach fought ferociously, but lacking substantial reinforcement, sooner or later they must break—as Colonel Taylor had promised.

But it had taken plenty of fighting to break them. For any American lucky enough to have survived an early morning landing on Omaha Beach, the day surely must have seemed endless. The sun, however, heralded an imminent end to the madness, as its descent in the western sky yielded elongated shadows on the bloody beach and a surprising chill in the air, causing many soldiers to shiver. A survivor could sort out his blurred memories of D-Day later—certainly there were enough of those to last a lifetime. But a lifetime of how long? Given the extraordinary toll in lives on Omaha Beach, and the long road to victory that lay ahead, there must have been many GIs at the forward edge of the beachhead who wondered that night if they would ever witness another sunset.

CHAPTER 14

To Rest or to Die

THE MOST HAZARDOUS JOB IN THE ARMY

World War II GIs used to say that the soldier's best friend was a skilled medic. On Omaha Beach, American medics, as well as physicians, had a multitude of opportunities to practice their craft, but to do so in full view of the enemy—the Geneva Convention notwithstanding—was not a healthful endeavor. Who would care for the caregivers if the caregivers themselves became casualties?

In a beachhead as narrow as Omaha's, medics and physicians found it nearly impossible to adhere to the army's standard medical practices on the battlefield. Under normal conditions, a medic's primary job was to keep wounded soldiers alive until they could be safely transported to a nearby aid station, and ultimately to a hospital where doctors would attend to them. But Omaha was anything but normal. The number of American casualties suffered in the first few hours of the invasion would have overwhelmed even ten times the actual number of medical personnel available on the beach. Furthermore, virtually every site considered as a potential aid station was under enemy fire. The transportation of wounded soldiers to aid stations was impracticable in any case due to casualties among litter-bearers and a dearth of litters. But even had sufficient men and gear been available to move the wounded, the enemy's fire would have made such attempts suicidal. As for those GIs wounded in the inland fighting around

Colleville, St. Laurent, and Vierville, the Americans' failure to open Omaha's five draws early on D-Day meant that the only routes between the beach and the interior had to traverse the bluffs, whose steep slopes were hardly feasible for the movement of wounded.

If there is one basic truth of military medicine, it is that the longer a wounded soldier is denied steady medical care, the greater the chance he will die. But there were no hospitals on Omaha Beach. The closest things to them were the frontline aid stations, but they were entirely overwhelmed by the work that had to be done. True, there were sick bays aboard warships and transports lying offshore. But how could the wounded be removed to those vessels? Moving hundreds of injured men across an open beach swept by enemy fire was hardly feasible. And from the perspective of naval landing craft crews, whose orders had said nothing about transporting wounded, adherence to strict timetables was of paramount importance; failure to keep on schedule could produce ruinous consequences. Furthermore, cramped and spartan landing craft could take only a few stretcher cases at a time, and in the two-hour journey back to a transport, boat crews could scarcely offer adequate medical attention. Although in some cases moving a severely wounded soldier back to a transport's sick bay was the only means of saving his life, removal of wounded from the beach by sea on a grand scale was not a realistic option. In the Omaha invasion plan, no one had anticipated that medical units would have to cope with such a large number of wounded men.

The only alternative was to drag the wounded to a spot at the foot of the bluffs where they would at least be minimally shielded from fire, offer basic medical care there, and hope for the best. If the wounded could hang on, more stable medical care would be available when the beachhead was secure. But many men could not hang on, and by the following day, they would no longer be looked after by doctors, but by Graves Registration personnel.

Headquarters, 16th Infantry, 1st Division
Unit Journal, 2300 hours, June 6, 1944
From Maj. [Charles] Tegtmeyer [CO, Medical Detachment] to Col. Ficchy: We are not able to evacuate any of our people. There are no evacuation facilities at the beach and something must be done.

Maj. Charles Tegtmeyer
Commander, Medical Detachment, 16th Infantry, Report, June 24, 1944
The landing craft made slight effort in the first 24 hours to evacuate wounded along the beach. Medical installations such as auxiliary surgical groups were

brought on shore too early without equipment, litters, blankets, or litter-bearers. During the first twelve hours of a beach assault, all medical emphasis should be placed on evacuation (litter and vehicle), and on emergency treatment only. The Collecting Company should not have been put all on one craft. They should have been distributed over at least two craft, if not three. The losses suffered by this group were such that they were rendered non-effective when they were needed most. Reserves of litter-bearers, litters, and blankets must be gotten to shore in some manner early to promptly replace losses in the initial waves. [Finally], the Geneva Convention is a failure. Many of our wounded aidmen were shot intentionally. The white brassard draws fire. The craft bringing in the Collecting Company, all of whom were wearing brassards, received more direct enemy fire than any other craft. Since the landing on the beach, several aidmen have been wounded by sniper fire. The Geneva Convention brassard makes the company aidman's job the most hazardous in the Army.

Lt. Col. Charles Horner
Commander, 3rd Battalion, 16th Infantry, 1st Division
The casualty ratio normally is about one [killed] to seven [wounded]. [On D-Day,] it was one-to-one. And the reason for that was that when these people were hit getting out of the boat or coming across the beach . . . [medics] couldn't get to them. And as a result they died when they might have been able to survive. One of my company commanders laid there for nearly 24 hours, and as a result he lost his foot. If we could have gotten him up to good medical facilities, we may have been able to save that foot.

Capt. Charles Clark
HQ Company, 16th Infantry, 1st Division, June 30, 1944
On the whole, the naval cooperation was excellent. However, there is one sore point in the landing that should be brought to the attention of small craft commanders. In many instances they refused to take casualties aboard their craft, disregarding the orders of both Army and Navy officers on shore. There were a number of cases where the wounded were carried through chest-deep water to within a few feet of the craft, when the skipper pulled up the ramp and took to sea. There were many dead American soldiers and sailors on the beach D+1 because of the refusal of the small craft to evacuate them, when a few more seconds of endangering their own lives would have saved the lives of many others.

Capt. Joseph Shelley
Medical officer, Company B, 104th Medical Battalion, 29th Division
I led my men ashore with instructions to do everything I did. We drew machine gun fire, which fortunately was firing on a fixed field, and we made the shingle by the

road without casualties. I lay down by a lieutenant who was shot through the abdomen. A bullet, passing through his steel helmet, had grazed his scalp. I dressed his wound and then started to look around. As I stuck my head up he said, "Doc, I wouldn't do that if I was you. That's how I got this bullet through my helmet."

1st Sgt. Herbert Goldberg
Medical Detachment History, 16th Infantry, 1st Division, July 14, 1945

At 1900 a count was made, and there was a total of 80 wounded men at the regimental aid station. The regimental section personnel dug foxholes for those who could not dig their own. Of the 80 wounded, five were serious, three of whom died during the night from shock and exposure—despite the use of blood plasma and blankets. Lt. Col. [John] Corley, CO, 3rd Battalion, 26th Infantry, passed the aid station and asked how things were. He was told that blankets were needed. One hour later the aid station had 100 blankets. Col. Corley had blankets taken from the bed-rolls of his men.

1st Lt. Jack Shea
Aide-de-camp to Brigadier General Cota, 29th Division, November 1944

The dead and dying soldiers had been collected from the beach and from the ground before the bluffs, and had been evacuated to the promenade. It was observed that medical corpsmen had limited facilities to tend these casualties, their efforts being mainly to take meager supplies on hand and distribute them as rationally as they could to the patients. This consisted of taking the blankets from those who had died and putting them on those who were wounded for protection from the chill night air. Some of the wounded had dug shallow trenches in the sandy soil bordering the promenade as protection from the artillery that still fell on the beach. . . . Some of the wounded had died, only to tumble into the shallow "graves" they had dug. A single medical ambulance, using cat-eye lights, was methodically picking up the living casualties and bringing them to a common collecting point near the ruins of the tank-barrier wall at the mouth of the Vierville exit. There a small medical staff tended their wounds and prepared them for evacuation by sea.

1st Lt. William Gniecko
29th Quartermaster Company, 29th Division

I was appointed the division's Graves Registration officer in March 1944. My first direct order from Gen. Gerhardt when I went back to the command post on D+1 was to clean up the beach of bodies. I started the Graves Registration boys and all idlers on the beach to help. The first cemetery was between the beach and the cliffs. Despite shells, and even small arms fire, the job went apace. Using a bulldozer, we buried 456 men just off the beach.

ROAMING IN THE GLOAMING

Nightfall on Omaha Beach did not yield tranquility, for darkness provided an opportunity for isolated pockets of German troops to escape the Americans' tightening grip on the beachhead. At dusk on D-Day, there was nothing close to the neat, continuous front line that invasion planners had hoped to achieve by the end of the first day; in truth, the Americans controlled only the soil on which they currently stood and the ground that was within range of a hand grenade toss. Throughout much of the beachhead that night, GIs discovered to their amazement that the enemy was just as likely to be behind them as to their front. The situation was far too volatile for anyone on either side to get more than just a few moments of sleep. But with adrenaline running so high, and the Norman night so brief, a good night's sleep was an impossibility anyway.

On the beachhead's eastern flank, the Germans had managed to hold on to much of Colleville and the nearby hamlet of Cabourg for the entire day. As a consequence, the enemy still controlled the vital beach exit connecting Colleville to the sea, and no American vehicles could reach the coast road by this route until the resilient German defenders were cleaned out. For the Germans, this was a victory of sorts, but the 1st Division's inland penetrations on either side of Colleville had nearly surrounded them. The American force so vastly outnumbered the surviving enemy defenders that their annihilation was virtually assured on the morrow.

There is hardly a factor in warfare that can change a soldier's state of mind more quickly than the realization that he is surrounded. Enemy soldiers in Colleville who reached that conclusion in the evening of June 6 faced a difficult choice. Several feisty Germans decided to fight it out the following morning, come what may. Many more had departed at sundown, heading southward through the tangled *bocage*, hoping to rekindle the battle at some later time. But numerous enemy troops wanted no more part in Hitler's war. An especially reluctant group of fifty-two grenadiers holed up in Cabourg, persuaded by Private First Class Milander—their German-speaking captive who had led a 16th Infantry patrol into Cabourg that afternoon—that surrender was their only option, decided to give up at first light. If only the Germans had been so submissive when the Americans first hit the beach that morning . . .

2nd Battalion, 18th Infantry, 1st Division
D-Day After-Action Report, july 1944

Companies went into position along an east-west road south of [Colleville]. Company F was the furthest east, Company G in the center, Company E, which came up shortly, was on the west flank, where it tied in with the 2nd Battalion, 16th

Infantry. The 3rd Battalion, 18th Infantry, came up later. In this position, which on the map was a ridge, but on the ground was perfectly flat and cut up by thick hedgerows into small fields and orchards, we found no enemy in front of us, but a large number of enemy behind us between our positions and Colleville. We had constant small skirmishes with small enemy positions. Just before dark, Company F pulled back, north of Company G. This formed a three-sided box around the enemy in and south of Colleville, and small firefights kept up all through the night as the enemy attempted to escape. In the morning all three rifle companies started working on the pocket of resistance, and by 0900 had taken over 160 prisoners and killed about 50 more of the enemy. Others trying to escape were taken care of by the 16th and 26th Infantry.

1st Battalion, 16th Infantry, 1st Division
D-Day After-Action Report, July 4, 1944
During the night, B Company was engaged almost continuously in a firefight on the right flank. Patrols maintained contact during the night with the 2nd Battalion, 16th Infantry and 2nd Battalion, 18th Infantry, on the left. Patrols were unable to gain contact with the 116th Infantry on the right.

Company L, 16th Infantry, 1st Division
U.S. Army Historical Division, interview with various Company L soldiers, July 1944
A patrol under Lt. Marincic was sent up the main road [from Le Grand Hameau] to reconnoiter Cabourg. It encountered heavy opposition en route and was unable to force its way into the town. S/Sgt. [Clovis] Madoux was killed in this action. At 2100 the company, preceded by a small covering patrol under T/Sgt. [John] Worozbyt took up defensive positions in orchards 600 yards southwest of Grand Hameau with the mission of protecting the right flank. During the night enemy infiltrating parties were encountered and driven off at dawn the next day. Small enemy groups were mopped up behind our position by the 5th section.

The confused military situation in the beachhead's central sector at sundown mirrored the conditions at Colleville. A stubborn German strong-point just west of St. Laurent had held up the advance of the 29th Division's 115th Infantry since late afternoon, but the 115th's 1st and 2nd Battalions had maneuvered around its southern edge and nearly surrounded it. Furthermore, the Americans' diffuse penetrations beyond the bluffs into the interior had also trapped scores of German defenders in the coastal strongpoints of the Les Moulins draw. As at Colleville, the Germans here faced a bleak future: They must fight it out against overpowering odds; attempt to flee; or lay down their arms.

Shortly before midnight, the 115th's 1st Battalion lost its commanding officer, Lt. Col. Richard Blatt. After leading his outfit in a flanking movement around St. Laurent, Blatt ordered his men to dig in for the night in the bewildering *bocage* about one-third of a mile south of town. The Germans were seemingly everywhere, and unfortunately for the GIs, the enemy somehow pinpointed the 1st Battalion's position with uncanny precision and laid down a mortar barrage at 11:30 P.M. that gave Blatt's men their first example of German military prowess. Blatt was walking beside Lt. Herbert Martin, a liaison officer from the 110th Field Artillery, when he was struck down.

PFC John Hooper
HQ Company, 1st Battalion, 115th Infantry, 29th Division
It was getting close to dusk, and we rested a few minutes. The battalion commander came up and indicated to our lieutenant that he was looking for a place to set down the weapons company [Company D] mortars. They went through an opening in the hedge and while scouting the adjacent field, German mortars began falling where Colonel Blatt and the mortar section were. The Germans must have had that field under observation. The colonel was mortally wounded.

PFC E. J. Hamill
Company D, 115th Infantry, 29th Division
Our Company D command post was on the same hedgerow with the battalion CP, as well as the aid station. . . . Night came on, and the rifle companies were several fields ahead. We dug deep foxholes. The night was like July 4th because of so much firing. . . . Company A had a roadblock on the Formigny road. Our runner came to our company CP and told our CO, Capt. [George] Nabb, that Col. Blatt had been wounded and was at the aid station. . . . Capt. Nabb went to the aid station to see him. A piece of shrapnel had hit him over the right ear and gone into his head. Capt. Nabb told me that Col. Blatt wanted his men treated first, which is what a good West Point officer would say. His wound was more serious than originally thought, so medics (with an escort) carried him back to the beach to a ship, which carried him to England. We learned later that he died on the ship.

S/Sgt. Lowry Brooks
HQ Company, 1st Battalion, 115th Infantry, 29th Division
When Col. Blatt was wounded, our battalion surgeon, Capt. Norval Carter, decided that the colonel must be evacuated to the beach as soon as possible. Blatt and Carter were close, and Dr. Carter chose to accompany him to the beach and act as a litter-bearer, even though this was normally the responsibility of privates from the medical detachment. It was a long walk back to the beach, and carrying

Col. Blatt could not have been easy. We found out later that Col. Blatt died, and they buried him in England.

Lt. Col. Richard Churchfield Blatt
Biographical inscription in 1933 West Point Yearbook "The Howitzer"
A West Pointer is more than a college graduate—more than an officer and a gentleman, if such is possible. Of the many molding influences, the Academic Department reigns supreme. It is in this predominant phase of cadet life that Dick Blatt stands foremost. Not as a scholar and not as one to whom academics come easily, but as one who has traveled an unusually rocky road to the end with far more success than those who can exhibit a pair of stars on their collars. This is a statement that only a West Pointer understands, by a West Pointer, and of a West Pointer.

At Vierville, on the beachhead's western flank, the positions of American and German troops at nightfall were more firmly defined than in Omaha's other sectors. Colonel Canham had managed to establish at least some semblance of a front line in this area, forming an arc on the south and west sides of Vierville manned by Rangers, fragments of his own 1st and 2nd Battalions, and elements of the 121st Engineers. But Canham worried that the apparent scarcity of American troops in this sector could invite an enemy counterattack, a tactic for which the enemy was renowned. Normally, Canham commanded more than 3,000 men, and augmentation from Rangers and engineers should have put that figure at over 4,000. But at sundown on D-Day, Canham could account for less than a quarter of that number in and around Vierville. Where was the rest of the Stonewall Brigade? Canham did not know, but that night he determined to find out, and until that time, the force under his direct control would hold their positions. As a result of Canham's decision, the disappointed Rangers would have to put off the scheduled rendezvous with their besieged brethren under Rudder at Pointe du Hoc until a later time.

Maj. Thomas Howie
S-3, 116th Infantry, 29th Division, June 9, 1944
Through a radio of the 743rd Tank Battalion, the liaison officer [Lieutenant Jones] contacted the remainder of the [116th] CP communications group under Capt. [James] Sink, and it was learned that the 2nd and 3rd Battalions had been badly shot up in crossing the beach and were in defensive positions in the vicinity of St. Laurent and Les Moulins. . . . The CO [Colonel Canham] decided the following

Omaha Beach at End of the Day, June 6, 1944

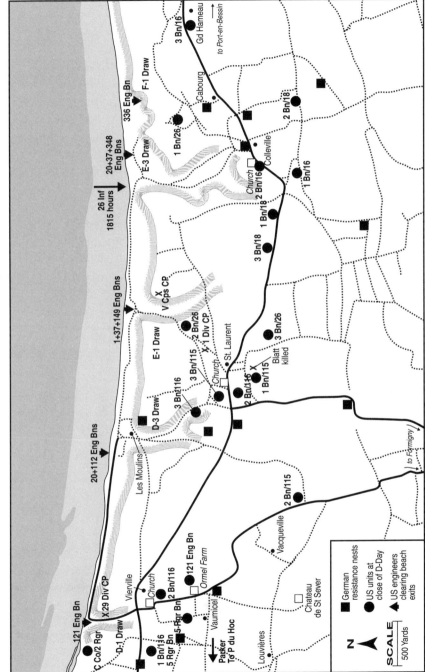

- 121 Eng Bn
- C Co/2 Rgr
- D-1 Draw
- X 29 Div CP
- Vierville
- Church
- 1 Bn/116
- 5 Rgr Bn
- 2 Bn/116
- 121 Eng Bn
- Vaumicel
- Ormel Farm
- Parker
- To P du Hoc
- Louvières
- Chateau de St Sever
- Vacqueville
- 2 Bn/115
- to Formigny
- Les Moulins
- 20+112 Eng Bns
- D-3 Draw
- 3 Bn/116
- Church
- St. Laurent
- 2 Bn/116
- X 1 Div CP
- 2 Bn/26
- E-1 Draw
- 3 Bn/115
- X V Cps CP
- 1-37+149 Eng Bns
- 2 Bn/4+6
- 1 Bn/115
- Blatt killed
- 3 Bn/26
- 26 Inf 1815 hours
- 20-37+348 Eng Bns
- E-3 Draw
- 3 Bn/18
- 1 Bn/18
- 2 Bn/18
- Colleville
- Church
- 2 Bn/16
- 1 Bn/16
- 336 Eng Bn
- F-1 Draw
- 1 Bn/26
- Cabourg
- 2 Bn/18
- 3 Bn/16
- Gd Hameau
- to Port-en-Bessin

N

SCALE
500 Yards

- ■ German resistance nests
- ● US units at close of D-Day
- ▲ US engineers clearing beach exits

morning at about 0600 to move the CP group back to St. Laurent, gather the 2nd and 3rd Battalions, and push inland toward our objective.

Capt. John Raaen
Commander, HQ Company, 5th Ranger Battalion

After organizing our defense and setting the guard, I ordered the men to dig in. At that moment I found out my worst mistake of the day. I had left my entrenching tool aboard the [HMS] *Prince Baudouin*! A couple of men volunteered to dig a hole for me, but no, I would have none of that. I tried to use my helmet as a scraper, but centuries of hard-packed clay yielded only a scratch or two. Night was falling, and I had to do something. I spied a haystack, more or less in the middle of the courtyard where I had been trying to dig. A haystack would be warm, the weather seemed like it was nearly freezing. The hay would slow down fragments little bit, so why not? I scooped away a little hay, lay down, and covered myself up. It was warm. Now I am a city boy, not a country boy, so I didn't know the difference between a haystack and a manure pile. I learned that difference in seconds. Every kind of biting insect in France was at me, hundreds of them. I came out like a shot.

Company C, 2nd Ranger Battalion
Company C History, "Roughing It with Charlie," 1945

Tech/Sgt. William Lindsay of Floral Park, New York, was in a concrete pillbox that received two direct hits. As a result, Sgt. Lindsay lost a tooth and was knocked silly by the concussion. Three times during the day, Sgt. Lindsay almost walked off the cliff; and that night he accused a full colonel of the 29th Division of stealing his rifle—and all the while Sgt. Lindsay had his rifle slung over his shoulder.

Lt. Col. Robert Ploger
Commander, 121st Engineer Combat Battalion, 29th Division

After we blew up the wall in front of the Vierville draw, Sgt. [John] Hickman and I made our way up the exit and beyond to the Vaumicel chateau. [Actually the Ormel farm, which was mistakenly labeled the "Chateau de Vaumicel" on army maps.] There were abandoned German trenches on the inland side of the building, and some of our engineers had already gathered there. Then I returned to the draw and reported to Gen. Gerhardt at the 29th Division CP in the quarry. Later, as it started to get dark, I was in an open field some distance from the chateau, and I met the V Corps deputy engineer officer. Somehow he had obtained two bottles of Calvados [a potent Norman apple brandy], which he urged me to try. I did—it was vile. We talked for about one-half hour. It was dark by then, but I had no desire to sleep.

Pvt. Rocco Russo
Company F, 116th Infantry, 29th Division

Gen. Cota put [PFC Louis] Simmons and me in a cemetery [adjacent to the Vierville church], where we dug a two-man foxhole; and with our bazooka, we were in a position to provide protection for the rest of the outfit against a possible German tank attack. It never did occur to us to get our bearings and identify our surroundings that night. Once night fell, the shadows around us began to move. We were really concerned, envisaging German soldiers creeping up on us. We tried to take turns sleeping, but even the exhaustion of the day was not enough to overcome our fear. The next morning we realized the shadows were due to two trees in the cemetery near our foxhole. We learned a lesson that night: the next time we dig in, we will check the area around us before it gets dark to get the layout of the land.

1st Lt. Joseph Ondre
Company A, 743rd Tank Battalion, October 1944

All the tanks of A Company had armored trailers filled with ammunition attached to them. But the resistance on the beach required us to jettison some of these trailers. Only six actually reached the bivouac area that we reached that night. Each of these trailers had 230 rounds of 75mm ammunition. Altogether we had about 51 tanks when we landed. But only about 30 got off the beach. All of the 743rd's tanks came off the beach through the Vierville exit. That night we tried to reorganize, but the casualties, especially among our officers, had been high, and it was pretty hard to knit ourselves together. The battalion commander, Lt. Col. John Upham, was injured, and in B Company four of their five officers had been killed. We entered the transit area [up the draw and beyond Vierville] just before dark on the night of D-Day and went into a bivouac circle. Here we were resupplied with ammo and gas, backed up the perimeter defense, and waited for orders.

Steel-nerved veterans and combat rookies alike spent an uneasy first night on Omaha Beach. After dark, almost anything that moved in the *bocage* beyond the beach became a target of American fire. But where exactly were the front lines? No one seemed to know. The most prudent course of action was to pick as safe a spot as possible, dig a foxhole, and sit still until dawn.

The aftermath. View of Omaha Beach near the E-1 draw on D+1, June 7. At least two dead GIs are visible on the sand. In the lower left, a thick belt of enemy barbed wire atop the shingle embankment can be seen. Numerous German beach obstacles are evident in the surf. U.S. ARMY SIGNAL CORPS, NATIONAL ARCHIVES.

1st Lt. Jack Shea
Aide-de-camp to Brigadier General Cota, 29th Division, November 1944
Throughout the hours of darkness between D-Day and D+1, it became apparent that many units of both the 1st and 29th Divisions engaged in minor firefights between themselves due to the promiscuous shooting of troops concerned. It was the opinion of both Gen. Cota and members of the 1st Division staff that much of the so-called "sniper" fire—allegedly enemy—originated from this source. It was infrequent that enemy soldiers were actually spotted by our infantry in this area.

Lt. Col. John Cooper
Commander, 110th Field Artillery Battalion, 29th Division
When darkness set in, I was with Lt. Col. Lou Smith [executive, 115th Infantry] just outside St. Laurent. We found what passed for a slit trench, really nothing more than a roadside drainage ditch, and decided to get some rest. We would need to be alert the next day. We lay in the trench, head-to-head, talking. As long as I talked, I felt all right. The instant we stopped talking, I trembled and shook like a leaf.

THE INSTANT MADE ETERNITY

No one had expected the Omaha invasion to be carried out flawlessly. But those who paused on the night of June 6 to reflect on the day's events must have been amazed at the discrepancy between expectation and reality. Nothing had gone right from the start. Bradley's promised "Greatest Show on Earth," courtesy of the Eighth Air Force's celebrated B-24 Liberators, had never materialized; the navy's rocket barrage prior to the assault hadn't hit anywhere near the enemy's strongpoints; the German coastal defenders were much more numerous and of higher quality than the plan had suggested; duplex drive tanks and DUKWs had sunk in alarming numbers while attempting to carry out the tasks for which they were designed; landing craft came in late and off-target.

And a lot of good men had been killed and wounded. Exactly how many, nobody knew for sure, and no one would establish a precise casualty figure in the weeks following the invasion. The military situation at nightfall on Omaha Beach was much too confused to permit careful record keeping. Countless soldiers had died in the sea or the surf and were never seen again. Others were piled in the remote sunken lanes and hedgerows of the *bocage* and would not be located for days. Some had been blown to bits and would never be identified. Wounded were scattered over the beach, the inland pastures, and ships heading back to England. When attempting to file their first morning reports after D-Day, perplexed company first sergeants surely must have shaken their heads with incredulity: Where was everybody?

The V Corps' initial reports wildly exaggerated casualties. One account submitted to General Gerow on June 8 stated that the 29th Division's 116th Infantry had a casualty total of 49 officers and 2,733 enlisted men—a figure that, if accurate, would have been nearly 90 percent of its authorized strength. With casualties like that, how could the Stonewall Brigade continue to press inland toward St. Lô? Fortunately for Gerow, such dreadful casualty figures were far off the mark.

U.S. Army Historical Division
D-Day Casualty Report, November 1944
Casualties for D-Day have never been stated officially. Because of confusion of reports and the lack of records, it is likely that the total will not be known. Most of the units involved reported losses by the week, beginning June 6, or by the month of June, thus making it impossible to have exact data. The matter was further com-

plicated because the first reports exaggerated losses as a result of the separation of sections, companies, and battalions of assault troops.

Col. Charles Canham
Summary of Actions, 116th Infantry, in initial D-Day assault, June 15, 1944

The closest estimate that can be made of casualties suffered by the Regiment in the initial assault of the beaches was conservatively 70 officers and 900 enlisted men out of a total of approximately 180 officers and 3,100 enlisted men of the Regiment who actually landed on D-Day. This figure was arrived at after scattered and missing had reported back to original units.

When the dust settled and U.S. Army historians prepared their official accounts of the invasion immediately after the war, they overturned accepted Omaha Beach casualty counts and provided new estimates based on fresh examinations of documents related to the invasion.

Lt. Col. Charles Taylor
U.S. Army Historical Division, "Omaha Beachhead," September 1945

Unit records for D-Day are necessarily incomplete or fragmentary, and losses in men and matériel cannot be established in accurate detail. First estimates of casualties were high, with an inflated percentage of "missing" as a result of the number of assault sections which were separated from their companies, sometimes for two or three days. On the basis of later, corrected returns, casualties for V Corps were in the neighborhood of 3,000 killed, wounded, and missing. The two assaulting regimental combat teams (16th and 116th) lost about 1,000 men each.

Gordon Harrison
U.S. Army, Office of the Chief of Military History, "Cross-Channel Attack," October 1950

The V Corps losses for [June 6] were about 2,000 killed, wounded, and missing. [Harrison footnoted this sentence with the following paragraph:] This is frankly a guess, based on a number of estimates of various dates and various headquarters, none of which agree. Under the Army's present casualty reporting system, it is unlikely that accurate figures of D-Day losses by unit will ever be available.

But in large measure, accurate figures are available, and inspection of the relevant documents yields the inescapable conclusion that Taylor's and Harrison's casualty figures are significantly undercounted. A more realistic estimate of killed, wounded, and missing in the Omaha Beach invasion, based on examinations of available after-action reports and unit histories of every ground, naval, and air unit that participated in the assault, is about 4,700 men out of a total of about 35,000 who came ashore on D-Day—an overall loss rate of more than 13 percent. Most units that came ashore in the first hour of the assault probably averaged a casualty percentage nearly triple that figure, and in a few cases—most notably Company A, 116th Infantry—the loss rate was still higher. However, due to imprecise unit records, it is almost impossible to determine precisely how many of the 4,700 casualties were killed outright, later died of their wounds, or were missing and declared dead months afterward. But it is virtually certain that of the total casualties suffered by the invaders on Omaha Beach, the percentage of those servicemen killed or who later died of wounds was significantly higher than in any other battle fought by the U.S. Army in Europe during World War II.

TO THE LAST SYLLABLE OF RECORDED TIME

Such dreadful losses confirm that the eighteen-hour battle on Omaha Beach on June 6, 1944, was indeed one of the U.S. Army's most costly one-day combats of World War II. That the Americans, with the critical aid of the Royal Navy, were the ultimate victors was undeniable, for despite Hitler's notorious Atlantic Wall, the Allies had succeeded in landing a large American ground force on Omaha Beach by the close of D-Day. As long as the Germans did not drive that force into the sea—and there was little fear of that after June 6—the battle was won. Along with the Allies' other four beachheads gained on D-Day, the top brass had the footholds on the Continent they needed to initiate the campaign they hoped would bring Nazi Germany to its knees within a year. General Marshall's "Great Offensive" in France, promised to the graduating class of West Point cadets gathered in the field house on May 29, 1942, had at last materialized.

On June 7, the war would resume, and thereafter Omaha Beach belonged to the ages. It would be up to historians to sift through reams of evidence to determine how the Americans had triumphed despite the tragedies that had marked the invasion's commencement. That evidence pointed to four main reasons for the American success: The Germans were surprised; the Americans applied overwhelming force; American soldiers were superbly prepared for the task; and the German defenses were incomplete.

Had only one of these four factors not held true on D-Day, an American victory would have been much more problematic; and had two or more not been true, the Omaha invasion in all likelihood would have failed.

Maintaining the secret of Operation Neptune's invasion sites for so long was a remarkable accomplishment and was the foundation of the Allied success on D-Day. Had the Germans known where the Allies would invade only a week, or even a few days, prior to the assault, they could have enhanced their defenses by a considerable degree. On Omaha, the Germans probably could have doubled or tripled the number of coastal defenders, and given the inherent strength of their fixed fortifications, that augmentation could have been decisive.

Furthermore, Generals Bradley and Gerow must be given credit for adhering to the salient principle that on D-Day, V Corps must pour as many troops as possible onto Omaha Beach by nightfall. Had Bradley and Gerow extended the preinvasion bombardment after dawn by an hour or more, the number of troops that could have been brought ashore on Omaha on June 6 would have been significantly reduced, and perhaps even more important, those troops would have had fewer daylight hours to accomplish their difficult missions. This factor was critical, and it is often eclipsed by speculation as to why the brief and highly flawed aerial and naval bombardment utterly failed to accomplish its goals. Colonel Taylor of the 16th Infantry had correctly assessed a fundamental facet of the Omaha plan: V Corps would throw troops at the enemy defenses until something broke—and that is precisely what happened.

That the enemy indeed eventually broke was due to both the Americans' overwhelming numerical advantage and the extraordinarily effective training of its assault troops. Wellington's success at Waterloo may have been gained, as the duke once stated, "on the playing fields of Eton"; but Gerow's victory on Omaha Beach was achieved on the training grounds of the Assault Training Center in Devon.

But even given the American advantage in numbers and training, planning for the Omaha invasion was an incredibly difficult task. The German coastal defenses were strong, and a successful landing of troops by sea directly in the face of those defenses required resourceful planning and inventive assault methods—otherwise another Gallipoli could result. But had Rommel had his way, the enemy's Omaha Beach defenses could have been much stronger than they actually were, and in this event, Gerow could have faced nearly insurmountable problems moving his troops from England to Normandy, then onto the beach, and subsequently off the beach. German pressure mines sown in the English Channel probably would have inflicted major harm to the assault convoys; thicker belts of beach obstacles, more effectively mined, would have made it much more challenging for coxswains to take their landing craft to the beach, even at low tide; more profuse bands of barbed wire at the head of the shingle and minefields in the draw mouths and bluff slopes would have slowed or entirely stopped the GIs from moving inland.

In retrospect, given the Americans' overwhelming weight of manpower and matériel, the American victory on Omaha Beach is habitually viewed as inevitable. It was not. Success was achieved only as a result of intense training, planning, deception—and the good fortune that the enemy did not prepare its defenses with equal fervor. Many elements of the invasion had gone grievously wrong; but the combination of spontaneous remedies on the part of those on the scene and a determination to carry on despite the original plan's flaws had overcome those wrongs. It had cost a lot of good men, but in the end, the plan worked.

For those who landed on Omaha Beach on D-Day, it was a battlefield. But for the vast number of troops who passed through it in subsequent weeks on the way to the front, it was also a supply base of almost unimaginable breadth. Even before the beach had been fully cleared of the enemy, American troops would begin off-loading war matériel on Omaha at a rate that would eventually rival the largest of America's harbors. This essential activity continued until November 1944, when the liberation of several sizable ports on the Continent had rendered Omaha redundant as a logistical hub.

In the grand scheme of the war, however, this was the essential reason American troops had to fight and die to win Omaha Beach, for without secure supply bases, America and Britain could not hope to carry out the relentless military campaign they had devised to defeat Germany. The Western Allies' five D-Day beachheads were the first of many entry points in northwest Europe for the war matériel that would sustain the campaign. What started out as a trickle on D-Day would swiftly grow into a torrent of men and supplies against which Hitler's worn-out military machine could not hope to stand.

But the war was far from over; and how much longer it would last, no one could say. After D-Day, however, Americans, Britons, and Canadians somehow found it infinitely easier to profess optimism, even certainty, about the ultimate termination of the European war in total Allied victory. Assuredly it was heartening to the soul to grasp that the dark years of the war were over and an end was in sight.

Gen. George Marshall
U.S. Army Chief of Staff, cable to President Roosevelt, June 14, 1944
Eisenhower and his staff are cool and confident, carrying out an affair of incredible magnitude and complication with superlative efficiency. I think we have these Huns at the top of the toboggan slide, and the full crash of the Russian offensive should put the skids under them. There will be hard fighting, and the enemy will seize every opportunity for a skillful counter-stroke, but I think he faces a grim prospect.

But from the perspective of the forlorn GIs who had survived the carnage of Omaha Beach, the victory provided little satisfaction. What military goal could ever be worth such a cost? Even a man with the eloquence of a Pericles or a Lincoln would strain to define why it all had to happen. But this time there would be no such men to provide definitions, and it would be years before the confession of an Omaha veteran that "I was there" would yield respectful glances and inquiries from listeners as to exactly what it was like. Of course, words could not possibly describe it adequately, and no one except the men who had lived through it could ever understand how fortunate were those who had survived to tell tales about it in their old age.

Every survivor of D-Day on Omaha Beach had witnessed ghastly sights that hung like black shrouds deep in their minds' recesses. Years later, even the most fleeting recollection of a bursting shell or a whizzing bullet could bring chills or wrenching despair: an excruciating wound, a close friend's death, a close call. Nothing a general or politician could ever say would make those firmly ingrained thoughts disappear. Most soldiers who landed on Omaha Beach were not heroes—those who truly were had in all probability been killed. But every passing year accentuated the melancholy contemplation that accompanied memories of Omaha Beach: Amid such carnage, how did I live while so many didn't make it?

PFC Ugo Giannini
29th Military Police Platoon, 29th Division, June 7, 1944
I retraced my way from the battered remains of Vierville-sur-Mer. I walked slowly, dragging my unwilling soul with me and forcing it to inhale the death odor. I was alone searching for my comrades, 37 men who were hurled ashore yesterday morning (or was it years ago?). I walked, stopped, resumed again, always against the visible signs of war. Which way did it go? . . . I wanted to forget, to stop thinking or feeling. I wanted to rest or die. A thin plaster of white mud, darker brown where it was still wet, painted my legs, my boots, my hands. And yes, it must have been inside of me too.

"The visible signs of war." A dead American soldier lies on Omaha Beach at low tide on D+1, June 7. Next to him, an enemy beach obstacle is embedded in the sand. The photo was taken between the Vierville and Les Moulins draws, in the area where Company C, 116th Infantry, and the 5th Rangers came ashore. U.S. ARMY SIGNAL CORPS, NATIONAL ARCHIVES.

Maj. Sidney Bingham
Commander, 2nd Battalion, 116th Infantry, 29th Division,
January 11, 1947
Everything that was done was done by small groups led by the real heroes of any war. Most of them were killed, and very, very few were decorated chiefly because no one was left to tell about what they did. The minefields behind the beach were strewn with these guys. They were lying around the hedgerows on top of the bluffs and, of course, they were piled—literally—on the beach proper.

But history can provide at least a little solace that there was some meaning to it all. Churchill had warned that the war was fought to prevent civilization from plummeting into "the abyss of a new Dark Age," and Buchenwald, Bergen-Belsen, Dachau, and the Final Solution had proved him right. D-Day was the decisive chapter of a twentieth-century *Iliad*, and when no one remains alive who can declare "I was there," the storytellers will carry on, in Homeric fashion, to preserve the tales of bygone warriors little different from those cast upon the shores of Troy. The D-Day epic will be preserved, told and retold for as long as there are people who are devoted to their ancestors—and to freedom.

They were there. And together they made the world a better place.

Capt. Joseph Dawson
Commander, Company G, 16th Infantry, 1st Division, June 16, 1944
My Dearest Family,

You must forgive me for not writing a detailed letter to you before now because there were certain things that occurred to prevent me from gathering my thoughts together long enough to inscribe them. However, my V-mail should have provided you with the dope that all is well, which is of course the main thing. My slight incapacitation is now coming along nicely and offers no presentable difficulty, so I am once more with my men and my heart is happy. One never realizes the utter loneliness of separation until he has had the privilege of living and being a part of the finest group of men on the face of the earth. . . . What I'm trying to say is that justice can never be properly accorded to the magnificent fortitude and heroism of the fine American soldier and man. He is without peer, and these past few days have implanted in the hearts of all a realization of the true greatness of these men. I say this because I've had an honor never to be equaled in being part of a group that will ever stand as a symbol of greatness to all who witnessed or know how they measured up to the supreme test without faltering or wavering. I cannot say more for my heart forbears it, but God is my witness that the men of my company lived, fought, and died in true glory. . . . All of which brings me down to the present and here amid the apple trees of this bit of France, with the symphony of war encompassing me, I have found peace of heart and soul never before attained in all my life, for here I am with the bravest, finest, grandest bunch of men that God ever breathed life into. Before it's all over, you will know that this is true and that this company is my life. God bless you one and all,

Joe

29th Division Veterans Association
Preamble to the 29th Division Association By-Laws
To perpetuate the friendships we cherish, to keep alive the spirit that never knew defeat, to glorify our dead, and to further keep before our country the record of the 29th Division in the World Wars.

Gen. Dwight Eisenhower
Supreme Commander, Allied Expeditionary Force, Speech, London Guildhall, July 12, 1945
Humility must always be the portion of any man who receives acclaim earned in the blood of his followers and the sacrifices of his friends.

Franklin D. Roosevelt
President of the United States, National Prayer, June 6, 1944
O Lord, give us faith. . . . With thy blessing, we shall prevail over the unholy forces of our enemy. Help us to conquer the apostles of greed and racial arrogancies. Lead us to the saving of our country, and with our sister nations into a world unity that will spell a sure peace—a peace invulnerable to the schemings of unworthy men. And a peace that will let all of men live in freedom, reaping the just rewards of their honest toil. Thy will be done, Almighty God. Amen.

Allied Casualties on Omaha Beach, June 6, 1944

Unit	Killed	Wounded	Missing	Total
1ST INFANTRY DIVISION				
16th Infantry Regiment	86	528	357	971
18th Infantry Regiment	12	147	45	204
1st Engineer Combat Battalion	4	27	6	37
1st Military Police Platoon	1	22	0	23
7th Field Artillery Battalion	4	14	3	21
1st Infantry Division HQ Company	0	2	0	2
32nd Field Artillery Battalion				28[a]
1st Medical Battalion				c. 40[b]
26th Infantry Regiment				c. 20[b]
TOTAL 1st INFANTRY DIVISION				1,346[b]
29TH INFANTRY DIVISION				
116th Infantry Regiment	247	576	184	1,007
115th Infantry Regiment	33	68	2	103
121st Engineer Combat Battalion	18	31	31	80
111th Field Artillery Battalion	17	26	4	47

Unit	Killed	Wounded	Missing	Total
104th Medical Battalion	2	8	10	20
29th Infantry Division HQ Company	0	1	0	1
175th Infantry Regiment	1	0	0	1
29th Reconnaissance Troop	3	0	0	3
29th Military Police Platoon				c. 10[b]
TOTAL 29th INFANTRY DIVISION				1,272
V CORPS/FIRST ARMY UNITS				
2nd and 5th Ranger Battalions	96	183	32	311[c]
146th Engineer Combat Battalion	84	112	0	196
299th Engineer Combat Battalion	71	c. 75	0	c. 146[d]
112th Engineer Combat Battalion	8	30	0	38
20th Engineer Combat Battalion	3	10	0	13
37th Engineer Combat Battalion				82[a]
336th Engineer Combat Battalion				30[a]
348th Engineer Combat Battalion				21[a]
149th Engineer Combat Battalion				c. 50[b]
147th Engineer Combat Battalion				c. 45[b]
397th Anti-Aircraft Artillery Battalion	17	71	32	120
467th Anti-Aircraft Artillery Battalion	8	31	0	39
197th Anti-Aircraft Artillery Battalion	5	12	0	17
81st Chemical Mortar Battalion	10	20	0	30
741st Tank Battalion	c. 45	c. 60	0	c. 105[b]
743rd Tank Battalion				c. 70[b]
745th Tank Battalion	1	0	0	1
61st Signal Battalion	1	3	0	4[e]
5th and 6th Engineer Special Brigades				c. 250[f]
TOTAL V CORPS/FIRST ARMY				1,568
U.S. NAVY/COAST GUARD AND ROYAL NAVY				
Naval Combat Demolition Units	24	32	15	71
6th Naval Beach Battalion	22	77	0	99
7th Naval Beach Battalion	19	10	0	29
USN/USCG Landing Craft Crews				c. 280[b]
RN Landing Craft Crews				c. 30[b]
Naval Shore Fire Control Parties				c. 15[b]
TOTAL NAVY/COAST GUARD				539

Unit	Killed	Wounded	Missing	Total
EIGHTH AIR FORCE				
2nd Bombardment Division	10	0	0	10
TOTAL EIGHTH AIR FORCE	10	0	0	10
GRAND TOTAL				4,720

Notes

[a] Indicated figure is casualty total only. Unit records do not differentiate among killed, wounded, and missing.

[b] Indicated figure is casualty approximation based on official unit records that do not specify number of killed, wounded, and missing.

[c] Indicated figure includes casualties suffered on June 7, and also includes casualties among Rudder's Ranger force at Pointe du Hoc.

[d] Company B, 299th Engineers landed on Utah Beach. Indicated 299th casualty total may include Company B on Utah.

[e] Indicated casualty figure is for twenty-four-man detachment under the command of Col. B. B. Talley, embarked in two DUKWs. Talley and his subordinates reported by radio their observations of events on the beach to General Gerow on his command ship *Ancon*.

[f] Indicated casualty total is approximation for all 5th and 6th Engineer Special Brigades units landing on Omaha Beach *except* for engineer combat battalions, each of which is given a separate casualty total in the above list. Among the miscellaneous Engineer Special Brigade units included in this casualty total are: signal, military police, quartermaster, medical, amphibious truck, and ordnance units. U.S. Navy units attached to Engineer Special Brigades are not included in this total.

Medal of Honor and Distinguished Service Cross Awards for Valor on Omaha Beach

The Medal of Honor is the highest military decoration that may be awarded to members of the armed forces of the United States. The U.S. Army's version of the Medal of Honor was established in 1862 by Congressional resolution, later approved by President Lincoln, to recognize soldiers who "shall most distinguish themselves by their gallantry in action, and other soldierlike qualities."

In recognition of their valor on Omaha Beach on June 6, 1944, the U.S. Army awarded Medals of Honor to three soldiers, all from the 1st Infantry Division. Two of these awards were posthumous. The citations are provided below in order of issuance.

Pvt. Carlton Barrett
HQ Company, 18th Infantry, 1st Division, General Orders,
October 2, 1944

For gallantry and intrepidity at the risk of his life above and beyond the call of duty on 6 June 1944, in the vicinity of St. Laurent-sur-Mer, France. On the morning of D-Day, Pvt. Barrett, landing in the face of extremely heavy enemy fire, was forced to wade ashore through neck-deep water. Disregarding the personal danger, he returned to the surf again and again to assist his floundering comrades and save them from drowning. Refusing to remain pinned down by the intense barrage of small arms and mortar fire poured at the landing points, Pvt. Barrett, working with fierce determination, saved many lives by carrying casualties to an evacuation boat lying offshore. In addition to his assigned mission as guide, he carried dispatches the length of the fire-swept beach; he assisted the wounded, he calmed the shocked; he arose as a leader in the stress of the occasion. His coolness and his dauntless, daring courage while constantly risking his life during a period of many hours had an inestimable effect on his comrades, and is in keeping with the highest traditions of the Army of the United States.

T/5 John Pinder
HQ Company, 16th Infantry, 1st Division, General Orders,
January 4, 1945 (posthumous)

For conspicuous gallantry and intrepidity at the risk of his life above and beyond the call of duty on 6 June 1944, in the vicinity of Colleville-sur-Mer, France. On D-Day, T/5 Pinder landed on the coast 100 yards offshore under devastating enemy machine gun and artillery fire which caused severe casualties among the boatload. Carrying a vitally important radio, he struggled towards shore in waist-deep water. Only a few yards from his craft he was hit by enemy fire and was gravely wounded. T/5 Pinder never stopped. He made shore and delivered the radio. Refusing to take cover afforded or to accept medical attention for his wounds, T/5 Pinder, though terribly weakened by loss of blood and in fierce pain, on three occasions went into the fire-swept surf to salvage communication equipment. He recovered many vital parts and equipment, including another workable radio. On the third trip he was again hit, suffering machine gun bullet wounds in the legs. Still this valiant soldier would not stop for rest or medical attention. Remaining exposed to heavy enemy fire, growing steadily weaker, he aided in establishing the vital radio communication on the beach. While so engaged this dauntless soldier was hit for the third time and killed. The indomitable courage and personal bravery of T/5 Pinder was a magnificent inspiration to the men with whom he served.

1st Lt. Jimmie Monteith, Jr.
Company L, 16th Infantry, 1st Division, General Orders, March 29, 1945
(posthumous)

For conspicuous gallantry and intrepidity at the risk of his life above and beyond the call of duty on 6 June 1944, in the vicinity of Colleville-sur-Mer, France. 1st Lt. Monteith landed with the initial assault waves on the coast of France under heavy enemy fire. Without regard to his own personal safety he continually moved up and down the beach reorganizing men for further assault. He then led the assault over a narrow protective ledge and across the flat, exposed terrain to the comparative safety of a cliff. Retracing his steps across the field to the beach, he moved over to where two tanks were buttoned-up and blind under violent enemy artillery and machine gun fire. Completely exposed to the intense fire, 1st Lieutenant Monteith led the tanks on foot through a minefield and into firing positions. Under his direction several enemy positions were destroyed. He then rejoined his company and under his leadership his men captured an advantageous position on the hill. Supervising the defense of his newly won position against repeated vicious counterattacks, he continued to ignore his own personal safety, repeatedly crossing the two or three hundred yards of open terrain under heavy fire to strengthen links in his defensive chain. When the enemy succeeded in completely surrounding 1st Lt. Monteith and his unit, and while leading the fight out of the situation, 1st Lt. Monteith was killed by enemy fire. The courage, gallantry, and intrepid leadership displayed by 1st Lt. Monteith is worthy of emulation.

In the U.S. Army, the Distinguished Service Cross (DSC) is second in precedence to the Medal of Honor. It was established in January 1918 by President Wilson upon the recommendation of General Pershing, commander of the American Expeditionary Force in World War I.

The U.S. Army awarded 153 DSCs to servicemen for valor on Omaha Beach. These men are listed alphabetically below, along with the units to which they belonged (when known). Some D-Day DSCs awarded to members of the 2nd Ranger Battalion were for valor in the action at Pointe du Hoc, four miles west of Omaha Beach, but are nonetheless included in this list. Furthermore, some DSCs were awarded for actions undertaken by the 116th Infantry and Rangers during their westward push from Omaha Beach to relieve Rudder's Rangers in their slender beachhead at Pointe du Hoc. This action took place on June 7 and 8, but these DSCs, too, are included in the following list.

Anderson, 2nd Lt. William. 146th Engineer Battalion
Anker, 2nd Lt. Leonard. 116th Infantry
Appleby, T/4 Stanley. 16th Infantry
Armellino, Capt. John. 16th Infantry
Armstrong, T/Sgt. L. 116th Infantry
Arnold, Capt. Edgar. 2nd Ranger Battalion
Austin, T/5 Billy. 149th Engineer Battalion
Barber, PFC Alexander. 5th Ranger Battalion
Beavers, 1st Lt. Harold. 743rd Tank Battalion
Beitler, Capt. Kenneth. 58th Armored Field Artillery Battalion
Belcher, Sgt. Julius. 2nd Ranger Battalion
Belmont, S/Sgt. Gail. 2nd Ranger Battalion

Benn, T/Sgt. William. 16th Infantry
Bennett, Lt. Col. Donald. 62nd Armored Field Artillery Battalion
Benton, S/Sgt. John. Infantry (no unit indicated)
Berkowitz, PFC Henry. 16th Infantry
Bingham, Maj. Sidney. 116th Infantry
Bleau, 2nd Lt. Kenneth. 16th Infantry
Bowen, PFC George. 16th Infantry
Briggs, Capt. Victor. 16th Infantry
Buschlen, Sgt. Arthur. 16th Infantry
Canham, Col. Charles. 116th Infantry
Cavaliere, Pvt. Peter. 16th Infantry
Clark, S/Sgt. Philip. 16th Infantry
Clark, T/5 Rex. 2nd Ranger Battalion
Clarke, Pvt. James. 116th Infantry
Coffman, S/Sgt. Ralph. 116th Infantry
Colson, Sgt. Clarence. 16th Infantry
Colwell, S/Sgt. Curtis. 16th Infantry
Cota, Brig. Gen. Norman. 29th Division
Cotter, Capt. John. 116th Infantry
Courtney, Sgt. William. 2nd Ranger Battalion
Cutler, 1st Lt. Robert. 16th Infantry
Dawson, 1st Lt. Francis. 5th Ranger Battalion
Dawson, Capt. Joseph. 16th Infantry
Dillon, 1st Lt. William. 16th Infantry
Dock, T/4 Lowell. 7th Field Artillery Battalion
Dove, Pvt. Vinton. 37th Engineer Battalion
Dreher, PFC William. 2nd Ranger Battalion
Elder, Capt. Ned. 743rd Tank Battalion
Ellis, T/Sgt. Calvin. 16th Infantry
Ferguson, 2nd Lt. Forest. 116th Infantry
Fitzsimmons, 1st Sgt. Lawrence. 16th Infantry
Fryer, Pvt. Gibson. 16th Infantry
Gallagher, PFC Richard. 16th Infantry
Gearing, 1st Lt. Edward. 116th Infantry
Gibbs, Lt. Col. George. 7th Field Artillery Battalion
Giles, 1st Lt. Carl. 16th Infantry
Goranson, Capt. Ralph. 2nd Ranger Battalion
Gregory, 1st Lt. Joseph. 146th Engineer Battalion
Griffen, PFC John. 16th Infantry
Habib, Sgt. George. 741st Tank Battalion
Hall, PFC Henry. 397th Anti-Aircraft Artillery Battalion

Hargrove, 1st Lt. Robert. 116th Infantry
Heenan, PFC John. 146th Engineer Battalion
Hicks, Lt. Col. Herbert. 16th Infantry
Isley, Lt. Col. Carl. 146th Engineer Battalion
James, Sgt. Theodore. 2nd Ranger Battalion
Jenkins, S/Sgt. Floyd. Infantry (no unit indicated)
Jewett, Maj. Milton. 299th Engineer Battalion
Johnson, Sgt. Denzil. 5th Ranger Battalion
Jones, PFC Aaron. 16th Infantry
Jones, 1st Lt. Henry. Infantry (no unit indicated)
Kehaly, 1st Lt. William. 146th Engineer Battalion
Kerchner, 2nd Lt. George. 2nd Ranger Battalion
Kidwell, Pvt. Kenneth. 81st Chemical Mortar Battalion
Lacy, 1st Lt. Chaplain Joseph. 5th Ranger Battalion
Lanterman, 1st Lt. Raymond. 146th Engineer Battalion
Lomell, 1st Sgt. Leonard. 2nd Ranger Battalion
Lovell, Sgt. Warden. 165th Signal Photo Company
MacConchie, 1st Lt. Howard. 18th Infantry
Mansfield, S/Sgt. Paul. 16th Infantry
Masny, Capt. Otto. 2nd Ranger Battalion
McElyea, 2nd Lt. Atwood. 16th Infantry
McKissick, T/5 Howard. 5th Ranger Battalion
McLaren, Pvt. Donald. 81st Chemical Mortar Battalion
Merendino, Capt. Thomas. 16th Infantry
Moody, 1st Lt. William. 2nd Ranger Battalion
Moody, Sgt. Willie. 5th Ranger Battalion
Morse, 2nd Lt. Verne. 116th Infantry
Mullins, Lt. Col. Thornton. 111th Field Artillery Battalion
Nicoli, Sgt. Raymond. 81st Chemical Mortar Battalion
O'Brien, Capt. Thomas. 16th Infantry
O'Neill, Lt. Col. John. Special Engineer Task Force
Orndorff, Sgt. Douglas. 116th Infantry
Panas, 1st Lt. James. 81st Chemical Mortar Battalion
Paolini, PFC Camillus. 18th Infantry
Parke, Pvt. Joseph. 16th Infantry
Parker, 1st Lt. Charles. 5th Ranger Battalion
Patterson, Sgt. Lyman. 116th Infantry
Pence, Capt. James. 16th Infantry
Perry, Capt. Edwin. 299th Engineer Battalion
Petersen, S/Sgt. Gerard. 743rd Tank Battalion
Peterson, Sgt. Kenneth. 16th Infantry

Peterson, PFC Victor. 16th Infantry
Philips, Capt. Vodra. 743rd Tank Battalion
Porter, Pvt. Benton. 81st Chemical Mortar Battalion
Pressley, 1st Sgt. William. 116th Infantry
Proffitt, T/Sgt. Carl. 116th Infantry
Radford, S/Sgt. David. 16th Infantry
Richards, Maj. William. 112th Engineer Battalion
Richmond, Capt. Kimball. 16th Infantry
Riggs, PFC William. 116th Infantry
Ritter, S/Sgt. Ozias. 116th Infantry
Roach, T/Sgt. John. 116th Infantry
Roberts, 2nd Lt. Eskell. 146th Engineer Battalion
Robinson, 1st Lt. James. 16th Infantry
Rodgers, PFC Thomas. Infantry (no unit indicated)
Rogers, T/Sgt. Howard. 116th Infantry
Rosen, PFC Sanford. 16th Infantry
Ross, 1st Lt. Robert. 37th Engineer Battalion
Ross, 2nd Lt. Wesley. 146th Engineer Battalion
Rudder, Lt. Col. James. 2nd Ranger Battalion
Runey, 1st Lt. Michael. 58th Armored Field Artillery Battalion
Savino, T/5 Felice. 81st Chemical Mortar Battalion
Schneider, S/Sgt. George. Engineers (no unit indicated)
Schneider, Lt. Col. Max. 5th Ranger Battalion
Schur, PFC Curtis. 149th Engineer Battalion
Settineri, Capt. John. 16th Infantry
Shaffer, T/5 Edward. 348th Engineer Battalion
Shelby, 1st Lt. John. 16th Infantry
Shindle, T/4 Elmer. 116th Infantry
Shoemaker, Pvt. William. 37th Engineer Battalion
Shorter, S/Sgt. Paul. 16th Infantry
Skaggs, Lt. Col. Robert. 741st Tank Battalion
Smulik, T/4 Bolick. 741st Tank Battalion
Spalding, 2nd Lt. John. 16th Infantry
Sproul, Capt. Archibald. 116th Infantry
Stephens, PFC Otto. 2nd Ranger Battalion
Stockwell, S/Sgt. Leeward. 16th Infantry
Streczyk, T/Sgt. Phillip. 16th Infantry
Strojny, S/Sgt. Raymond. 16th Infantry
Sullivan, Maj. Richard. 5th Ranger Battalion
Sweeney, PFC Lawrence. 741st Tank Battalion
Talley, Col. Benjamin. V Corps

Taylor, Col. George. 16th Infantry
Taylor, 2nd Lt. Walter. 116th Infantry
Tegtmeyer, Maj. Charles. 16th Infantry
Thompson, Col. Paul. 6th Engineer Special Brigade
Tucker, Pvt. Albert. 146th Engineer Battalion
Upham, Lt. Col. John. 743rd Tank Battalion
Van de Voort, 2nd Lt. Leo. 116th Infantry
Washington, Maj. William. 16th Infantry
Wells, S/Sgt. James. 16th Infantry
White, T/Sgt. John. 2nd Ranger Battalion
Whittington, Capt. George. 5th Ranger Battalion
Wilk, PFC Theodore. 16th Infantry
Williams, 1st Lt. Alfred. Infantry (no unit indicated)
Williams, 1st Lt. William. 116th Infantry
Woodward, Capt. Robert. 7th Field Artillery Battalion
Wozenski, Capt. Edward. 16th Infantry
Wyman, Brig. Gen. Willard. 1st Infantry Division
Zantow, 1st Lt. Forrest. 116th Infantry

U.S. Army awards for extraordinary valor in World War II were the result of a complex and lengthy evaluation process. For a soldier to be considered for a Medal of Honor or DSC, that soldier's unit had to submit carefully prepared paperwork to higher headquarters, usually the corps or army to which the unit belonged. This paperwork was required to contain details of the action in question, including written statements by as many soldiers as possible who had witnessed the supposed deeds of valor. The presentation of paperwork in support of a unit's appeal for a Medal of Honor or DSC was critical: The collected details of the action and eyewitness accounts were examined thoroughly by a board of three senior officers, who would ultimately decide by unanimous or majority vote whether the unit's appeal was approved, rejected, or reduced to a lesser medal.

Several of the 153 DSCs awarded for valor on Omaha Beach were actually the result of appeals for Medals of Honor that were downgraded to DSCs by vote of the three-officer evaluation board. Indeed, without the personal intervention of General Eisenhower, only two men—not three—would have been granted Medals of Honor for valor on Omaha Beach. An evaluation board had at first recommended that the 16th Infantry's Medal of Honor application for Company L's Lt. Jimmie Monteith be downgraded to a DSC, but nearly six months after D-Day, a handwritten note from Ike supporting a Medal of Honor for Monteith settled the issue.

One can only speculate as to why, in a battle of such intensity and significance as Omaha Beach, only three applications for decorations resulted in Medals of Honor—all in the 1st Infantry Division. According to the officer boards examining each appeal, perhaps only those three actions satisfied the clearly stated requirements for "conspicuous gallantry and intrepidity at risk of life above and beyond the call of duty." However, the battle-hardened 1st Infantry Division, which had fought in two major campaigns in the Mediterranean theater prior to D-Day, was presumably much more familiar and adept with the process by which military decorations were applied for and awarded than units new to combat. Once the Omaha invasion was over, the Fighting First's staffs knew exactly what to do to gain official recognition of its soldiers' extraordinary courage on D-Day, and they jumped to the task with celerity and professionalism. The result was three Medals of Honor and fifty-three DSCs for June 6 alone. The 1st Division's fifty-three D-Day DSCs amount to slightly more than 1 percent of all U.S. Army DSCs awarded throughout World War II.

In comparison, most of the other outfits that participated in the Omaha invasion filed far fewer appeals for decorations. For example, the Fighting First's partner in the Omaha assault, the 29th Division, received no Medals of Honor and about half the number of DSCs (twenty-seven) as the 1st Division for its D-Day actions, despite the fact the 1st and 29th contributed roughly equal numbers of men to the invasion. Indeed, this pattern continued until the end of the war in Europe: In the European theater of operations (ETO), the army granted the 1st Division roughly 4,300 decorations of Silver Star or higher, while the 29th Division was accorded only 877—this despite the fact that the 29th suffered about 5,000 more casualties in the ETO than the 1st and was in action for roughly the same time period.

And yet there is one person in the 29th Division whose actions on Omaha Beach were so worthy of the Medal of Honor that it is astonishing that he was never even considered for it. Dozens of eyewitness accounts, only a portion of which are included in this book, establish beyond any doubt that Brig. Gen. Norman D. Cota, the 29th's assistant division commander, repeatedly performed extraordinary feats of valor that were instrumental in rescuing the seemingly unsolvable and deadly situation faced by first-wave assault troops on the western sector of Omaha Beach at about 8:00 A.M. on D-Day. Cota's exploits in encouraging the troops to leave the beach and move up the bluffs, which ultimately led to the capture of Vierville and the opening of the Vierville draw, surely fulfilled the Medal of Honor requirements for "conspicuous gallantry and intrepidity at risk of life above and beyond the call of duty." In spite of overwhelming evidence corroborating Cota's performance, however, he was awarded not the Medal of Honor, but the DSC.

Officer boards established to evaluate petitions for decorations in Normandy may have maintained an unspoken understanding that senior officers of colonel rank and above should be considered for awards no higher than the DSC, limiting Medals of Honor to officers and men whose duties required them to be present more or less continuously in the front lines. Such a theory would also account for the army's failure to grant a Medal of Honor to the 16th Infantry's CO, Col. George Taylor, who performed acts of heroism on D-Day almost identical to Cota's on an adjacent beach sector, with equally beneficial results. The only exception to the senior officer rule on D-Day was Brig. Gen. Theodore Roosevelt, Jr., the 4th Infantry Division's assistant division commander and son of the former president, who was granted the Medal of Honor in September 1944 for his D-Day actions on Utah Beach. The award was posthumous, as Roosevelt had died of a heart attack in July.

The facts are irrefutable that for most of D-Day, Omaha Beach was a great leveler of rank. Everyone, from general to private, was in equal danger every second; there was no such thing as a secure command post anywhere on the beach where colonels and generals could calmly deliberate their next moves, with runners rushing in and out bearing dispatches to and from the distant front. By necessity, Cota and Taylor fought all day on Omaha Beach not as a conventional general and colonel, but as *de facto* platoon leaders or company commanders—positions typically held by young officers half the ages of the two older men. Cota's and Taylor's extraordinary actions on D-Day, by any measure, contributed mightily to the invasion's ultimate success.

The U.S. Army should seriously consider upgrading the DSC awards for General Cota and Colonel Taylor to Medals of Honor. This is especially appropriate now, in the twenty-first century, when careful retrospect of sixty years' duration yields mounting recognition that the Omaha Beach invasion was a pivotal test of America's resolve and arguably its most decisive moment in World War II. Cota's and Taylor's remarkable accomplishments on Omaha Beach on June 6, 1944, are critical reminders that military leadership—well timed, expertly and courageously applied—is the key to success in war. Today their actions are worthy of far broader recognition and gratitude, for without them the end result of the Omaha invasion might have been much different.

A grateful nation must remember.

U.S. Army and U.S. Navy First-Wave Units on Omaha Beach

The following U.S. Army and U.S. Navy units composed the initial assault waves on Omaha Beach on June 6, 1944, starting at H-Hour, or 6:30 A.M.

741ST TANK BATTALION
Lt. Col. Robert Skaggs

Company A (16 tanks, 8 tank dozers on 8 LCT[A]): Capt. Cecil Thomas

Company B (16 DD tanks on 4 LCT): Capt. James Thornton

Company C (16 DD tanks on 4 LCT): Capt. Charles Young

743RD TANK BATTALION
Lt. Col. John Upham

Company A (16 tanks, 8 tank dozers on 8 LCT[A]): Capt. Vodra Philips

Company B (16 DD tanks on 4 LCT): Capt. Charles Ehmka

Company C (16 DD tanks on 4 LCT): Capt. Ned Elder

16TH INFANTRY REGIMENT, 1ST INFANTRY DIVISION
Col. George Taylor
Regimental Staff
Executive Officer: Lt. Col. John Matthews
S-1 (Personnel): Capt. William Friedman
S-2 (Intelligence): Maj. John Lauten
S-3 (Operations): Maj. Carl Plitt
S-4 (Supply): Maj. Leonard Godfray
Surgeon: Maj. Charles Tegtmeyer

1st Battalion (Transport: USS Samuel Chase, USCG)
Lt. Col. Edmund Driscoll
Company A: Capt. James Pence
Company B: Capt. Thomas Merendino
Company C: Capt. Victor Briggs
Company D: Capt. Polydore Dion

2nd Battalion (Transport: USS Henrico)
Lt. Col. Herbert Hicks
Company E: Capt. Ed Wozenski
Company F: Capt. John Finke
Company G: Capt. Joseph Dawson
Company H: Capt. Robert Irvine

3rd Battalion (Transport: SS Empire Anvil [British])
Lt. Col. Charles Horner
Company I: Capt. Kimball Richmond
Company K: Capt. Anthony Prucnal
Company L: Capt. John Armellino
Company M: Capt. Emil Edmonds

116TH INFANTRY REGIMENT, 29TH INFANTRY DIVISION
Col. Charles Canham
Regimental Staff
Executive Officer: Lt. Col. Harold Cassell
S-1 (Personnel): Capt. Morris Ernst
S-2 (Intelligence): Maj. Asbury Jackson

S-3 (Operations): Maj. Thomas Howie
S-4 (Supply): Maj. John Sours
Surgeon: Maj. Millard Buckley

1st Battalion (Transport: SS Empire Javelin [British])
Lt. Col. John Metcalfe
Company A: Capt. Taylor Fellers
Company B: Capt. Ettore Zappacosta
Company C: Capt. Berthier Hawks
Company D: Capt. Walter Schilling

2nd Battalion (Transport: USS Thomas Jefferson)
Maj. Sidney Bingham
Company E: Capt. Lawrence Madill
Company F: Capt. William Callahan
Company G: Capt. Eccles Scott
Company H: Capt. George Boyd

3rd Battalion (Transport: USS Charles Carroll)
Lt. Col. Lawrence Meeks
Company I: Capt. Mifflin Clowe
Company K: Capt. William Pingley
Company L: Capt. Charles East
Company M: Capt. Charles Kidd

COMPANY C, 2ND RANGER BATTALION
Capt. Ralph Goranson
(Transport: HMS Prince Charles)
1st Platoon: 1st Lt. William Moody
2nd Platoon: 1st Lt. Sidney Salomon

146TH ENGINEER COMBAT BATTALION
Lt. Col. Carl Isley
Gap Assault Teams
Team 1: Lieutenant Kehaly
Team 2: Lieutenant Anderson
Team 3: Lieutenant Schill
Team 4: Lieutenant Shively
Team 5: Lieutenant Caldwell
Team 6: Lieutenant Roberts

Team 7: Lieutenant Bartholomew
Team 8: Lieutenant Ross
Team 9: Lieutenant Lanterman
Team 10: Lieutenant Gregory
Team A: Lieutenant Meier
Team B: Lieutenant Rollins
Team C: Lieutenant Latendresse
Team D: Lieutenant Trescher

299TH ENGINEER COMBAT BATTALION
Maj. Milton Jewett
Gap Assault Teams
Team 11: Captain Manniko
Team 12: Lt. J. Wood
Team 13: Lieutenant Batchelor
Team 14: Lt. P. Wood
Team 15: Lieutenant McGuire
Team 16: Lieutenant Hobson
Team E: Lieutenant Donahoo
Team F: Captain Perry
Team G: Staff Sergeant Luehrs
Team H: Captain Bunting

U.S. NAVY NAVAL COMBAT DEMOLITION UNITS (NCDU)
Lt. Cmdr. Joseph Gibbons
NCDU 11: Chief Freeman (attached to Team 1)
NCDU 24: Lieutenant (jg) Culver (attached to Team 2)
NCDU 27: Lieutenant (jg) Holtman (attached to Team 3)
NCDU 41: Lieutenant (jg) Nichols (attached to Team 4)
NCDU 42: Warrant Officer Thompson (attached to Team 5)
NCDU 43: Lieutenant (jg) Jenkins (attached to Team 6)
NCDU 140: Warrant Officer Hill (attached to Team 7)
NCDU 137: Ensign Blean (attached to Team 8)
NCDU 44: Warrant Officer Raynor (attached to Team 9)
NCDU 45: Ensign Karnowski (attached to Team 10)
NCDU 46: Ensign Bussell (attached to Team 11)
NCDU 22: Lieutenant Cooper (attached to Team 12)
NCDU 23: Lieutenant (jg) Vetter (attached to Team 13)
NCDU 141: Ensign Gouinlock (attached to Team 14)
NCDU 138: Ensign Allen (attached to Team 15)

NCDU 142: Ensign Stocking (attached to Team 16)
NCDU 133: Ensign Mitchell (attached to Team A)
NCDU 130: Ensign Chaney (attached to Team B)
NCDU 128: Ensign Duquette (attached to Team D)
NCDU 131: Ensign Inman (attached to Team F)
NCDU 129: Ensign Peterson (attached to Team H)

Composition of Typical Assault Boat Team, 16th and 116th Infantry

Troops from the 16th and 116th Infantry Regiments composing the initial assault waves on Omaha Beach were conveyed to the beach in U.S. Navy or Coast Guard LCVP or Royal Navy LCA landing craft. Typically, each LCVP/LCA carried a team of thirty-one troops organized in the following manner:

One Boat Team Leader (1st or 2nd Lieutenant)
- With M-1 carbine and SCR-536 walkie-talkie

One Assistant Boat Team Leader (Technical or Staff Sergeant)
- With M-1 Garand rifle

One 5-man Rifle Team
- Each with M-1 Garand rifle
- Two with bangalore torpedoes

One 4-man Wire-Cutting Team
- Each with M-1 Garand rifle and wire cutters
- Two with bangalore torpedoes

Two 2-man BAR Teams
- Two with Browning automatic rifles
- Two with M-1 Garand rifles and extra BAR ammunition

One 4-man Mortar Team
- One with 60-millimeter mortar and M-1911 .45 Colt pistol
- Three with M-1 carbine and extra mortar ammunition

Two 2-man Bazooka Teams
- Two with bazooka and M-1 carbine
- Two with M-1 Garand rifles and extra bazooka ammunition

One 2-man Flamethrower Team
- One with flamethrower and M-1911 .45 Colt pistol
- One with M-1 Garand rifle, nitrogen tank, and extra fuel

One 5-man Demolition Team
- Each with M-1 Garand rifle
- Primacord, TNT, satchel/pole charges, detonators divided among team

One Medic (some boat teams did not have a medic)
- With medical supply kit
- Unarmed

The boat team leader took position at the front of the boat with his five-man rifle team. The assistant boat team leader remained at the back of the boat with the five-man demolition team and medic (if any). In one of the six or seven landing craft constituting a rifle or heavy weapons company, the normal thirty-one-man boat team was supplemented by the company commander (usually a captain) and his radio operator, who carried an SCR-300 backpack radio.

The above boat team organization was typical of rifle companies only. Heavy weapons companies (Companies D, H, and M in U.S. Army infantry regiments) used a different method, substituting a heavy machine gun team for the BAR teams and a heavy mortar team for the bazooka and flamethrower teams.

In addition to the thirty-one army troops, each landing craft carried a four-man (sometimes three) navy crew:

One Coxswain
- On LCVP, steered from exposed position at aft on port side
- On LCA, steered from armored cabin in bow

One Bowman
- Stood in front of boat to open and close ramp (and armored door on LCA)

- Aided in lowering and raising LCVP/LCA from transport's davits
- Sometimes replaced by officer acting as three- or six-boat wave leader

One Sternman (Sternsheetsman in Royal Navy)
- Stood in stern to operate machine gun if necessary
- Aided in lowering and raising LCVP/LCA from transport's davits
- Sometimes replaced by radioman (signalman in RN) in wave leaders' boats

One Engineer (Stoker in Royal Navy)
- Operated machinery in engine compartment at stern, hidden from view

Uniform and Equipment of Boat Team Leader, 16th and 116th Infantry

B oat team leaders in the 16th and 116th Infantry (generally 1st or 2nd lieutenants) were typically outfitted with the following uniform items and equipment on D-Day. (All uniform items were treated with a protective chemical to prevent enemy chemical agents from penetrating through the fabric to the skin.)

UNIFORM

Wool drawers, long
Wool trousers
Wool undershirt
Flannel shirt
Suspenders
Wool socks
Leggings
Service shoes (sometimes paratrooper boots)
Field jacket
Assault vest, with attached pouches and packs
Helmet, with netting and liner
Two arm brassards (used for chemical detection)
Dog tags

EQUIPMENT

Pistol belt, with carbine and pistol ammunition pouches
Entrenching tool, with cover
M-1 carbine
M-1911 .45 pistol, with holster
Hand grenades
SCR-536 walkie-talkie
Flotation belt (kept one-third inflated)
Map case
Binoculars, with case
Gas mask, with case
First-aid pouch
Trench knife
Canteen, with cup
Utensils
Compass
Blanket
Raincoat
Three K rations
Three D rations

Notes

To recount a thorough story of the Omaha Beach invasion, I strove to draw source materials from documents written as close as possible in time to June 6, 1944. Based on my personal collection of such materials—an ongoing research effort that has now endured for more than a quarter century—I knew even before starting the manuscript that most details pertaining to the invasion are encompassed, generally in meticulous fashion, by the reams of unit journals, after-action reports, postcombat interviews, correspondence, U.S. Army medal citations, and postwar unit histories (invariably written by participants) available in public archival repositories in the United States. Indeed, the challenge posed to any serious Omaha Beach researcher is not the availability of primary source information, but the availability of time to examine and analyze the vast amount of paperwork the invasion generated. The truth of the invasion is somewhere within those papers, but to decipher that truth is a vast undertaking.

Information assembled from secondary sources and veterans' recollections decades after D-Day were also useful in the preparation of this book, but I tended to use such information only if primary sources could corroborate it. As a rule, the closer in time to D-Day an account was prepared, the more I trusted it. This is not to say, however, that original archival records covered every detail of the Omaha invasion. They did not. Several glaring gaps in the Omaha time line existed that primary sources could not fill. For example, the oft-told story of the landing of Company A, 116th Infantry, at H-Hour on Dog Green beach has very few archival records that accurately portray the company's fate because so few men survived the debacle and hardly any witnesses noted down accounts of worth to an historian. Consequently, in secondary sources, many descriptions of Company A's landing are not factual, and those errors are perpetuated by historians who continue to base their research on flawed accounts.

But the historiography of Omaha Beach changed forever when several Royal Navy veterans of the landing came forward in the late 1990s to provide their recollections of D-Day. Most of the 116th Infantry's 1st Battalion was brought ashore by British landing craft, but not once had American historians tapped Royal Navy veterans to piece together an accurate portrayal of precisely what happened on Dog Green at 6:30 A.M. on June 6, 1944. One veteran, Sub-Lt. Jimmy Green, was one of the last people to see Capt. Taylor Fellers, CO of Company A, alive. Consequently, Green's account is invaluable because, for the first time in fifty-five years, details of Company A's first moments on the beach finally came to light.

Altogether, I knew that an accurate and complete history of the Omaha landing could not be rushed. There were simply too many documents to pore over, accounts to piece together, new sources to discover and evaluate. I resolved to begin the manuscript only when I had collected and catalogued sufficient documents to support all of the hundreds of significant events I could reconstruct on Omaha on D-Day. Furthermore, I suspected that the writing of the manuscript would be a learn-as-you-go experience, and I was right. The effort was analogous to starting a monumental jigsaw puzzle. Progress seemed impossible at first because such a vast array of information was available, and each informational piece had to fit flawlessly in place with others. But the more I pieced together, the more the historical puzzle cleared up. And when all the pieces were finally assembled, a broader historical picture emerged, a depiction consisting of a multitude of stories fit together in the larger framework of one of the most decisive military operations in history.

Much of the original source material for the book is found at the National Archives and Records Administration in College Park, Maryland. However, as the Omaha landing was an effort combining ground, naval, and air forces to achieve a military goal, some information specific to particular service branches is located in those branches' own historical repositories. Samuel Eliot Morison's research notes for *The Invasion of France and Germany* (volume 11 in his *History of U.S. Naval Operations in World War II*) can be found at the Naval Historical Center, Operational Archives Branch, in the Washington Navy Yard. At the U.S. Air Force History Office at Bolling Air Force Base, also in Washington D.C., I examined Eighth Air Force mission orders and action reports relating to Omaha. The U.S. Army Military History Institute at Carlisle Barracks, Pennsylvania, has an excellent collection of rare unit histories, sometimes down to company level, written by unit members during the occupation of Germany immediately after V-E Day in May 1945—when memories of the war were still fresh.

In short, one could spend a lifetime searching for and reading archival documents relating to Omaha and still not come close to discerning the full story of the invasion. I have no doubt that deep in the alcoves of the various military archives holding D-Day material, there is much more to be discovered, and in the decades ahead, new information surely will be unearthed by those willing to commit the necessary time to the task.

Anyone writing World War II history cannot fail to appreciate how fortunate he or she is to live at a time when the participants themselves may be contacted directly for their memories of those great historical events. When there are no more such men, the historian's task will become inestimably more complex. I have discovered the answers to hundreds of thorny historical puzzles relating to Omaha Beach at veterans' reunions, solutions that in many instances could not have been determined through conventional research alone. The reunions are always the highlights of my annual research journeys.

But one of the greatest aids to the World War II historian has only evolved over the past decade: the Internet. It never ceases to amaze me how many members of the World War II generation are accessible by e-mail. Their willingness to adapt to new technology has made my job infinitely easier than it was when I wrote *Beyond the Beachhead* in 1988, a time when virtually no World War II veterans were using the Internet. (Admittedly, neither was I.) The answers to tricky historical questions sometimes came to me so promptly by electronic mail that I could not help contemplating the day—probably in the near future—when the historian need never leave his chair to write the definitive history of a great battle.

One day I needed the name of a tank driver from the 741st Tank Battalion. Thanks to Al Heintzleman and his 741st Tank Battalion website, I had the answer directly from Al within ten minutes of making the query. (An autographed copy of Al's invaluable 741st history followed in the mail shortly.) In all my Omaha research, I had neither met nor corresponded with a single man who knew Lt. Jimmie Monteith, the 16th Infantry Medal of Honor winner on D-Day. But within twenty-four hours of my initial search on the Internet to find such a person, I was corresponding by e-mail with John Sweeney, who knew Lieutenant Monteith personally and was in his LCA when it landed on Omaha. The replies to so many Omaha questions came via the Internet that I find it difficult to conceive how I carried out World War II research in the days before e-mail. It is not just the speed by which cyberspace enhances research; more important is an awareness that a vast amount of new historical information, heretofore virtually impossible to obtain, is now literally at a writer's fingertips.

A unique and noteworthy collection of D-Day veterans' memories is to be found in the Cornelius Ryan Memorial Collection of World War II Papers at the Ohio University Library in Athens. This vast set of papers includes the research materials gathered by Ryan for his classic D-Day history *The Longest Day*, published in 1959. In the mid-1950s, Ryan sent out thousands of questionnaires to D-Day veterans of both sides, and the collection includes the responses he received over the years, sorted by nationality and unit. When they filled out Ryan's questionnaires, the respondents who had landed on Omaha Beach were still young men, and D-Day was little more than a decade old. Ryan was one of the first historians to probe the veterans' D-Day experiences, and their personal views of the invasion are sometimes remarkably frank. In truth, all D-Day historians must be monumentally grateful for Cornelius Ryan's early efforts.

I make no apologies for telling the Omaha Beach story mostly from the Allied perspective. Aside from numerous German accounts from the point of view of their high command, there are astonishingly few versions of the Omaha battle from German soldiers who manned the coastal defenses on D-Day. Many of those that are available are unspecific in nature and cannot be fit as precisely into the June 6 time line as the Allied accounts. The paucity of German accounts of the fighting derives from the fact that comparatively few German soldiers manned the Omaha defenses on D-Day, and a large percentage of those did not survive the American onslaught. Many of the survivors had been decidedly reluctant to serve Hitler and were so numbed by their Omaha experience that they had no desire whatsoever in later years to recall that traumatic experience. It is a historical axiom that the winners of battles write their histories. Perhaps Omaha Beach proves that the losers for the most part are simply incapable of doing so.

The following section provides the sources for all of the book's firsthand accounts and unit records. Citations provide the originator of the account, the first few words of that account, and a reference specifying its source(s). Archival repositories and other sources from which I drew much of my material are abbreviated as follows:

AC: Author's collection

ACAR: Author's collection, archival records, original location unknown

ACUM: Author's collection, veteran's unpublished manuscript

AOR: Army Operational Records, (a part of National Archives Record Group 407)

CA: Correspondence with author

CI: Combat Interview files (a part of National Archives Record Group 407)

CMH: Center of Military History, Fort McNair, Washington, DC

DDE: Dwight D. Eisenhower Library, Abilene, KS

DDEP: Dwight D. Eisenhower Papers, Johns Hopkins University Press

FB: Fort Benning Infantry School Library, Fort Benning, GA

FDM: Col. Robert R. McCormick Research Center of the First Division Museum at Cantigny, Wheaton, IL

FRA: Fifth Regiment Armory, Museum of the MD National Guard, Baltimore, MD

FRUS: Foreign Relations of the U.S., Cairo and Tehran Conferences

GCM: George C. Marshall Foundation, Lexington, VA

GCMP: Papers of George Catlett Marshall, Johns Hopkins University Press

HI: Hospital Interview files (a part of National Archives Record Group 407)

IA: Interview by author

MHI: Military History Institute, Carlisle Barracks, PA

NA: National Archives and Records Administration II, College Park, MD

NHC: Naval Historical Center, Operational Archives Branch, Washington Navy Yard, Washington, DC

OUCR: Cornelius Ryan Memorial Collection of WWII Papers, Mahn Center for Archives and Special Collections, Alden Library, Ohio University, Athens, OH

PIP: Pre-Invasion Planning files (a part of National Archives Record Group 407)
SIX: 16th Regiment Association, Fort Washington, MD
SUR: WWII Surveys, Military History Institute, Carlisle Barracks, PA
TWN: *Twenty-Niner* (newsletter of the 29th Division Association)
USAF: U.S. Air Force History Support Office, Bolling AFB, Washington, DC
USCG: U.S. Coast Guard Historian's Office, Washington, DC
USNA: U.S. Naval Administration in WWII: The Invasion of Normandy (vol. 5)
VMI: Virginia Military Institute Library, Lexington, VA
WWW: World Wide Web sites

Also, the following other abbreviations are used:

AAA: Anti-aircraft artillery battalion
AF: Air Force
CMB: Chemical mortar battalion
CP: Corps
DSC: Distinguished Service Cross
ECB: Engineer combat battalion
ESB: Engineer special brigade
FAB: Field artillery battalion
ID: Infantry division
IR: Infantry regiment
MH: Medal of Honor
NBB: Naval beach battalion
PG: Photographic Group
RB: Ranger battalion
RG: National Archives Record Group
TB: Tank battalion
TF: Task force
TRG: Tactical Reconnaissance Group
USMA: U.S. Military Academy
USN: U.S. Navy

CHAPTER 1: THE END OF THE BEGINNING
We Will Land in France (pages 1–6)

Eisenhower, career: In 1940, Eisenhower served as executive officer of the 15th Infantry at Fort Lewis, Washington, simultaneously commanding its 1st Battalion. **Alexander**, *mentally and physically*, Alexander to Montgomery letter 3/29/43, quoted in Hamilton, *Master of the Battlefield*, p. 212. **Marshall**, *had the U.S. initiated*, Marshall interview with Forrest Pogue 11/15/56, GCM. **Marshall**, *once said that*, Marshall interview with Pogue 10/5/56, GCM. **Marshall**, *This struggle will*, GCMP, vol. 3, pp. 212–14.

It Won't Work (pages 6–14)

Churchill, *While I was always willing*, from Churchill, *The Second World War*, p. 429. **Brooke**, *Well there it is*, NA, RG 331, Box 56, as quoted by Morgan in his address to COSSAC staff, 4/17/43. **Morgan**, *I am to plan nothing less*, NA, RG 331, Box 56, as quoted by Morgan in his address to COSSAC staff, 4/17/43. **Morgan**, *Essentially what we are trying*, CMH, *History of COSSAC*, p. 6. **Morgan**, *The Pas de Calais is*, MHI, Arthur Nevins Papers. **Morgan**, *I have come to the conclusion*, MHI, Arthur Nevins Papers. **Calvados**, Another theory is that the name Calvados derives from the Latin words *calva dorsa*, "bleak hills." **Stalin**, *We Russians believe*, FRUS Cairo and Tehran, pp. 497–506. **Roosevelt**, *The immediate appointment*, letter reproduced in Eisenhower, *Crusade in Europe*, p. 208. **Marshall**, *Consider only Overlord*, GCMP, vol. 4, p. 445. **Eisenhower**, *I have now had*, DDEP, The War Years, vol. 3, p. 1673.

CHAPTER 2: REALISM, NOT PESSIMISM
A Man Named Gee (pages 15–24)

Gerow, *In my opinion*, VMI, Gerow file. **Eisenhower**, *I am quite well*, DDEP, The War Years, vol. 1, p. 566. **Roberts**, *Gerow expected a lot*, MHI, J. Milnor Roberts Papers. **Eisenhower**, *I can never get over*, VMI, Gerow file. **Butcher**, *Gee said he wasn't pessimistic*, Butcher, *My Three Years with Eisenhower*, p. 530. **Tehran Conference**, *General Marshall said*, FRUS, Cairo and Tehran, pp. 527–28. **Crerar**, *Although at the time*, quoted in Stacey, *Six Years of War*, p. 402. Of the 6,100 troops involved in the Dieppe raid, nearly 5,000 were Canadian; the rest were British with the exception of a few U.S. Rangers and Free French commandos. **Gerow**, *The whole success*, NA, RG 407 PIP, V CP. **Gerow**, *The thing that concerns me*, NA, RG 407, Box 24309. **Chase**, *This was approximately*, Bass, *Spirits of the Sand*, p. 47. **Thompson**, *Engineers had a great deal*, Conference, Fort Belvoir, VA, *Engineers in the Normandy Invasion*. **Gerow**, *The plan of the V Corps*, NA, RG 407 PIP, V CP.

No Mission Too Difficult (pages 24–32)

Mason, *Sincerity just oozed*, FDM, Mason file. Last sentence (*Huebner had the God-given*) quoted in Rogers, *A Study of Leadership in the 1st Infantry Division in WWII*, p. 84. **Huebner**, *Somebody in this Division*, FDM, quoted by Mason. **Andrus**, *Training and planning*, quoted in Rogers, pp. 65–66. **Hangsterfer**, *Some of our catchwords*, Group W D-Day twentieth anniversary radio broadcast, June 1964. **Eisenhower**, *You are one of the finest*, quoted in Clay, *Blood and Sacrifice*, p. 203. **Bingham**, *The men of the 116th*, CA, 4/8/87. **Ritter**, *I don't think there ever*, Group W D-Day twentieth anniversary radio broadcast, June 1964. **Gerhardt**, *For a new outfit*, NA, RG 319, CMH working papers, *Cross Channel Attack* correspondence. **Carter**, *We realize that*, Walter Carter, *Elmer Norval Carter: A Profile*, ACUM. **Parker**, *I was driven*, Parker, ACUM. **Gerow**, *You have been selected*, Ross, *146th Engineer Combat Battalion*.

CHAPTER 3: FESTUNG EUROPA
Defend Everything, Defend Nothing (pages 33–40)

Hitler, *Most dangerous for us*, NA, RG 319, CMH working papers, *Cross Channel Attack* correspondence. **Rommel**, *You know, Bayerlein*, Liddell-Hart, *The Rommel Papers*, pp. 451–52. **Jodl**, *My most profound*, Wilmot, *The Struggle for Europe*, p. 160. **Hitler**, *For the last two and one-half*, Harrison, *Cross Channel Attack*, pp. 464–67. **Supreme Headquarters**, *Germany's only hope*, NA, RG 331, SHAEF Papers, Box 58. **Rommel**, *The enemy most likely*, FRA, Atlantic Wall Inspection Report. **von Rundstedt**, *Rommel was a brave man*, Liddell-Hart, *The German Generals Talk*, pp. 228, 234. **Speer**, *Given the great length*, Speer, *Inside the Third Reich*, pp. 352–53. **von Schweppenburg**, *The Atlantic Wall*, NA, RG 338, MS B-720. **Rommel**, *If in spite of the enemy's*, Liddell-Hart, *The Rommel Papers*, p. 468.

Look upon My Works Ye Mighty and Despair (pages 40–47)

Subtitle from Shelley poem *Ozymandias*. **Japanese Attaché**, *Since his inspection*, Hinsley, *British Intelligence in the Second World War*, vol. 3, part 2, pp. 787–92. **V Corps**, *The concave shape*, MHI, *Intelligence Operations of the V Corps in Europe*, p. 23. **Rommel**, *Minefields will contain*, FRA, Atlantic Wall Inspection Report. **Talley**, *In addition to the minefields*, NA, RG 319, CMH working papers, *Cross Channel Attack* correspondence. **Rommel**, *Here and there*, FRA, Atlantic Wall Inspection Report. **Army Talks**, *They would like for you to think*, MHI, Charles Corlett Papers. **Special Tactical Study**, *Troops employed in coastal defenses*, FRA.

Someone Had Blundered (pages 47–51)

Subtitle from Tennyson's poem *The Charge of the Light Brigade*. **16/1**, *From one of the first*, NA, RG 407 AOR, 1 ID. **Heintze**, *These Frenchmen*, TWN, 7/02. **Ziegelmann**, *It* *became generally*, NA, RG 319, MS B-432. **V Corps**, *Probable enemy action*, NA, RG 407 PIP, V CP. **Dickson**, *was transmitted to V Corps*, Dickson, *G-2 Journal*. **21st Army Group**, *For some time now*, Hinsley, *British Intelligence in the Second World War*, vol. 3, part 2, p. 842.

CHAPTER 4: FORTUNE FAVORS THE BOLD
Mother Nature's Warriors (pages 52–55)

Omaha Beach, *Natural Conditions*, NA, RG 38, TF 122. **Gerow**, *Objectives*, NA, RG 407 PIP, V CP.

Young Men Looking Old (pages 55–64)

Hall, *Several subordinate*, NA, RG 38. **Ninth AF**, *P-38s had been chosen*, GCM, *Report of Ninth Air Force Operations on D-Day*, p. 29. **Terranella**, *We all felt we had*, ACAR. **Bryan**, *The ship was crowded*, NA, RG 407 HI. **Army Talks**, *As you move onward*, MHI, Charles Corlett Papers. **Carter**, *Well, the further*, Carter, *Elmer Norval Carter: A Profile*, by Walter Carter, ACUM. **Bour**, *Personally the one thing*, OUCR, Box 11, Folder 13. **Lewis**, *At about 1700*, USCG, Website, www.uscg.mil. **Hall**, *Having participated in*, OUCR, Box 15, Folder 33. **Minesweeping**, Background: NHC, *USNA*, p. 433; also, NHC, S. E. Morison Papers, see article by Capt. E. McEathron on U.S. minecraft in Operation Neptune used by Morison in preparation for his work *The Invasion of France and Germany*. **Stark**, *In order to assure*, NHC, *USNA*, p. 439. **Special Tactical Study**, *Mines were laid*, FRA. **Hitler**, *The Commander-in-Chief*, Transcripts of *Führer Conferences on Matters Dealing with the German Navy*, translations by Office of Naval Intelligence of original copies discovered in German Navy Archives at Tambach in 1945. Microfilm copy at University of North Carolina at Chapel Hill. **Kirk**, *It can be said*, NA, RG 38, TF 122 Action Report.

For a Short Moment in the Annals of Time (pages 64–70)

Ramsay, *It was always*, NHC, quoted in *USNA*, p. 516. **Omaha Beach Offshore Currents**, *Offshore Currents*, NA, RG 38, TF 122 monograph. **Crook**, *The PCs' job*, Stillwell, *Assault on Normandy*, pp. 64–65. **Omaha Map**, *Note to coxswain*, FRA. **67 TRG**, *What is believed*, USAF, 67 TRG files. **10 PG**, *Heading the list*, USAF, 10 PG files. **10 PG**, *Port-en-Bessin to*, USAF, 10 PG files. **Ziegelmann**, *I must say*, NA, RG 319, MS B-433. **Schilling**, *This is the Real McCoy*, Slaughter, *Wartime Memories*, ACUM. **Pratt**, *The picture of*, MHI, Robert Pratt Papers. **Moglia**, *Some were convinced*, OUCR, Box 12, Folder 12. **McClintock**, *I slept for*, OUCR, Box 18, Folder 20. **Spalding**, *We cheered each other*, OUCR, Box 12, Folder 40. **Stevens**, *Ray said he wasn't*, IA.

CHAPTER 5: THE GREATEST SHOW ON EARTH
A Beach Drenched with Fire (pages 71–79)

Bradley, *The attack will*, NA, RG 407, Box 24309. **Combined Operations HQ**, *The lesson of greatest importance*, quoted in Stacey, *Six Years of War*, p. 399. **V Corps**, *Every house*, NA, RG 407 PIP, V CP. **Butcher**, *Gerow seemed*, Butcher, *My Three Years with Eisenhower*, p. 530. **Bingham**, *General Omar Bradley*, CA, 4/8/87. **Sherrod**, *The facts were cruel*, Sherrod, *Tarawa*, p. 162. **Hall**, *In general it is believed*, NA, RG 38. **Willow Run**, 500 B-24s per month, Davis, *FDR: The War President*, p. 615. **Eighth AF**, *Heavy bomber operations*, GCM, *8th AF Tactical Operations in Support of Landings in Normandy*, pp. 1–5. **Spaatz**, *The weather here*, quoted in Davis, *Carl A. Spaatz and the Air War in Europe*, pp. 305–6. **Smith**, *I explained*, USAF, Smith oral history interview, June 1976, pp. 89–90. **V Corps**, *Details of bombing*, NA, RG 407 PIP, V CP. **Eighth AF**, *Col. De Russey*, NA, CMH working papers, *Cross Channel Attack* correspondence. **100-Pound Bombs**, Effectiveness, see McFarland, *America's Pursuit of Precision Bombing*, pp. 169, 224–25. **Eighth AF**, *The probability that*, GCM, *8th AF Tactical Operations in Support of Landings in Normandy*, pp. 1–5.

A Great Thunder from the Sea (pages 79–85)

Force O, Bombardment Group, FRA, Force O Order of Battle. **Pratt**, *Around us the vaporous*, MHI, Robert Pratt Papers. **Hicken**, *We went right in front*, CA, 2003. **Whitehead**, *We headed for the beach*, quoted in Wilson, *D-Day*, p. 208. **McNabb**, *There were a number*, NA, RG 407 HI. **USS Texas**, NA, RG 38. **USS Doyle**, *Commenced indirect fire*, quoted in Kirkland, *Destroyers at Normandy*, prologue. **Murdoch**, *As we went toward*, FRA, Joseph Ewing research files.

The Best Laid Schemes Go Oft Astray (pages 85–96)

Subtitle from Burns poem *To a Mouse*. **96 Wing**, *Greatest possible care*, USAF, 96 Combat Wing F.O. 81. **Eighth AF**, *It was deemed*, GCM, *8th AF Tactical Operations in Support of Landings in Normandy*. **Eighth AF**, *Safety features represented*, GCM, *8th AF Tactical Operations in Support of Landings in Normandy*, pp. 1–5. **Ardery**, *We were briefed*, Ardery, *Bomber Pilot*, p. 206. **96 Wing**, *Single aircraft*, USAF, 96 Combat Wing F.O. 81. **Anonymous Airman**, *Who could think of food*, WWW, John Howland, *Pathfinders and the 8th Air Force*, www.381st.org. **Polking**, *We were together*, USAF, 14th Combat Wing, Critique of June 1944 Missions. **Gilbert**, *The B-17*, WWW, www.b24.net, Gilbert interview with G. Hatton, 9/16/89. **20 Wing**, *Flights will depart*, USAF, 20th Combat Wing F.O. 127. **Gibson**, *You can envision*, Group W D-Day twentieth anniversary radio broadcast, June 1964. **Johnson**, *I thought our plan*, USAF, 14th Combat Wing, Critique of June 1944 Missions. (General Johnson held the

Medal of Honor for his outstanding performance during the Ploesti raid.) **Ardery,** *I called the bombardier*, Ardery, *Bomber Pilot*, p. 209. **Bradley,** *In bombing through the overcoat*, Bradley, *A Soldier's Story*, p. 268. **Sabin,** *In the midst*, Stillwell, *Assault on Normandy*, p. 59.

CHAPTER 6: FORLORN HOPE
A Device Called Duplex Drive (pages 97–104)

Gerow, *I don't know*, NA, RG 407, Box 24309. **Duncan,** *The following are limitations*, NA, RG 407, Box 24377. **Rockwell,** *I should like*, NA, RG 407, Box 24377. **Sledge,** *I recall the complete*, OUCR, Box 12, Folder 39. **Force O,** *Weather permitting*, Force O Operations Neptune orders, NA, RG 38. **741 TB,** *You are 5,500 yards*, MHI, Robert Rowe Papers, USN. **Metcalfe,** *The tank corps men*, MHI, Robert Rowe Papers, USN. **741 TB,** *At approximately H-60*, NA AOR, 741 TB. (Captain Thornton was killed in September 1944.) **Barry,** *No signal was received*, MHI, Robert Rowe Papers, USN. **Duncan,** *Any Force 4 sea*, TWN, Letter to editor. **Rockwell,** *It was apparent*, NA, RG 38. **Ragan,** *I saw the yellow flags*, Heintzleman, *The Story of Vitamin Baker*, p. 24. **Harkey,** *I am not proud*, MHI, Robert Rowe Papers, USN.

Over There, Again (pages 104–109)

Sabin, *As we were behind*, NA, RG 38. **Sabin,** *During the approach*, NA, RG 38. **Hicken,** *On Dog Green*, CA, 2003. **Kaufmann,** *While on the beach*, WWW, Kaufmann, *LCT(A)s at Normandy on D-Day*. **Cook,** *After beaching*, MHI, Robert Rowe Papers, USN. **White,** *We beached a little*, MHI, Robert Rowe Papers, LCT reports. **Fair,** *The ramp was dropped*, NA, RG 407, Box 16703, 741 TB. (Sergeant Fair was killed later in the war.) **Schiller,** *Lt. Gaetera Barcelona's tank*, NA, RG 407, Box 16703, 741 TB. **743 TB,** *The LCT on the extreme right*, NA, RG 407 AOR, 743 TB. **Jarvis,** *When we first came*, OUCR, Box 18, Folder 13.

CHAPTER 7: THE MOMENTOUS NOW
Top Men at Their Craft (pages 110–117)

Green, *It was approaching*, Green, *D-Day Experiences*, ACUM. Green's actual first name is George. "Jimmy" is a Royal Navy nickname typically applied to the first officer of a ship or other naval organization, "Jimmy the One." **McCormick,** *Going into shore*, OUCR, Box 12. **Spalding,** *The Navy had been*, MHI, Robert Rowe collection, Box 24. (Spalding's interview was conducted by Sgt. Forrest Pogue.) **Goranson,** *I was fortunate*, correspondence with K. Elsby, 2/19/00, AC. On Army maps the location was designated Pointe et Raz de la Percée—*Raz* is a French word for an exceptionally strong coastal current. Neptune orders specified that a German observation tower at

Percée would be a notable landmark, but the enemy had dismantled the tower about two weeks prior to D-Day. **Rudder**, *You have the toughest*, MHI, interview with Goranson, Robert Rowe collection. **Golas**, *Gee fellas*, MHI, *The 2nd Ranger Battalion: Roughing It with Charlie*, p. 26. **Goranson**, *I told the men*, correspondence with K. Elsby, 2/19/00, AC. **Salomon**, *After going*, correspondence with K. Elsby, 1/21/00, AC. **Noyes**, *We went out*, OUCR, Box 10, Folder 14. **Stephens**, *Proceeding across*, NA, RG 338, First Army Awards. **Goranson**, *After we had crossed*, correspondence with K. Elsby, 2/19/00, AC.

Captain Fellers's Boys (pages 117–123)

Green, *As we neared*, Green, *D-Day Experiences*, ACUM. **Fellers**, *I am beginning*, quoted in Geroux, "The Suicide Wave," *Richmond Times-Dispatch*. **Schenk**, *All that will save us*, Geroux, "The Suicide Wave," *Richmond Times-Dispatch*. **Barnes**, *I had heard*, Barnes, *Fragments of My Life*, p. 65. **A/116/29**, *Lt. Edward Tidrick*, FRA, 29 ID *Group Critique Notes*. **A/116/29**, *A medical boat team*, FRA, 29 ID *Group Critique Notes*. Information on Breeden from Baumgarten, *Eyewitness on Omaha Beach*. Several members of the 29th Recon Troop were also onboard Nance's LCA, three of whom were killed. **Elmere Wright**, Baseball prowess: TWN, Rowell, William. *The 116th's Plymouth Yankees: 1943 ETO World Series Champions*, 3/99, p. 27. Three members of the 116th's baseball team were killed on Omaha Beach: Wright, T/Sgt. Frank Draper of Company A, and PFC Louis Alberigo of Company F. Some observers considered these three the best players on the team. Also, IA, Ray Nance 8/4/03. **Bedford Bulletin**, *The war was brought*, "The War Comes Closer," *Bedford Bulletin Weekly*, 7/20/44, p. 6.

Obedient to Their Commands We Lie (pages 123–128)

Subtitle from Simonides' epitaph, "Go tell the Spartans. . . ," considered by one observer as "the noblest group of words uttered by man." **Robertson**, *Most of my boat team*, CA, 1991. **Bruno**, *We didn't expect*, FRA, 29 ID *Group Critique Notes*. **Russo**, *We landed in three*, Russo, *My Memories of WWII*, ACUM. **Robertson**, *I went in*, CA, 1984. **Russo**, *I looked to my right*, Russo, *My Memories of WWII*, ACUM. **Callahan**, *I went in*, OUCR, Box 6, Folder 10. **Fettinger**, *The men were standing*, FRA, 29 ID *Group Critique Notes*. **Russo**, *In a little while*, Russo, *My Memories of WWII*, ACUM.

The Third Time Around (pages 129–134)

Taylor, *There will be lots*, ACAR. **3/16/1**, *The alert company commander*, NA, RG 407 CI, 1 ID. **3/16/1**, *The Company L*, NA, RG 407 CI, 1 ID. **Sweeney**, *All of a sudden*, CA, 2003.

To Move Ever Forward (pages 134–139)

Subtitle from 116th Infantry motto, "Ever Forward." **Wozenski**, *Nearing the shore*, OUCR, Box 12, Folder 55. **Fitzsimmons**, *The men kept yelling*, NA, RG 407 CI, 1 ID. **McCormick**, *One of our BAR*, OUCR, Box 12. **F/16/1**, *The 5th section*, NA, RG 407 CI, 1 ID. **Wozenski**, *The boats were hurriedly*, OUCR, Box 12, Folder 55. **E/116/29**, *The company CO*, FRA, 29 ID *Group Critique Notes*. **Smith**, *I remember debarking*, ACUM. **E/16/1**, *Streczyk's section*, NA, RG 407 CI, 1 ID. **Spalding**, *Sgt. Streczyk and the medic*, MHI, Robert Rowe collection, Box 24; interview by Pogue.

CHAPTER 8: CLEAR THE WAY
The Time Is Short (pages 140–146)

Gerow, *I am rather disturbed*, NA, RG 407 PIP, V CP. **Kean**, *I have your letter*, NA, RG 407 PIP, V CP. **HQ V CP**, *It was agreed*, NA, RG 407 PIP, V CP. **McDonough**, *Army objections raised*, NA, RG 407 PIP, V CP. **Operation Neptune**, *Sixteen gap assault teams*, NA, RG 407 PIP, V CP. **HQ 1 ID**, *Fundamentally each gap*, Ross, *146th Engineer Combat Battalion*, Appendix 1. **Bigot-Neptune Omaha Beach Map**, *Underwater obstacles*, NA, RG 331, SHAEF G-2, Normandy beach intelligence. **Jewett**, *Each demolition man*, OUCR, Box 18, Folder 14. **Ross**, *The wooden obstacles*, Ross, 146th *Engineer Combat Battalion*, p. 20. **Hicken**, *Heads failed*, CA, 2001. **299 ECB**, *Part of the LCT*, NA, RG 407 AOR, Box 18664, 299 ECB.

Blowin' Up a Storm (pages 146–152)

Ross, *Our LCM crew*, Ross, *146th Engineer Combat Battalion*, p. 24. **299 ECB**, *Team 11*, NA, RG 407 AOR, Box 18664, 299 ECB. **146 ECB**, *The team touched down*, Ross, *146th Engineer Combat Battalion*, p. 39. **299 ECB**, *The ramp dropped*, NA, RG 407, Entry 427, Box 24238. **Hurlbut**, *Everything's nice and quiet*, WWW, interview with Aaron Elson, 1998, www.tankbooks.com. **146 ECB**, *Team C*, Ross, *146th Engineer Combat Battalion*, p. 42. **Karnowski**, *Lt. Gregory*, TWN, letter from T. Chatas quoting Dwyer, "The D-Day Demolitioneers," *Washington Times*. **146 ECB**, *The operation*, Ross, *146th Engineer Combat Battalion*, p. 37. **Hall**, *How do we get*, quoted in Godson, *Viking of Assault*, p. 131.

Castles on Their Collars (pages 152–156)

Ploger, *I suppose that*, IA, 9/6/98. **Cvitanovitch**, *Most of the boys*, OUCR, Box 6, Folder 2. **Gara**, *Our mission*, Conference, Fort Belvoir, VA, *Engineers in the Normandy Invasion*. **Neptune**, *Establish and operate*, quoted from Conference, Fort Belvoir, VA, *Engineers in the Normandy Invasion*. **Thompson**, *A unit getting a new*, Conference, Fort Belvoir, VA, *Engineers in the Normandy Invasion*. **149 ECB**, *The operation was not*, NA, RG 407 AOR. **6 NBB**, *The 6th NBB's job was to*, NA, RG 407 AOR. **37 ECB**, *The mission of*, NA, RG 407 AOR.

CHAPTER 9: BULLETS LIKE RAIN
Only an 88 Could Be That Mean (pages 157–163)

Sales, *I was the radio operator*, correspondence with K. Elsby, 2000, AC. **HQ/1/116/29**, *Nowlin with the communications*, FRA, 29 ID *Group Critique Notes*. **Kobe**, *I was with the mortar*, CA, 7/4/89. **Slaughter**, *I didn't care*, Slaughter, *Wartime Memories*, ACUM. **McNabb**, *I could see pretty clearly*, NA, RG 407 HI. **Bingham**, *On the way in*, letter, 1/11/47, AC.

What Do You Do in the Infantry? (pages 163–168)

Subtitle from Glenn Miller AAF Band tune by Loesser. **H/16/1**, *The company reached*, NA, RG 407 CI, 1 ID. **Deery**, *In the LCA*, OUCR, Box 11, Folder 28. The Latin sentence is from Horace's satires, Book I, Satire IV, Lines 103–5. Translation provided courtesy of Dr. Anthony Buccini, Department of Linguistics, University of Chicago. **Fraser**, *At about 0400*, McPherson, *A History of the Royal Navy and Royal Marine Minor Landing Craft Flotillas in WWII*, ACUM. **Joseph**, *The day after*, OUCR, Box 11, Folder 46. **Bour**, *Our LCVP ramp*, OUCR, Box 11, Folder 13. **Hall**, *The beach was in*, SIX, Hall, A Memoir of WWII, p. 18. **Advance CP, 16th Infantry**, *The Advance CP*, MHI, Robert Rowe Papers, 1 ID. **Talley**, *I explained to my men*, Talley, *D-Day Plus 10 Years*, ACUM; and CA, 7/3/87. **G/16/1**, *The water was still*, NA, RG 407 CI, 1 ID.

Praise the Lord (pages 168–176)

Hicken, *We managed to pull*, CA, 2003. **Hawks**, *Everything went according to plan*, NA, RG 407 HI. (Captain Hawks was killed later in the war.) **C/116/29**, *As the boat neared*, NA, RG 407 CI, 29 ID, interview by Lieutenant Shea. **Polyniak**, *With all the training*, CA, 1999. **Raaen**, *Ranger Force C*, CA, 1/30/03. **A&B/2 RB**, *As a Company A LCA*, NA, RG 407 CI, 5 RB, interview by Lt. Col. Charles Taylor. **Arnold**, *After reaching the edge*, OUCR, Box 10, Folder 17. **Edlin**, *Sgt. Klaus*, OUCR, Box 10, Folder 25. **Epstein**, *I was shoulder-to-shoulder*, CA, 2/4/03. **Raaen**, *Waves lashed at us*, Raaen, *The 5th Rangers Have Landed Intact*, ACUM. **Burke**, *We were lying*, OUCR, Box 10, Folder 21. **Parker**, *The coxswain*, Parker, ACUM. **Raaen**, *This was our Ranger chaplain*, Raaen, *The Story of Father Lacy*, ACUM.

Lousy Civilian Ideas (pages 176–181)

Liebling, *The crews probably*, originally published in *The New Yorker*, July 1, 1944, *Cross-Channel Trip*. **Vyn**, *Upon approach to Dog White*, USCG, WWW, www.uscg.mil, *Coast Guard History*. **Walker**, *The skipper of LCI-91*, Walker, *With the Stonewallers*, ACUM. **Lewis**, *Tracer shells*, USCG, WWW, www.uscg.mil, *Coast Guard History*. **Shepard**, *Ahead of us*, USCG, WWW, www.uscg.mil, *Coast Guard History*.

The Times That Try Men's Souls (pages 181–190)

Grossman, *I had a very fatalistic*, Grossman, *Forty Days in France*, ACUM. **Meeks**, *I had my hand*, TWN, 11/92, p. 14. **K/116/29**, *The company was to come*, FRA, 29 ID *Group Critique Notes*. **Branham**, *We had a little Italian*, IA, 1991. **M/116/29**, *Company M came ashore*, FRA, 29 ID *Group Critique Notes*. **Anderson**, *Morale was terrific*, OUCR, Box 6, Folder 4. **Dillon**, *We were to land*, Dillon, *Pearl Harbor to Normandy and Beyond*, ACUM. **HQ/1/16/1**, *The forward CP*, NA, RG 407 CI, 1 ID. **Adams**, *As we approached*, Stillwell, *Assault on Normandy*, pp. 72–73. **Beach**, *Boats were lowered*, NA, RG 407 CI, 1 ID. **Foley**, *As Pvt. Carlton Barrett*, quoted in Barrett MH file, NA, RG 338, First Army Awards. **Montague**, *The low silhouette*, NA, RG 407 AOR.

CHAPTER 10: MOVE OR DIE
A General Named Dutch (pages 191–197)

Shea, *Moderate small arms*, NA, RG 407 CI, 29 ID, Box 24034. (Shea wrote two drafts of his experiences as General Cota's aide; the later, or November 1944, version is the one quoted in this book.) **Buckley**, *When I got up*, Slaughter, *Wartime Memories*, ACUM. **Howie**, *It was the consensus*, FRA, *Summary of Actions 116th Infantry in Initial Assault*. (Howie was killed on July 17, 1944.) **Shea**, *In each of the bays*, NA, RG 407 CI, 29 ID, Box 24034. **Bedell**, *Cota was waving*, NA, RG 407 CI, 29 ID. (Lieutenant Shea did this interview after he had left the 29th Division to become a U.S. Army historical officer.) **Huesser**, *Cota came up to us*, NA, RG 407 CI, 29 ID. **Herring**, *Before Cota reached Schneider*, quoted in Raaen, *Landed Intact*, p. 29, ACUM. **Sullivan**, *The activities of Gen. Cota*, OUCR, Box 10, Folder 54. **Raaen**, *As I got ready*, Raaen, *Landed Intact*, ACUM. **Cota**, *I well remember*, AC, letter provided courtesy of John Raaen.

Guests of the Third Reich (pages 198–200)

Deery, *Sergeant Ken Finn*, OUCR, Box 11, Folder 28. **HQ/16/1**, *Col. Taylor came in*, NA, RG 407 CI, 1 ID. **Friedman**, *Col. Taylor then commanding*, OUCR, Box 11, Folder 35. **Taylor**, *Col. George A. Taylor*, NA, RG 338, First Army Awards. **Michaud**, *While participating*, quoted in Pinder MH file, NA, RG 338, First Army Awards.

Angels on Their Shoulders (pages 200–207)

Spalding, *Sgt. Fred Bisco kept saying*, MHI, Robert Rowe collection, Box 24; interview by Pogue. **Spalding**, *At this point*, MHI, Robert Rowe collection, Box 24; interview by Pogue. **G/16/1**, *A minefield lay behind*, NA, RG 407 CI, 1 ID. **Neighbor**, *We soon discovered*, TWN, Neighbor, *One Man's War Story*, 3/95, p. 21. **Wozenski**, *In climbing the bluff*, OUCR, Box 12, Folder 55. **Herman**, *Capt. James Pence stood up*, OUCR, Box 11, Folder 38. **Dillon**, *As we got to the top*, Dillon, *Pearl Harbor to Normandy and Beyond*, ACUM. **Smith**, *The only thing that got us*, NA, RG 407 CI, 1 ID. **1/16/1**, *A Company was on the right*, NA, RG 407 CI, 1 ID.

So Much Owed to So Few (pages 207–213)

L/16/1, *The assault on the beach*, NA, RG 407 CI, 1 ID. **Martin**, *When the troops were pinned*, quoted in Monteith MH file, NA, RG 338, First Army Awards. **L/16/1**, *The sections attacking*, NA, RG 407 CI, 1 ID. **741 TB**, *0830 hours*, NA, RG 407 AOR, 741 TB. **USS Doyle**, *Stopped 800 yards*, quoted in Kirkland, *Destroyers at Normandy*, p. 50. **Strojny**, *I saw that our sector*, OUCR, Box 12, Folder 41. **F/16/1**, *Sgt. Strojny took up*, NA, RG 407 CI, 1 ID. **F/16/1**, *Seeing the pillbox in flames*, NA, RG 407 CI, 1 ID.

Ducks in a Shooting Gallery (pages 213–217)

Salomon, *I ran a short distance*, correspondence with K. Elsby, 1/21/00, AC. **C/2 RB**, *Separated from*, NA, RG 407 CI, 5 RB, interview by Taylor. **C/2 RB**, *On the other side*, MHI, *The 2nd Ranger Battalion: Roughing It with Charlie*, p. 27. **B/116/29**, *The beach was strewn*, FRA, 29 ID *Group Critique Notes*.

On the Upward Trail (pages 217–220)

Shea, *Cota had found*, NA CI, RG 407, 29 ID, Box 24034. **C/116/29**, *To the right of the company*, FRA, 29 ID *Group Critique Notes*. **Shea**, *The first soldier to go*, NA, RG 407 CI, 29 ID, Box 24034. **Ploger**, *While I was walking*, CA, 4/7/00. **Polyniak**, *Our boat team*, CA, 2/17/03. **C/116/29**, *Company C slipped through*, NA, RG 407 CI, 29 ID, interview by Shea. **Hawks**, *One thing happened*, NA, RG 407 HI, July 1944. **Shea**, *Our CP was scattered*, NA, RG 407 CI, 29 ID, Box 24034.

Rangers Led the Way (pages 220–229)

A/2 RB, *Put in charge*, NA, RG 407 CI, 2 RB, interview by Taylor. **Edlin**, *It seemed to me*, OUCR, Box 10, Folder 25. **A/2 RB**, *Sgt. White found Ray*, NA, RG 407 CI, 2 RB, interview by Taylor. Names of other Rangers who climbed the bluff with White and Ray were provided by Robert Edlin. **Edlin**, *The bravest men I ever saw*, CA, 7/21/03. **B/2 RB**, *The plan had been*, NA, RG 407 CI, 2 RB, interview by Taylor. **D/116/29**, *Morse and his men*, NA, RG 407 CI, 29 ID, interview by Shea. **Raaen**, *Not ten yards to my right*, Raaen, *Landed Intact*, ACUM. **5 RB**, *Capt. Edward Luther of E Company*, NA, RG 407 CI, 5 RB, interview by Taylor. **Raaen**, *By now Col. Schneider*, Raaen, *Landed Intact*, ACUM. **Raaen**, *The advance had slowed*, Raaen, *Landed Intact*, ACUM.

They Had Not Yet Begun to Fight (pages 229–236)

Bingham, *An impression*, CA, 4/8/87. **Bush**, *The men were beat up*, FRA, 29 ID *Group Critique Notes*. **2/116/29**, *At the patch of shingle*, NA, RG 407 CI, 29 ID, interview by Pogue. **111 FA/29**, *Capt. Richard Bush*, FRA, 29 ID *Group Critique Notes*. **Thompson**, *The attack on a vital*, NA, RG 338, First Army Awards. **Bingham**, *The ground floor*, OUCR, interview by Ryan, 4/7/58, Box 6, Folder 8. **Thompson**, *A couple of weeks*, Conference, Fort Belvoir, VA, *Engineers in the Normandy Invasion*.

L/116/29, *On getting to the shingle*, FRA, 29 ID *Group Critique Notes*. **Smith**, *I started up the bluff*, FB, Smith monograph, *Operations of 3/116 on Omaha Beach*. **Grossman**, *The bluff was booby-trapped*, Grossman, *Forty Days in France*, ACUM. **Branham**, *I carried an M-1*, IA, 1991. **Meeks**, *My command group*, TWN, 11/92, p. 14. **I/116/29**, *Sgt. Vincent Corsini found*, FRA, 29 ID *Group Critique Notes*.

CHAPTER 11: EVERYONE AN INFANTRYMAN
The Graveness of the Hour (pages 237–239)
Bradley, *I reluctantly contemplated*, Bradley, *A Soldier's Story*, p. 271. **Anonymous**, *Early reports received*, NA, RG 319, CMH working papers, *Cross Channel Attack* correspondence. **Pratt**, *Col. Talley*, MHI, Robert Pratt Papers. **Huebner**, *As far as the 116th*, FDM, interview in *Bridgehead Sentinel*, summer 1964. **Plitt**, *The most outstanding*, NA, RG 407 AOR, 1 ID. **Mullins**, *To hell with*, FRA, 29 ID *Group Critique Notes*.

The Legion of Lost Souls (pages 239–246)
Hintze, *The CP/Fire Direction*, ACUM. **Hickman**, *In the hold of*, TWN, 7/98. **81 CMB**, *Company A in support*, NA, RG 407 AOR, 81 CMB. **397 AAA**, *At 0645 we saw*, NA, RG 407 AOR, Box 17097, 397 AAA. **197 AAA**, *The 197th learned*, NA, RG 407 AOR, 197 AAA. **Ferguson**, *Lt. Ferguson reached*, NA, RG 338, First Army Awards. **Shelley**, *I met Lt. Forest Ferguson*, CA, 4/18/89. **743 TB**, *In the D-Day plan*, MHI, *Move Out, Verify*, pp. 26–27. **Skaggs**, *The government paid*, quoted by Captain Deery, NA, RG 407 CI, 1 ID. **King**, *At about 10:00*, NA, RG 319, CMH working papers, *Cross Channel Attack* correspondence.

We're Going In (pages 246–250)
Whitehead, *I lay on the beach*, Knickerbocker, *Danger Forward*, pp. 212–13. **Spalding**, *We were now in*, MHI, Robert Rowe collection, Box 24; interview by Pogue.

Dead Corpsmen Can't Save Lives (pages 250–256)
2/18/1, *After passing*, NA, RG 407 AOR, 1 ID. **Argo**, *Suddenly all hell*, WWW, Argo D-Day memoirs, www.jun6dday.com. **2/18/1**, *The beach shingle*, NA, RG 407 AOR, 1 ID. **Gibbs**, *Displaying superb courage*, NA, RG 338, First Army Awards. **Alvarez**, *Someone pointed out*, MHI, 1 ID SUR. **USS Frankford**, *Fire was commenced*, quoted in Kirkland, *Destroyers at Normandy*, p. 50. **Hoffer**, *From our defiladed*, NA, RG 407 AOR, 741 TB. **Fair**, *I noticed the tide*, NA, RG 407 AOR, 741 TB. **467 AAA**, *An M15 halftrack*, NA, RG 407 AOR, Box 17202, 467 AAA. **Talley**, *It is suggested*, NA, RG 319, CMH working papers, *Cross Channel Attack* correspondence. **1 ECB**, *Slowly the enemy*, MHI, *Eight Stars to Victory*, p. 63. **741 TB**, *Ordered by Headquarters*, NA, RG 407 AOR, 741 TB.

Citizens of Death's Gray Land (pages 256–264)

Subtitle from Sassoon's poem *Dreamers*. **Wilch**, *I want to go*, CA, 5/9/91. **HQ V CP**, *Land 115th RCT*, NA, RG 407 AOR, V CP. **HQ 1 ID**, *From Commanding General* (both 1131 and 1146 entries), OUCR, Box 11, Folder 1. **Wright**, *As we approached*, ACAR. **Cooper**, *I was on LCI-411*, IA, 1987. **Terranella**, *Just as we dropped*, ACAR. **Zarfass**, *As I took my first step*, Binkoski, *The 115th Infantry Regiment in WWII*, p. 17. **Clark**, *A floating body*, ACAR. **Eckert**, *I would have qualified*, IA, 1991. **Henry**, *We were in the center*, TWN, Henry, *LCIs and the 115th*, 7/00. **Cooper**, *We found a hole*, IA, 1987. **Eckert**, *There was a path*, IA, 1991. **2/18/1**, *The battalion went*, NA, RG 407 AOR, 1 ID. **McGregor**, *The 1st Battalion*, NA, RG 407 AOR, 1 ID. **Gurka**, *The 3rd Battalion*, NA, RG 407 AOR, 1 ID.

Cohorts of the Damned (pages 264–266)

Subtitle from Kipling's *Barrack Room Ballads*. **Gercke**, *A narrow path*, letter to Major Stremlau, NA, RG 407. **Shea**, *From a point just below*, NA, RG 407 CI, 29 ID, Box 24034.

CHAPTER 12: BEYOND THE BEACH
How You Tell the Men from the Boys (pages 267–274)

Ziegelmann, *Shortly after 8:00 A.M. I succeeded*, NA, RG 319, MS B-432. **C/116/29**, *1st Lt. Robert Bedell*, NA, RG 407 CI, 29 ID, interview by Shea. **C/116/29**, *While in the town*, FRA, 29 ID *Group Critique Notes*. **5 RB**, *When Col. Schneider*, NA, RG 407 CI, 5 RB, interview by Taylor. **C/116/29**, *Cota had seen the column*, NA, RG 407 CI, 29 ID, interview by Shea. **5 RB**, *Company B now started*, NA, RG 407 CI, 5 RB, interview by Taylor.

Suppose You Go Find Out (pages 274–279)

Howie, *Communications were completely*, FRA, *Summary of Actions 116th Infantry in Initial Assault*. **Hawks**, *We tried to crack*, NA, RG 407 HI. **Weast**, *Next to an orchard*, OUCR, Box 10, Folder 37. **Thornhill**, *West of Vierville we lost*, OUCR, Box 10, Folder 33. **MacAllister**, *I proceeded into Vierville*, CA, 3/21/00. **Shea**, *For the past 25*, NA, RG 407 CI, 29 ID, Box 24034. **Coiker**, *On the plateau*, ACAR. **USS McCook**, *Commenced firing*, quoted in Kirkland, *Destroyers at Normandy*, p. 55. **USS Thompson**, *Commenced demolition*, quoted in Kirkland, *Destroyers at Normandy*, p. 55. **HQ 1 ID**, *From Dog Green*, OUCR, Box 11, Folder 1. **Shea**, *Keep a sharp eye*, NA, RG 407 CI, 29 ID, Box 24034. **MacAllister**, *On the way down*, CA, 3/21/00. **Shea**, *Reaching the promenade*, NA, RG 407 CI, 29 ID, Box 24034.

Kill-Crazy (pages 279–282)

B/116/29, *At the chateau*, FRA, 29 ID *Group Critique Notes*. **A/5 RB**, *It was evident*, NA, RG 407 CI, 5 RB, interview by Taylor. **Parker**, *When I first arrived*, Parker, ACUM.

Bienvenue à France (pages 282–289)

Washington, *I can remember*, SIX, interview, 4/29/84. **Dawson**, *As I ran out*, SIX, interview, 4/29/84. **G/16/1**, *The 1st section*, NA, RG 407 CI, 1 ID. **Wozenski**, *Two skeleton sections*, NA, RG 407 CI, 1 ID. **Spalding**, *In the middle of the afternoon*, OUCR, Box 12, Folder 40. **Bieder**, *We finally found*, WWW, *Men of the 16th Infantry*, www.warchronicle.com, interview with David Allender. **1/16/1**, *1330 hours found*, NA, RG 407 CI, 1 ID. **Fulk**, *Lt. Brown*, NA, RG 407 AOR, 1 ID. **2/18/1**, *The battalion moved*, NA, RG 407 AOR, 1 ID. **USS Harding**, *Received orders to*, quoted in Kirkland, *Destroyers at Normandy*, p. 61; also WWW, Benson-Livermore class destroyers website, USS *Harding* action reports and war diaries. **Washington**, *I actually thought*, OUCR, Box 12, Folder 50. **Dawson**, *At 4:00*, FDM, transcript of interview by John Votaw, 4/16/91. **Pilck**, *When we were near*, MHI, 1 ID SUR. **Bryant**, *We didn't know*, NHC, interview with S. E. Morison, Morison Papers. **Stark**, *Every firing ship*, NHC, USNA, p. 470. **Board of Admiralty**, *It must be appreciated*, NA, RG 331, Entry 23, SHAEF Papers, Box 43.

This Man Was Good (pages 289–294)

Jones, *In that sector*, quoted in Monteith MH file, NA, RG 338, First Army Awards. **Martin**, *When Lt. Monteith*, quoted in Monteith file, NA, RG 338, First Army Awards. **Worozbyt**, *Shortly before my platoon*, OUCR, Box 12, Folder 54. **Smith**, *Gen. Eisenhower*, quoted in Monteith file, NA, RG 338, First Army Awards. **Eisenhower**, *Bedell*, quoted in Monteith file, NA, RG 338, First Army Awards. **3/16/1**, *Capt. Richmond*, NA, RG 407 CI, 1 ID. **Richmond**, *Without hesitation*, NA, RG 338, First Army Awards.

The Present Is All You Have (pages 294–301)

Subtitle from Whittier's poem *My Soul and I*. **Shea**, *Most of the enemy fire*, NA, RG 407 CI, 29 ID, Box 24034. **L/116/29**, *Lt. Donald Anderson*, FRA, 29 ID *Group Critique Notes*. **Anderson**, *I was shot*, OUCR, Box 6, Folder 4. **I/116/29**, *At the top*, NA, RG 407 CI, 29 ID, interview by Taylor. **L/116/29**, *Company L spent*, NA, RG 407 CI, 29 ID, interview by Taylor. **McGrath**, *When L Company*, FRA, 29 ID *Group Critique Notes*. **Grossman**, *We were pinned*, Grossman, *Forty Days in France*, ACUM. **Garcia**, *With PFC Armand Berthiaume*, TWN, 7/95. **USS Thompson**, *Rocket guns*, quoted in Kirkland, *Destroyers at Normandy*, p. 54.

Are You Ready for It? (pages 301–306)

Wilch, *Company E was*, CA, 5/9/91. **115/29**, *St. Laurent was a mass*, Binkoski, *The 115th Infantry Regiment in WWII*, p. 19. **Phillips**, *It struck me*, OUCR, Box 6, Folder 44. **McGrath**, *With me was a captain*, FRA, 29 ID *Group Critique Notes*. **Kaiser**, *T/5 Walter Brown*, Binkoski, *The 115th Infantry*, p. 23. **115/29**, *When the 2nd Battalion*, Binkoski, *The 115th Infantry*, p. 21. **741 TB**, *One headquarters tank*, NA, RG 407 AOR, 741 TB. **Shea**, *A sergeant of the 115th*, NA, RG 407 CI, 29 ID, Box 24034. **58 AFA**, *By 1830 hours*, MHI, *The 58th Armored Field Artillery Battalion in WWII*. **Cooper**, *At about 9:00*, IA, 1987. **Wyman**, *To Gen. Huebner*, OUCR, Box 11, Folder 1.

CHAPTER 13: A FULL MEASURE OF DEVOTION
Hanging Breathless On Thy Fate (pages 307–317)

Subtitle from Longfellow's poem *The Building of the Ship*. **Bach**, *1215 hours*, quoted in Shea, NA, RG 407 CI, 29 ID, Box 24034. **Talley**, *We walked up the beach*, Talley, *D-Day Plus 10 Years*, ACUM; CA, 7/3/87. **Talley**, *To Gen. Gerow*, CA, 7/3/87. **Shea**, *Cota turned*, NA, RG 407 CI, 29 ID, Box 24034. **Ploger**, *Word reached me*, CA, 4/7/00. **149 ECB**, *Clearing up of the beach*, NA, RG 407 AOR, 149 ECB. **McGrath**, *At 2030*, FRA, 29 ID *Group Critique Notes*. **Callahan**, *An Engineer Special Brigade*, OUCR, Box 6, Folder 10. **Montague**, *On the beach*, NA, RG 407 AOR, 37 ECB. **Montague**, *Capt. Louis Drnovich*, NA, RG 407 AOR, 37 ECB. **348/5 ESB**, *Work on E-3 began*, NA, RG 407 AOR, 348 ECB. **336/5 ESB**, *There was no attempt*, NA, RG 407 AOR, 336 ECB. **336/5 ESB**, *The 336th began*, NA, RG 407 AOR, 336 ECB. **336/5 ESB**, *Two tanks blew their tracks*, NA, RG 407 AOR, 336 ECB.

The General They Called Coach (pages 317–325)

Force O, *1715 hours*, FRA. **HQ 1 ID**, *The Division command post*, OUCR, Box 11, Folder 1. **Pratt**, *It seemed that*, MHI, Robert Pratt Papers. **Crook**, *In the late afternoon*, Stillwell, *Assault on Normandy*, p. 67. **Talley**, *Gen. Gerhardt made*, CA, 6/15/87. **Irvin**, *We met no organized*, FRA. **Ballard**, *I asked for a volunteer*, FRA. **Pratt**, *Gen. Gerow decided*, MHI, Robert Pratt Papers. **Marshall**, *The support of destroyers*, quoted from Fraser, *Operation Report Neptune: Provisional Engineer Special Brigade Group*, p. 93. **USS Harding**, *Received visual message*, quoted in Kirkland, *Destroyers at Normandy*, p. 60; also www.geocities.com/bristolclass/hardingrep.html, Benson-Livermore class destroyers website, USS *Harding* action reports. **1/116/29**, *In the late morning*, FRA, 29 ID *Group Critique Notes*. **HQ 1 ID**, *From 1st Battalion*, OUCR, Box 11, Folder 1. **Dallas**, *Goddamn it*, OUCR, Box 6.

Something Has Got to Break (pages 325–328)

Daniel, *We were pretty relaxed*, OUCR, Box 11, Folder 27; also, *Just after the attack*, MHI, 1 ID SUR. **Seitz**, *The 26th Infantry*, NA, RG 407 CI, 1 ID. **Bridges**, *We landed very soon*, NA, RG 319, CMH working papers, *Omaha Beachhead* correspondence.

CHAPTER 14: TO REST OR TO DIE
The Most Hazardous Job in the Army (pages 329–332)
HQ/16/1, *From Maj. Tegtmeyer*, DDE, WWW, www.eisenhower.utexas.edu. **Tegtmeyer**, *The landing craft*, NA, RG 407 AOR, 1 ID. **Horner**, *The casualty ratio*, SIX, interview, 4/29/84. **Clark**, *On the whole*, FRA, *Comments and Criticisms of Operation Neptune*. **Shelley**, *I led my men*, CA, 4/18/89. **Goldberg**, *At 1900*, NA, RG 407 AOR, 1 ID. **Shea**, *The dead and dying*, NA, RG 407 CI, 29 ID, Box 24034. **Gniecko**, *I was appointed*, AC, letter to Robert M. Miller, 9/2/90.

Roaming in the Gloaming (pages 333–340)
Subtitle from H. Lauder song. **2/18/1**, *Companies went into*, NA, RG 407 AOR, 1 ID. **1/16/1**, *During the night*, NA, RG 407 CI, 1 ID. **L/16/1**, *A patrol under Lt. Marincic*, NA, RG 407 CI, 1 ID. **Hooper**, *It was getting close*, Hooper, *Recollections of an Infantryman*, ACUM. **Hamill**, *Our Company D*, Hamill, *A Combat Infantryman's Experiences*, ACUM. **Brooks**, *When Col. Blatt was wounded*, IA, 9/97. **Blatt**, *A West Pointer is*, USMA Library. **Howie**, *Through a radio*, FRA, *Summary of Actions 116th Infantry in Initial Assault*. **Raaen**, *After organizing our defense*, Raaen, *Landed Intact*, ACUM. **C/2 RB**, *T/Sgt. William Lindsay*, MHI, *The 2nd Ranger Battalion: Roughing It with Charlie*, p. 29. **Ploger**, *After we blew up*, IA, 9/6/98. **Russo**, *Gen. Cota put Simmons*, Russo, *My Memories of WWII*, ACUM. **Ondre**, *All the tanks*, quoted in Shea's account, NA, RG 407 CI, 29 ID, Box 24034. **Shea**, *Throughout the hours*, NA, RG 407 CI, 29 ID, Box 24034. **Cooper**, *When darkness set in*, IA, 1987.

The Instant Made Eternity (pages 341–343)
Subtitle from Browning poem *The Last Ride Together*. **U.S. Army**, *Casualties for D-Day*, NA, RG 319, CMH working papers, *Omaha Beachhead* correspondence. **Canham**, *The closest estimate*, FRA, *Summary of Actions 116th Infantry in Initial Assault*. **Taylor**, *Unit records for D-Day*, Taylor, *Omaha Beachhead*, pp. 108–9. **Harrison**, *The V Corps losses*, Harrison, *Cross Channel Attack*, p. 330.

To the Last Syllable of Recorded Time (pages 343–349)
Subtitle from Shakespeare's *Macbeth*, Act V. **Marshall**, *Eisenhower and his staff*, GCMP, vol. 4, p. 480. **Giannini**, *I retraced my way*, CA, thanks to Maxine Giannini. **Bingham**, *Everything that was done*, letter, 1/11/47, AC. **Dawson**, *My Dearest Family*, FDM, Dawson files. **29th Division**, *To perpetuate*, TWN. **Eisenhower**, *Humility must always*, Bartlett, *Familiar Quotations*, 14th ed., p. 1016. **Roosevelt**, *O Lord give us faith*, WWW, Franklin D. Roosevelt Presidential Library and Museum, www.fdrlibrary.marist.edu/audio.html.

Bibliography

Ardery, Philip. *Bomber Pilot*. Lexington: University Press of KY, 1978.

Balkoski, Joseph. *Beyond the Beachhead: The 29th Infantry Division in Normandy*. Harrisburg, PA: Stackpole Books, 1989.

———. *The Maryland National Guard: A History of Maryland's Military Forces*. Baltimore: Maryland National Guard, 1992.

Barnes, John. *Fragments of My Life: With Company A, 116th Infantry Regiment*. Holland Patent, NY: JAM Publications, 2000.

Bass, Richard. *The Brigades of Neptune: U.S. Army Engineer Special Brigades in Normandy*. Exeter: Lee Publishing, 1994.

———. *Spirits of the Sand: A History of the U.S. Army Assault Training Center*. Exeter: Lee Publishing, 1991.

Baumgarten, Harold. *Eyewitness on Omaha Beach*. Jacksonville, FL: Halrit, 2000.

Bennett, Donald. *Honor Untarnished: A West Point Graduate's Memoir of World War II*. New York: Doherty Associates, 2003.

Bennett, Ralph. *Ultra in the West: The Normandy Campaign of 1944–45*. New York: Scribner's, 1979.

Berger, Sid. *Breaching Fortress Europe: The Story of U.S. Engineers in Normandy on D-Day*. Dubuque, IA: Kendall Hunt, 1994.

Bernage, Georges. *Omaha Beach*. Bayeux, France: Heimdal, 2001.

Binkoski, Joseph, and Arthur Plaut. *The 115th Infantry in WWII.* Washington, DC: Infantry Journal Press, 1948.

Bland, Larry, ed. *George C. Marshall: Interviews and Reminiscences for Forrest C. Pogue.* Lexington, KY: George C. Marshall Foundation, 1996.

———, ed. *The Papers of George Catlett Marshall,* vols. 3 and 4. Baltimore: Johns Hopkins, 1991.

Bradley, Omar. *A Soldier's Story.* New York: Henry Holt, 1951.

Bradley, Omar, with Clay Blair. *A General's Life.* New York: Simon and Schuster, 1983.

Butcher, Harry. *My Three Years with Eisenhower.* New York: Simon and Schuster, 1946.

Cawthon, Charles. *Other Clay.* Niwot, CO: University Press of CO, 1990.

Chandler, Alfred, ed. *The Papers of Dwight David Eisenhower: The War Years.* Baltimore: Johns Hopkins, 1970.

Chandler, David, and James Collins, eds. *The D-Day Encyclopedia.* New York: Simon and Schuster, 1994.

Churchill, Winston. *The Second World War.* New York: Time, Inc., 1959.

Clay, Steven. *Blood and Sacrifice: The History of the 16th Infantry Regiment from the Civil War Through the Gulf War.* Chicago: Cantigny 1st Division Foundation, 2001.

———. *Roll of Honor: 16th Infantry Regiment Casualties, 1862–1991.* Chicago: Cantigny 1st Division Foundation, 2001.

Cochrane, Robert. "The Story of the 29th Division," *Baltimore Sun,* April-May 1945.

Cooper, John. *The History of the 110th Field Artillery.* Baltimore: Maryland Historical Society, 1953.

Craven, Wesley, and James Cate. *The Army Air Forces in WWII.* Vol. 3, *Europe: Argument to V-E Day.* Chicago: University of Chicago, 1951.

Daniel, Derrill. *Landings at Oran, Gela, and Omaha Beaches: An Infantry Battalion CO's Observations.* Privately published, 1950. Copy at MHI.

Davis, Kenneth. *FDR: The War President, 1940–1943.* New York: Random House, 2000.

Davis, Richard. *Carl A. Spaatz and the Air War in Europe.* Washington, DC: Center for Air Force History, 1993.

Delve, Ken. *D-Day: The Air Battle.* London: Arms and Armour, 1994.

Dickson, Benjamin. *G-2 Journal: From Algiers to the Elbe.* Privately published: USMA Library, Special Collections.

Ehrman, John. *Grand Strategy,* vol. 5. London: HMSO, 1956.

Eisenhower, Dwight. *Crusade in Europe*. New York: Doubleday, 1948.

Elliott, Peter. *Allied Minesweeping in WWII*. Annapolis, MD: Naval Institute Press, 1979.

ETO Observers Board. *Observations on the Invasion of France and Fall of Cherbourg*, Report 23, 1944. Copy at MHI.

Eubank, Keith. *Summit at Tehran: The Untold Story*. New York: Morrow, 1985.

Ewing, Joseph. *Twenty-Nine Let's Go!* Washington, DC: Infantry Journal Press, 1948.

Fane, Francis, and Don Moore. *The Naked Warriors: The Story of the U.S. Navy's Frogmen*. Annapolis, MD: U.S. Naval Institute, 1995.

Fifth (V) Corps. *V Corps Operations in the ETO*, 1945. Copy at MHI.

————. *Intelligence Operations of the V Corps in Europe*. Copy at MHI.

Folkestad, William. *The View from the Turret: The 743rd Tank Battalion During WWII*. Shippensburg, PA: Burd Street, 1996.

Frank, Stanley. "First Stop—Omaha Beach." *Saturday Evening Post*, June 1945.

Fraser, Ian. *Operation Report Neptune: Provisional Engineer Special Brigade Group*. Historical Division, U.S. Army, September 1944. Copy at CMH.

Freeman, Roger. *The Mighty Eighth*. London: Cassell, 2000.

————. *The Mighty Eighth War Manual*. London: Cassell, 2001.

Gawne, Jonathan. *Spearheading D-Day*. Paris: Histoire & Collections, 1998.

Geroux, William. "Sacrifice," *Richmond Times-Dispatch*, May 28, 2000.

————. "The Suicide Wave," *Richmond Times-Dispatch*, June 2001.

Godson, Susan. *Viking of Assault: Admiral John L. Hall and Amphibious Warfare*. Washington, DC: University Press of America, 1982.

Hamilton, Nigel. *Master of the Battlefield: Monty's War Years, 1942–1944*. New York: McGraw Hill, 1983.

Harris, Sir Arthur. *Despatch on War Operations*. London: Cass, 1995.

Harrison, Gordon. *Cross Channel Attack*. Washington, DC: Chief of Military History, 1951.

Heintzleman, Al, ed. *The 741st Tank Battalion*. Privately published, 1982.

Hinsley, F. H. et al. *British Intelligence in the Second World War*, vol. 3, pt. 2. London: HMSO, 1984.

Institut Geographique National. *Pointe du Hoc—Omaha Beach*. 1:25,000 Serie Bleu map, Paris: IGN, 2000.

Isby, David, ed. *Fighting the Invasion: The German Army at D-Day*. London: Greenhill, 2000.

Jackson, W. G. F. *Overlord: Normandy, 1944.* Newark: University of Delaware, 1978.

Kirkland, William. *Destroyers at Normandy: Naval Gunfire Support at Omaha Beach.* Washington, DC: Naval Historical Foundation, 1994.

Knickerbocker, H. R., et al. *Danger Forward: The Story of the First Division in WWII.* Atlanta: Albert Love, 1947.

Lewis, Adrian. *Omaha Beach: A Flawed Victory.* Chapel Hill: University of NC, 2001.

Liddell-Hart, B. H., ed. *The German Generals Talk.* New York: Morrow, 1948.

———. *The Rommel Papers.* New York: Harcourt, Brace, 1953.

Liebling, A.J. "Cross-Channel Trip," *New Yorker*, July 1, 8, and 15, 1944.

McDonald, JoAnna. *The Faces of D-Day.* Redondo Beach CA: Rank and File, 2000.

McFarland, Stephen. *America's Pursuit of Precision Bombing, 1910–1945.* Washington, DC: Smithsonian, 1995.

McPherson, Donald. *A History of the Royal Navy and Royal Marine Minor Landing Craft Flotillas in WWII.* Unpublished manuscript, author's collection.

Morgan, Sir Frederick. *Overture to Overlord.* New York: Doubleday, 1950.

Morison, Samuel E. *The Invasion of France and Germany, 1944–1945.* Boston: Little Brown, 1962.

Parrish, Thomas. *Roosevelt and Marshall: Partners in Politics and War.* New York: Morrow, 1989.

Pogue, Forrest. *George C. Marshall: Ordeal and Hope, 1939–1942.* New York: Penguin, 1993.

———. *George C. Marshall: Organizer of Victory, 1943–1945.* New York: Penguin, 1993.

———. *Pogue's War: Diaries of a WWII Combat Historian.* Lexington, KY: University Press of KY, 2001.

———. *The Supreme Command.* Washington, DC: Chief of Military History, 1954.

Price, Scott. *The U.S. Coast Guard at Normandy.* U.S. Coast Guard Historian's Office Website, www.uscg.mil, 2003.

Rogers, Robert. *A Study of Leadership in the 1st Infantry Division in WWII: Terry Allen and Clarence Huebner.* Privately published, 1965. Copy at MHI.

Ross, Wesley. *The 146th Engineer Combat Battalion: Essayons.* Privately published, 2000.

Ryan, Cornelius. *The Longest Day*. New York: Simon and Schuster, 1959.

Sherrod, Robert. *Tarawa*. New York: Pocket Books, 1944.

Speer, Albert. *Inside the Third Reich*. New York: Macmillan, 1970.

Stacey, C. P. *Six Years of War: Official History of the Canadian Army in the Second World War*, vol. 1. Ottawa, Ontario: Queen's Printer, 1955.

Stanton, Shelby. *WWII Order of Battle*. New York: Galahad, 1984.

Stillwell, Paul. *Assault on Normandy: First-Person Accounts from the Sea Services*. Annapolis, MD: U.S. Naval Institute, 1994.

Sullivan, John. *Overlord's Eagles: Operations of the U.S. Army Air Forces in the Invasion of Normandy in World War II*. London: McFarland, 1997.

Taylor, Charles. *Omaha Beachhead*. Washington, DC: Center of Military History, 1984.

Thompson, Paul. "D-Day on Omaha Beach." *Infantry Journal*, June 1945.

Twenty-Ninth Infantry Division. *Group Critique Notes: Combat Interviews with Members of 116th Infantry*. France: 29th Division HQ, 1944.

U.S. Army Air Force. *The Effectiveness of 3rd Phase Tactical Air Operations in the ETO, 5 May 1944–8 May 1945*. Germany: AAF Evaluation Board, August 1945.

U.S. Coast Guard. *The Coast Guard at War*, vol. 11. Washington, DC: U.S. Coast Guard, 1946.

U.S. Department of State. *Foreign Relations of the U.S., Diplomatic Papers: The Conferences at Cairo and Teheran, 1943*. Washington, DC: GPO, 1961.

U.S. Navy. *U.S. Naval Administration in WWII, The Invasion of Normandy*, vol. 5. Washington, DC: U.S. Navy, 1945.

Walker, Robert. *With the Stonewallers*. Privately published, 1997.

Wilmot, Chester. *The Struggle for Europe*. London: Collins, 1952.

Wilson, Theodore, ed. *D-Day, 1944*. Abilene: University Press of KS, 1994.

Acknowledgments

A long time ago, my favorite professor offered me a bit of advice. This elderly educator, a highly courteous and cultured Hungarian émigré, told me that the premier trait of any historian who wishes to do great work is an ability to listen. These simple words of wisdom struck me as entirely sensible then; and now, thirty-three years later, they retain their freshness and relevance.

If, as John Donne wrote, no man is an island, then neither is the historian. The ultimate objective of history is to define past human activities honestly; and no one can perform this seemingly straightforward task well without speaking to the people who undertook those activities or becoming wholly familiar with the works of those who have explored those subjects before. Fortunately for those historians devoted to D-Day, we live in an age in which we can do both. If, as my old professor declared, historical proficiency is based on listening, I feel unreservedly lucky that in telling this story of Omaha Beach, I have been able to listen and learn from both those servicemen who experienced it and those historians who have investigated the subject in detail before me.

Our perspective of D-Day today would be completely different—and much less accurate—had it not been for the small group of historians the army wisely assigned in the summer of 1944 to the task of gathering relevant unit reports and conducting interviews with invasion participants. The three most notable of these men were Lt. Col. Charles Taylor, a former Harvard history professor; 1st Lt. Jack Shea, once General Cota's aide and a participant in the Omaha invasion; and Sgt. Forrest Pogue, later author of a brilliant four-volume biography of George C. Marshall. I became so familiar with the handwritten notes made by these men during their combat interviews—sometimes undertaken near the front lines only a few weeks after the invasion—that I came to recognize their occasionally unreadable penmanship. (This was fortunate, as none of them as a matter of course noted their own names on the notes.) Sadly, I never had the good fortune of meeting Taylor or Shea, but one of the supreme highlights of my professional life was talking extensively with Pogue at an army history conference, during which he vividly described interviewing Maj. Sidney Bingham—a major figure in this book—in a frontline dugout with a poncho draped over their heads to prevent rain from dripping on Pogue's notepad. My debt to Taylor, Shea, and Pogue is immense.

Similarly, all current D-Day historians cannot fail to acknowledge the work of Cornelius Ryan, author of the renowned *The Longest Day*. That Ryan was a superlative historian as well as a great writer is evident by the care he took to preserve his voluminous D-Day interviews and records, all of which are superbly maintained and open to researchers at the Mahn Center for Archives and Special Collections, Alden Library, Ohio University, in Athens. I offer thanks to Doug McCabe, curator of the Ryan collection, for his valuable help on this book.

Of the dozens of people who assisted me on this project, my most profound debt of gratitude surely must go to Kevan Elsby, my steadfast friend from Britain and fellow Omaha Beach scholar. Years ago, Kevan and I agreed that an accurate depiction of the Omaha Beach invasion must be written, and we should be the people to do it. Ever since, we have dedicated ourselves to that task and have freely and frequently exchanged information by post and e-mail. At times, however, when life's harsh realities intervened, my spirit sagged to a point at which such a vast project seemed overwhelming and utterly unfeasible. But Kevan's enthusiasm was contagious, and generally a simple exchange of e-mails pertaining to the many little-known truths of Omaha Beach was all I needed to rekindle my dedication to the task.

Kevan's father-in-law is Jimmy Green, the Royal Navy sub-lieutenant in charge of the first wave of landing craft to touch down on Dog Green beach on D-Day. In the past, the story of Omaha Beach has been told only from the American perspective, but thanks to Kevan, the significant British contributions to the landing have at last been uncovered. Every American

Ranger who landed on Omaha Beach or at Pointe du Hoc on D-Day was conveyed to shore in a British landing craft, as were many 1st and 29th Division GIs. Kevan's thorough correspondence with the many American veterans brought to the beach by the Royal Navy shed entirely new light on the invasion and was indispensable to me in the preparation of this book.

I also offer my sincere appreciation to four U.S. Army colonels (active and retired), all of whom contributed mightily to this project. Steve Clay, author of the superb history of the 16th Infantry, *Blood and Sacrifice*, provided immeasurable assistance by loaning me his archival records pertaining to the 16th on D-Day. Steve and I also attended a 1999 U.S. Army Normandy staff ride, and my discussions with him during that trip clarified several issues concerning the 16th Infantry's role on Omaha Beach. Tom Bowers guided me to several little-known but highly revealing sources at the National Archives in College Park, Maryland, such as the collected notes and correspondence of the U.S. Army historians who wrote the army's official histories of the D-Day landings in the postwar years. Roger Cirillo, one of the world's leading experts on the U.S. Army in World War II in the European theater, kindly reviewed my manuscript and offered invaluable suggestions to improve it. Mark Reardon of the Center of Military History, author of the seminal Normandy history *Victory at Mortain*, did the same—and also located and copied for me several important monographs at Fort Benning written by Omaha veterans as part of the Advanced Infantry Officers Course in the postwar years.

I must also thank Jon Gawne, author of the outstanding book *Spearheading D-Day*, for his vital contribution of Omaha photographs from his immense and priceless collection. Tim Nenninger, the chief of Modern Military Records at the National Archives, provided indispensable help in tracking down important Omaha documents, as did Dr. Richard Sommers and David Keough of the U.S. Army Military History Institute at Carlisle Barracks, Pennsylvania, and Andrew Woods of the Robert McCormick Research Center at the 1st Division Museum in Wheaton, Illinois.

Others who assisted me appreciably on this book were Paul Stillwell and Peggy Wooldridge of the U.S. Naval Institute; Susan Lintelmann of the U.S. Military Academy Library; Dr. Anthony Buccini; Donald McPherson, author of *A History of the Royal Navy and Royal Marine Minor Landing Craft Flotillas in World War II*; Stewart Bryant; Maxine Giannini; Curt Vickery; Bob Mullauer; Laurent Lefebvre; Walter Carter; David Allender; Lee Rawlinson; Aaron Elson; Adam Bryant; Doug Whatley; and H. Steven Blum, a former commander of the 29th Infantry Division.

I am saddened by the thought that most of the Omaha veterans I have corresponded with and interviewed over more than twenty years are now deceased. I dedicated my last book, *Beyond the Beachhead*, to John P. Cooper, the CO of the 29th Division's 110th Field Artillery Battalion on D-Day, and although General Cooper did not live to see me start this book, the lengthy interviews I conducted with him in the 1980s pertaining to D-Day were of inestimable help to me in understanding Omaha Beach. The same could be said for Sidney V. Bingham, the CO of the 2nd Battalion, 116th Infantry. Bingham died a few years after the release of *Beyond the Beachhead*, but I will never forget his kindness to me over the years as I questioned him at length about his Omaha Beach experiences. I miss both of these kind gentlemen acutely.

There are many other veterans whose contributions were so considerable that I feel obligated to single them out. I owe an enormous debt of gratitude to Maj. Gen. (Ret.) John Raaen, CO of Headquarters Company, 5th Ranger Battalion on D-Day, for his vast knowledge of the Omaha Beach landing and his patience and thoroughness in answering my hundreds of D-Day questions submitted to him by e-mail over the past several years. My large "Raaen" file, consisting of our collected correspondence related to Omaha Beach, usually contained the answers to any perplexing questions that arose as I wrote this book.

Victor Hicken, the officer-in-command of the U.S. Navy's LCT(A)-2227—one of the first Allied landing craft to touch down on Omaha Beach on D-Day—provided constant inspiration during this project. Victor, a distinguished historian in his own right and author of the classic book *Illinois in the Civil War*, gave me an invaluable perspective as both a D-Day participant and a professional historian, and I am proud to call him my friend.

Robert Ploger, CO of the 121st Engineer Combat Battalion on D-Day, supplied me with a vast amount of information related to engineer operations on Omaha Beach, for which I will always be grateful. Alas, General Ploger did not live to see this book reach fruition. His son and daughter-in-law were killed in the September 11 terrorist attacks, and he passed away shortly after that terrible day in our history. But Ploger's contribution to victory on Omaha Beach will never be forgotten.

Al Heintzleman of the 741st Tank Battalion generously offered considerable help on any question relating to tank operations on Omaha Beach. The 146th Engineers' Wes Ross did the same for any issues pertaining to the extraordinarily dangerous demolition engineer operations on D-Day, in which he actively participated. Cal Collier, a former World War II bomber pilot (and notable military historian), and John Howland, a B-17 pathfinder navigator, kindly gave me much useful information related to air operations on D-Day. The late Larry Noel, a U.S. Navy LCT officer in the Omaha landing, used to be a neighbor of mine in Fairfield, Pennsylvania, and he visited my home on several occasions to provide especially informative material on LCT D-Day operations.

I am indebted to former Rangers Ralph Goranson, Bob Edlin, Sidney Salomon, Tom Herring, Herb Epstein, Charles Parker, and Frank South for their substantial contributions to this project. It was men such as these who were the original executors of General Cota's legendary directive, "Rangers, lead the way!"—now the motto of current U.S. Army Rangers—and who are still supremely loyal to the Ranger creed sixty years after Omaha Beach. Jack Sweeney, a veteran of Company L, 16th Infantry, exchanged many e-mails with me concerning his D-Day experiences, and I am most thankful for it. Jack served with Medal of Honor winner Jimmie Monteith of the 1st Division, and his comments on Monteith were enlightening.

Joe Ewing, author of the renowned World War II history *29 Let's Go!*, was willing to discuss secrets of historical research with me on countless occasions, and I will always be obliged to him. There are not many moments of unadulterated pleasure when exploring musty boxes of old records, but finding Lt. Joe Ewing's personal World War II diary in a foot-locker deep in the recesses of Baltimore's Fifth Regiment Armory and returning that memento to him nearly fifty years later was one of those moments. I am also beholden to Jimmy Green, the Royal Navy Volunteer Reserve wave leader who brought Company A, 116th Infantry, ashore, for his dedication to uncovering the truth of the Omaha invasion.

Ever since the publication of *Beyond the Beachhead* in 1989, I have been proud to be a friend of Bob Slaughter, veteran of D Company, 116th Infantry, on D-Day and the man who first proposed a National D-Day Memorial. That memorial was dedicated by President George W. Bush in June 2001 in Bedford, Virginia, but I remember Bob energetically talking about it more than a decade before, when it was nothing more than a vision in his gleaming eyes. Without Bob, that vision never would have become a reality. Bob kindly read through my manuscript and offered much sound advice.

Harold Baumgarten, Walter Bieder, Joseph Binkoski, Felix Branham, Lowry Brooks, August Bruno, Thomas Cadwalader, Vincent Digaetano, Walter Eckert, Norman Grossman, E. J. Hamill, John Hickman, John Hooper, Chuck Hurlbut, Mike Ingrisano, Jr., George Kobe, John MacAllister, Robert M. Miller, Ray Nance, Chuck Neighbor, Arthur Plaut, John Polyniak, John Robertson, Walter Rosenblum, Rocco Russo, Bob Sales, Murphy Scott, Joseph Shelley, Roy Stevens, Benjamin B. Talley, Robert Walker, and Frank Warynovic are D-Day veterans who contributed markedly to this book. My profound appreciation to all.

At Stackpole Books, I would like to thank Judith Schnell and Leigh Ann Berry for their firm support and encouragement over the years; and my editor, Chris Evans, for convincing me that it was finally time to write this book—after I had been thinking and talking about it for more than a decade. Also at Stackpole, editorial assistant Dave Reisch and artist Wendy Reynolds contributed significantly to the fulfillment of this project.

And then there is my family: wife, Joyce, and daughters, Leah and Emma. Eternal thanks for appreciating that your husband and dad has an everlasting ardor to ensure that the world does not forget.

As the words of the well-known World War II song proclaim: Bless 'em all.

Index

404

3 1170 00654 0433